BCL

D0759779

Multicultural Teaching:

A Handbook of Activities, Information, and Resources

Pamela L. Tiedt
Stanford University

and

Iris M. Tiedt
University of Santa Clara

Allyn and Bacon, Inc.
Boston • London • Sydney

Library of Congress Cataloging in Publication Data

Tiedt, Pamela L
    Multicultural teaching.

    "Resources for multilingual/multicultural approaches to teaching": p.
    Includes indexes.
    1. Intercultural education—United States. 2. Language arts (Elementary) I. Tiedt, Iris M., joint author. II. Title.
LC1099.T53   372.6′044   78–25870

ISBN (Hardbound): 0–205–06445–0
ISBN (Paperbound): 0–205–06522–8

Printed in the United States of America

Contents

Chapter 5: *TEACHING WITH A MULTICULTURAL CALENDAR: ACTIVITIES AND INFORMATION* **174**

Chapter 6: *CREATING TEACHING MATERIALS FOR MULTICULTURAL APPROACHES* **229**

To the
Teacher

Multicultural Teaching offers ideas that enable any classroom teacher to promote understanding in the classroom through varied learning experiences focusing on language and culture. A comprehensive handbook, it should be invaluable to the bilingual teacher who needs activities, information, and resources that introduce both cultural and linguistic variety. Emphasis is placed on developing understandings about ethnic groups within the United States, for example, Black Americans, Irish Americans, Jewish Americans, and Chicanos. The book is designed to benefit children who are members of minority groups by providing activities with which they can identify and by making them feel an important part of the class group. The approaches to teaching included in this book will also benefit white, English-speaking children by teaching them to value their own ethnic backgrounds as well as by expanding their awareness of the diverse groups in American society. Teaching respect and appreciation for cultural diversity, which includes linguistic diversity, should be an important objective in all classrooms.

While the chief aim of this book is to provide teaching strategies, it is essential also to give teachers who are not expert in this field certain basic information, to update their awareness of current developments. The introductory chapter, therefore, summarizes such information as definition of terms, relevant laws, and the development of thinking in this field. Chapters deal specifically with the development of the child's self-esteem, language, and intergroup relations. Selected references and sources of additional information are included at the end of each chapter as well as in a special chapter at the end of the book.

An outstanding feature of this handbook is "The Multicultural Calendar," which the teacher can use immediately. This section includes activities and information that focus on celebrating the people and events that appear each month on the calendar—birthdays, holidays, significant legislation.

A second feature that teachers will find particularly helpful is a fully developed "learning module" designed to promote understanding of Chinese-Americans. An example that teachers can use as a model for preparing other studies, this module is presented in a chapter on preparing teaching materials. Teachers are shown how to develop learning centers and to create learning materials specific to their individual classroom needs.

In using this text, the professor may wish to emphasize such learning experiences as:

1. reading suggested literature
2. preparing annotated bibliographies
3. researching local community resources
4. creating learning centers
5. developing modules about specific groups

Teaching strategies, information, booklists, important dates, addresses of organizations—all are compiled in this handy source book. Here is a book all teachers will want to have available.

We wish to thank those who helped us in preparing this manuscript. Dr. Bertha Perez (Texas State University) and Yetive Bradley (Oakland Public School District) read the manuscript and provided helpful criticism; Dr. Sidney W. Tiedt (San José State University) supplied information and encouragement; Rosalind Ratliff typed the manuscript and created ideas for illustrations.

Pamela L. Tiedt
Iris M. Tiedt

UNDERSTANDING

1

Teaching for Multicultural Understanding

*A man bleeds, suffers, despairs not as an
American or a Russian or a Chinese, but in his
innermost being as a member of a single human
race.*

Adlai Stevenson

Never before has there been such an emphasis on equality for all Americans no matter what their race, sex, age, national origins, or the language they speak. Legislation has been passed designed to provide equal opportunity for education. Efforts have been made to eliminate discriminatory practices in hiring and firing. Women and members of minority groups are holding greater numbers of political positions. Still we have a long way to go before every person in the United States can feel equally valued.

Multicultural Teaching has been prepared to help classroom teachers at all levels and in all geographic locations to promote greater multicultural understanding. It has also been designed to aid both bilingual and monolingual teachers in introducing a variety of language experiences that enrich learning and also promote understanding. Education has always been the hope for enlightenment. Through implementing the information and teaching strategies described in this book teachers should move toward developing a curriculum that will help students to:

1. recognize the positive nature of our pluralistic society with its cultural and ethnic diversity

2. appreciate the contributions of all groups to the richness of our national culture
3. extend awareness of their own origins and that of others in the United States

The emphasis in this book is on presenting the rich tapestry of American culture and the great language variety that exists within that culture. The ideas presented here belong in the curriculum of all bilingual programs because bilingual students, and teachers, too, need to be aware of the diversity of languages and cultures represented in the United States. Furthermore, these ideas belong in every elementary and junior high school classroom in the country because all students need learning experiences designed to make them proud of the rich culture we Americans have inherited. All students need to develop a greater understanding, compassion, and appreciation for themselves as well as for the others with whom they inhabit this earth.

HOW NATIONAL THINKING HAS CHANGED

The contemporary teacher is responsible for education that reaches into many facets of sociology, psychology, and the humanities. No teacher can be equally well grounded in all fields of endeavor and thought. The purpose of this section, therefore, is to summarize the evolution of thinking regarding bilingual education, equality of treatment for members of minority groups, and the plural and diverse nature of the American culture.

Changing philosophy expressed in the literature of the field, legislation at state and national levels, and even changing terminology has a direct effect on practice in the schools. The melting-pot theory is outdated. Racist and sexist discrimination is taboo. All students have a right to equality of education—these are but some of the issues that teachers must contend with today.

The Outdated Melting-pot Theory

For many years it was popular to speak of the United States as "the great melting pot." Immigrants from other countries were expected to adopt English and submerge their differences into the American culture. Habits and traditions retained from the Old Country were often ridiculed as evidence of incomplete adaptation to American life by the second generation, the new Americans.

The term "melting pot" came from a play by that name which was written by Israel Zangwill in 1909. The following quotation illustrates the prevailing American nationalist sentiment that created the image of a homogeneous culture.

America is God's Crucible, the great Melting Pot where all the races of Europe are melting and reforming! Here you stand, good folk, think I, when I see them at Ellis Island, here you stand in your fifty groups with your fifty languages and histories, and your fifty hatreds and rivalries, but you won't be long like that, brothers, for these are the fires of God. A fig for your feuds and vendettas! Germans and Frenchmen, Irishmen and English-

men, Jews and Russians—into the Crucible with you all! God is making the American ...
The real American has not yet arrived. He is only in the Crucible, I tell you—he will
be the fusion of all races, the coming superman.

Israel Zangwill, *The Melting Pot* (play), 1909

The melting-pot theory is inappropriate today because the presence of cultural diversity is recognized as a strength, not a weakness. This country is not perceived today as a melting pot but rather a tossed salad, with various groups contributing to the national culture while maintaining their distinct identity. As a result, individuals can be proud of their ethnic heritage instead of ashamed of their differences.

Language is a crucial aspect of this concern for preserving the heritage of different groups. Pressure to include languages besides English in the school curriculum comes from members of many groups who feel that their language is an essential part of their culture. In addition, others have pointed out the students' right to their own language and have identified the close tie between valuing one's language and self-esteem. The following chart summarizes the evolution of thinking about language in the United States during the twentieth century.

America is a Tossed Salad!

EVOLUTION OF THINKING
ABOUT LANGUAGE IN THE UNITED STATES

Prior to 1914
Many community schools existed to teach a specific language such as German. Saturday classes were common.

1918
World War I brought about reactions against Germany and a resurgence of patriotic feeling; use of "English only" in schools legislated in many states.

1945
World War II led to realization of need for knowledge of foreign languages; teaching of foreign languages in schools encouraged.

1953
UNESCO published a monograph advocating use of the mother tongue to teach students; not widely accepted in the United States.

1958
Russian launching of Sputnik frightened U.S. leaders who turned to schools. National Defense Education Act (NDEA) passed to help U.S. schools keep up with Russian education. Aid given to promote key subject areas including teaching of foreign languages.

1963
Dade County, Florida, initiated bilingual program for Spanish-speaking Cuban children coming to Miami. Interest spread to other states.

1965
Elementary and Secondary Education Act (ESEA): Funds granted to schools to upgrade education in many areas including English instruction (modern grammar, linguistics).

1968
Bilingual Education Act: Title VII of ESEA promoted bilingual programs in schools.

1971
Massachusetts Bilingual Education Act: Massachusetts was first state to pass law mandating bilingual education for non-English-speaking children (NES). Other states followed.

1973
Bilingual Education Reform Act: Updated 1968 law; mandated language instruction as well as study of history and culture in bilingual programs.

1974
U.S. Supreme Court Decision: *Lau v. Nichols*—NES students have a legal right to bilingual instruction as part of "equal educational opportunity."

Development of Bilingual Education

Until recently, schools reflected the melting-pot theory which assumed that all people should be assimilated into *the* American culture. This attitude became particularly strong following World War I, and it persisted. School personnel insisted on the use of English only, and children were reprimanded for speaking another language. Speakers of other languages were clearly scorned and made to feel ashamed of their native language. Since language is an important aspect of personal identity, children were hurt by this attitude, and, not surprisingly, they dropped out of school as soon as possible. In 1966, a well-known study by James Coleman, *Equality of Education Opportunity* (U.S. Office of Education), showed, too, that those who completed high school scored far below national norms.

It is estimated today that more than 5 million school children speak languages other than English. That they do need help is substantiated by the dropout rates. Although English-speaking students tend to complete twelve years of schooling, the average years for other groups is much lower: Mexican-Americans, 8.1 years; Puerto Ricans, 8.6 years; Native Americans, 9.8 years.*

Today, with the support of federal and state funding, efforts are being made to promote bilingual programs that include, rather than exclude, the native languages of all students. This effort must be made across the curriculum at all levels, however, if it is to be truly successful. (See the discussion in Chapter 2.)

Although bilingual education has been generally accepted as desirable, there are still controversial issues. Controversy revolves around these questions: For whom is bilingual education intended? How shall bilingual education be carried out? How long should bilingual programs last? What is the ultimate goal of bilingual education?

The answer to these questions depends on your philosophy of education and your perception of what our society should be like, for bilingual education reflects not only pedagogy but also politics. Many advocates of bilingual education accept the use of the home language for instruction during beginning school experiences while the non-English-speaking (NES) student is learning English in an ESL (English as a Second Language) program. With this approach, English is gradually used for instruction as the native language is phased out.

Others support full language maintenance throughout at least the elementary school years, a dual language approach. In this program the classroom teacher should be fully competent to teach in the language spoken by many students as well as in English. The dual language approach would have English-speaking children learn a new language while NES children learn English. As children learn the languages, they also learn about the two cultures involved. Thus, all children are acquiring a second language and facing similar problems. This should minimize the inferiority felt by members of the minority group.

There are, of course, real problems for any bilingual program to overcome. Obtaining well-qualified teachers (skilled in both languages as well as teaching

---

* K. J. Shender, "Bilingual Ed," *Learning*, October 1976.

methodology) is not easy. Many parents, furthermore, do not support this bilingual education for various reasons. Some minority parents, for example, want their children to be Americanized as quickly as possible; they feel, and perhaps rightly so, that their children are being penalized in such programs. Another obstacle to parental acceptance of bilingual education is that such programs have been associated with "the disadvantaged" and "compensatory education," terms that were used in federally funded projects. Many parents do not want their children to be involved in programs that bear this stigmatized label. An extensive program to educate the public would have to be undertaken to overcome this kind of opposition and to stress the advantages of knowing more than one language.

BILINGUAL PROGRAMS SPONSORED BY HEW
Forty-six Languages Represented

Native American Languages

Indian
Apache
Cherokee
Choctaw
Cree
Crow
Eelaponke
Havasupai
Keresan
Lakota
Miccosukee-Seminole
Mohawk
Navajo
Northern Cheyenne
Paiute
Papago
Passamaquoddy
Seminole-Creek
Tewa
Ute
Walapai

Eskimo
Aleut
Central Yupik
Gwichin
Inupik

European Languages

French
Canadian French
Haitian Creole
Greek
Italian
Pennsylvania Dutch (Germanic)
Polish
Portuguese
Spanish
Russian
Yiddish

Other Languages
Arabic
Hebrew
Punjabi (India)
Samoan
Cambodian
Chinese
Ilocano (Philippines)
Japanese
Korean
Tagalog (Philippines)
Vietnamese

SOURCE: Department of Health, Education and Welfare.

Ideally, some say, our country would be a dual language society. Everyone should know at least one other language besides English. In 1976, however, the Office of Education funded bilingual programs across the country that involved forty-six different languages. Obviously, selecting just one language other than English, for example, Spanish, would not solve the problems of native speakers of the other forty-five languages. Teachers in bilingual programs, parents, and students themselves should know that bilingual education encompasses the wide variety of languages listed on the preceding chart.

As we note the varied languages for which bilingual programs exist, there are further questions to be discussed. Although Chinese is listed as a single language, there is more than one Chinese language. Cantonese and Mandarin, for example, are mutually unintelligible as spoken languages although they share the same written form. Many Chinese in this country speak Cantonese although a form of Mandarin is the official language of China. Are children from Haiti being taught Parisian French or the Haitian Creole? What about students who speak Canadian French, a distinctly different variety of French? Plainly, as we venture into bilingual education, we need more sophisticated information about language. In Chapter 3 we provide information about the complexity of language which is the concern of all teachers.

Bilingual education is here to stay no matter what the problems for it has been mandated by law. It has expanded, furthermore, beyond the initial emphasis on language to bilingual-bicultural approaches. This broader emphasis has been further extended to include all cultural concerns, for example, white ethnic origins or religious beliefs. Gradually we have become aware that it is important for all individuals to take pride in their origins and cultural diversity.

Teachers need to know more about the history of bilingual education and the important concepts involved. They need to prepare, furthermore, to teach broader multicultural understandings, for multicultural education has evolved from the first thrust to aid minority groups and those who speak languages other than English. Linguistic and cultural variety must be an important consideration in all curriculum planning.

Issues Underlying Multicultural Education

Many laws and court decisions paved the way for bilingual education and the current trend toward multicultural teaching. If we examine legislation and court cases, we see the same evolution of theory and philosophy regarding the rights of the individual that we have already discussed related specifically to language. Contemporary court decisions have in certain instances overthrown earlier legislation related, for example, to human rights and equality of educational opportunity. Today there is a strong push toward multicultural approaches to teaching at all levels.

What are the issues involved? Legal actions affecting the education of minorities, persons of varied cultural backgrounds, and the economically disadvantaged

A Fable

In a house there was a cat, always ready to run after a mouse, but with no luck at all.

One day, in the usual chase the mouse found its way into a little hole and the cat was left with no alternative than to wait hopefully outside.

A few moments later the mouse heard a dog barking and automatically came to the conclusion that if there was a dog in the house, the cat would have to go. So he came out only to fall in the cat's grasp.

"But where is the dog?"—asked the trembling mouse.

"There isn't any dog—it was only me imitating a barking dog," explained the happy cat, and after a pause added, "My dear fellow, if you don't speak at least two languages, you can't get anywhere nowadays."

Reprinted from *BBC Modern English*, Vol. 2, No. 10, p. 34, December 1976.

are all relevant. The chronology of such events might rightly begin with the benchmark case of *Brown v. Topeka Board of Education*. In 1954 this Supreme Court decision stated that segregated schools are unequal. State laws providing separate schools for black and white students were declared unconstitutional.

Following this decision came legislation establishing the U.S. Commission on Civil Rights in 1957. This independent, bipartisan agency was charged to "Investigate complaints alleging denial of the right to vote by reason of race, color, religion, sex, or national origin, or by reason of fraudulent practices."

This commission published *A Better Chance to Learn: Bilingual-Bicultural Education,* a report designed for educators as a "means for equalizing educational opportunity for language minority students." This overview published in 1975 summarizes efforts to help students in school who speak languages other than English. Clearly this agency sees language and culture as basic considerations in providing equal rights.

In 1968 the Bilingual Education Act (BEA) was passed as Title VII of the Elementary and Secondary Education Act. The intent of this law was clarified by President Lyndon B. Johnson:

This bill authorizes a new effort to prevent dropouts; new programs for handicapped children; new planning help for rural schools. It also contains a special provision establishing bilingual education programs for children whose first language is not English. Thousands of children of Latin descent, young Indians, and others will get a better start—a better chance—in school . . .

Efforts to enforce such legislation also appeared. The Office of Civil Rights Guidelines, for example, indicated that affirmative efforts to give special training for NES students were required as a condition to receiving federal aid to public schools in 1970. The text read:

Where inability to speak and understand the English language excludes national origin-minority group children from effective participation in the education program offered by a school district, the district must take affirmative steps to rectify the language deficiency in order to open its instructional program to these students.

A related issue is the treatment of women in the United States. In 1972, Title IX, an amendment to the Civil Rights Act, stated that "No person in the United States shall, on the basis of sex, be excluded from participation in, be denied the benefits of, or be subjected to discrimination under any education program or activity receiving federal financial assistance."

The most significant case related to multicultural bilingual education, however, is *Lau v. Nichols,* a Supreme Court case that is pressuring all school districts to provide for linguistic and cultural diversity. In 1974 it charged a school district as follows:

The failure of the San Francisco school system to provide English language instruction to approximately 1,800 students of Chinese ancestry who do not speak English, or to provide them with other adequate instructional procedures, denies them a meaningful opportunity to participate in the public educational program and thus violates . . . the Civil Rights Act of 1964 . . .

This class-action suit against the San Francisco Unified School District led to a decision that school districts must provide education in languages that meet the needs of students who attend the school. Thus began plans to teach students in their native language, whether it be Yupik or Tagalog, and to provide ESL programs specifically designed for each group.

These laws stressed human rights and the need for bilingual education. Out of this thrust came multicultural approaches to teaching that recognized the need for awareness of our culturally diverse society. Teachers in bilingual classrooms are asked to present both linguistic and cultural instruction. Social studies classes must today present multicultural perspectives of sociology and history. Language arts instructors are expected to enrich their classrooms with multicultural literature and language information.

Legislation and court decisions reflect the thinking of our times. It is important to realize, on the other hand, that laws alone do not effect change. What you do in your classroom may, however, serve to break down stereotypes, promote multicultural understandings, and make a crucial difference in the personal development of many individual students. This handbook, *Multicultural Teaching*, is designed to provide activities, information, and resources that will aid you in reaching those goals.

Clarification of Terminology

As thinking has changed, terminology has also changed. Furthermore, as changes have been made, there has also been controversy about which terms are acceptable. More militant members of ethnic groups have at times preferred one term while less militant members of the same group use another. Such terms as Chicano, Mexican-American, and Hispanic American are widely used today, and each has its own rationale.

Teachers must be aware of changing terminology. We demonstrate our awareness of how thinking has changed by our own use of appropriate terms. The once widely accepted term "culturally disadvantaged," for example, is no longer acceptable because many people are aware of its loaded implications. We recognize that all groups have cultures that are unique, and, at the same time, have much in common. "Disadvantaged" is an evaluative term that assumes a standard against which all cultures are judged and has led to the assumption that minority groups do not have a culture of their own. Following is a brief discussion of terminology that may need clarification.

Asian Americans. The more specific terms Chinese Americans or Japanese Americans are acceptable, too. The use of Oriental has fallen into disrepute because it connotes stereotyped views, for example, "the inscrutable Oriental."

Black Americans. Many Blacks accept the term Negro which is the Spanish word for black. Others who wish to stress their African origins prefer Afro-American. In general Black American or Afro-American is acceptable. Certainly, such derogatory terms as colored, darky, nigger, and so on are not acceptable.

Chicano or Mexican-American. The term Chicano was adopted by leaders who wished to stress that they are developing a unique culture in this country. The term Mexican-American is preferred by some groups. At times there are references to the brown movement, but the term is not widely used.

Native Americans. The terms Amerindian, Indian, and Native American are used. The only problem with using Native American is that it is nonspecific, including many Indian tribes as well as a number of Eskimo groups. If possible, it is preferable to designate a specific tribe such as Hopi or Aleut.

Race. The term race is frequently misused. Race is not synonymous with nationality, a language spoken, or a culture. It is incorrect, therefore, to speak of the Jewish race, the English-speaking race, or the Negro race. For many years it was the practice to identify three races: European (white), African (black), and Asian (yellow). As scientific information about blood types grew, a number of major races have been identified. Sometimes called geographical races, nine groups are identified as follows:

> African (Negroid)—Collection of related persons living south of the Sahara. American Negroes are mostly of this origin.
>
> American Indian (Amerindian or American Mongoloid)—Related to the Asian geographical race. Only group in the Western hemisphere for many years.
>
> Asian (Mongoloid)—Persons in continental Asia except for those in South Asia and the Middle East; includes Japan, Taiwan, the Philippines, Indonesia.
>
> Australian (Australian aborigine or Australoid)—A group of people in Australia.
>
> European (Caucasoid)—Located in Europe, the Middle East, and north of the Sahara. Includes persons living on other continents.
>
> Indian—Persons in South Asia from the Himalayas to the Indian Ocean.
>
> Melanesian (Melanesian-Papuan)—Dark-skinned persons living in New Britain, New Guinea, and the Solomon Islands.
>
> Micronesian—Dark-skinned persons living on islands in the Pacific: Carolines, Gilberts, Marianas, and Marshalls.
>
> Polynesian—Many persons living in the Pacific Islands such as Hawaii, Easter Island, and the Ellice Islands.

For a general discussion of this topic, refer to an up-to-date encyclopedia such as *World Book.*

Frequently people express confusion about how to handle the capitalization of ethnic terms, particularly those that include the word "black." There clearly is a need for some logical consistency. It is also important to respect the wishes of the persons involved. Taking these points into consideration, we have decided on the following practices.

Since many Blacks prefer to substitute that term for Negroes, we capitalize both Negroes and/or Blacks as names for a distinct group. The singular forms would also then be capitalized as proper nouns, Negro and Black.

The term Black American is analogous to Irish American and Jewish American and is capitalized in similar fashion. Black is not capitalized, however, when used as an ordinary adjective as in black car, black man, black child. The word "chicano" would follow the same pattern, as in Chicanos and chicano child.

THE ROLE OF THE TEACHER

Equal treatment of the people in our society has become a realistic concern at all levels of education. Teachers who deal with the humanistic elements of education have both a responsibility and an opportunity to guide students toward greater awareness of the multifaceted nature of the U.S. population. We need to work actively in our classrooms to dispel stereotyped perceptions of members of different groups and resulting behaviors that tend to demean any human beings.

You can show students how to:

1. use language that is free of racist and sexist terms or labels
2. recognize careless use of language and stereotyped perceptions of people that can hurt human beings and limit their potential
3. talk about people as individual human beings who have varied characteristics not limited by sex, race, class, or ethnic background

You can lead students gradually to greater awareness without being preachy or hostile. Every teacher can, for example:

- model appropriate behavior and usage of language
- initiate discussion of questionable practices or language to promote awareness
- plan lessons designed to break down stereotyped thinking
- select nonstereotyped text materials

The Teacher as a Model

You model appropriate language and behavior every day in the classroom. Referring to groups of people by acceptable names such as Blacks, Caucasians, Irish Americans, and Native Americans, for example, demonstrates your respect for members of these ethnic groups no matter what your own origins are. The kinds of expectations that you have for the various students in your class should reflect realistic assessment of each child's abilities and should not be influenced by skin color or national origins. Your real feelings and attitudes toward other human beings will be revealed through your language and behavior no matter what you say, and students will "read you loud and clear." Be sure the message you are sending is the one you really mean to send.

You do not have to be bilingual in order to introduce concepts about various languages and dialects in your classroom. It is important that students become aware, for example, of the wide variety of languages that Americans use daily across the country. As shown on the chart on page 6, the Office of Education has recognized a need for bilingual programs in forty-six different languages in the United States. Even though you may have a bilingual program in your school, it probably deals with only one of those forty-six languages. It is important for children and also for teachers to recognize that English is not the only language spoken in the United States and that other kinds of bilingual programs exist, too.

If you are a monolingual teacher, you can bring in speakers of varied languages to broaden student perspectives. Not only will visitors introduce different languages, but they can also share ideas and values from other cultures. Your role can be to facilitate this kind of interaction, to explore the resources of your community, and to plan learning experiences designed to teach children about the multilingual/multicultural nature of our population. The child participating in a Chinese bilingual program should know that elsewhere in the United States children are working in Tewa, Spanish, French, Tagalog, or Aleut. Where do people speak these languages? What do they sound like? Let's find out.

If you are fluent in a second language, or even if you know a little about another language, you can share your knowledge. Naturally we do not expect children to become bilingual by brief exposures to phrases in several languages, but learning to say Tovarishch (Russian—friend), ¡Hasta luego! (Spanish—So long!), or Gesundheit! (German—To your good health!) opens doors to new knowledge that can be fascinating to young language learners and exposes them to multicultural concepts.

Sharing stories from different cultures, too, offers a way of expanding student horizons. Folklore from Russia (discover the wicked Baba Yaga), Native American Indians (laugh over the stories of Coyote the Trickster), Black Africa (look for Anansi the spider), or lore from the American West (Pecos Bill and Paul Bunyan) can be enjoyed equally by students and teachers.

The Effect of Teacher Expectations

Studies of fully bilingual programs, such as the one in Dade County, Florida, show that students are eager to go to school. They are enthusiastic about learning a second language. Why do all students who are learning a second language not show the same enthusiasm? The answer may lie in teacher attitudes.

In true bilingual programs, *teachers assume that students will be successful.* Teachers are enthusiastic about the English-speaking child's first efforts to speak or to read Spanish. They are equally positive and supportive as the Spanish-speaking child begins to speak or read English. This expectation of success and appreciation of individual efforts is, of course, communicated to the children. They feel good, and they do succeed!

Contrast the attitude of a teacher who has several non-English-speaking children in a classroom of English-speaking children. These NES children probably go to a special ESL class to learn English. Often the classroom teacher does not know how to help these students. She or he obviously feels ill at ease with them. Teachers frequently tend to overcorrect the NES students' attempts to speak English. The situation is uncomfortable and nonsupportive for both student and teacher. Students feel negative and they do not succeed.

A well-known study that suggests possible effects of teacher expectations on student performance has been published under the title *Pygmalion in the Classroom* by Robert Rosenthal and Lenore Jacobson (Holt, 1968). Twenty percent of the children in an elementary school in northern California were identified to teachers as having great potential for intellectual growth. Actually, these children's names were selected at random, so they had no greater potential than any other random group in the school. The teachers, however, perceived the children as having great potential and this belief seemed to color their expectations for these children. After eight months in the classroom, this group made significant gains in IQ score compared to the children who had not been singled out. Apparently, the teachers' attitudes and expectations, although never explicitly verbalized, were communicated to the children. The teachers' expectations served as a self-fulfilling prophecy: *teachers expected the children to succeed and they did.*

Many things influence a teacher's expectations. Labels such as "slow," "educationally handicapped," and "mentally retarded" written in a cumulative folder are dangerous if they provide a set of expectations that actually limits the possibilities for children. Test scores can have the same limiting effect. Skin color, socioeconomic level, or a child's surname are other determinants of limited expectations. If children are to succeed, we must be aware of the damaging effect of such subtle expectations. Teachers need to ignore test scores, avoid using labels, and work hard to project honest appreciation of student achievements.

Planning Multicultural Experiences

As you develop a multicultural program, remember that no set of published materials constitutes a "program." You design the program to meet the needs of your particular students. Commercial instructional materials may then be included in your program as they fit. A well-designed program will draw from many resources and include a wide range of activities for varied difficulty levels.

To begin developing a program, first determine the goals and objectives you want to meet. What do you want students to learn? Our goals can be grouped into the following six aspects of cognitive and affective learning:

Valuing Students will respect and appreciate the diversity of our pluralistic society.

Describing Students will identify and describe groups within the population of the United States and note their contributions.

Relating Students will make connections, noting similarities among people, their universal needs and behaviors.

Discriminating Students will identify differences among individuals, observing that no two persons are exactly alike.

Generalizing Students will state understandings gained from discussion, inductive exploration or ideas abstracted from literature.

Judging Students will critique or evaluate experiences such as literature read.

These six goals can be developed with students at all levels. They begin simply but explicitly with children in the preschool years, and they spiral upward and outward as children grow. Students in high school and college will be expanding these same skills as they apply their abilities with greater sophistication based on knowledge, maturity, and experience. Each goal can be used with any content, furthermore, and should engage the student in thinking, listening, speaking, reading, and writing—the essential language skills.*

For each of these goals we need to spell out specific objectives related to multicultural understandings. Practically, it is best to state these objectives in terms of student performance: What will the student do? Once we have decided on the performance objectives, we can design learning experiences that will bring about the desired performance. These learning experiences can be presented on task cards to be used in a learning center in an individualized approach. Following are examples of objectives you might want to include in your multicultural/multilingual program and sample activities that can be presented on task cards. The activities cited are for upper elementary levels. Adapt the same activities for primary or junior high levels.

Valuing

Objective: Students will discuss characters in books as human beings with varied needs.

TASK CARD ACTIVITY

Read one of the following books (middle grade level):

Blue Willow, by Doris Gates

Cotton in My Sack, by Lois Lenski

Johnny Hong of Chinatown, by Clyde Bulla

---

* Reprinted from *Reading Ideas,* March 1977, p. 8.

And Now Miguel, by Joseph Krumgold

Berries Goodman, by Emily Neville

The Shy One, by Dorothy Nattran

Describe the main character in the book you read. Include his/her other feelings and behavior as well as physical appearance. How do you feel about this person?

Describing

Objective: Students will retell a folktale that has been read or heard.

TASK CARD ACTIVITY

Choose a folktale from one of these countries:

Mexico	Ireland
Italy	France
Japan	

Read the story. Then prepare to retell the story for recording on a cassette. Other students can listen to your story at the Listening Center.

Relating

Objective: Students will note similarities between their lives and those of other children.

TASK CARD ACTIVITY

Read the book *I Wish I Had an Afro,* by John Shearer. Write a description of Little John's life with his mother and father. How is Little John's life similar to yours?

Discriminating

Objective: Students will discuss the difference between various terms used to describe individuals and groups in our society.

TASK CARD ACTIVITY

Discuss the difference between these terms. How do people feel about these terms? Which would you rather be called?

heavy—fat—plump
slow—stupid—dumb
Asian American—Chinaman—Oriental
Negro—Black American—colored
Indian—Native American
woman—broad—old lady

Generalizing

Objective: Students will roleplay situations that are not necessarily familiar to them.

TASK CARD ACTIVITY

Choose people to roleplay this situation with you.
Time: Wednesday evening about 7:30 p.m.
Place: In the Hartley living room
Characters: Joe—black boy of 15
              Mildred—his sister, 12
              Mother—works as waitress
              Father—cabdriver
Situation: Joe wants to go off with his friends after dinner. Mother says he should help clear up the dinner dishes and do his homework instead.

Judging

Objective: Students evaluate the objectivity of the author of a biography.

TASK CARD ACTIVITY

Compare an encyclopedia description of George Washington Carver's early years with that of at least one biography. What kinds of words does the author use to describe Mr. Carver?

Obviously, you will need to generate many more activities for each goal and objective. The same kinds of activities can be developed for students at all levels. Throughout this book you will find activities that fit each of these goals.

Planning Lessons to Combat Stereotypes

Develop activities to help students analyze specific stereotypes. For a first experience, choose a simple, noncontroversial generalization: Red signals danger.

Working in small groups, have students list as many ideas as possible that support this statement, such as firetrucks are red. After ten minutes, switch the focus to collecting data that negates this statement, such as giving someone red roses shows you love them.

Over a period of time present similar lessons as you gradually examine more crucial stereotypes. The following sequence moves from less controversial to more controversial issues designed to aid students in becoming aware of the danger inherent in most generalizations:

1. Wolves are bad animals.
2. Fat people are jolly.
3. Good mothers stay home with their children.
4. Indians live in teepees and steal horses.
5. Black people are superior athletes.

Celebrate the contributions of different groups to the development of the United States but beware of featuring the contributions of specific cultural groups *only* on special days, for example: Cinco de Mayo, a Christmas Piñata, Thanksgiving with the Indians, Chinese New Year, a Black History Week. Although these events appear on the multicultural calendar (see Chapter 5) and should not be ignored, be sure that the contributions of different ethnic groups are brought into the classroom throughout the year. In order to avoid stereotyping the attributes or characteristics of specific groups, deliberately point out Blacks, for example, who are not athletes or musicians.

As much as possible, focus studies on topics that are general in nature, such as education, music, science, or sports. Focusing on broad themes permits students to discover the contributions of individuals from many races or ethnic groups. A study of American music, for instance, offers an opportunity to teach folk songs and dances from many countries, to study typical musical instruments, and to research contemporary trends in music that reflect the contributions of different cultures. Make it clear that developments in medicine, government, or literature depend on contributions from Americans who represent different geographic regions, varied educational backgrounds, and diverse beliefs.

Be careful also to avoid featuring only heroes or heroines, the few special people whose names are well known. Prepare a display, for example, based on Walt Whitman's well-known poem, "I Hear America Singing." Use the title of the poem as a caption.

I HEAR AMERICA SINGING

I hear America singing, the varied carols I hear,
Those of the mechanics, each singing his as it
    should be blithe and strong,
The carpenter singing his as he measures his
    plank or beam,
The mason singing his as he makes ready for
    work or leaves off work,
The boatman singing what belongs to him in his

boat, the deck hand singing on the steam-
   boat deck,
The shoemaker singing as he sits on his bench,
   the hatter singing as he stands,
The wood-cutter's song, the ploughboy's on his
   way in the morning, or at noon intermission
   or at sundown,
The delicious singing of the mother, or the
   young wife at work, or the girl sewing or
   washing,
Each sings what belongs to him or her and to
   none else,
The day what belongs to the day—at night the
   party of young fellows, robust, friendly,
Singing with open mouths their strong melodi-
   ous songs.

Walt Whitman

Around the poem display pictures of Americans at work. Include members of different ethnic groups as well as people performing nonstereotyped jobs such as a woman working on lines for the telephone company or a black father caring for his children.

Prepare a poster like this to stimulate a discussion of prejudice:

ECIDUJERP

No matter how you look at it,
it still spells PREJUDICE!

Many topics that are introduced or debated in the newspaper will provide good discussion material for older students. For example, occupational status commonly determines the standing of individuals and groups in the United States. Dr. Arthur Jensen reported a study in 1976 of the relative status of various groups in the United States. Adjusting these figures to the proportion each ethnic group represents within the total population, Jensen ranked the contributions to American professions (occupational status) of various ethnic groups in this order (1) Chinese-Americans, (2) Jewish-Americans, (3) Japanese-Americans, (4) all other White Americans, (5) American Indians, (6) Black Americans.

This report should prove provocative as students learn to question methodology and to interpret studies they encounter. Ask students to discuss the following questions in relation to Jensen's findings:

1. During what years were Japanese-Americans imprisoned in the United States?
2. At what time was it illegal for Chinese-Americans to own land on the West coast?
3. When were Jews killed or imprisoned in Germany?

How can the answers to these questions be reconciled with the findings reported by Jensen in 1976?

Encourage students to bring in clippings to share, to question contemporary events, and to express their opinions. Teach them to live by the words of Patrick Henry: "I may not agree with you, but I will defend unto death your right to say it."

Handling Difficult Classroom Problems

If you live in a community composed of several racial and/or ethnic groups, racial tensions probably surface repeatedly in housing and job discrimination. Your students live in this community, too, and are aware of these tensions. Almost every day, incidents reflecting hostile group relations are reported in the news. Elementary students watch the news on television and hear adults discuss national and local events.

An important part of the teacher's role is to bring these controversial events into the classroom. Although it will be uncomfortable for teachers and students to discuss such controversial issues, silence is no alternative. By the time children begin school, they have well-developed stereotypes of many groups in the population (age, sex, racial, ethnic), based not on experience but on information from parents, other adults, older children, and the media. If these stereotypes are not talked about in class, they will continue to exist and spread, supported by teacher silence.

You may not want to bring up an uncomfortable subject because it might make certain students in the class uncomfortable; or because hostilities might arise between different groups; or because, face it, you feel uncomfortable. Feeling comfortable is an indulgence only white, middle-class people can afford. The group of students who might be made uncomfortable by being singled out for discussion are the nonwhite, nonmiddle-class students. However, these students probably already feel uncomfortable. Racist attitudes and behaviors can exist in the classroom even when not consciously recognized. The hostile feelings of students toward other students, because they belong to a particular group, surface in a discussion of this topic. But an apparently calm classroom can conceal repressed hostilities and conflicts. Lack of discussion makes the task of dissipating these intergroup hostilities more difficult. Disturbing the superficial peace is the only effective method of resolution.

As a teacher, you may feel inadequate to handle such a serious and heavily emotional discussion. There are the fears of losing control of the class, of letting the class get too noisy, of not knowing how to answer student questions, and of getting emotionally involved yourself. These are all legitimate fears to take into account in planning class discussion. When you feel uncomfortable, you communicate uneasiness to the class which makes it difficult to get students to relax, talk honestly, and share feelings. When you pretend to feel at ease or claim to hold beliefs that are not consistent with your actions in class, students generally perceive the inconsistency and thereby lose respect for the beliefs you profess.

Tell me, I forget.

Show me, I remember.

Involve me, I understand.

Ancient Chinese Proverb

There are many solutions to classroom discussions of difficult topics other than avoiding them. One possibility is to invite a person experienced in leading such discussions to talk with the class. Groups such as the National Organization for Women offer speakers experienced in consciousness-raising techniques, precisely what you are attempting to do with the class. Community action groups or branches of national racial or ethnic organizations are sources of names of people to contact for speaking to the class. And while students become informed, you can learn from these people the delicate skill of leading a discussion: specifically, creating an accepting climate and developing student awareness of the stereotypes we hold and the harmful nature of stereotypes. Another possible approach is teaming with another teacher. You could share responsibility for discussions as you gradually accumulate knowledge and experience, work with each other's classrooms, and support each other's efforts.

At times you and members of your class will be confronted with questionable student behavior or language. Perhaps a situation will arise in the classroom or students may report an event they witnessed. Take advantage of the opportunity to discuss this type of problem with the class. You might find it appropriate, for instance, to discuss why people object to the use of such terms as Jap, broad, Spick, or honky. Students who can express their personal reactions to such language will have moved a long way toward achieving a caring, respectful attitude toward each other as individuals. They will also have established an acceptable mode for dealing with controversial or emotion-laden issues.

Developing a Community Resource List

Many excellent sources of multicultural information are available right in your own community. Sometimes an organization has produced a list of possible contacts for materials, resources, or speakers. Your public library may have this information already compiled. If not, begin developing a list of your own. The best place to start is the telephone directory. Look for national organizations that have branches in a big city close to you. Possible names to look for include National Association for the Advancement of Colored People (NAACP) and National Conference of Christians and Jews. Look also under group names to see what services are offered. Try Chicano, American Indian, Mexican-American, Native American, La Raza, Black, Afro-American, and so on.

Another important resource is the local community college or university. Write or call them for information about possible ethnic studies departments or organizations for students of different ethnic backgrounds. Check the catalogs to see whether courses are taught in the history or culture of a particular group that might be of interest to your students. Sometimes the teachers of courses can be of help in locating more materials and information as well as perhaps providing contacts with other people in the community. They might also come to speak to the class.

In some communities, local service organizations may be aware of the special needs of minorities. Find out whether the YWCA, National Organization for

Women, League of Women Voters, Junior League, and other similar organizations offer special programs that might be useful to your students. State teacher organizations, adult education programs, and state/county/city human relations commissions are other groups that should be especially responsive to local conditions and interested in helping teachers in the classroom.

Throughout this book we suggest explicit ways of incorporating multicultural/multilingual activities across the curriculum. Developing a multicultural/multilingual approach in your classroom can be very exciting and should provide a whole new perspective for all aspects of your curriculum. Invite your students to accompany you as you embark on this adventure. Bon voyage!

SOURCES TO INVESTIGATE

Human and Anti-Human Values in Children's Books. Council on Interracial Books for Children, Inc., 1841 Broadway, N.Y. 10023, 1976.

United States Commission on Civil Rights. *A Better Chance to Learn: Bilingual-Bicultural Education.* U.S. Commission on Civil Rights Clearinghouse Publication, no. 51, May 1975.

Sheils, Merrill, et al. "Teaching in English—Plus." *Newsweek,* February 7, 1977, pp. 64–65.

Sibelman, Larry. "Bilingual Education: A Mosaic of Controversy." *American Teacher,* December 1976, pp. 13, 22–23.

Bilingual-Bicultural Education and English-as-a-Second-Language Education: A Framework for Elementary and Secondary Schools. California State Board of Education, Bureau of Publications, 1974.

2

Building Positive Concepts of Self and Others

Human beings have a natural potentiality to learn.

Carl Rogers, *Freedom to Learn*

In order for children to learn, they must perceive themselves as competent human beings who can succeed at the tasks they undertake. A major goal for education, therefore, is to help children develop positive self-concepts, to view themselves as worthwhile persons, and to perform accordingly. Because this emphasis is especially crucial for children from minority groups we have placed this chapter second in this book.

Children who feel good about themselves will project this feeling of worth to others. They can accept other children and adults. Because there is constant pressure to conform, to be "like everyone else," we need to teach children to value diversity, particularly linguistic and cultural diversity, and to view being different as a positive quality. The secure individual does not fear that which is different, but welcomes difference as challenging, exciting, and personally fulfilling. We need to teach this attitude consciously in the classroom.

Developing positive self-concepts is an essential concern of bilingual programs, but it is also a primary concern for all of education. The activities described in this chapter are designed to promote the self-esteem of children who come from diverse backgrounds. Through such experiences, children should learn to:

1. see themselves as worthwhile human beings
2. recognize their origin and cultural background as an asset
3. attack meaningful tasks with the expectation of success
4. interact positively with other children in the classroom
5. recognize that the cultural backgrounds of others are valuable aspects of the pluralistic American society

Although we have devoted a full chapter to developing positive concepts of self and others, you will find that this emphasis permeates the entire book. This chapter is divided into three sections. First we discuss the teacher's role in promoting student self-esteem. The second part of the chapter presents activities designed to help students learn to know and value themselves, and the third section concentrates on applying positive perceptions to other diverse people.

THE TEACHER'S ROLE

Young children approach life eagerly, positively, no matter what their backgrounds. Self-confidently they reach out to learn. They work hard to learn, for example, the complexities of language and how to function in their social environment—family, neighborhood, and later, school. What happens in school has a significant effect on the development of this natural potentiality to learn. Teacher expectations directly influence children's performance. For children from low-income homes or from minority ethnic groups, this effect can be particularly adverse.

> Love and self-worth are so intertwined that they may properly be related through the use of the term *identity*. Thus we may say that the single basic need that people have is the requirement for an identity; the belief that we are someone in distinction to others, and that the someone is important and worthwhile. Then *love* and *self-worth may be considered the two pathways* that mankind has discovered that lead to a successful identity.
>
> William Glasser, M.D., *Schools Without Failure*

A six-year study of children from low-income homes by Virginia Shipman and others investigated "how home and school work together to influence the child's development." * Preliminary findings reported in 1976 reveal:

1. "Disadvantaged" and middle-class children enter school with the same average level of self-esteem.

---

* Virginia Shipman, et al., *Young Children and Their First School Experiences*, Educational Testing Service, 1976.

2. After three years of schooling children from low-income homes experience a significant drop in level of self-esteem compared to children from middle-class homes.
3. Although there is a loss of self-confidence, children from low-income homes still feel positive at this stage rather than negative about their ability to take care of themselves.

The Shipman study clarifies the characteristics of children from low-income homes. Studying more than 1,000 children from 1969–1975, she found that children from low-income homes:

1. enter school with as broad a range of abilities as any other group
2. have as much self-esteem as children from other groups
3. come from homes containing the same range of positive and negative influences on learning as do middle-class children

These findings should help teachers rid themselves of the misconceptions that low socioeconomic status automatically means cultural deprivation and little value for learning. They also emphasize the need for viewing each child as an individual.

What does this study tell us about the process of schooling? The implications of this study for the classroom relate to teacher expectations for children from low-income homes. As Shipman notes, "It gets down to what happens in the classroom between the teacher and the child—how much encouragement that child is given, how much stimulation and warmth." Teachers who have low expectations for students may have an adverse effect on children's performance.

Teacher expectations based on income level or cultural background are not the only factors affecting student performance. Teachers need to consider the advantages the English-speaking child has on entering most U.S. schools compared to the NES child.

English-speaking child

1. Language used is familiar.
2. Teaching materials are presented in English, and the child learns to read English.
3. Child's self-esteem is supported by successful experiences in school.
4. He/she graduates from high school and may enter college.

Non-English-speaking child

1. Language used is strange.
2. Expected to use materials presented in English; the child may be illiterate in his/her native language.
3. Child feels unhappy, is unsuccessful in school, and cannot wait to go home.
4. He/she drops out of school as soon as possible.

We need to be aware of these differences in how children may regard the school experience. The role of the teacher should be to minimize the ways the NES students feel at a disadvantage because language is closely allied with the students' self-concept. The activities in Chapter 3 also, therefore, support the development of positive self-concepts.

Children who have experienced failure and frustration as members of minority groups may perceive themselves as having limited ability or little chance of success and may not even try a task before saying, "I can't." They have internalized this negative perception of themselves, and this attitude will influence their whole development, their approach to life. In this chapter we will focus on the child who needs to be revitalized, reassured. Our task is not easy even if we begin working with a young child at the age of four or five; it becomes increasingly difficult as the child grows older. In order to develop in a child a positive attitude toward self, we need to examine teaching strategies used in the classroom to make certain that school experiences do actually develop self-esteem. In the following section we present activities designed to promote positive self-concepts for all children, but especially for those who need a special boost.

DEVELOPING POSITIVE SELF-CONCEPTS

Strategies used in the classroom do make a difference. Approaches to evaluation in all subject areas of the curriculum, for example, affect children's self-concepts. Teachers who are aware of the potential effects of school experiences on children will select strategies designed to make children feel good about going to school. In this section we describe ways of developing positive self-concepts for children of all ages. Most of the activities can be adapted for different ages so no grade levels are indicated. The activities are designed to meet specific objectives. Children will learn:

- to feel a welcome part of a class group
- to know that their cultural background is valued
- to perceive themselves as good persons
- to dare to try new tasks with the expectation of success

The teacher plays a crucial role in welcoming children to school. We need to extend a welcome to each child, making each one feel at ease in the classroom. This is important at the beginning of the school year, particularly for children entering school for the first time. It is even more important for children who enter a classroom after the year has already begun, for children (and adults, too) experience great difficulty breaking into a group that has already been formed. The activities suggested in this section are designed to make children feel a sense of belonging, of being "wanted."

Welcoming the Child

Make a welcome message as clear as possible by displaying the word on a bulletin board display, thus:

If you have Spanish-speaking children in your room, use BIENVENIDO.

The Meaning of Welcome

Talk about the word "welcome" as a way of drawing students' attention to the meaning of the display. For younger students, talk about what the word means—what do we mean when we tell someone "You're welcome" after someone thanks us for something? Children might note that welcome is a friendly expression; it conveys pleasure, gladness, friendship. The discussion might add a special dimension to the use of this simple expression that we say without thinking.

Older students might compile a list of expressions that include the word welcome, for example:

> *Welcome,* stranger!
> to give someone a warm *welcome*
> to wear out one's *welcome*
> you're quite *welcome*
> *Welcome* Wagon

They might be interested, too, in knowing the origins of this word, which comes from the Scandinavian languages and appears in Icelandic as "velkominn."

"You're Welcome" in Other Languages

Point out, too, how the response "you're welcome" is expressed in other languages. In French the word is "bienvenue" and in Spanish it is similar, "bienvenido"; both translate directly into "well come." In some languages "you're welcome" is expressed by the same word that means "please." In German please is "bitte" and thank you is "bitteschön" to which the response is "bitte" again. In Russian, too, the same word (pronounced "puh zhal' stuh") means please and you're welcome; thank you is "spuh se' buh." (Remember that Russian is written with a different alphabet, but you might try these approximate pronunciations orally.)

A Welcome Wagon in Your School

Challenge a group of older students to organize a welcome wagon that would assume responsibility for personally and officially welcoming newcomers to the school. Students of all levels could be part of this team effort. Encourage students to brainstorm possibilities for making students feel at home in their new surroundings. They might ask themselves: "What would make me feel good about coming to a new school?" Ideas include:

Introducing the student to several children who live near him or her.

Meet the child at the principal's office to express a welcome and to introduce him or her to the classroom teacher.

Give the newcomer a small gift:

1. A welcome card made by students.
2. A flower to pin on (if everyone knows this symbol, they can be encouraged to smile their own welcome or to say, "Hello").

An Affective Acrostic

This get-acquainted activity focuses on adjectives and promotes vocabulary while it breaks down the stiffness of persons in any group. Ask each person to print his or her name on a sheet of paper, thus:

C
L
A
R
A

Then they are to write adjectives that describe themselves and begin with each letter of their name. Above all, they are to make themselves sound great! Encourage them to brag as they use ostentatiously extravagant words, as in this example:

D elightful
O ptimistic
N atural
A mbitious
L evel-headed
D ramatic

Permit students to use dictionaries and to help each other as they complete their acrostics. Then have several students share their acrostics aloud. If someone needs help in finding a really good word, ask the group to suggest an even better adjective. Comment on how great each list of adjectives makes the owner sound!

Mount the acrostics on pieces of colored construction paper cut into interesting shapes according to individual desires. Display them on the bulletin board where students can read them.

Reading for Personal Growth

Point out to students how independent reading about others can be supportive as you share the lives of people who have experiences you identify with. Relate the way reading has helped you.

Share this quotation from James Baldwin with older students;

You think your pain and your heartbreak are unprecedented in the history of the world, but then you read. It was books that taught me that the things that tormented me the most were the very things that connected me with all the people who were alive, or who had ever been alive.

Reading Aloud

Read books aloud occasionally about students that have problems. Talk about them with the group. Books you might use include:

Primary

Stevie by John Steptoe. Harper & Row, 1969. Young black boy resents having Stevie in his home but misses him when he is gone.

A Father Like That by Charlotte Zolotow. Harper & Row, 1971. Small boy without a father.

The Quarreling Book by Charlotte Zolotow. Harper & Row, 1963. A chain of reactions begins when Father forgets to kiss Mother good-bye.

Crow Boy by Taro Yashima. Viking, 1955. A young Japanese boy feels rejected at school until an understanding teacher helps.

I Love My Mother by Paul Zindel. Harper & Row, 1972. Boy shares feelings with his mother.

The Adventures of Obadiah by Brinton Turkel. Viking, 1972. Young Quaker boy living in colonial Nantucket faces problem of lying; see other books about Obadiah.

Upper Elementary

Shadow of a Bull by Maia Wojciechowska. Atheneum, 1964. Son of a great Spanish bullfighter fears being a coward.

Journey to Topaz; A Story of the Japanese-American Evacuation by Yoshiko

Uchida. Scribner's, 1971. Yuki and her family were interned in Utah during World War II.

Plain Girl by Virginia Sorenson. Harcourt Brace Jovanovich, 1955. An Amish girl learns to think for herself.

Berries Goodman by Emily C. Neville. Harper & Row, 1965. Two city boys learn the meaning of prejudice, in this case, against Jews.

Kate by Jean Little. Harper & Row, 1971. In this sequel to *Look Through My Window,* Kate learns to value her Jewish heritage.

And Now Miguel by Joseph Krumgold. Crowell, 1953. Moving story of New Mexican sheepherders and Miguel's problems of growing up.

It's Okay to be Afraid

Introduce the subject of being afraid by reading a book such as *There's a Nightmare in My Closet* by Mercer Mayer (Dial). Then ask each student to write a sentence or two about something they are really afraid of. You participate, too. With no names attached, each paper is folded up tightly and put in a box. You might say:

> Now that you have your fear written on paper, I want you to fold it up tight and put it in this box. (Collect everyone's fears.)

> Here we have everybody's fears collected in a box. Sometimes the things we're afraid of are only fearsome because we can't talk about them. We keep them hidden inside us. Today we're going to bring some of these fears out in the sunshine where we can look at them. I'm going to ask somebody to pick up one of these fears and read it right out loud. If the one that's drawn is yours, you don't have to tell anyone because your name isn't on the paper.

Discuss the fear that is drawn from the box—how many of you have been afraid of the dark when you go to bed? What did you do about it? Repeat this activity as long as the group is interested. Then set the box aside for further discussion the next day.

The "Me" Collage

Have students clip magazines as they prepare a collage that reveals things about their lives. Talk about the things they might include, for example:

> Birthplace—picture, part of a map
> Baby pictures
> Things they like—food, sports
> Their family—people, pets
> Where they have lived or traveled

Words can be included as well as pictures to help tell others in the classroom more about themselves. Clippings are pasted on a large piece of colored construction paper or cardboard. A frame can be attached after the collage is completed, thus:

Have students write a brief biographical description which can be attached to the collage or read aloud to the class. These collages make interesting displays for Open House when parents visit the school. Record each student's presentation of the biographical sketch that accompanies his or her collage. Play the tape continuously as parents visit the rooms. Post an order of the presentations on the board so people can tell when their child will be heard.

Open-ended Writing

Provide open-ended sentences for students to complete either orally or in writing. Such ideas as the following help children probe their feelings and to express them with little fear of sharing:

> I feel really happy when . . .
> When I get big, I am going to . . .
> Once I got really scared because . . .
> When I'm all alone, I pretend . . .
> I get really mad when . . .

What I Like about My Life

Encourage children to talk about what they like about their lives and what they do not like. Ask the following questions:

1. Can you think of somebody who has a worse life than you?
2. Name one thing you think is really great about your life.
3. If you could change one thing in your life, what would you change?

Ten Things about Me

A good activity for the beginning of the year is having each student write ten things about himself or herself. Students can list anything, for example:

Joel Davis

I get up at 5:30 each morning to deliver papers.
I live next to Julie and Carl.
My favorite food is fried chicken and mashed potatoes.

Introducing

Students can exchange the lists they wrote in the previous activity. Working in small groups, each person then introduces the student whose paper he or she received. The student introducing Joel might say, for instance:

I'd like you to meet Joel Davis. He gets up at 5:30 every morning to deliver newspapers. Just imagine! I'm still sleeping at that time. His favorite food is fried chicken and mashed potatoes . . .

Taking Care of Yourself

Ask children the question used in the Shipman study described at the beginning of this chapter: Can you usually take care of yourself? For preschool and primary grade children, ask the question orally to each individual. For students in third grade or older the most accurate results will also be obtained through individual questioning. You might achieve a different objective by preparing this question on an assessment sheet like this to move the child beyond consideration of the question asked:

Can you usually take care of yourself?   Yes _____

No _____

Tell about a time when you were able to take care of yourself.

_____

_____

_____

After students have written their responses, encourage them to share the responses with others. This type of sharing is supportive. In this case it should reinforce feelings of strength.

In the Shipman study fewer than one-third of the third graders questioned, answered "Yes" (25.5 percent low income; 29.5 percent more affluent). Clearly we need to teach all students to feel secure in their ability to cope.

Feeling Inadequate

To help children talk about their feelings of inadequacy, follow up the previous discussion with this direction:

Tell about a time when you were not able to take care of yourself. How did you feel? What happened? Encourage students to share. Tell them of a time you felt inadequate.

Bragging Is In!

Just for fun, have students write as many wonderful, extravagant statements about themselves as they can. Encourage them to try to outdo each other, as shown here:

ANTONIO ROMANO

I am the handsomest fellow on my block, in the class, in the whole school! I am so handsome that I can't stand to look at myself in the mirror in the morning. I get dressed with my eyes closed.

I am so smart that the teachers and the principal ask me for advice and sometimes I tell them a few things. And besides being handsome and smart, I am strong — strong enough to lift a car up and check the wheels. I am so strong my mother and father are afraid to yell at me. They let me have whatever I want to eat.

Students who have negative self-images need to engage in such exercises repeatedly. Force them to stress positive attributes even if they are fantasies like these. Encourage them to assert themselves.

TEACHING STRATEGIES THAT BUILD ESTEEM

1. *Provide positive reinforcement.* Every child needs to hear the words: "You did a good job." See that tasks assigned are within the abilities of the student. Value what the child does accomplish and be sure to tell him or her that you do: "You really worked hard, Joe."
2. *Recognize children as individuals daily.* Be sure that each child is reached directly in some way every day. Keep a special list of the children in your class. Toward the end of the day glance down this list quickly. Have you had some direct contact with each child? If not, make a point of saying something pleasant to the children you have missed before they leave: "My, María, we really had a busy day, didn't we?"
3. *Project liking for children.* Smile at children. Tell the children in your room that you are glad to be working with them. You might share the charming little books *I Like You* or *Hooray for Us!* by Sandol Warburg with groups of middle grade or junior high students.
4. *Publicize student work.* Bulletin board displays or published collections of student writing should include something by each person in the class. Let each student select the work to be displayed.
5. *Plan for success.* See that learning experiences you plan can be accomplished successfully. Provide help as needed yourself or use peers and aides.
6. *Recognize and encourage differences.* Provide opportunities for children to be different, to select projects or activities that are unique to their home environments.

The Fantasy Trip

Taking a fantasy trip can be an interesting personal experience. It also provides stimulating material for group discussion. Here are two ideas to use at different times. Speak slowly with pauses between sentences so children have time to follow the fantasy trip.

1. Close your eyes. Think back to the time when you began school. Think of a time when something nice happened to you in school. How did you feel? Now think of a time when something unpleasant happened. How did you feel? Now change the situation. Make the teacher say something to make it all right. What would you have liked the teacher to say? (Pause) Open your eyes when you are ready.

2. Put your head on the desk and close your eyes. Imagine you are floating on a cloud high above the earth. The sun is shining. There is a warm breeze. What do you see as you float along? (Pause) Can you see the land? What is it like? Are there people? What are they doing? Would you like to join them? Float down from the cloud if you like. Would you like to stay there? If not, hop on your cloud and float away. Now float back home and open your eyes when you are back.

After a fantasy trip, discuss how students felt. Encourage them to share their experiences. For older students a fantasy trip can be a launching pad for writing as students describe the trip and their feelings. Use this strategy for introducing various symbolic struggles: climbing a mountain, taking one step at a time, or thinking positively. Use the story of *The Little Engine That Could* for primary children.

A Chart Story

Print this story on a chart so children can read it and talk about this idea.

ACCEPTING YOURSELF

A second-grader in Tennessee made a good start toward a sense of self-esteem when he submitted an essay, "My Face," to his teacher.

"My face has two brown eyes," the seven-year-old began. "It has a nose and two cheeks. And two ears and a mouth.

"I like my face. I'm glad that my face is just like it is.

"It is not bad, it is not good, but just right."

Liking ourselves is essential to a healthy love of self which is the basis for loving others.

Take a good look at yourself. Discover and accept what has been given you. It may not be as much as you might like to see. But growth depends on an acceptance of what you have and where you are starting from.

Christopher News Notes, no. 187, May, 1971

The Color of Me

Cut a number of strips of paper in a variety of colors, for instance red, yellow, green, blue, purple, orange, brown, gray, black, white. For a class of thirty, you may need twenty pieces of each color.

Ask children to close their eyes. Then say, "Imagine that you are looking at a painting of yourself. What color would you be? If you could choose one color, what color would you choose to be you?" Have children come to the table on which the colored strips of paper are spread out to choose the color they identify with. Divide in small groups to talk about the colors selected and what they mean to each person.

Writing Personal Essays

Have each child mount the strip of paper chosen on a sheet of composition paper. They can explain why they see themselves as this color by writing a short personal essay beginning with these words: I think I am _____ because . . .

This is a very revealing step toward self-awareness and will provide insight into the child's self-perception. This is not the type of writing to display on the wall, but children may voluntarily share their writing in small groups. Be careful not to make evaluative comments, saying only perhaps, "Thank you for sharing, Paula." Such open disclosures are healthy for all students and should be encouraged, but never forced.

I Am a Hamburger

Children can become more aware of themselves by selecting other things they identify with. In addition to color, have children answer these kinds of questions: What food are you? What kind of car are you? What kind of building are you?

After each person has answered the questions on paper, have them talk about the questions in small groups where each person can participate directly. Although the choices are revealing in many ways, usually people are not threatened by this neutral approach. Sometimes this occasions laughter as children share the humor of someone's choice. Like most people, children enjoy talking about themselves. They may contribute such metaphoric ideas as these:

> Joe: I think I'm a peanut because you have to crack me open to find out what's good inside.
>
> Terry: I'm a big office building because I like to be in charge and to be where the action is.
>
> Sara: I'm a little red Triumph, snappy with a lot of get up and go!

My Lifeline

Have students draw a series of mountain peaks across a sheet of paper, like this:

Tell them that this line represents their life. What are the big peaks in their life? What are the smaller peaks. Have them identify the peaks in their lifeline as they write on each mountain.

This idea can be extended by describing their usual daily existence across the base of the mountains. A few fantasies can be added on clouds: Someday I'd like to...

Journals, Diaries, or Logs

An excellent way to promote writing fluency is personal writing that can be kept in a journal. Schedule ten minutes each day for journal writing. Children who have trouble beginning can simply write what they are thinking or saying to you:

I can't seem to get started with writing a journal. The teacher says I should write, but I can't think of anything interesting to write. That happens to me sometimes. My mind just goes blank, so what do you do?

Children should be encouraged to write anything they want, but at times you may suggest a topic for the day, for example:

Once I dreamed...
If I had ten dollars, I would...
Sometimes I get so angry that...
Once upon a time...
On the way to school...
Freedom is...

A Dialogue with Your Students

Most students want you to read what they write. Read each child's journal once a week, if possible. Do not edit it, but do write comments about the ideas expressed. Open up a personal dialogue between you and the student. You will get to know your students better through journal writing. Other writing can serve the same purpose, too. Make it clear that journals are private, not to be read by other students or the teacher without permission.

My Name

Talk about names with children. Discuss how they feel about their first names, how their names were chosen, what names mean.

Have children make designs based on their first names like the one on the following page.

Color the name designs for display on the bulletin board. This design makes a good cover for a personal collection of writing.

Choosing Names

Ask children where they got their first names. Are they named after someone, perhaps an aunt or grandfather? Perhaps someone has a family name, like Jamison, or an invented name composed of both parents' names, such as Rayella.

You might discuss how they feel about their names. Ask them to write about one of these topics:

I like my first name because _____.

I wish I could change my first name because _____.

If I could choose a name for myself, it would be _____

because _____.

If I had a baby, I would name it _____ because _____

_____.

Naming Customs

Talk about different customs of naming children. Children will be interested in knowing about the use of the names of saints by Catholic families or the Jewish practice of naming children after dead grandparents. Ask children to share information from their personal experience.

What People Call You

Observe that some families use pet names or nicknames. Others scorn the use of nicknames. In the South children are commonly called by both the first and middle names, for example, James Leroy or Nancy Kathryn.

Ask students: What does your mother call you? How about your friends? Discuss what children like to be called. Ask children what they would like you to call them in school. Practice pronouncing these names as the children do until you can say even names less familiar to you easily.

Surnames

Discuss surnames. What are they? Where do they come from? Have children state their surnames as you write them on the board. Observe the variety of names in the classroom. Some are long, and some are short. Some have only one syllable (Wong) while others contain several syllables (Asakura, Rodríguez, Anderson).

Use surnames in classroom learning experiences. Have students line up alphabetically for lunch. Younger students can line up according to the first letter only while older students check the second and third letters as needed for more precise order.

Discuss the characteristics of surnames. "Mc" and "Mac" names originated in Ireland and Scotland. Names that end in "son" mean "son of" as in Peterson. Let students make generalizations about the names represented in their classroom such as:

We have many Spanish names:

> Castañeda
> Chávez
> Feliciano
> Vásquez

Chinese names are short.

> Wang
> Lee
> Ching

A Study of Names

If students become especially interested in names, you might want to begin a more extensive study of American names. Look for the following books which provide information about the meanings of common names and their origins:

> *Our Names: Where They Came from and What They Mean* by Eloise Lambert and Mario Pei. Lothrop, 1960.
> *How Surnames Began* by C. M. Mathews. Lutterworth Press, 1967.

Books of first names are available in the public library to assist parents who are selecting names for new babies.

Family Roots

Students can ask their families about the history of the family as they develop a chart like this:

My Family		
	Name Birthplace Date	
Mother		
Father		
Brothers		
Sisters		
	Mother's Family Name Birthplace Date	
Mother		
Father		
Brothers		
Sisters		
	Father's Family Name Birthplace Date	
Mother		
Father		
Brothers		
Sisters		

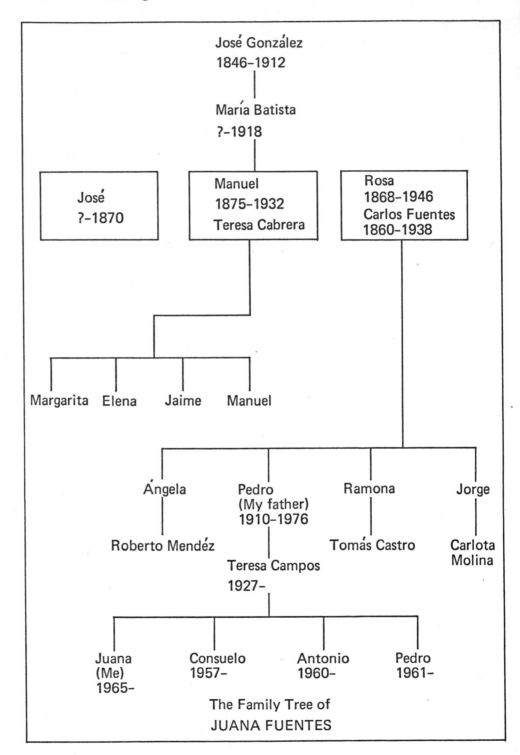

José González
1846–1912

María Batista
?–1918

José
?–1870

Manuel
1875–1932
Teresa Cabrera

Rosa
1868–1946
Carlos Fuentes
1860–1938

Margarita   Elena   Jaime   Manuel

Ángela   Pedro   Ramona   Jorge
(My father)
1910–1976

Roberto Mendéz   Tomás Castro   Carlota
Molina

Teresa Campos
1927–

Juana   Consuelo   Antonio   Pedro
(Me)   1957–   1960–   1961–
1965–

The Family Tree of
JUANA FUENTES

A Family Tree

Children can construct a family tree using the information they collect. They should interview their parents and grandparents to find as much about the family as possible.

When introducing this kind of activity, be aware that some parents might be offended by this "invasion of privacy." It is important, therefore, to discuss the project in the classroom first so children have a clear sense of your intent, namely, developing *pride in the family,* the importance of remembering our forefathers, our *roots.* You might, for example, tell the group something of your own origins. Parents who saw the televised version of *Roots* will be especially interested in this project.

What Is Genealogy?

Introduce the big word "genealogy" (notice the spelling) which means the study of lineage, family history. Many people trace their family history as a matter of pride. Today there are societies focusing on this study. Discuss lineal descent which is important in royal families such as in England. Students might find out the order of succession following Queen Elizabeth II to the British throne.

An interesting book for upper elementary and junior high students is *Who Do You Think You Are? Digging for Your Family Roots* by Suzanne Hilton (Westminster Press, 1976).

Curriculum Materials

A number of commercial materials have been produced specifically to meet the needs of children in developing self-esteem. You might want to examine the following:

About Me: A Curriculum for a Developing Self by Harold Wells and John T. Canfield. Encyclopedia Britannica, 425 N. Michigan Ave., Chicago, IL 60611. For grades four to six. Titles include: *I Know Who I Am, I Know My Strengths, I Can Set and Achieve Goals, I Try to Be Myself, I Am in Charge of Becoming Myself.*

I Have Feelings by Terry Berger. Behavioral Publications, 2852 Broadway, New York, NY 10025. Ages four to nine. Covers seventeen different feelings, both good and bad, such as anger, sorrow, joy, grief.

STRATEGIES TO AVOID

1. *Activities in which there is only one winner.* Consider all the losers in the old-fashioned spelling bee. Work in teams or family groupings together. How many words did we spell right? (A math problem.) How many pages did we read today?
2. *Publicizing the "A" papers or those that got 100 percent on the spelling test.* The children who need a boost are being ignored. Display work in which all can

be included—original poetry, designs for book covers, maps drawn for geography.

3. *Putting grades on every paper a child completes.* Explain to parents that traditional ABC grades can get in the way of a child's progress. Stamp children's writing "Creative Writing—Not To Be Graded" if **parents** need assurance that you are checking student work.

4. *Teaching to mastery.* Expecting any child to read a passage or a list of words without error is unrealistic and can be defeating. Even good readers make errors as they read. They may correct themselves later if the meaning is confused. If there is no problem with the meaning, children should be encouraged to move along as quickly as possible as they develop fluency. Fluency and enjoyment of reading are more important objectives than 100-percent accuracy.

5. *Expecting the same answer to everything.* Stress questions that encourage divergent thinking, original answers. Also show students that there may be many ways to solve a problem even in arithmetic.

DEVELOPING POSITIVE PERCEPTIONS OF OTHERS

In his book *Surviving the Future,* historian Arnold Toynbee discusses what education for the future should be like. He stresses the need to value the contributions of all:

It is in the interest of both the individual and society that each individual's particular gifts should be helped to bear fruit for the benefit of both the individual and society. We cannot, of course, have completely different systems of education for each individual; yet, as far as possible, the individual's very subtly distinctive personality should be taken into account in giving him his education.

We can help children develop positive perceptions of others through our practices in the classroom. Our own attitudes toward children serve as models for their behavior. Demonstrated through the words we speak, selection of children to perform classroom tasks, and evaluative remarks we make, these attitudes are clearly interpreted by youngsters. It is important, therefore, that we display positive attitudes toward the children with whom we work. This is important in any classroom, but it is essential in bilingual/multicultural programs.

All children need interaction in group situations. They need the response of group members and recognition of themselves as accepted members of a group. The group offers security as well as opportunity for new experiences. These universal needs should be considered as we design a curriculum for any subject area or for any specific group of children. Individualized programs must not ignore the individual's need for group interaction.

The activities presented in this section have been selected to help children learn to:

• respect each other as individuals
• interact successfully within a group
• work cooperatively toward a common goal
• value the contributions of other people

A Class Directory

Type a list of the students' names to give to the children in your room. You may include their addresses, birthdays, or other information that might interest the children as they become acquainted. They will be highly motivated to read this directory even though names of students and streets may be difficult.

Have students introduce themselves according to this listing. They may simply say: I am Juan Rodríguez. I live on Fairglen Avenue. Or, they might add other information such as what they like to do on Saturday or where they were born. Ask the students what they would like to know about each other and what each is willing to share. Combine this activity with those about names at the beginning of this chapter.

Share a Parable

Read this short story to students. Discuss its meaning.

HOW DO YOU KNOW?

One day Soshi was walking on the bank of a river with a friend. "How delightfully the fishes are enjoying themselves in the water!" exclaimed Soshi. His friend spoke to him thus: "You are not a fish; how do you know that the fishes are enjoying themselves?" "You are not myself," returned Soshi; "how do you know that I do not know that the fishes are enjoying themselves?"

Okakura Kakuzo

Share a Compliment Today

"There's something good about everyone." Discuss this topic with your students.

Then divide into small groups of five to six students. Each student has a sheet of paper on which he prints his or her name. Students pass their paper to the person on the left. Each one then writes a compliment, something nice, about the person whose name is on the sheet, thus:

TERESA VALDEZ

Teresa is always smiling.
She has pretty long black hair.
Teresa is a friendly person.

After everyone has finished writing the first compliment, the sheets are passed again. This process is repeated until each person has his or her own compliment sheet to keep. What a good feeling for everyone in the room!

Role Playing

Taking roles in varied situations is a good way to open up discussion and to encourage group participation. Suggest open-ended situations that are nonthreatening; for example:

1. Cast:
   Teacher: Mrs. Rodríguez
   Principal: Mr. Phillips
   Student: Juan
   Student: Tomás

   Situation: Two Puerto Rican students are suspected of breaking windows in the school building.

2. Cast:
   Mildred
   Frances
   María

   Situation: Three girls walking to school are discussing who will be invited to a party they are planning.

Students can suggest other situations they would like to act out. After the role-playing session, discuss the subject and how the situation was portrayed. Let others try the same situation to see how they would interpret it differently.

Family Grouping

To avoid undesirable individual competition and to promote cooperation, at times divide the class into family groupings. Each family supports its members and assists them in completing work. Weekly progress reports might include, for example, the total number of words we spelled right on the weekly test, the total number of lines we wrote in our journals, a summary of new science ideas we learned, the number of books we read.

Family grouping provides support for each individual. It ensures that each child is directly involved with other children in a caring situation. In establishing family grouping you may need to discuss how a family operates, for instance, how we help each other. Discuss ways of helping effectively, not just giving a person answers, for instance, but helping them learn.

Which Would You Rather Be?

Provide a list of characteristics from which students choose those they would most like to have. Each student gets a copy to mark individually. Before marking their papers, discuss the meaning of each item.

WHAT KIND OF PERSON WOULD YOU LIKE TO BE?

Mark 1 before the word that is most important to you. Mark 2 before the next most important, and so on. The number 14 will mark the thing that is least important to you. I would like to be:

_____ Polite		_____ Loving
_____ Dependable		_____ Creative
_____ Hard-working		_____ Brave
_____ Cheerful		_____ Capable
_____ Neat		_____ Respectful
_____ Helpful to others		_____ Truthful
_____ Smart		_____ Open-minded

After papers are marked (with no names attached), have students tally the results on the board. This can be done with students keeping their own papers. Simply tally the number who marked 1, 2, or 3 for each item. Then tally the number who marked 12, 13, or 14 for each item. This gives you an indication of the high-valued and low-valued items as well as those that were not considered important. Discuss the results for a very provocative interchange.

Something Special

Step 1. Collect enough lemons (or walnuts) so that each person in a group can have one. Number the lemons with a black felt pen. With eyes closed each person draws a lemon from the bag. The leader records the number of the lemon selected. Holding the lemon under the table so it is not seen, each person spends several minutes feeling the lemon, exploring its texture, size, and distinguishing marks. Then each lemon is returned, sight unseen, into the bag.

Step 2. Have students jot down ideas about their lemon, thus:

> *Lemon:*
> Egg-shaped,
> Fits snugly in my hand,
> Scarred across the middle,
> A lump on one end.

The written ideas produce a kind of free-verse poem.

Step 3. Each student reaches in the bag to select his or her lemon, again without looking. Amazingly, most people quickly identify the right lemon!

Step 4. Discuss the experience. Obviously, even lemons are not all alike. Like people, each one is special!

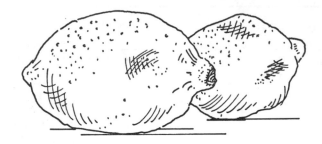

Meet Your Neighbor

A good follow-up to "Something Special" is this activity which focuses on the students.

Step 1. Divide the group in pairs. Each pair of students turns toward each other. Each student is to tell the other about something exciting that happened to him or her.

Step 2. The two students in each pair turn their backs to each other. Then each person writes the answers to these questions:

a) What is your partner wearing today?
b) What color are his/her eyes?
c) Describe his/her face.

Step 3. Students turn toward each other. Usually, they discover how unobservant they are. Discuss how we look at people without really seeing them.

One Big Machine

Form a big circle holding hands. Perform together as one big machine according to directions given by the leader. Tell children what they are going to do; count to three; then the machine performs together, thus:

> Take in lots of air—1, 2, 3 (Breathe deeply)
> Swing arms upward—1, 2, 3 (Move arms up)
> Three steps forward—1, 2, 3 (Step forward)
> Sway right, left, right, left—1, 2, 3 (Sway together)

This group activity provides good experience in working together. Everyone contributes.

Different Viewpoints

Help students become aware of the different ways we may perceive the same thing. Choose any simple object—an apple, a book, a potted plant. Hold the object up before the group, saying: "What is this?" After identifying the object, ask students to write a description of the object using as much detail as possible. Have a number of students read their descriptions aloud as you observe how the descriptions vary. Discuss why our descriptions of the same object differ so much —our background of experiences, a specific aspect of the object that catches our attention, the angle from which we see the object. Discuss whether there is one "right" or "best" way to describe the object.

What Really Happened?

Related to the preceding idea is the description of an event. Arrange to have two people enter your classroom unexpectedly, argue with each other loudly, even push each other around a bit, and then leave abruptly. Have students, who have witnessed the event, write a description of what happened from their point of view. Again, share the descriptions, note how they differ, and discuss why their descriptions are different. Your students can plan other situations to act out for a similar activity.

"The Blind Men and the Elephant"

Older students can read the poem "The Blind Men and the Elephant" which they will probably find amusing. Here is a good demonstration of what causes difference of opinion—limited information, not looking at the whole problem or subject, jumping to conclusions. Students might draw a series of large pictures to illustrate this poem. They can display the pictures as they read or speak the poem together. This poem can also be presented through readers' theater.

THE BLIND MEN AND THE ELEPHANT

It was six men of Indostan
  To learning much inclined,
Who went to see the Elephant
  (Though all of them were blind),
That each by observation
  Might satisfy his mind.

The First approached the Elephant,
  And happening to fall
Against his broad and sturdy side,
  At once began to bawl:
"God bless me! but the Elephant
  Is very like a wall!"

The Second, feeling of the tusk,
  Cried, "Ho! what have we here
So very round and smooth and sharp?
  To me 'tis mighty clear
This wonder of an Elephant
  Is very like a spear!"

The Third approached the animal,
    And happening to take
The squirming trunk within his hands,
    Thus boldly up and spake:
"I see," quoth he, "the Elephant
    Is very like a snake!"

The Fourth reached out his eager hand,
    And felt about the knee.
"What most this wondrous beast is like
    Is mighty plain," quoth he;
" 'Tis clear enough the Elephant
    Is very like a tree!"

The Fifth, who chanced to touch the ear
    Said, "E'en the blindest man
Can tell what this resembles most;
    Deny the fact who can,
This marvel of an Elephant
    Is very like a fan!"

The Sixth no sooner had begun
    About the beast to grope,
Than, seizing on the swinging tail
    That fell within his scope,
"I see," quoth he, "the Elephant
    Is very like a rope!"

And so these men of Indostan
    Disputed loud and long,
Each in his own opinion
    Exceeding stiff and strong.
Though each was partly in the right,
    And all were in the wrong!

                                    John G. Saxe

Bibliotherapy

Sharing a good book can be a way of stimulating discussion about needs that children have in common. Read books aloud for this purpose; for example, *North Town* by Lorenz Graham for grades four and up or *Stevie* by John Steptoe for primary grades. These books happen to be about Black characters, but children will identify with them as human beings who are experiencing things familiar to them.

Other good books that reveal the universal needs and feelings include:

Primary Grades

Sam by Ann Scott (McGraw-Hill, 1967). Sam gets in trouble all the time until his family realizes that he needs a job he can do successfully.

What Can I Do? by Norma Simon (Whitman, 1969). A little Puerto Rican girl is looking for something to contribute.

The Knee-Baby by Mary Jarrell (Farrar, Straus & Giroux, 1973). Accepting a new baby is not easy.

Ebbie by Eve Rice (Morrow, 1975). Eddie resents being called Ebbie after he is able to pronounce his own name distinctly.

Books for Older Students

Lizzie Lies a Lot by Elizabeth Levy (Delacorte, 1976). Third-graders will be able to understand Lizzie's need to add glamour to her life.

The Meat in the Sandwich by Alice Bach (Harper & Row, 1975). Ten-year-old Mike creates a fantasy world to make his life more interesting.

It's Like This, Cat by Emily Neville (Harper & Row, 1963). Adolescent Dave Mitchell learns to get along with his father.

Universal Problems Children Face

Children today need to be able to talk about varied problems that were not so freely discussed even five years ago. Death and divorce are two topics that we can talk about in the classroom as an aid to students who are faced with these events in their lives. Books can often serve to provide a realistic perspective as well as to open up the topic for students who may find it difficult to introduce such topics to the teacher. Many fine books written for young people handle these subjects sensitively.

DIVORCED OR SINGLE-PARENT FAMILIES

Primary Grades

Me Day by Joan Lexau (Dial, 1971)

I Love My Mother by Paul Zindel (Harper & Row, 1975)

Jenny's Revenge by Anne N. Baldwin (Four Winds, 1974)

Books for Older Students

A Month of Sundays (Watts, 1972)

I Know You, Al and *A Girl Called Al* by Constance Greene (Viking, 1975, 1969)

Last Night I Saw Andromeda by Charlotte Anker (Walck, 1975)

When the Sad One Comes to Stay by Florence P. Heide (Lippincott, 1975)

DEATH AND RELATIONSHIP WITH AGED PEOPLE

Primary Grades

Nana Upstairs and Nana Downstairs by Tomie De Paola (Putnam, 1973)

My Grandson Lew by Charlotte Zolotow (Harper & Row, 1974)

Nonna by Jennifer Bartoli (Harvey House, 1975)

Annie and the Old One by Miska Miles (Little, Brown, 1971)

Books for Older Students

Away Is So Far by Toby Talbot (Four Winds, 1974)

Good Times by Lucille Clifton (Random House, 1969)

Where the Lilies Bloom by Vera and Bill Cleaver (Lippincott, 1969)

A Taste of Blackberries by Doris B. Smith (Crowell, 1973)

Hang Tough, Paul Mather by Alfred Slote (Lippincott, 1973)

Talking about Friendship

Having friends is an important part of every child's life. Read the small book *A Friend Is Someone Who Likes You* by Joan Anglund (Harcourt Brace Jovanovich, 1958). After discussing ideas about what a friend is, have students write other endings for this line:

A friend is . . .

(someone who thinks you're neat,

a person who chooses you first, etc.).

Compile their ideas in an illustrated book which can be placed on the reading table where everyone can read it at leisure. Such class-produced books can then be placed in the school library.

Getting Along with Others

Choose books about friendships and getting along with others to read aloud to the class. Encourage students to talk about the problems of getting along together. Good selections are the following:

Young children:

Cohen, Miriam. *Best Friends.* Macmillan, 1971.

———. *Will I Have a Friend?* Macmillan, 1967.

Kantrowitz, Mildred. *I Wonder If Herbie's Home Yet.* Parents, 1971.

Zolotow, Charlotte. *Janey.* Harper & Row, 1973.

Sherman, Ivan. *I Do Not Like It When My Friend Comes to Visit.* Harcourt Brace Jovanovich, 1973.

Middle School:

Burch, Robert. *Queenie Peavy.* Viking, 1966.

Clifton, Lucille. *The Times They Used to Be.* Holt, Rinehart and Winston, 1974.

Coles, Robert. *Dead End School.* Little, Brown, 1968.

Corcoran, Barbara. *Sam.* Atheneum, 1967.

Fox, Paula. *Portrait of Ivan.* Bradbury, 1969.

Little, Jean. *One to Grow On*. Little, Brown, 1969.

Rockwell, Thomas. *How to Eat Fried Worms*. Watts, 1973.

Sachs, Marilyn. *Peter and Veronica*. Doubleday, 1969.

Sharmat, Marjorie Weinman. *Getting Something on Maggie Marmelstein*. Harper & Row, 1971.

Smith, Doris B. *Tough Chauncey*. Morrow, 1974.

Stolz, Mary S. *A Wonderful, Terrible Time*. Harper & Row, 1967.

———. *The Noonday Friends*. Harper & Row, 1965.

Wallace, Barbara Brooks. *Victoria*. Follett, 1972.

Topic for Thought

Discuss the Chinese proverb presented on the opposite page. Have students notice the progression from *right* to *peace*. Students can discuss the importance of peace and how it can be brought about.

This poetic presentation can also be used as a model for student writing. They can follow this pattern:

> If there is _____,
> There will be _____.

Two-line free verse poems can be produced like this:

> If there is prejudice anywhere,
> There will be unhappiness.

Repeating this pattern produces additional verses. The verses could be rhymed, thus:

> If there is one friend in your life,
> There will be singing.
> If there is love in your life,
> There will be joy-bells ringing.

Children Who Are Different

Focusing attention on children who are physically disabled may open the door to understanding children who are different for various reasons—because of beliefs, appearance, or ways of behaving. Read some of the following:

Me Too by Vera and Bill Cleaver (Lippincott, 1973)—retarded twin

Don't Feel Sorry for Paul by Bernard Wolf (Lippincott, 1974)—artificial hands and feet

The Nothing Place by Eleanor Spence (Harper & Row, 1973)—deafness

If there is right in the soul,
There will be beauty in the person;
If there is beauty in the person,
There will be harmony in the home;
If there is harmony in the home,
There will be order in the nation;
If there is order in the nation,
There will be peace in the world.

Chinese Proverb

Deenie by July Blume (Bradbury, 1972)—wearing a brace
Door in the Wall by Margerite De Angeli (Doubleday, 1949)—paralysis
Don't Take Teddy by Babbis Freis-Baastad (Scribner's, 1967)—retarded
Take Wing by Jean Little (Little, Brown, 1968)—retarded
Let the Balloon Go by Ivan Southall (St. Martin's, 1968)—spastic
A Racecourse for Andy by Patricia Wrightson (Harcourt Brace Jovanovich, 1968)
—retarded

Happiness Is a Warm Puppy

Use the book *Happiness Is a Warm Puppy* by Charles Schulz (Determined Press) to motivate students to write about what happiness is to them. Each student selects one thing that represents happiness and illustrates it on an $8\frac{1}{2} \times 11$ inch sheet of paper. Then bind the sheets together to make a book: Happiness is . . . Students will enjoy sharing their ideas.

Give Yourself a Present

If you could give yourself a present, what would you choose? This question should start a lively discussion. After students have talked about their ideas, ask them to write about the present they would choose. Ask them to describe the present and to tell why they selected that particular thing. The present could be drawn followed by sharing the illustration orally in small groups.

Class Survey

Have students in your room complete the following questionnaire.

Name _____

Address _____

Who lives with you?

_____

_____

Where were you born? _____

What is your birthday? _____

How many different countries have you traveled in? Name them.

_____

Name the different states you have lived in:

_____

_____

How long have you lived in this state? _____

What languages do you speak? _____

Discuss the questionnaire with students. Add questions they would like to know the answers to. Caution: Whenever you ask personal questions in a school activity, permit students to pass or to omit information that makes them feel uncomfortable.

Compiling the Data Collected

After the survey is completed, have small groups of students compile the data collected. Each group can make a graph, a map, or a poster, some way of presenting the information collected about the class. Here are a few ideas for the statistics gathered:

1. Make a map of the school area and locate each student's home. Pinpoint the location of each student's home.
2. How many people were born in each state?
3. Which students were born in the same month? Make a poster listing class birthdays to celebrate during the year.
4. Which countries have students traveled to? How many students have traveled to the same countries?
5. Which states have students lived in? How many students have lived in specific states?
6. How many people were born in your state? How long have class members lived in the state?

Post the findings of this survey on a large bulletin board. Students will be very much interested in reading the information.

Writing as a Way of Sharing

All children can write successfully, but we may need to provide assistance at first by printing or typing stories for children to help them gain confidence and skill. This is an excellent job for an aide. When taking dictation, follow the language of the student, but use standard conventional spelling. For children who speak other languages, provide assistance in the language spoken.

Remember to provide positive comments about anything children produce. If you want to encourage writing, first focus on developing fluency, just getting words on paper. Sharing what they write helps students get to know and understand each other. As they share, they also become excited about writing as a way of telling the stories they have inside them!

Cross-level Tutoring

Having older students work with younger ones as tutors is highly beneficial for both groups. High school students can work in junior high and elementary classrooms. Junior high and upper elementary can work in primary grades. Choose students from different ethnic groups to promote cross-cultural awareness. Students who speak languages other than English could be especially helpful.

Cross-age tutoring is not just for the brightest students. Those who may be having trouble reading or who need a psychological boost can function very well as tutors with younger children. Nothing is more gratifying than a young child's appreciative comments. They love having the attention of older students.

Young tutors may need some teacher guidance, but there are many classroom activities they can assist in ably, for example, printing dictated stories, listening to children read, spelling words for children who are writing, reading books to children, or recording a story on tape for children to listen to.

SUPPORTIVE EVALUATION TECHNIQUES

Your attitude toward children is reflected in the methods you use for evaluation of any work they do. Effective techniques that avoid the failure syndrome include the following:

1. *Self-evaluation.* As much as possible, have students check their own work. Provide answer sheets so they can discover mistakes immediately. Stress reading items over again as needed, and correcting errors. If you eliminate yourself from this kind of "grading," you cease to be the ogre who has all the "right" answers.
2. *Individual conferences.* Have a short conference with each student once a week, if possible. Five minutes of individual attention does a lot for children who need support. This is a good time for examining children's writing or talking about the library book they are currently reading.
3. *Send a letter to parents.* Several times during the year, send a letter to each parent commending at least one thing their child has accomplished. Children will be glad to take a Good Work Letter home. Be sure to write this letter in the language of the home even if you have to prepare several translations.
4. *Accentuate the positive!* Count up what students do accomplish, not what they fail to achieve or the mistakes they make. Compare:

    Wow, you spelled thirteen words out of fifteen correctly!

    Too bad, you missed two words out of fifteen today.

SOURCES TO INVESTIGATE

Brown, George. *Human Teaching for Human Learning.* Viking, 1971. ($8.50)

Canfield, Jack, and Harold Wells. *100 Ways to Enhance Self-concept in the Classroom.* Prentice-Hall, 1976.

Glasser, William. *Schools without Failure.* Harper & Row, 1969.

Ginott, Haim. *Teacher and Child.* Macmillan, 1972.

Gordon, Thomas. *T.E.T.: Teacher Effectiveness Training.* Wyden, 1974. ($9.95)

Holt, John. *How Children Fail.* Delta, 1966.

Human Values and Understanding. U.S. Government Printing Office, 1976. (55¢)

Moffett, James. *A Student-Centered Curriculum, Grades K-13: A Handbook for Teachers.* Houghton-Mifflin, 1968, 1976.

Schrank, Jeffrey. *Teaching Human Beings: 101 Subversive Activities for the Classroom.* Beacon, 1972. ($3.45)

Simon, Sidney, et al. *Values Clarification.* Hart, 1972.

Tiedt, Iris, and Sidney Tiedt. *Creative Writing Ideas.* Contemporary Press, 1975. Box 1524, San Jose, CA 95109. ($1.50)

Tiedt, Sidney, and Iris Tiedt. *Language Arts Activities in the Classroom.* Allyn and Bacon. 1978. ($6.95)

3

Focusing on Language

The limits of my language mean the limits of my world.

|Ludwig Wittgenstein

The United States is an English-speaking country. We sometimes assume, therefore, that people in this country are monolinguals, people who speak only one language, and that English is the only language of the country. Few of us are fully aware of the diversity of languages actually spoken in this country.

LANGUAGES SPOKEN IN THE UNITED STATES

The accompanying chart shows states that have considerable numbers of speakers of specific languages. It is easy to see that some languages are concentrated in certain areas. Did you know that a large number of Basque speakers live in Idaho, for example? Within a state the languages are not distributed evenly, however, and the populations speaking these languages may be very different. Some languages may be limited to a group of older generation speakers, while others represent groups of recent immigrants, and still others are groups who have maintained their language across several generations.

The data reported on this chart do not tell us the full story of languages in the United States. They do not indicate, for example, the great variety and number of Native American languages spoken throughout the country. Recent figures show, furthermore, that Spanish, the most widely spoken language other than

LANGUAGE LOCATION

Location	Language
Arizona	Spanish, Uto-Aztecan
California	German, Italian, Spanish, Polish, Yiddish, French, Russian, Hungarian, Swedish, Greek, Norwegian, Dutch, Japanese, Chinese, Serbo-Croatian, Portuguese, Danish, Arabic, Tagalog, Armenian, Turkish, Persian, Malay (Indonesian), Scandinavian, Basque, Mandarin, Gypsy (Romani)
Florida	Spanish
Hawaii	Japanese, Tagalog, Polynesian
Idaho	Basque
Illinois	German, Italian, Spanish, Polish, Yiddish, Russian, Swedish, Greek, Norwegian, Slovak, Dutch, Ukrainian, Lithuanian, Czech, Serbo-Croatian, Danish, Balto-Slavic
Maine	French, Amerindian
Massachusetts	Italian, Polish, Yiddish, French, Swedish, Greek, Lithuanian, Portuguese, Celtic, Armenian, Albanian, Breton
Michigan	German, Polish, French, Hungarian, Dutch, Finnish, Arabic, Balto-Slavic, Near E. Arabic dialects, Amerindian, Iraqi, Algonquin, Gypsy (Romani)
Minnesota	Swedish, Norwegian, Finnish
Montana	Algonquin
New Hampshire	French
New Jersey	German, Italian, Polish, Yiddish, Russian, Hungarian, Slovak, Dutch, Ukrainian
New York	German, Italian, Spanish, Polish, Yiddish, French, Russian, Hungarian, Swedish, Greek, Norwegian, Slovak, Dutch, Ukrainian, Lithuanian, Czech, Chinese, Portuguese, Danish, Finnish, Arabic, Rumanian, Balto-Slavic, Celtic, Hebrew, Armenian, Near E. Arabic dialects, Turkish, Uralic, Albanian, Persian, Scandinavian, Amerindian, Dalmatian, Breton, Mandarin, Egyptian, Georgian, Gypsy (Romani), Athabascan
Ohio	German, Polish, Hungarian, Greek, Slovak, Czech, Serbo-Croatian, Slovenian
Pennsylvania	German, Italian, Polish, Yiddish, Russian, Hungarian, Greek, Slovak, Ukrainian, Lithuanian, Serbo-Croatian
Rhode Island	French, Portuguese
Texas	Spanish
Washington	Swedish, Norwegian, Scandinavian, Amerindian
Wisconsin	German

ADAPTED FROM: Theodore Andersson and Mildred Boyer. *Bilingual Schooling in the United States.* U.S. Office of Education, 1970, pp. 26–27.

English, has over 4 million speakers. This information is of great importance to the classroom teacher. Students need to learn this aspect of the history, geography, and sociology of the United States.

All teachers can expect to have non-English-speaking students in their class at some point. Even when all the students in a class speak English, some may have another language as their first language or the language they use at home. Students whose only language is English, furthermore, need to be exposed to other languages and to be made aware of the importance of other languages in this country. In fact, teachers will find what everyone who has studied a foreign language knows—that one of the best ways to stimulate interest in one's own language is to study another one.

The increased concern for encouraging cultural pluralism means that any teacher's involvement with students who speak languages other than English extends beyond teaching them English. This book does not, therefore, focus on teaching English as a second language. Language is an important aspect of culture, and respect for the culture of different groups includes respect for their languages. As we discuss how to value the student and the student's culture, we must remember the importance of valuing the student's own language, specifically, not just the language the student *should* know but all the aspects of the language the student already knows and can use.

The purpose of this chapter is to open up the possibilities for exploring language in the classroom. The information presented here will:

1. introduce concepts about language to the teacher
2. provide activities that integrate non-English speakers into the class
3. expose monolingual English speakers to other languages
4. develop student awareness of and respect for different ways of speaking
5. use language as a way of exploring other cultures

The chapter is divided into three parts. The first part presents background information for the teacher about language and bilingualism. The second focuses on ideas for the study of language diversity in the classroom. The third section introduces ideas for promoting understanding of the varieties of English used in a classroom with special attention to Black English.

THE NATURE OF LANGUAGE

One of the first steps in discussing language is to clarify what we mean when we talk about language. Each of the following sentences illustrates an approach to the meaning of the word "language."

1. Maria speaks several *languages* fluently.
2. Teachers don't speak our *language*.
3. You'd better watch your *language!*
4. Researchers have studied children's acquisition of *language* from one to five years of age.

5. All of the *language* arts are interrelated.
6. Numbers are a universal *language*.
7. Even the way we cross our legs is an important aspect of body *language*.
8. Everyone knows that doctors speak a different *language*.
9. Dolphins have a complex *language* that enables them to communicate at great distances.
10. Hemingway's use of *language* is a model for young writers.

Each sentence uses the same word but look at the variety of ideas expressed.

1. language = human system of vocal communication, historically associated with a particular group and culture
2. language = understanding based on similar background or experience
3. language = manner in which people speak, usually with reference to correctness or other social standard
4. language = knowledge that sounds can be combined into meaningful patterns, not confined to a particular language
5. language = subject of study; specifically, skills taught in school such as reading, spelling, handwriting
6. language = method of communicating ideas through a system of symbols
7. language = transmission of meaning or intent
8. language = vocabulary and usage associated with particular occupational or social group
9. language = means of communication used by animals
10. language = style of speaking or writing characteristic of an individual

This section will explore different approaches to language. It will cover ways to look at language capacity, language use in a particular context, how languages vary and how they are similar, and what we mean by the ability to know more than one language.

Psychology and Language

Some linguists study language as a property of the human mind. This approach depends on the distinction between "language" and "speech." "Speech" refers to our actual utterances while "language" refers to the abstract ability to use language, a capacity that we all possess no matter how we use it or what we say. For linguists, this language/speech distinction becomes a distinction between "competence" (knowledge of the possible ways of constructing sentences in a language) and "performance" (actual speech). What a person actually says at any particular moment (performance) represents only a small sample of the ability of any speaker of the language to produce an infinite variety of sentences (competence). In order to study language, then, one studies *ability* rather than samples of utterances. Our use of language is based not on imitation or repetition of utterances but on an ability to create new utterances based on our knowledge of the language structure, the grammar system of a language. This perspective emphasizes the equality and universality of language capacity or competence.

The way children learn language illustrates the natural human capacity for language. Individual differences are insignificant compared to the fact that children learn language before they come to school just as children learn to walk, with the same ease and unfolding of ability. Differences in language use increase as children are exposed to different experiences, but the potential for language remains the same.

Sociology and Language

Sociolinguists approach language from a different perspective, seeing language as a means of communication. This use of language includes not only the words used but also tone of voice, position of body, and relationship between participants. How we interpret an utterance depends on the social context in which it is used. A speaker's language capacity is the ability to know when and where to say what and to whom. This is called "communicative competence." Appropriate use of language depends upon such factors as relative status of speaker and hearer, sex, age, social class/occupation, topic, and environment.

The major difference between child and adult speakers of a language is that children do not yet know how to use language appropriately. Children begin learning the social requirements of language use from the earliest stages of language acquisition. One of the first distinctions they learn is that you talk differently to babies than to adults. However, children are usually not exposed to many different language contexts until they are in school. They need to learn, for example, how the way you talk in class is different from the way you talk on the playground. This ability to adapt speech to different contexts is one that we adults may take for granted. Because we are not aware of the extent to which we vary our speech, we do not fully appreciate the language-learning task facing children. We cannot always understand the reasons for student mistakes until we see mistakes as indications of their trying to learn which features of speech are appropriate in what contexts. This is an essential aspect of language learning that continues to be developed throughout the school years.

The School and Language

A very different concept of language is represented by the idea that schools should teach children "language." If children's language abilities develop naturally, what is the role of the teacher in assisting this kind of development? First of all, the teacher can provide language experiences for the child. Children's grasp of language at the oral level leads to success in writing and reading language. Also, children need to be exposed to a variety of language input in order to learn standards of correctness and appropriateness. The more the child reads, listens, and speaks, the more about language the child will learn.

The other aspect of the teacher's role is to understand the nature of student mistakes. Whether the "mistake" is grammatically incorrect or represents inappropriate usage, it is not a random error but indicates the state of the child's knowledge about language. Mistakes made by students are frequently the best sources of information for the teacher about what students know of how language works (grammar) and how they are applying this knowledge. Consequently, students' mistakes should not be treated as examples of being "wrong" but as instances of learning experiences. Just marking mistakes on student papers is not helpful when students do not know why it was wrong and what they should have done instead. We need to provide more experiences in hearing and speaking language from which children can abstract concepts of grammar and usage. This is true for all children, but especially for those learning English as a second language.

Language Variety

One of the tasks of linguistics is to describe the structure of various languages. On the basis of language structure and history, languages are classified together into families. Languages that superficially may seem very different are considered part of the same family; English belongs to the family, for example, that includes German, French, Russian, Greek, and Sanskrit. Languages that belong to other families can be expected to appear even more different from English, for example, Japanese, Arabic, Hungarian, and Swahili. Examples of ways in which languages differ include the following:

1. Out of a limited number of possible sounds, no languages use precisely the same group of sounds. Many sounds do not occur in English and, therefore, sound strange to ears accustomed to English. However, no sounds are unusual or uncommon. All are found in the major languages of the world.
2. Some languages have a system for classifying nouns. Often this is based on gender. Objects are arbitrarily assigned to one of two groups called masculine and feminine (as in Spanish), or to one of three groups: masculine, feminine, and neuter (as in German and Russian). This use of gender is not equivalent to the division of humans into male and female. For example, in German, madchen (maiden) and fraulein (young woman) are both neuter. Different languages may assign the same object different genders. The word for table is "tisch" in German (masculine) and "mesa" in Spanish (feminine). In languages with gender, pronouns usually agree in gender with the nouns to which they refer. In addition, adjectives usually have different endings depending on the gender and number (singular or plural) of the noun modified. Note this example in French:

ils	préfèrent	les	tasses	blanches
they	*prefer*	*the*	*cups*	*white*
(3rd person, masculine, plural)	(3rd person, plural)	(plural)	(feminine, plural)	(feminine, plural)

In this sentence, the pronoun "ils" could refer to "les hommes" (men, masculine, plural) or to "les chats" (cats, masculine, plural) but not to "les femmes" (women, feminine, plural). Therefore, French speakers easily confuse the English he/she/it contrast and use he/she for inanimate objects. Examples of languages with a noun classification system not based on gender are the Bantu (African) languages. In these languages nouns are grouped into categories based primarily on the physical shape of the object; for example, long and thin, small and round.

3. The concept of *word* differs from language to language. The Japanese word "ikimasu," for example, carries the potential meaning of these English words:

Japanese: ikimasu

$$\text{English:} \begin{Bmatrix} \text{I} \\ \text{you} \\ \text{he} \\ \text{she} \\ \text{we} \\ \text{they} \end{Bmatrix} \begin{Bmatrix} \text{am} \\ \text{is} \\ \text{are} \end{Bmatrix} \text{going}$$

Japanese speakers decide who is going from the context of the conversation.

An example of the concept of word taken from the Yana Indian language in northern California* is even more complicated:

yābanaumawildjigummaha'nigi

yā = several people move
banauma = everybody
wil = across
dji = to the West
gumma = indeed
ha' = let us
nigi = we

Try reading these definitions as a "sentence."

Even with the parts of the long word defined, we still do not understand it, because we arrange our thoughts differently and do not repeat words as the Yanas did. An English sentence that conveys the same meaning as the Yana word might go like this:

Let us each move to the West.

4. Word order differs in various languages. In English, adjectives usually precede the noun described. Compare these phrases in English and Spanish:

English	*Spanish*
the blue book	el libro azul
	(the book blue)

---

* J. N. Hook, *The Story of American English*, Harcourt Brace Jovanovich, 1972, p. 2.

5. Word order affects meaning in English, as is clear in these sentences:

> The dog bit the man.
> The man bit the dog.

In other languages special endings carry meaning so the words can be arranged in any order. For example, this Latin sentence says "Peter (subject ending *us*) sees Paul (object ending *um*)" no matter what the order.

> Petr*us* videt Paul*um*.
> Paul*um* Petr*us* videt.
> Videt Paul*um* Petr*us*.

Language Universals

Currently the emphasis in linguistics is away from the specification of language differences and toward the discovery of language universals. Through in-depth study of one language, linguists seek to describe structure that is common to all human languages and eventually to make claims about the nature of the human mind.

While languages differ in vocabulary for cultural and historical reasons, all languages have the same expressive potential. There is no such thing as a primitive language, just as there is no such thing as a primitive people. All human languages and all human cultures are rich and complex and capable of adapting to different circumstances. A language may not express some concepts that are considered important in our society, such as the linear notion of time, but it can develop the vocabulary to express any of these concepts if the speakers of the language consider it necessary. The use of formerly unwritten native African languages to conduct all the affairs of law, government, and education is an example of the flexibility of language. Another example is Hebrew, a dead language (not learned by anyone as a first language), which was revived for use as a national language in Israel. These languages have suddenly developed masses of new vocabulary as they expand to meet the demands placed on them. All languages possess the capacity to adapt to such new uses.

Bilingualism

We call a person who speaks two languages "bilingual." What does this really mean? The term bilingual covers a variety of types of language knowledge and use. People often use bilingual without specifying what they mean. The following are examples of different kinds of language behavior that have been called bilingualism. Which would you consider bilingualism?

1. People who study a second language in school. They may read it slowly, write it with difficulty, and speak it painfully. English speakers often know French or German this way.

2. People who can understand much of another language when it is spoken but cannot read, write, or speak it themselves. These people may have grown up with grandparents who spoke Ukrainian or Japanese as a first language, for instance, and English poorly or not at all. The parents knew both languages but the children learned only enough to understand the grandparents without being able to use the language.

3. People who learn a second language when they are older, often adults. This is common among people who move to another country or do business with other countries. Although the second language is spoken often, they may retain a foreign accent. Their degree of knowledge of the second language is limited by the contexts in which they use it: only for business and never at home, only with strangers and never with friends in conversation, or only in reading and writing and never in speaking.

4. People who learn two languages while young. These people can use both languages for a wide range of situations and functions, although each language may become associated with particular topics. When there is a large community of people who share two languages, such as English and Spanish, people may switch frequently from one to another even in the middle of a sentence. This natural language behavior is called code-switching.

5. People who can translate, sentence for sentence, from one language to another. This is the rarest group. The difficulty of the task, even for those who use several languages easily, is the reason there are few simultaneous translators. This skill is not a normal part of social interaction.

These examples represent different degrees of bilingualism. Factors affecting bilingualism include the following: whether the language was learned first or second, when the language was learned (child or adult), and for what situations and functions the language is used.

Bilingualism plays an important role in language change and language spread. Historically, languages in contact influence each other. This influence cannot occur if languages exist side by side but separately. However, when people begin to communicate with neighbors who speak another language, each learns the other's language. Because some people are bilingual, their knowledge of one language can influence the other. Individual changes then spread to monolingual speakers.

The high percentage of French words in English resulted in part from the language contact and bilingualism that began in 1066 with the French-speaking (Norman) invasion of England. English has subsequently been enriched by words from many different languages as English speakers learned other languages. Spanish, although originally from Spain, has developed independently in Latin America with distinctive differences because of long separation and isolation. In addition, Latin American Spanish has been influenced by contact with Native American languages. Many Spanish/English bilinguals have lived in the United States long enough for their Spanish to be influenced by English. The Spanish spoken in the United States varies regionally depending on where the original

Spanish speakers came from, the length of time they have lived in the United States, the amount of bilingualism in the community, and the variety (dialect) of English spoken locally. The English spoken by the non-Spanish inhabitants has hardly been influenced at all by Spanish because fewer people learn Spanish as a second language.

Bilingualism is an important part of life for many people in the United States. Pretending that everyone is or should be solely English-speaking means ignoring the diversity and wealth of language experience in this country. If you disregard the presence of other languages besides English in your area or community, you risk denying your students the ability to participate fully and to communicate with others in their community.

Two Approaches to Bilingual Education

Two different strategies are currently being used in bilingual education: (1) the *transitional* program in which the native language is gradually replaced by English and (2) the *maintenance* program in which both the native language and English are maintained throughout. The transitional approach is clearly designed to aid the non-English-speaking (NES) student who needs to learn English quickly in order to function in an English-speaking classroom. The maintenance program, on the other hand, places equal value on two languages and assumes that all children can benefit from learning a second language. Under this system NES children are not penalized because, while they are learning English, the other students are learning another language, too.

A well-planned maintenance bilingual program provides for instruction in the minority language for all students, at least in the lower grades. NES students feel included in the mainstream curriculum and are supported by the positive approach of the program. Spanish-speaking students, for example, learn to read in Spanish first before they are expected to read in English. Spanish is easier for them because it is more familiar and the phoneme to grapheme correspondence is regular. The transition to reading in English is made easily later. The maintenance bilingual program also benefits the English-speaking students. In addition to the opportunity to learn another language, they are learning about the culture as well. English-speaking students are challenged, not threatened, by this experience. As NES students acquire fluency in English, both languages can be used interchangeably for instruction. In the fully bilingual approach, all students learn to speak, read, and write both languages.

One major problem for proponents of bilingual education has been people's attitudes towards bilinguals and those who do not speak English. The presence of NES students in schools has been seen as a problem and bilingual or ESL programs have been considered expensive extras rather than the right of the students involved. Often, NES students are perceived as unintelligent because they do not know English, while eradicating the native language is viewed as a better solution than bilingualism. We might note however, that bilingualism is a considered disability only for students learning English as a second language. For English-speaking high school students, learning another language such as French is supposedly an asset. Spanish is taught painfully in high schools to many students who might have learned it naturally as children if they had been in bilingual programs.

What is the goal of bilingual education programs for this country? Bilingual education programs aim to foster the coexistence of many languages, respecting the right of different groups to maintain their own language. The programs provide evidence that knowledge of two languages does not hinder a person's ability to use either one of the languages. English has never been the sole language spoken in this country, but the fact that many people are bilingual has not been acknowledged by schools. Recognition of the presence of bilingualism and encouragement of the increasing development of bilingualism is crucial if schools are to serve students and the community.

LANGUAGE ACTIVITIES IN THE CLASSROOM

It is essential that *all* students become aware of the diversity of languages present in the United States and that they learn to respect and value the ability to speak more than one language. This is important for bilingual and English-speaking students alike. This section of the chapter includes (1) strategies for developing positive attitudes toward language diversity and (2) a special focus on activities related to the Spanish language and speakers of Spanish in the United States.

No attempt is made, on the other hand, to include the teaching of English as a second language. Such instruction requires more extensive training and different coverage. A number of texts have been written for that express purpose, for example, *Teaching English as a Second Language* by M. Finocchiaro (Harper & Row). Teaching specific languages such as Spanish, French, Yupik, or Tagalog would also require more extensive development than space permits although many of the ideas presented in this book could be adapted to such language instruction.

EXPLORING LANGUAGE DIVERSITY

We can help students of all ages become aware of the diversity of language that exists in the United States. Do they know, for example, that 4 million U.S. citizens speak Spanish? Have they ever heard of such languages as Tagalog, Basque, or Romani? Somewhere in the elementary school curriculum this information should be included. The activities in this section are designed to promote the teaching of such language learning that should be an integral part of both social studies and language arts.

Discussing the Value of Knowing More than One Language

Open discussions about languages in our country will aid students in recognizing the issues involved. Discuss the following topics:

1. List the advantages of knowing a second language. List the disadvantages. (Are there any?)
2. How many different languages are spoken in your area? Do you know someone who speaks more than one language?
3. What languages would you like to learn? Why?

Our Language Family

Many words in English are related to words in other languages, not because they are borrowed but because the words in all of these languages came from the same source. English and many of the languages spoken in Europe and India belong to the language family called Indo-European. Students are sure to notice the family resemblances when you present lists that compare familiar words such as mother and father in languages that belong to this family.

English	*mother*	*father*
Irish	mathair	athair
Spanish	madre	padre
French	mère	père
Italian	madre	padre
Portuguese	mae	pai
German	mutter	vater
Swedish	moder	fader
Russian	maty	otyets
Dutch	moeder	vader
Latin	mater	pater
Greek	meter	pater
Sanskrit	mata	pita

Contrast:

Hebrew	imma	av

What language does English most resemble? (German) Many of the languages listed may be unfamiliar to the students. Discuss with the class where these languages are spoken.

The Language Tree

Prepare a bulletin board to provide information about the family of Indo-European languages spoken by half the world's population and the relationship of English to other languages. Construct a large tree out of construction paper, with eight branches representing the main groups:

Albanian

Armenian

Balto-Slavic: Russian, Polish, Serbo-Croatian, Czech, Ukrainian, Bulgarian, Lithuanian

Celtic: Irish, Scots Gaelic, Welsh, Breton, Cornish

Greek

Indo-Iranian: Hindi, Urdu, Bengali, Persian

Romance: French, Italian, Spanish, Portuguese, Rumanian

Germanic: German, English, Dutch, Danish, Norwegian, Swedish

Tocharian ⎫
Hittite ⎭ extinct languages

Have students research what languages belong to each branch. Where does English fit in? Hittite and Tocharian died out a long time ago and are known today only through archaeological discoveries. Latin is no longer learned by anyone as a first language. Other languages have died out recently (such as Cornish) or are now dying out (Breton). Which are the most populous branches? In what countries are these languages spoken?

Exploring Different Languages

When the tree is constructed and the branches labeled with some of the major languages they include, have students add life to the tree by discovering words in these different languages. (See pages 73–74 for suggestions to get them started.) Students can look up words or use words they have found in books. Provide "leaves" cut out of construction paper on which to write words to place on the tree according to the "branch" they belong to.

Exercises such as looking up the word for *ten* in many languages will help demonstrate to students the relationship among these languages; their similarities and differences. Here are some examples to begin with. Check dictionaries and encyclopedias for more.

English	*ten*
French	dix
Italian	dieci
Spanish	diez
Portuguese	dez
Rumanian	zece
German	zehn
Dutch	tien
Swedish	tio
Danish	ti
Norwegian	ti

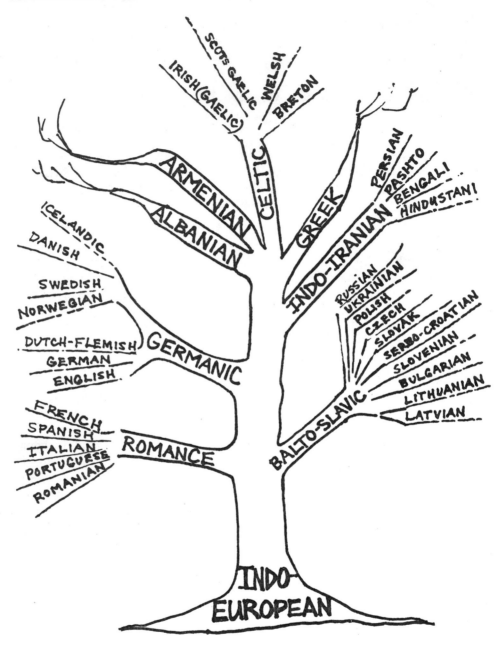

The World's Language Families

Ask students to name languages that do not belong to the Indo-European language family. (Check names against the Indo-European family tree you constructed.) Names they may suggest include:

Chinese	(Sino-Tibetan)
Japanese	(Japanese and Korean)
Hebrew	(Hamito-Semitic)
Navajo	(American Indian)
Hungarian	(Ural-Altaic)

After the class has accumulated a list, have them look up the languages to find out which languages are related to each other. There are many language families besides the Indo-European and some include languages with many speakers.* Students may be surprised to learn that Chinese and Japanese are not related but belong to separate families. Many American Indian languages belong to distinctly different language families as well.

Have students research how many people speak each language. They can prepare a chart of the most widely spoken languages in the world. Figures can be obtained by counting the population of countries that speak a particular language, or you can use information on what languages people learn as a second language. Check figures in almanacs and encyclopedias. Because the population of China is large, more people grow up speaking Chinese than any other language. However, English is the most widely used second language.

English Borrowings

English is a mixture of many languages. Although English is historically related to German, it has been heavily influenced by French and has borrowed words from many of the other languages it has been in contact with. Words that were borrowed a long time ago are now considered part of English. Words borrowed recently usually show their foreign origins. When students look up word origins in the dictionary, point out that any word that does not come from Old English must have been borrowed into English at some time.

List a number of borrowed words on the board for students. How many of the words do they know? Can they guess what language each word was borrowed from? Borrowed words include:

Language	*Word*
Malay	ketchup
Arabic	alcohol
German	kindergarten, sauerkraut
French	souvenir, menu, encore

---

* Other language families include Malayo-Polynesian, Bantu, and Dravidian.

Language	*Word*
Hindi	shampoo
Spanish	bonanza, mosquito
Dutch	cole slaw, sleigh
American Indian	squash, raccoon
Italian	macaroni, piano
Yiddish	kosher
Japanese	kimono
Scandinavian	smorgasbord

After you have discussed these words with the students, prepare a display showing the origins of the words. Use a map of the world pinned to the bulletin board with the words printed on cards placed near their country of origin. Or mount the Indo-European tree on the bulletin board and place the borrowed words on leaf shapes attached to the proper branches. Discuss how the display shows which languages have contributed most to the English language. Why are some languages represented more than others? Speculate on why these words might have been borrowed.

English in Other Languages

Just as English has borrowed many words for new things, so other languages have borrowed words from English for objects or ideas that came from English-speaking people. Familiar appearing or sounding words can be found in French, Japanese, Russian, Spanish, and many other languages. Ask students to guess what the following words are.

le pique-nique	(French, picnic)
le coquetel	(French, cocktail)
el ampayer	(Spanish, umpire)
los jonroneros	(Spanish, homerun hitters)
jiipu	(Japanese, jeeps)
gamu	(Japanese, chewing gum)
garu-furendo	(Japanese, girlfriend)
futbol	(Russian, football)
parken	(German, to park)
hitchhiken	(German, to hitchhike)

Numbers Around the World

Prepare a chart for the bulletin board featuring numbers and their names in different languages. Write large numerals from one to ten along the side and next to them write the names in several languages including English. If possible, use languages that are represented in the classroom or in the community. Read the names to the students so that they know how to pronounce them. If there are students in the class who know other languages besides English, use number words from those languages frequently enough to familiarize the other students with the words in contexts where the meaning is clear.

	English	Spanish	French	German
1	one	uno	un	eins
2	two	dos	deux	zwei
3	three	tres	trois	drei
4	four	cuatro	quatre	vier
5	five	cinco	cinq	funf
6	six	seis	six	sechs
7	seven	siete	sept	sieben
8	eight	ocho	huit	acht
9	nine	nueve	neuf	neun
10	ten	diez	dix	zehn

Students can easily see similarities between the words in different languages. Discuss why words are similar and what it means for languages to be related.

The Language of Numerals

Numerals (number symbols) are special because they represent a universal language. Many people who speak different languages use the Arabic numeral system. People who cannot understand one another's language can communicate through numerals and mathematics: $2 + 2 = 4$ is true whether written on a blackboard in the Philippines, Ghana, or the United States. How many countries use the Arabic system? What other systems do countries use?

Have students investigate the history of our number system. How did Arabic numerals represent an improvement over Roman numerals? The Arabs were sophisticated mathematicians before Christ and developed positional notation (the importance of place) and the idea of zero (the place holder). Our word "algebra," meaning "the number," comes from Arabic and reflects their contributions. Many other words were borrowed from Arabic. Examples are albatross, alcohol, and alfalfa. Their beginning, *al,* is Arabic for *the.*

Other Symbols that Cross Language Barriers

Numerals are universal because they are symbols. Ask students to list other symbols that communicate information and can be understood by speakers of different languages. Students might suggest some of the following:

dollar sign	stop lights
skull and crossbones (poison)	music notation
	road signs

Interesting tables of signs and symbols are available in some dictionaries, for example, *The World Book Dictionary*. Different fields such as astronomy, chemistry, electrical engineering, astrology, and chess use symbols that are international.

Secret Languages

Children enjoy using secret languages because they sound mysterious and not everyone can understand them. Ask students whether they know secret languages such as Pig Latin, for example. Many children learn to use Pig Latin easily but it is very difficult for an outsider to understand. How many students have felt left out because everyone else was speaking a secret language that they could not understand? Compare this to the problems faced by a NES student entering an English-speaking class.

Have students explore secret languages and practice them. Examples are discussed in *The Lore and Language of Schoolchildren* by Iona and Peter Opie (Oxford University Press, 1959). This kind of language play helps develop awareness of English word structure.

Learn Fingerspelling

Another kind of special language is a silent language, the language of hands. This kind of language is used by deaf people and takes the place of speech. Although ASL (American Sign Language or Ameslan) uses signs that generally correspond to English words, it also has signs for each letter (fingerspelling). Fingerspelling is sometimes called the manual alphabet. Anyone can quickly learn to fingerspell and the exercise helps practice English speaking. Students enjoy being able to signal each other secretly, across a noisy room, and without making a sound. Several books present fingerspelling for beginners. *Handtalk* by Remy Charlip, Mary Beth, and George Ancona (Parents Magazine Press, 1974) includes photographs of a person signing.

Sign Language

Discuss the differences between sign language and spoken language. What are the advantages of sign language? What are the advantages of spoken language? What language is best when you are: eating, under water, on the phone? Students may not believe that sign language is a "real" language. Present some of the following information about sign.

FACTS ABOUT SIGN LANGUAGE

There are different sign languages used in different countries, just as there are spoken languages. People who use American Sign Language (ASL) cannot understand people who use British Sign Language.

ASL is not a word-for-word translation of English. Signed English is used for simultaneous translation and matches spoken English more closely.

Children who are deaf learn ASL as a first language, similar to the way hearing children learn a spoken language. Signers (people who use sign) can express themselves as well in sign as hearing people in a spoken language.

Exploring Sign

Invite a hearing person who knows sign to speak to the class and demonstrate signing. (Try facilities for the deaf, teachers of sign language, and relatives of deaf people.) If students watch closely, they will be able to guess what some of the signs mean.

Drink—fingers shaped around glass move to mouth

See—two fingers move away from eyes

Nose, Mouth—point to them on face

Find out what services are available for deaf people. Sometimes television news programs have simultaneous sign translations. Discuss with students why these services are necessary. Wouldn't printing the news on the screen as subtitles work?

Signed poetry can become a dance. The shape of the movements contributes to the poem in the same way as the shape affects a written poem. The National Theater of the Deaf combines sign language and movement for a striking, dramatic presentation. If these facilities for the deaf are in your area, try to arrange for a local group to give a performance totally in sign.

Different Writing Systems

There are three basic types of writing systems. Alphabetic systems use symbols to represent individual sounds. Syllabaries have separate symbols for consonant-vowel pairs. Pictographic or ideographic systems represent entire words or ideas with a single symbol. Bring in examples of each type of writing (in print or handwritten) to show students how languages differ. Include some of the following:

Alphabetic: *Cyrillic,* used for Russian and other Slavic languages, based on the Greek alphabet.

Hebrew, an alphabet without written vowels, similar to Arabic.

Syllabary: *Japanese,* despite adoption of some Chinese characters, still primarily uses *Kana,* syllable-based.

Pictographic: *Chinese,* with large numbers of distinct characters, very difficult to memorize and write, is now being simplified and standardized by Chinese government.

Discuss with students implications of these differences in writing systems. Consider, for example, how dictionaries would be organized. How would Hebrew students learn new words, written without the spoken vowels? The complex Chinese system is better for the Chinese than an alphabetic system. Speakers of different Chinese languages who cannot understand each other's spoken language can communicate through using the same writing system. How might these different writing systems make translation into English difficult?

Investigate the history of the English alphabet. Students can research where our letters came from and how they have changed. English is not purely alphabetic, however. Our numerals are examples of pictographic writing because each symbol stands for a word. Find out where our numerals came from.

Esperanto

The following paragraph is written in Esperanto. Write it on the board and read it to the class. (It is pronounced approximately like Spanish—follow the rules given on pages 82–83). See how much students can understand.

La inteligenta persono lernas la interlingvon Esperanto rapide kaj facile. Esperanto estas la moderna, kultura lingvo por la internacia mondo. Simpla, flekselbla, praktika solvo de la problemo de universala interkompreno, Esperanto meritas vian seriozan konsideron. Lernu la interlingvon Esperanto!

Esperanto is an artificial language invented to be used as an international language. It is easy to learn and easy to understand because it is completely regular. Spanish-speaking students will find Esperanto much easier to understand than will English-speaking students because it is based on the Romance languages.

Bring books about Esperanto to the class. Students can learn enough from several lessons to read the paragraph above. They will enjoy practicing the new language and using it in interesting ways. They can write to each other in Esperanto and perform simple translation exercises. In addition, they will learn more about how their own language is constructed by comparing it with Esperanto.

Discuss why Esperanto was created. Is there a need for an international language? Why doesn't everyone know English? What are the advantages and disadvantages of Esperanto? Esperanto is only one of a large number of artificial international languages. Ask students if they think any of these proposed languages will succeed. Have students investigate the history of Esperanto and other artificial languages (Interlingua, for example).

Greetings

We have other ways of communicating with people besides talking with them. When we greet someone, we not only say hello, hi, or how ya doin', but we also shake hands, kiss, or slap one another on the back. What we do depends on the

particular situation—where we are, how well we know each other, and other social factors. Have students suggest some of the different ways we greet each other
nonverbally and when each behavior is appropriate. Discuss ideas of appropriateness and how these might vary from individual to individual.

Other cultures have different conventions for greeting. Japanese people bow
to each other and the depth of the bow indicates relative status. Eskimos rub
noses. Can students think of any others? People in some cultures hug each other
more than most Americans do. Compile a list of American greetings. Ask students to write a description of various greetings as if they had to teach a foreigner
how to greet people American style.

Body Language

An important aspect of the way we communicate is how we use our body. The
expression on our faces or how we stand can affect how other people interpret
what we say. However, we are not as conscious of the messages we communicate
with our bodies as we are of our verbal expression. People from other cultures
have different ways of expressing themselves in body language. Part of learning
a new language is learning the cultural expectations of what to do with your
body.

Try these exercises with students to make them more aware of how we all
use body language.

1. *Eye Contact.* Divide students into pairs. Have one person talk while the
   other person refuses to look the speaker in the face. Stop after a short period
   and reverse. Now have the listener stare at the speaker and try to maintain
   eye contact. Stop and discuss. Who felt most uncomfortable and why?
2. *Facial Expression.* Give students a list of "happy" sentences and "sad" sentences. Have them say happy sentences (a friend gave me a present) with
   frowns, and sad sentences (the class guinea pig died) with smiles. What happens? How do listeners react?
3. *Personal Space.* When we talk with people, we usually stand a certain distance away. Have students experiment with trying to move closer to people
   as they talk. Discuss the reactions they report back to the class. Did the other
   people notice what was going on?

A good book for young children is *Face Talk, Hand Talk, Body Talk* by Sue
Castle (Doubleday, 1977).

Kinesics

The study of body language is called kinesics and it has received much popular
attention recently. Study has centered around cross-cultural differences, particularly in the areas of eye contact and personal space. Information on such differences would be extremely helpful for anyone who has students from different
cultural backgrounds in a class. Investigate such books as *Body Language* by

Julius Fast, *Kinesics and the Art of Non-Verbal Communication* by Ray Bird-whistell, and *Our Silent Language* by Edward Hall.

Advanced students will enjoy researching this topic. Have them demonstrate their findings to the class. Humorous skits could be written, for example, to show what might happen when persons from different cultures meet.

Nobody Speaks My Language

Give students a taste of what foreigners experience by setting up the classroom as a foreign country. For a brief period, everyone (including the teacher) will pretend that they cannot understand what anyone else says (or writes). Hide all written material so that students will not see anything in a familiar language. Students will have to communicate by pointing, gesturing, and acting out.

At the end of the specified time, discuss how everyone felt. How would this experience be similar to or different from that of a foreigner coming to this country for the first time? Was there anything they wanted to communicate but could not? How could they help someone in a similar situation?

A Local Language Survey

Do students know what languages are spoken in their area? Begin with the local place names. What languages have influenced local names? Ask families. What languages are spoken in the students' families? Do students know people who speak different languages?

Make a map or chart of the area on which to record the information students find. Have them research local history to see what the earliest languages were. Were there any Native American groups living nearby? What language did they speak and what happened to them? Ask who the first settlers were and what languages they brought with them. Trace the language history down to the present time. Students should be able to discover what the major local language groups are and how long their speakers have been in the area.

Once the major languages are identified, this can become an important resource for further study. Plan lessons around examples from these languages. Bring people in who speak various languages so that students can hear what the languages sound like.

FOCUSING ON SPANISH

Spanish is the most commonly spoken language in the United States other than English. Spanish-speaking Americans have their roots in Mexico, Spain, Puerto Rico, Cuba, and other countries. Most Spanish speakers are spread throughout California and the Southwest. However, students may be surprised to learn that there are large groups of Spanish speakers in Colorado, Massachusetts, and Florida, for example. In addition, almost all major cities such as Chicago and

New York have large Spanish-speaking communities. All children should be aware of the Spanish language and the variety of Spanish-speaking cultures represented in the United States.

The following activities are designed to acquaint all students with the Spanish language. They can be used with bilingual programs or classrooms in which only English is spoken. You can use these activities easily whether or not you know Spanish. Encourage Spanish-speaking students to contribute vocabulary and pronunciation information and reward them for their knowledge. If you have no Spanish-speaking students, bring in Spanish language teaching tapes or records for the class to become accustomed to Spanish sounds. The activities given here are not intended to teach students Spanish. They are useful to make non-Spanish speakers aware of Spanish as an interesting and important language and to assure Spanish-speaking students that their ability to speak two languages is valued. Although the activities refer specifically to Spanish, they can be adapted for use with any language. Examples of possible adaptations are given, as on page 93. Activities related to the Chinese language can be found in Chapter 6.

Comparing Alphabets

Show students how the Spanish alphabet is similar to the English alphabet. Show them how it differs. Write or print the letters on the board, circling the letters that are added, thus:

a	b	c	(ch)	d	e	f
g	h	i	j	k	l	(ll)
m	n	(ñ)	o	p	q	r
(rr)	s	t	u	v	w	x
y	z					

Explain that the letters k and w are used in the Spanish language only when words have been borrowed from other languages (kilómetro and Washington).

Letter Names

What are the names of the letters of the alphabet? English-speaking children will be interested in learning how Spanish-speaking children say the alphabet. Have a child who speaks Spanish say these letters slowly for the group. This is more effective than reading or saying them yourself, for it makes the student aware that knowledge of Spanish can be important in school.

Spanish Letter Names

a	ä	n	ānā
b	bā	ñ	ānyā
c	sā	o	ō
ch	chā	p	pā
d	dā	q	kü
e	ā	r	ārā
f	āffā	rr	ārrā
g	hā	s	āsā
h	āchā	t	tā
i	ē	u	ü
j	hōtä	v	bā
k	kä	w	düblä bā
l	ālā	x	ākēs
ll	āyā	y	ē grē · āgä (Greek i)
m	āmā	z	sätä

Comparing Phonemes and Graphemes

After examining the alphabet letters that are used in writing Spanish, show students the phonemes used in speaking Spanish, some of which are similar to English but none of which are exactly the same. Also show them corresponding graphemes for these phonemes. Here they will notice many differences between Spanish and English, as shown in this chart:

CONSONANTS	SPANISH	ENGLISH
b	también	rib
	abrir	like v, but with lips almost touching
c	casa	case (before a, o, u)
	nación	cent (before e, i)
ch	chico	church
d	donde	down
	madre	the
f	familia	family
g	gente	like exaggerated h (before e, i)
	gordo	game
h	hacer	silent
j	jugar	like exaggerated h
k	kilómetro	kitchen
l	lástima	little
ll	llena	yellow ⎫
		million ⎬ (regional variation)
m	mañana	morning
n	nada	nothing

CONSONANTS	SPANISH	ENGLISH
n	niño	ca<u>ny</u>on
p	piña	su<u>pp</u>er
q	queso	<u>k</u>ey
r	pero	<u>r</u>ich
	rico	trilled r
rr	perro	trilled r
s	sala	<u>s</u>ad
t	trabajar	<u>t</u>ime
v	enviar	like <u>b</u> in tambien
	la vaca	like <u>b</u> in abrir
w	Wáshington	<u>w</u>ash
x	examen	e<u>x</u>am
	extranjero	<u>s</u>ound
	México	<u>h</u>it
y	yo	<u>y</u>es
z	zapato	<u>s</u>ave

VOWELS

a	padre	f<u>a</u>ther
e	es	th<u>ey</u>
i	nida	pol<u>i</u>ce
o	poco	p<u>o</u>em
u	luna	sp<u>oo</u>n
	querer	silent after <u>q</u>
ai, ay	traiga	n<u>i</u>ce
au	auto	m<u>ou</u>se
ei, ey	aceituna	tr<u>ay</u>
eu	deuda	<u>ay</u> plus <u>oo</u>
ia, ya	hacia	<u>y</u>onder
ie, ye	nieve	<u>y</u>es
io, yo	dios	<u>y</u>elk
iu	ciudad	<u>y</u>ule
oi, oy	soy	<u>b</u>oy
ua	guante	<u>w</u>ander
ue	vuelve	<u>w</u>eight
y	y	<u>e</u>ven
ui, uy	muy	<u>w</u>e
uo	cuota	<u>wo</u>e

Spanish Pronunciation

Whether or not you have ever studied Spanish, it is important to be able to pronounce the Spanish that you introduce in your classroom as easily as possible. Use the chart of Spanish phonemes to become familiar with Spanish sounds. Ask Spanish-speaking students to share their knowledge of Spanish and contribute words or demonstrate pronunciations. There is no reason for you as the teacher to be afraid of making mistakes. You can help by making an effort to try Spanish words without having to speak Spanish fluently. Taking at least an introductory Spanish class is, of course, recommended for any teacher's professional development.

Varieties of Spanish

The information on Spanish presented in this book is very general. There are many varieties of Spanish spoken in the United States, depending on where the speakers live, how long they have lived in this country, and where they came from originally. Spanish in the Southwest is different from Spanish in the Midwest (Chicago), the Northeast, and Florida. Even in New York City, there are important cultural and linguistic differences between persons from Puerto Rico, Cuba, Dominican Republic, Colombia, Ecuador, Peru, Mexico, Venezuela, Bolivia, and other South American communities.

The differences in the Spanish of Latin America are primarily vocabulary and pronunciation. Some vocabulary differences are due to influence from local Indian languages, others to independent development of Spanish.

The following are examples of different words used in Latin America for *boy*.

Mexico	chamaco
Cuba	chico
Guatemala	patojo
El Salvador	cipote
Panama	chico
Colombia	pelado
Argentina	pibe
Chile	cabro

Pronunciation also varies regionally. The following are some of the differences found.

syllable final *s* becomes *h* or disappears—*estos* is [éhtoh] or [éto]

ll becomes same as *y*—*valla* and *vaya* are alike

syllable final *r* sounds like *l*—*puerta* is [pwelta], *comer* is [komel]

Introduce vocabulary specific to local Spanish-speaking groups by having a variety of children's books available. Many books, written about members of particular groups, take pride in presenting common Spanish words that are special to that group. The following are some suggestions. Include as many books on the locally represented groups as possible.

Puerto Ricans in New York

Yagua Days by Cruz Martel (Dial, 1976)

Friday Night Is Papa Night by Ruth Sonneborn (Viking, 1970)

El Bronx Remembered by Nicholasa Mohr (Harper & Row, 1975)

Southwest United States
Juan Patricio by Barbara Todd (Putna, 1972)
Indian Paintbrush by Edna Chandler (Whitman, 1975)

California
Rosa by Leo Politi (Scribner's, 1963)
Barrio Boy by Ernesto Galarza (University of Notre Dame, 1971)

Spanish Words We Know

Students may be surprised to see how many Spanish words they know. If Spanish is frequently used in the community, students should have no trouble recalling words seen on signs and heard in conversations. Have students list words they know as you write them on the board. Do they know what the words mean? Words they might suggest include

amigos	fiesta	siesta
adiós	tortilla	piñata

Do any stores in the community have signs in Spanish? Where do they hear Spanish spoken? What does "Aquí se habla Español" mean? ("Spanish is spoken here.") Are there any Spanish place names or street names in the community?

Listening to Spanish

An easy way to become accustomed to hearing Spanish spoken is to listen to local radio programs in Spanish. Bring a radio to class and allow students to listen for short periods every day. Or leave it on while students are working on different tasks so that they can listen to the Spanish music.

Exposing students to Spanish helps them to become more aware of Spanish as an interesting language that is used by large groups of people in the United States. Spanish-speaking students will hear different accents and learn more about Spanish. Both groups will become more familiar with other cultures, particularly through listening to the music.

Spanish Borrowings

English has borrowed extensively from Spanish, particularly in the Southwest. List examples of borrowings on the board. Do students know what these words mean? What kinds of words have been borrowed? Discuss why borrowings might take place. The following are examples of borrowings from Spanish.

arroyo	chili	stampede
bronco	avocado	frijole
rodeo	vanilla	mesa
sombrero	adobe	sierra
burro	alfalfa	tortilla
canyon	mustang	San Francisco
lasso	plaza	Los Angeles

Have students research Spanish borrowings. What do the original Spanish words look like? What happens to the words when they enter English?

Indian Borrowings

The Spanish spoken in Latin America is distinctively different from the Spanish of Spain because of the influence of the Native American languages. Many words borrowed into English from Spanish come originally from these languages. "Chocolate" was borrowed from Nahuatl, the Aztec language, into Mexican Spanish and then into English. As students research Spanish borrowings, have them notice examples of Native American words. The following are examples of words borrowed from Guaraní, a language spoken in Paraguay, into English: tapioca, maracas, jaguar, jacaranda, tapir, and toucan.

Spanish spoken in this country differs from the rest of Latin America because it has continued to borrow from the Native American languages and it has also been influenced by English.

Spanish Folklore

An important aspect of studying Spanish language and culture is Spanish folklore. This folklore reflects Spanish, English, and Indian influences and is unique to the Spanish-speaking culture as well as an important part of the American experience. Folklore includes stories (cuentos), sayings (dichos), songs, music, legends (leyendas), and drama. Special types of songs are corridos, mañanitas, and rancheras. Many legends center around La Bruja (the Witch) and La Curandera (the Healer).

Provide examples of different kinds of folklore and discuss the ritualized characteristics of each form. Encourage students to research more examples. Because all of the stories and songs are short, they are particularly suitable for presenting in front of the class. Several students can take turns telling stories that are spooky or humorous. You can also obtain records of traditional ballads and songs to play.

Suggested references and resources for exploring Chicano or Mexican-American folklore include:

Campa, Arthur. *Spanish Folk-Poetry in New Mexico*. University of New Mexico Press, 1946.

Dobie, Frank S. *Southwestern Lore*. Southwest Press, 1931.

Dorson, Richard. *Buying the Wind: Regional Folklore in the United States*. University of Chicago Press, 1964.

Espinosa, Gilberto. *Heroes, Hexes and Haunted Halls*. Calvin Horn, 1972.

Espinosa, José. *Spanish Folk-Tales from New Mexico*. Kraus Reprint Co., 1969.

Valdez, Luis, and Stan Steiner. *An Anthology of Mexican American Literature*. Knopf, 1972.

Spanish Synonyms for English Words

Have you ever thought that knowing a Spanish word for one used in English is simply adding another synonym to our list of words that mean the same thing? As children learn synonyms for big, for example, why not include several Spanish words, as shown here?

Big
large
ancho (wide)
immense
gordo (fat)
tremendous
grande

The last word is similar to the English word "grand," but it has two syllables. It may not be totally strange to students who have heard of such phrases as El Rancho Grande.

Provide examples of synonyms in other languages that the class is studying or students know. Have students think of different ways to express "strong" in English and add a few words from German, for example.

Strong
stark (G.)
powerful
nachdrücklich (G.)
vigorous
forceful
kräftig (G.)
energetic

Clarifying Concepts of Grammar

As you teach children about English grammar, point out the importance of word order in English. Children can easily tell the difference between these two English sentences.

The tiger chased the hunter.
The hunter chased the tiger.

They can also tell you which of these sentences sounds most appropriate:

A yellow butterfly lit on the flower.
A butterfly yellow lit on the flower.

Their judgments are based on the knowledge of English grammar which they have learned since they were born. If they had been born in a Spanish-speaking home, they would have learned different ways of arranging language. In Spanish, for example, the adjective does follow the noun as in the last sentence above. *Juan lives in the blue house* would be written with the adjective blue (azúl) following house (casa), thus:

Juan vive en la casa azúl.

Other languages have different ways of arranging words in a sentence. Japanese speakers learning English make mistakes by directly translating normal Japanese sentences into English, as in the following:

John house in lives.
I ball saw.

In Japanese, the verb is placed at the end of a sentence and the object immediately follows the subject. Post-positions are used instead of prepositions and particles are attached to nouns to indicate, for example, the topic of the sentence.

Spanish on the Map

The importance of Spanish-speaking people in the history of this country can be easily seen in the names on the map. Project a copy of a U.S. map on the wall with the opaque projector so that all the students can see the names marked on the map. Have students find examples of Spanish place names. Talk about how you can tell whether a name is Spanish or not. If the first word is "San" or "Santa" the name is probably a Spanish saint name. What would these names be in English? (San Francisco/St. Francis, San Antonio/St. Anthony, for example.)

Look at different areas of the country separately. Students will notice that more Spanish names occur in certain areas. Which areas have more Spanish names and why?

As students search for Spanish names, they will notice other groups of foreign names. There are a number of French names in Louisiana, for example. Why? Ask students if they can think why the names used on the map might reflect the history of a region. Does the presence of Spanish names in an area necessarily mean that there are Spanish-speaking people living there?

Cognates

When languages are related, they contain many cognates (words that are the same or almost identical in each language). While English is not directly related to the Romance languages (French, Spanish, Italian, Portuguese, etc.) it shares many cognates with these languages. List Spanish words that have English cognates. For example:

curiosidad	diccionario	aeroplano
formalidad	información	cemento
sociedad	gasolina	violencia
nacionalidad	avenida	federal
famoso	moderna	civilizado
delicioso	imposible	hotel
bicicleta	puntuación	foto

Have students guess the meaning of these Spanish words. Maintain a list of cognates on the bulletin board as students discover them. Searching for cognates and figuring out their meanings encourages students to pay attention to the forms of English words as well. Students can spot patterns in the similarities and differences between Spanish and English cognates, for example: Spanish -dad = English -ty.

Remember that although these words are spelled alike, they sound different when spoken. Because of the different pronunciation systems of the languages, it is sometimes harder to spot cognates in speech than in reading.

There are many Spanish and English cognates because English was heavily influenced by French and borrowed extensively from Latin. Have students check other Romance languages to find more examples of cognates. The following are examples from Italian:

associazione	compagnia
atmosfera	emergenza
automobile	licenza
caffè	memoria
violino	oceano
colore	fonografo
dentista	stomaco

False Friends

"False friends" is the translation of "faux amis," the French term for misleading cognates. One of the problems of working with related languages such as English and Spanish is that words may have a similar appearance in both languages but have different meanings. "Asistir" does not mean "to assist" in Spanish but "to attend." Librería means bookstore, not library (which is "biblioteca"). And in many languages, the words for "first floor" refer to what Americans call the "second floor" (our first floor is their "ground floor").

As your class works with different languages, be suspicious of these "false friends." Maintain a list of examples you run across so that students won't be fooled.

Studies in Spanish and English

Many subjects studied in class have similar names in English and Spanish. When you prepare a bulletin board for a particular subject or write the name of a subject on the board, write it in English and Spanish. Say both words so that students are familiar with the sound of the words. When you introduce a subject, alternate the English name with the Spanish name. The similarities between the English and the Spanish words are sufficient so that students will not become confused by the use of both. Here are some examples to begin with. Others can be found in any dictionary.

geografía	geography
historia	history
aritmética	arithmetic
arte	art
música	music
ciencia	science

Spanish Sayings

Collect Spanish proverbs, jokes, and riddles to display on the bulletin board. Use them to stimulate interest as students eagerly read the board to find new sayings. Include English translations so that everyone can enjoy the sayings. Solicit contributions from students, as well. They will appreciate seeing familiar sayings on the bulletin board. After students have read the sayings, discuss what they mean.

Pasajero nervioso: ¿Piloto, por favor, se caen estes aeroplanos con frecuencia?
Piloto: No, solamente una vez.

Nervous passenger: Excuse me, pilot, do these planes crash often?
Pilot: No, only once.

A la mejor cocinera se le va un tomate entero.
Even the best cook drops a tomato in whole once in a while.

Barriga llena, corazón contento.
A full stomach means a contented heart.

The Color Wheel

A Spanish color wheel is helpful to show students the names for colors which they know. Make a large poster to display on the wall like this:

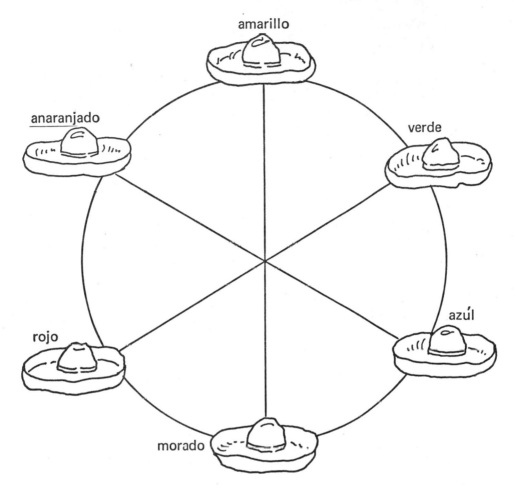

Los Colóres

Spanish colors:

morado—purple	anaranjado—orange
azúl—blue	rojo—red
verde—green	negro—black
amarillo—yellow	blanco—white

    This idea can be easily adapted for use with any language spoken by students in the class. With languages such as Tagalog and Navajo, it is often difficult to find printed materials for use with students. Prepare a variety of displays similar to the color wheel showing basic vocabulary. Include numbers, days of the week, and words used in the classroom.

Spanish Review

Help students practice Spanish vocabulary they have learned or seen by preparing review charts. Construct a slip chart with common Spanish words written on the front. Students read the Spanish, say it aloud, give the English equivalent and check their response by pulling the tab that shows the proper English word below each Spanish example. These are especially useful for practicing limited sets of words such as numbers and days of the week.

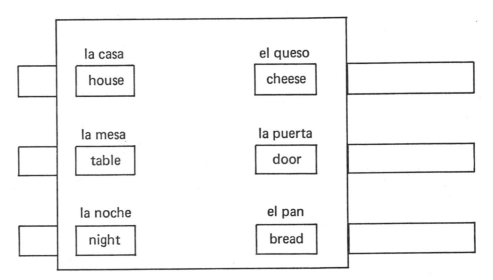

Charts can also be made with pictures of objects on the front. Students review by saying the name of the object in Spanish and then lifting the picture (which is attached at the top) to read the correct answer. Use these charts for independent student review or small group work. Both kinds of charts are useful for practicing English with NES students as well.

Spanish in the Classroom

As you work with Spanish in the classroom, whether or not you have Spanish-speaking students, you will need to have books on Spanish available for students. Two easy to use, accessible books are:

How Do You Say It? In English, Spanish, and French by Frank Martin. Platt and Munk, 1973.

Mi Diccionario Ilustrado by Marion Monroe. Scott, Foresman.

Words in Context

An easy way to introduce a new language, whether English to a Spanish-speaking student or Spanish to an English-speaking one, is to give the unfamiliar words in a sentence that makes their meaning clear. Ask students what they think the italicized words in the following sentences mean.

1. I write with a *lápiz* because I can erase my mistakes.
2. The *árbol* is tall and has large leaves.
3. How many pages have you read in your *libro*?
4. Because it was cold outside, she put gloves on her *manos*.
5. After school, we can check out books from the *biblioteca*.

This exercise can be used with other languages and different grade levels. Use a dictionary to construct other sentences. Here are some sentences for older students with German words. (Note that German capitalizes all nouns.)

1. An *Apfel* a day keeps the doctor away.
2. The *Hund* is man's best friend.
3. His *Bellen* is worse than his bite.
4. A *Masche* in time saves nine.

(Answers. Spanish: 1, pencil; 2, tree; 3, book; 4, hands; 5, library.
German: 1, apple; 2, dog; 3, bark; 4, stitch.)

Idioms

Every language has a set of special expressions, called idioms, that are not meant to be taken literally. Idioms are especially difficult for people learning a new language because, even if they understand the words, they do not know what the phrase means. Have students collect idioms that they know or discover in Spanish. Post examples on the board with student drawings illustrating literal interpretation of the idioms. Begin with the following:

hacer el papel—to play a part (literally, make a paper)

tomar el pelo—to be kidding (literally, take the hair)

me hace pedazos—thrills me (literally, makes me pieces)

As students look for Spanish idioms, they will become more aware of idioms in English. Encourage them to collect English idioms and illustrate them. These can be used for working with students learning English as a second language. Have students prepare a dictionary of English idioms. Include the idiom, a humorous illustration, its meaning, and an example using it in a sentence. Idioms that might be used are the following: all tied up, put your foot in it, raining cats and dogs, and to be broke.

Beginning English Dictionaries

As students develop a collection of English idioms, they may want to prepare a more extensive dictionary for NES students. Discuss what words and phrases should be included. Ask students what they would want to know if they were learning English. Assign students to collect and write down specific groups of words. Include basic vocabulary, words used at school, and slang. Have students study how other dictionaries are made. Decide how to present pronunciation (if necessary), meanings, and examples of uses.

This dictionary can be a long-term class project. If kept in a large notebook, students can add pages as they think of new words and topics. The notebook could also contain information on the school, class rules, and student activities.

Tongue-Twisters

The word for tongue-twister in Spanish is "trabalengua." Challenge students to say the following example:

Tres tristes tigres trillaron trigo en un trigal.
(Three sad tigers threshing wheat in a wheat field.)

Collect examples of tongue-twisters from different languages. Share some interesting ones in English, too, for the benefit of all students. Spanish-speaking students might find the following examples helpful in developing the pronunciation of specific English sounds:

Six silent snakes slithering slowly southward.
Eight gray geese grazing gaily into Greece.
The sun shines on shop signs.
Thrice times three; twice times two.

An interesting source of varied tongue-twisters is *A Twister of Twists, A Tangler of Tongues* by Alvin Schwartz (Lippincott, 1972).

Language Activities for Primary Grades

An easy way to introduce young children to words from other languages is to use synonyms for words in English. At times choose functional words such as numbers, days of the week, or names.

In addition, however, introduce words that are related to English words, as shown on the task card on p. 95. "El fútbol" and "el auto," for example, are clearly borrowed Americanisms. "El libro" and "el árbol" have Latin origins in common with English words (library and arboretum or Arbor Day).

At the oral level, encourage preschoolers and primary grade children to use greetings and other useful phrases from different languages as a natural part of their talking.

Wunderbar! (Wonderful! German)
Adiós, amigo. (Goodby, friend. Spanish)
Ja. Si. Oui. (Yes. German and Scandinavian languages, Spanish, French)
Tenga cuidado! Prenez garde! Attenzione! (Be careful! Spanish, French, Italian)

Other expressions are listed throughout this chapter.

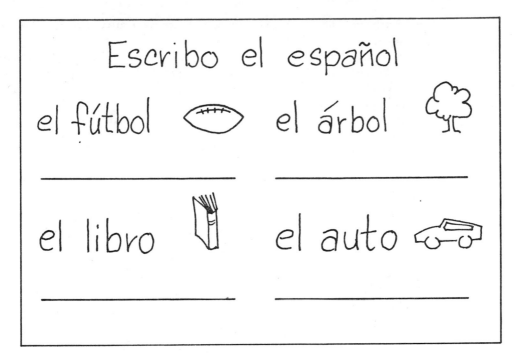

Escribo el español

el fútbol _____ el árbol

_____ _____

el libro _____ el auto

_____ _____

Aspects of Spanish that May Cause Problems for Children Learning English

1. Strong influence of the Spanish *ch* on the English *sh* is a common problem. When *sh* is introduced because of its proximity in sound, the student may appear to say *share* for *chair* and *shoes* for *choose*.

2. In Spanish, *b* and *v* are exactly alike phonetically; each has two sounds. The use of one sound or the other is governed by accompanying sounds as follows:

   a. Sound one is made by the buzzing of both lips (e.g., *Ella boto la caja; Ella voto ayer*). The letters *b* or *v* surrounded by vowel sounds must be buzzed.

   b. Sound two is *b* as in boy (e.g., *El bote se caja; El vaso se caja*). Both sound like the *b* in boy. When *b* or *v* begins an utterance or is not surrounded by vowel sounds it is pronounced as the *b* in boy.

3. Spanish uses one word for *it is* (*es*) and for *there are* and *there is* (*hay*). Examples: *It is* a nice day (*Es un dia agradable*). *There are* many children at school (*Hay muchos niños en la escuela*). There *is* a teacher in the classroom (*Hay un profesor en la clase*).

4. In Spanish, articles are placed in some positions where English does not require them: *Veo al doctor Brown* (I see *the* Dr. Brown); *Asi es la vida* (That's *the* life).

5. In Spanish the adjective usually follows the noun and must agree with it in gender and number: *Yo tengo zapatos blancos* (I have shoes white).

6. There are five vowels in Spanish. The corresponding sounds in English are as follows: *a* as in father; *e* as in step; *i* as in machine; *o* as in over; and *u* as in ooze. The short vowel sounds *a, i, o,* and *u* are not used in Spanish.

7. The adverb, not the direct object, usually comes right after the verb. Example: I immediately saw ... (*Yo* v̲i̲ *immediatamente ...*).

8. The consonanat sounds *v, b, d, t, g, h, j, l, r, w, v,* and *z* are not pronounced the same in Spanish as in English. Knowledge of the point of articulation for the production of these sounds is necessary.

9. Beginning and ending sounds.

   a. Spanish words never begin with consonant clusters identified in italics as follows: *s*peak, *s*tay, *s*care, *s*chool, *s*treet, *s*pring, *s*cratch, *s*phere, *s*low, *s*mall, *s*nail, *s*velte. Speakers of Spanish add an initial vowel sound *e* as, for example, in *e*speak, *e*street.

   b. Spanish words can end in any of the five vowels—a, e, i, o, u—or the consonants listed as follows:

l	*pape̲l*	
d	*verda̲d*	*car̲a*
r	*seño̲r*	*com̲e*
z	*zari̲z*	*cas̲i*
j	*relo̲j*	*tod̲o*
y	*esto̲y*	*t̲u*
n	*so̲n*	
s	*casa̲s*	

   Note: Speakers of Spanish have difficulty with ending sounds such as *m, p, k, c, b, d, f, g, j, l, t, v,* and *x* (voiced *z*). They also have difficulty in pronouncing the 371 consonant-cluster endings used in English.

10. Some factors of intonation such as pitch and stress that can cause problems in communication are the following:

    a. *Stress.* Spanish words are stressed as follows:

       1) Stress on the last syllable: *pa pél, vi vi rás, te le vi sión, ciu dád*
       2) Stress on the next to last syllable: *cá sa, ma dé ra, clá ro*
       3) Stress on the third to last syllable: *jó ve nes, áng e les, te lé fo no*
       4) Stress on the fourth to last syllable: *llé va te los, mánd a se lo, có me te los*

       Most Spanish words are stressed on the last syllable (Group A words) or next to last syllable (Group B words). In contrast, English words are usually stressed on the first or second syllable; e.g., *constant* (*constante*), *telephone* (*telefono*). In English, long words may have two or even three stresses. Spanish uses only one stress except for adverbs ending in *mente* (e.g., *facilmente, rapidamente*).

    b. *Tone system.* English and Spanish have four tone levels. Spanish normally operates on the lower three levels except in cases of extreme anger or alarm. Then the fourth (upper) pitch is used. English usually operates on all four levels.

11. Spelling differences. Although many Latin derivatives are common to Spanish and English, **there** are some interferences between spelling systems. Teachers should help **students** with the transfer of cognate vocabulary. Spanish does *not* use the doubled **consonants** or combination of consonants; i.e., *bb, dd, ff, gg, mm, pp, ss, tt, zz, th, gh, ph, sh,* or *hn*.

SOURCE: *Framework in Reading for the Elementary and Secondary Schools in California.* California State Department of Education, 1973.

VARIETIES OF ENGLISH IN THE CLASSROOM

When we speak of studying English or teaching English to NES students, it is important to remember that people vary in how they speak English. Of course, all individuals speak differently. However, people from different areas of the country characteristically speak in distinctive ways. These differences are called regional dialects. Often people who have had more formal education speak differently from those with less. Differences such as these are called social dialects. Dialects are defined as *variation according to user*. In addition, all of us vary our speech in specific ways depending on the situation. This stylistic variation, also called register, is defined as *variation according to use*. Because dialects and registers represent regular patterns of speech, we can identify them readily and label the speaker as coming from New York, for example, or the speech as being formal.

This section is divided into two parts. The first deals with dialects and activities for developing student awareness of English dialects. It includes a special focus on Black English, an important dialect of English. The second part covers register or stylistic variation. It provides activities to help students expand their use of different registers.

INTRODUCING DIALECTOLOGY

Dialectology is the study of dialects—what they consist of, who speaks them and where, and how they developed. Because all languages are composed of a number of different dialects, the choice of the dialect that will be taught in schools, the "standard dialect," is an arbitrary one. The standard dialect is not necessarily *better* than the other dialects but it is the one generally used for pronunciation guides in dictionaries, training radio announcers, and producing rhymed poetry, for example. Most people speak several dialects because they learned one dialect at home and another at school. They are bidialectal because they use the standard dialect in order to get jobs and appear educated while at the same time they need the other in order to be accepted by people in their own community or social group. Some dialects have acquired a negative evaluation, so that no matter how well educated a speaker of that dialect is, she or he will be heard as poorly educated, lower class, or stupid. Examples of these are the Bronx (New York) dialect, Black English, and southern speech. Popular attitudes towards low status dialects are obvious when the dialects are caricatured in jokes or the media.

Dialects can differ from each other in pronunciation, vocabulary, or syntax. Examples of pronunciation differences include the addition of an *r*, identified as a Boston dialect, and the replacement of *th* by *d*, as found in some New York dialects. Vocabulary differences are illustrated by the various regional terms for a large sandwich: hoagie, grinder, hero, dagwood, poor boy. One of the most common syntactic differences is the use of the double negative, as heard in Black English (I don't got no book = I don't have a book). Dialects that differ substantially from "standard English" (SE) in pronunciation and syntax are usually called nonstandard dialects. This term reflects only the degree of difference from

SE and does not mean that speakers of these dialects are less intelligent or less capable than speakers of SE.

Black English (BE) is often called a nonstandard dialect. The origin of BE is a subject of dispute but BE probably resulted from contact between African languages and English. What we call BE is really a collection of features that identify the dialect as different from SE, yet are not used by any BE speakers all of the time. Instead, BE and SE can be considered two ends of a continuum where individual speakers vary toward one end or another, depending on the situation. The frequency with which features of BE appear determines to a great extent whether the speech is labeled BE.

We All Speak Dialects

It is important that students realize that we all speak different dialects. Even the most highly educated persons differ in the way they pronounce words. Have students try pronouncing the following words as they compare the varied ways of saying them:

greasy	here	car
bath	dog	because
aunt	get	idea

The wide variation in pronunciation is important to keep in mind and to draw to the attention of students as you work together in the classroom. It is particularly evident as the teacher pronounces spelling words. For words that present obvious difficulty, you might have a student or two pronounce the same word aloud.

Consider particularly the problem of the vowels in Mary, merry, and marry. Some students may pronounce these as three different words. Other students say them with two homonyms or even as three homonyms. Remember to allow for student differences in pronunciation when teaching spelling and reading rules.

Regional Dialects

Practice listening for regional variation with the record *Our Changing Language* (McGraw-Hill) by Evelyn Gott and Raven I. McDavid, Jr. (available from The National Council of Teachers of English, 1111 Kenyon Road, Urbana, IL 61801). On one side of this record there are recordings of high school students reading a story that contains many words that are pronounced differently. Each student is from a different city in the United States, and the speech variation is fascinating. Students who are from these geographic regions will identify their own speech characteristics as they listen.

To demonstrate the difference in speech in your own classroom, have a number of children read the same passage onto a tape. Then play the tape. Discuss what kinds of variation are noted. Which words are pronounced differently?

Have students compare their pronunciations of the following words:

right	child	park
house	Mary	here
fit	were	log
bath	fire	sorry

The reverse side of *Our Changing Language* shows how English has changed historically. It includes a passage that compares English as spoken in England with that of the United States, showing students how vocabulary also changes.

Regional Vocabulary Differences

Many common objects have different names in different parts of the country. Early dialectologists (people who investigated regional differences in pronunciation and vocabulary) developed maps that showed the spread of words for particular objects. Conduct a miniature experiment in dialectology and see how many different regional terms you can find. Ask students:

What do you call a carbonated drink?
  (soda, pop, sodapop)
What do you call a place where you can get a drink of water?
  (fountain, bubbler)
What do you call something you fry eggs in?
  (skillet, frying pan, spider, fry pan)
What do you call an animal with a stripe down its back?
  (skunk, polecat, pussy)

Discuss the regional patterns you find. Do students from the same area use the same terms? Why or why not? Depending on how many different regions the students represent, can you divide the United States into several main dialect areas?

Students might be interested in seeing dialect atlases that have been prepared. There are atlases for most areas of the United States but the first one ever published, the *Linguistic Atlas of New England* (Hans Kurath), includes many interesting maps. Use these as sources of information on more regional differences in vocabulary and pronunciation.

Stump the Teacher

Encourage student interest in dialect differences or regionalisms by having them collect special words or phrases that they hear around the community. How many can they find that you do not know? How many that other students do not know? Have them report their findings orally, with definitions, for the class, or develop a bulletin board to record information gathered about language in the area. As students discuss their words, ask them who might use which words. Suggest different groupings, such as young people, old people, people new to the community, or members of specific ethnic groups. Use this activity to develop the ideas of speech variation within a community and appropriate speech for different groups.

British-American Differences

The English spoken in Britain is made up of various dialects also. It is interesting to point out differences between English spoken in the United States and that spoken in Great Britain. Although you may not wish to investigate the full range of British dialects, you can have students investigate variations in vocabulary; for example:

American English	British English
pharmacist	chemist
bathrobe	dressing gown
pullover sweater	jumper
canned fruit	tinned fruit
undershirt	vest
cookie	biscuit
truck	lorry
elevator	lift
thumb tacks	drawing pins
garbage collector	dustman
subway	underground, tube
underpants	pants
pants	trousers
firecracker	squib
trunk (of car)	boot

In many cases, the British words are familiar but less common. However, some words have very different meanings in Britain and the United States.

Spelling across the Atlantic

Write several of the following familiar words on the board for students to read and pronounce. Wait for students to notice something strange about these words. Tell them that these represent British rather than American spellings. Can they identify the differences?

gaol	colour	grey
kerb	practise	civilise
tyres	programme	behaviour

Discuss the use of spelling conventions with the students. Why do we insist that everyone spell the same way?

British English in Books

Have students search for additional examples of British English. Reading books written by British authors will bring out more items. Suggest titles to upper-grade students, for example, books by these British authors:

> Lucy Boston
> > *The Children of Green Knowe*
> > *A Stranger at Green Knowe*
>
> Joan Aiken
> > *The Wolves of Willoughby Chase*
> > *Black Hearts in Battersea*

"Wrong" has no meaning in describing the use of language.

Students' Right to Their Own Language

The following is a statement prepared by the National Council of Teachers of English in response to the controversy over how to teach speakers of Black English. Read this to the students and discuss it. Do they agree with the position expressed? What do they think teachers should do?

We affirm the students' right to their own patterns and varieties of language—the dialects of their nurture or whatever dialects in which they find their own identity and style. Language scholars long ago denied that the myth of a standard American dialect has any validity. The claim that any one dialect is unacceptable amounts to an attempt of one social group to exert its dominance over another. Such a claim leads to false advice for speakers and writers, and immoral advice for humans. A nation proud of its diverse heritage and its cultural and racial variety will preserve its heritage of dialects. We affirm strongly that teachers must have the experiences and training that will enable them to respect diversity and uphold the right of students to their own language.

Strange Dialects

What would English look like if we spelled it the way we talked? For one thing, we would be able to indicate differences in the way people talk, such as dialect differences. Investigate this topic with students. A favorite game is to write definitions of words from a strange dialect. The unsuspecting reader has to say the words aloud in order to figure out the meaning of this foreign English. Challenge students to figure out the following examples.

Strine

1. Tiger—"Tiger look at this."
2. Retrine—"How to speak Strine without retrine."
3. Air fridge—"The air fridge man in the street."
4. Baked necks—"Baked necks or fright shops for breakfast."

(Hint: Strine means Australian English. Try saying the sentences several times aloud.)

American examples are also used. The following are supposed to be accurate representations of Texas talk. Can students understand these sentences?

Texas talk

1. offen—"Now stan still so ah can shoot that apple offen yore had."
2. main—"That there is one main man."
3. cheer—"Yawl come riot cheer this minute."

Now that students are familiar with these dialects, have them write similar versions of their own speech. They can develop dialogues or write definitions for incomprehensible words. The spelling is meant to be creative but it has to represent the pronunciation closely enough for another person to say it correctly. Students will become more aware of how, in rapid speech, we slide together words that must be separated in learning to spell and write properly.

Pronunciation Variants

Because people speak differently, there is no single "correct" pronunciation for many words. Dictionaries are beginning to list variant pronunciations without indicating that one is better than the others. Instead of trying to eradicate differences, allow for them and discuss them with students. Advanced students can check dictionaries for examples of pronunciation variants. Provide dictionaries such as *Webster's Unabridged* and *American Heritage Dictionary* (available in an inexpensive paperback) for them to compare. How do students pronounce the following words? What pronunciation(s) do the dictionaries give?

secretive:	see kreé tiv	seé kre tiv
abdomen:	ab̌ do men	ab' dō̌ men
conversant:	kon vér sant	kón ver sant
lamentable:	lám entable	la mén table

Black English and Written English

In order to learn to read, students must learn the specialized variety of language used in books. However, Black English (BE)-speaking students find book language extremely different from the language they are familiar with. Help students work with the differences between spoken and written English. Write examples of common sentences found in books on the board. Have students suggest how they would say it in natural speech. Try to obtain versions in both BE and standard spoken English. Include some of the following to illustrate the differences between speaking and writing BE and SE.

Written	*Spoken*	
	Standard English	Black English
A book is on the desk.	There's a book on the desk.	It's a book on the desk.
The man was hit on the head.	The guy got hit on the head.	The guy got hit upside the head.
Nobody can come.	There isn't anyone who can come.	Ain't nobody can come.

Black English in Books

Many contemporary writers attempt to reproduce the sound of BE in their books. Some just include black slang and others incorporate both vocabulary and grammatical features of BE. Unfortunately, no written version can accurately portray spoken BE, just as standard spoken English is very different from written English. However, these books have the advantage of sounding more familiar to BE speakers and are sometimes easier to read than standard English. They also are important for introducing other students to BE because the context makes the meaning of unfamiliar words and constructions clear.

Read passages from some of the following to the class and discuss the language used. How do students feel? Does it sound realistic or familiar? Do they understand what the people are saying? Why would someone want to write like that?

Brenda Wilkinson. *Ludell*. Harper & Row, 1975.

Eloise Greenfield. *She Come Bringing Me That Little Baby Girl*. Lippincott, 1974.

Jol Steptoe. *Train Ride*. Harper & Row, 1971.

John Shearer. *I Wish I Had an Afro*. Cowles, 1970.

Reading and Writing Standard English

Many BE-speaking students are able to translate SE into BE. They learn SE from hearing it used on television, for example, and they read sentences written in SE by changing them into BE. This practice of reading "She got a ball" for the printed sentence "She has a ball" is not a reading comprehension mistake but an indication of the translation process.*

---

* Such translation happens when students understand what they read and report their comprehension in language familiar to them. Thus, many students will read "Mother goes to work" as "Mommy goes to work."

Discovering Regularities

Usually students, while translating readily from SE to BE, are not aware of the patterns involved and, therefore, cannot translate from BE to SE. In order to learn to use SE in appropriate situations, students need to develop conscious control of the translation rules. Focus attention on specific differences by having students compare materials written in BE and SE. Look for dialect poems by Paul Laurence Dunbar, for example, or the speeches of Simple, a character created by Langston Hughes. Read them aloud and **discuss** with students how these selections would sound in SE. What generalizations can students suggest about the differences between SE and BE? Encourage students to be specific by listing equivalent SE and BE constructions on the board.

Analyzing Differences

After students have begun to notice regular differences, have them tape examples of SE and BE speech for further analysis. Try to obtain a full range of variation from SE to BE. For younger students, develop short role-play situations for taping in class, assigning individuals specific roles such as student, older brother, teacher, storekeeper, and doctor.

Older students can explore the speech variation heard in the community. Brainstorm a list of people who represent different varieties. Who talks the most "black"? Who the most "white"? Include members of the class, people students know, personalities familiar through the media, and characters seen on television. From the list, select a representative sampling of speech for students to tape. (Note that the ethics of taping speech suggest that hidden tape recorders not be used and that participants be informed of the tape recorder and their permission given before they are taped. Because most people are self-conscious about being taped, students will have the best chance of obtaining natural speech.)

Use these tapes as a background for discussion with students. BE- and SE-speaking students can each benefit from this exercise in listening carefully to the other's speech. Have students write rules for both BE and SE based on the tapes. What distinctions do some people make in speech that others do not? Comparing the speech of different people will help students learn to hear distinctions that they do not make. Depending on student abilities and interest, the class can write detailed descriptions of BE and SE, identifying areas of important differences and including aspects of pronunciation, vocabulary, word order, and speaking style. This study will help students learn to use SE well, enabling them to predict translation problems by approaching SE as a "foreign language." Teachers can also **use the** descriptions to reduce confusion in spelling, for example. Student **problems in hearing** and spelling correctly can be avoided by learning "silent" **letters (as in "desk,"** pronounced "des") and homonyms ("coal/cold," pronounced **alike).**

Use Your Own Language

One way for speakers of Black English to become more involved in the material they read is to have them write their own. The first step is to get them talking and telling stories. Pay attention to what stories students like to tell each other; for example, ghost stories. Encourage them to tell a favorite story, one they heard or that happened to them, to someone who can write it down (or tape it as long as they also have an audience). This activity is especially useful for involving older students in other classes as transcribers for the stories.

Collect these stories in a book so that all students can read them. As students become more involved in telling their stories, the language will be livelier and the stories more interesting.

Verbal Games

Black English is an important part of black culture, particularly in the verbal street games. Many black students do not participate in class because they feel the classroom is an alien environment, where people speak a different kind of language from the one they know. Encourage all students to become involved by talking about the verbal games they are familiar with. Signifying, sounding, rapping, and playing the dozens are all names for a number of different activities involving verbal facility. Ask different students to define these terms and give examples. What does it take to be good at these? Can students think of related verbal games from nonblack cultures? (All children play at ritual insults to some extent.) While the examples students give may sound offensive, an important part of the performance is to not take anything personally but to "give as good as you get." These forms of verbal duelling are really skill contests and the person who takes offense is not playing the game right.

Discussion of verbal games is important in the classroom because it gives everyone a chance to talk about something they know and are good at. The goal is to get students involved in classroom activities. Everyone can participate in the exaggeration and bragging required. Have students suggest completions for the following frame.

You're so low _____

You're so low that you slide under the door.

You're so low that everyone thinks your head's below your feet.

African Words

When Blacks were first brought to this country as slaves, they spoke many different languages. Because they could not understand each other, it was difficult to preserve their different native languages against the influence of English. It is not surprising, therefore, that few African words were borrowed into English. Even when a word appears to be originally African, it is difficult or impossible to pin down the source language.

Prepare a bulletin board to reflect the African contribution to English. List some of the following:

tote—to carry
jubilant, jubilee (from "juba," a dance)
gumbo
goober—peanut (from "guba")
voodoo
cooter—tortoise (from "kuta")
OK (origin unknown—possibly from yaw kay)
hip—with it
guy—man

Learn Swahili

Students enjoy learning about another language. Offer them the challenge of learning Swahili, one of the major languages of Africa. Several books present Swahili for students.

Muriel Feelings. *Moja Means One*. Dial, 1971.

————. *Jambo Means Hello*. Dial, 1974.

Have these books available for students to read. Prepare task cards for them to use with the books. Include some of varied difficulty, ranging from matching the words *one* through *ten* with the corresponding Swahili words to writing a paragraph using as many Swahili words as possible.

Modeling Standard English

Although many BE-speaking students understand SE, it is often difficult for them to practice their knowledge. In their experience, black people speak BE and white people SE. Provide experience in speaking SE by using puppets or masks with older students. Many students find it easier to take the role of another person when they have a puppet to speak through. Assigning students specific roles to play helps them understand that SE is more appropriate than BE in certain situations. Having to talk like an important business executive encourages students to use their knowledge of SE, even if they only hear it on television. Role-play speech has an advantage because it allows students to identify structural differences between BE and SE and to practice switching between them without losing ability to function verbally in the black community. Having students memorize rules or translate individual sentences is confusing and less effective because the same sentences can mean one thing in BE and another in SE.

Students need to have models of black people who can use both BE and SE in order to show them why it is important to learn both. Invite a person from the community to speak to the students about black talk and SE. It is important to reassure students that learning to use SE appropriately does not have to mean giving up the ability to talk black. Naturally, the teacher of black students should become familiar with BE, both the structural characteristics and the way it is used in the community, in order to work effectively with students.

Learning Black English

One major problem teachers have in dealing with BE-speaking students is lack of familiarity with BE. What may appear to be mistakes in the use of SE are often actually features of BE. If teachers are not aware of these differences, they will have trouble understanding the students and making themselves understood.

There are a number of recent books that discuss Black English—its structure, use, history, and differences from standard English. The following are recommended resources:

Robbins, Burling. *English in Black and White.* Holt, Rinehart and Winston, 1973.

Dillard, J. L. *Black English.* Random House, 1972.

Differences Between Black English and Standard English

In talking of black dialects, one must be careful to recognize that not all black Americans speak dialects that are labelled "Black English." Also, remember that there are variant dialects within the general term: Black English. These generalizations may be helpful if Black English is unfamiliar to you.

1. *It* will often be used for *there* (e.g., "It's a book on the table" instead of "There's a book on the table").
2. The verb will tend to be missing where a contraction is commonly used in standard English, especially in the present tense (e.g., "I here" and "We going").
3. More than a single negative form is acceptable in the black English vernacular (e.g., "I don't take no stuff from nobody").
4. Two or more consonant sounds appearing at the end of words in standard English tend to be reduced in the black English vernacular (e.g., *tes* for test and *des* for desk). The reduction of consonant clusters affects words that end in *s* (e.g., plurals, third person singular forms, and possessives like its and father's). The reduction also affects verbs in the past tense ending in -ed.
5. Words in which a medial or final *th* appears often change pronunciation in the black English dialect (e.g., *wit* or *wif* for with and *muver* for mother).
6. There are words in which *r* and *l* appear in medial or final positions in standard English. These sounds are often absent in the Black English dialect.
7. Labels and concepts different from the dominant English dialect are generated from a variety of different experiences (e.g., the use of *bad* to mean good).

SOURCE: *Framework in Reading for the Elementary and Secondary Schools in California.* California State Department of Education, 1973.

In addition, a few more specific points might be helpful. Black English does not distinguish gender. The form *he* is used for "he, she, it." Black English has a verb form not found in Standard English. *Be* is used to mean the habitual aspect. It does not change for person or tense. Singular and plural are often not distinguished in nouns in Black English. Instead, the pronoun can follow the noun to indicate number (e.g., The boy he . . . , Those guys them . . .).

SPEECH REGISTERS

Closely related to dialectology is the study of style or register variation—identifying what features comprise distinct registers, which registers are used in which situations, and what factors affect register choice. Every speaker of a language can use a great variety of registers. This control of a repertoire of registers and the ability to select the appropriate register from one's repertoire is a part of communicative competence, general knowledge of how to use language appropriately. The term appropriateness is used throughout discussions of register because choice of a register is based on consideration of a number of factors such as sex, age, relative status, and topic, and there is no "correct" decision. An inappropriate choice of register is usually recognized as a misunderstanding of the situation rather than as "incorrect."

Registers differ from each other in the same way as dialects—pronunciation, vocabulary, and syntax. When speaking informally, we tend to shorten the verb ending -ing to -in, for example. Baby talk register (how adults talk to babies) is recognized by special vocabulary such as choo-choo train and gitchy-gitchy goo; dropping of articles, prepositions, and verbs (Ellie want nap now?); and raised pitch. Syntactic differences are clear in the register of legal writing characterized by long sentences made up of many relative clauses. Related registers have features in common. For example, baby talk, pet talk, lover talk, and talk to foreigners have many features in common, showing an association of ideas. Registers are usually identified not by the presence or absence of specific features but by the frequency of usage of their representative features.

Study of register shows us that the difference between spoken and written language is an important part of our knowledge of language. Teachers need to be aware that the language used in books, the written representation of language, is an unfamiliar register for students. Children learn what registers are and how to use them through exposure to various registers. The teacher has an important role in teaching students about different registers by providing as many different experiences with language as possible. For example, the best way to teach students how to use written language is to read books aloud to them.

Levels of Language

Although students can identify when the style of someone's speech is inappropriate to the occasion, they may not be aware of the many stylistic distinctions we make all the time in the way we speak. Discuss possible differences in levels of language such as formal or informal, scientific or casual. When would we use each of these? Ask students to identify situations in which they would talk differently. Situations can be affected by the following factors: (1) person(s) talked to, (2) topic of conversation, (3) location of talk, and (4) relative status—age or occupation, for example. What groups in our society have distinctive ways of talking? Mention occupational groups (doctors) and social or ethnic groups (Blacks), for example.

Older students can translate passages from one level to another for practice in appropriate language. Ask students how a Mother Goose rhyme would sound if it were written by a scientist in very formal and elaborate language. Allow each student to compose versions of Mother Goose rhymes and try to stump the others. The longer the words used, the more unfamiliar the passages sound. Have them consult a thesaurus and dictionary for useful practice in finding synonyms. Can they guess what familiar first line this adaptation represents?

Scintillate, scintillate seemingly minuscule orb.
(Twinkle, twinkle little star.)

Sex Differences in Style

Another factor affecting how people speak is the sex of the participants. Women and men speak differently and adjust their speech depending on whether they are speaking to women or men. We are all aware of the sex role stereotypes of speech. Discuss with students their ideas on how men and women talk. Ask them if they think boys and girls talk differently. What are some of these differences?

Have students write two dialogues, one of two girls talking about what they did on the weekend and another of two boys discussing the same topic. Keep them short but allow each student to have a chance at suggesting the girls' and boys' conversations. If students have trouble thinking of ideas, develop a class version with students contributing single lines of dialogue. Afterward, have pairs of students read the dialogues aloud. It is often most effective when girls read the boys' version and vice versa. Discuss the differences in these conversations. Do all boys and girls really talk this way? What would happen if a girl talked like a boy and vice versa?

Younger students may express their ideas more easily through puppets. Use pairs of girls, boys, or mother/father puppets to enable students to act out their interpretation of female and male speech. Discuss how they know these differences exist. Is this how their parents or their friends talk? Usually written dialogues or puppet plays produce stereotypes or exaggerated representations of how different people speak. Contrast students' examples with real conversations, obtained by taping or writing down what students actually say in class. Can students tell whether the speakers are girls or boys?

Roleplay and Language

The best way to show students how to use language appropriately in new situations is to have them act out the situation in roleplay before they encounter an actual problem. Make an unfamiliar situation, such as interviewing an adult, less frightening by having students run through their roles, developing possible problems, discussing with the class how to solve them, and encouraging students by showing them how to be successful.

Work with younger students on practicing basic conversational skills. Set specific tasks such as asking another student to lend you crayons. With puppets or in small groups, have students act out simple situations. Vary details of the task so that students have to modify their approach and use language appropriate to the situation. How would they borrow crayons from a new student, for example? When all students have had a chance, allow students to suggest ways they could improve their own performance. Roleplay can also be used to practice common school situations and improve student self-confidence. Have students enact being called to the principal's office for something they did or did not do, or being sick and having to go see the nurse. Both roles can be played by students or the teacher and student can alternate roles.

Older students derive enjoyment and experience from roleplaying open-ended situations. Have them practice situations in which appropriate language is important such as apologizing and requesting a favor. Vary the seriousness of the situation and the relationship to the person addressed.

These activities provide essential experience in appropriate use of language for students who are learning English as a second language. An excellent resource for further work with roleplay is Fannie Shaftel's *Roleplaying for the Social Studies* (Prentice-Hall, 1968).

Connotations

Knowing the connotation of a word involves knowing when to use it appropriately. In order to choose between words (synonyms), students need to be conscious of possible connotations. Begin with a word or an idea. How would students apply it to themselves, to their friends, to others? Develop a chart such as the following:

I am:	firm	cautious	thrifty
You are:	stubborn	timid	a tightwad
She or he is:	pig-headed	chicken	a skinflint

When working with synonyms, brainstorm a long list of examples. Have students arrange the words in a scale, from most to least, or worst to best, for example. Accept individual differences because reactions to words differ, based on personal experiences. Discuss the connotations of these words.

Ask students to write a headline describing how one school's team won a game over another school. How many different words could they find to replace "win"? Which words would they use if they favored the winning team? The losing team? Which words would be best if the score was close? If the margin was large? What other factors might influence the choice of words? Consider some of the following possibilities: beat, closeout, smash, trounce, whip, sail over, or edge.

Groups of synonyms can also be arranged in humorous measurement scales. Have students develop a list of expressions used to mean "small," for example. They can turn this list into a table of relative weight, as in the following:

$$5 \text{ tittles} = 1 \text{ jot}$$
$$5 \text{ jots} = 1 \text{ drop}$$
$$10 \text{ drops} = 1 \text{ smidgen}$$
$$3 \text{ smidgens} = 1 \text{ touch}$$

Euphemisms

Euphemisms are a special category of synonyms. They are words used to disguise the real meaning. Have students collect examples of euphemisms. Look at advertisements, occupational titles, business names, and anything related to death. What are the real equivalents for these euphemisms? Why would people use one form and not another? For what style of speech would each be appropriate?

Occupations dealing with death provide a large source of euphemisms. Do students know what the following words mean?

mortician	(undertaker)
loved one	(dead person, corpse)
casket	(coffin)
interment	(burial)
memorial garden	(graveyard)

Discuss with students the purpose of these euphemisms. Do they protect the undertaker, the bereaved family, or no one?

Other areas in which to look for euphemisms are the "forgotten groups" in our society. Senior citizens is a euphemism for old people. What do we call poor people? Are there other groups for which we use euphemisms?

Slang

Although slang is not considered a usual part of the language arts curriculum, it is an essential part of the student's language. The language that students find familiar and comfortable is often labeled slang by teachers. However, this attitude not only reflects lack of respect for the child's language but misses the important role of slang in the transmission of culture. Read the following quotes to students and discuss.

Slang is language that takes off its coat, spits on its hands, and goes to work.

Carl Sandburg

All slang is metaphor, and all metaphor is poetry.

G. K. Chesterton

Proverbs

Slang can be considered another level of language, appropriate for use in specific situations. It increases the choice of ways by which we can express an idea. Proverbs are traditionally expressed in archaic language, yet the ideas represented are universal. Have students suggest how they would translate simple proverbs into slang. Are there expressions in "street talk" that cover the same ideas as the proverbs? How many different ways can students think of to restate the following proverb in familiar language?

Do unto others as you would have them do unto you.

Discuss the differences in what these expressions communicate, depending on whether they use slang or archaic language. Which would be appropriate when and why?

Stale Slang

Slang can be difficult to use because it goes out of date quickly. Ask students to contribute examples of slang words and expressions that they use frequently. Have them describe what these mean. How long do they think these expressions will last? Give them a list of slang words from the 1960s. How many of these words do they know or hear used?

hip	flower child	hot rod	rip off
cool	cat	dragster	dropping acid
with it	chick	chopper	going steady

Present examples of slang from another period, such as the 1940s, and have students discover the meanings by interviewing older people they know.

tin Lizzie	off the cob	a Jackson
to spoon	flivver	you shred it, wheat
rumble seat	cooking on the front burner	

Students can report to the class their findings of how and when these expressions were used.

Yiddish Slang

Yiddish is a rich language, used by people with a tradition of storytellers and colorful characters, and it represents an important source of slang for English. Talk with students about the many words we have adopted from Yiddish. Some words will be familiar to all students, others primarily to students from areas with large Jewish populations, such as New York and Los Angeles. How many students know what the following words mean, as they are used in English?

schlemiel	nudnik	shtick
kibbitz	nebbish	shnoz
chutzpah	yenta	

Ask students if they know any other Yiddish words, for example, for food.

Cockney Slang

Slang can begin by a group of people's adopting special vocabulary in order to distinguish them from other groups. The Cockneys, people living in a particular neighborhood of London, are easily recognizable by their distinctive pronunciation and special slang. Give students some of the following examples.

Use your *loaf!* (head)
Going home to the *trouble and strife.* (wife)

Can students figure out how this slang works? Words are replaced by phrases that rhyme with the original. *Trouble and strife* equals *wife; loaf of bread* is shortened to loaf, for *head.* Loaf has also been used in American slang for head. Have students make up more examples and put them into sentences so that others can guess what they mean.

Local Slang

Slang can also be based on shared experiences, family tradition, and ethnic background. People in the town of Booneville, California, population 1,000 (in 1969), developed a unique vocabulary in 1892 called Boont. Here are some of the terms they used.

zeese	coffee, after J. C., a cook who made strong coffee
ottin'	working, after Otto, an industrious logger
charlie ball	embarrass, after Charlie Ball, too shy to talk
forbes	50 cents, short for four bits
wee	small, from Scotch-Irish dialect
kimmie	man, from Scotch-Irish
tweed	young man, from Scotch-Irish
boche	deer, from a Pomo (Indian) word
perel	rain, looks like pearls
croppies	sheep, because they crop the grass

List these on the board for students and describe how they originated. Are there any special terms that students use among friends or in the same class, for example? How might these have developed? Boont vocabulary came from characteristics associated with particular people or places, memories of shared events, and a common ethnic heritage. Have students think of examples of these word coinages in their own speech.

Children's Folklore

Although students are not aware of it, their use of sayings and rhymes is considered important by folklorists and is a rich source of information on children's culture. Have students recite rhymes they use for counting. How many different ones do they know? Do any students know rhymes that no one else does? Read students' examples of different British counting rhymes so that they can see what other students use. *Lore and Language of School Children* by Iona and Peter Opie (Oxford University Press, 1959) is an excellent source for all types of British children's folklore. Their work indicates that many children's rhymes are spread across both Britain and the United States and are very old.

Another set of rhymes to explore with students is jump-rope rhymes. If any students have come from another area or another school, ask them whether the other students used different rhymes. Discuss how students learned the rhymes they know and how these rhymes might spread to other schools. *The Whim-Wham Book* by Duncan Emrich (Four Winds, 1975), a collection of folklore contributed by children, includes examples from across the country.

There are other children's language games that provide insight into cultural differences. Specifically, ritual verbal games used by Blacks are important aspects of black culture. Ask black students to describe black verbal games, such as playing the dozens, to the class. If you develop an atmosphere of sincere interest and desire for information, the black students will be glad to share their special knowledge because they are making an important contribution to the class.

Superstitions reveal the different ethnic and cultural backgrounds of students. Children's superstitions are evidence of the persistence of ethnic traditions. Have students name examples of superstitions they believe or have heard. Collect their contributions (written or dictated) into a book and display for everyone to read. This book can motivate further student research on folklore and folk beliefs in the community. Alvin Schwartz's *Cross Your Fingers, Spit in Your Hat* (Lippincott, 1974) is a humorous and useful collection of superstitions and other beliefs.

SOURCES TO INVESTIGATE

Cazden, Courtney, Vera John, and Dell Hymes. *Functions of Language in the Classroom.* Teachers College Press, 1972.

Ching, Doris C. *Reading and the Bilingual Child.* IRA, 1976.

Cullinan, Bernice E. *Black Dialects & Reading.* ERIC Clearinghouse on Reading and Communication Skills, NCTE, 1974.

Davidson, Jessica. *Is That Mother in the Bottle? Where Language Came From and Where It Is Going.* Watts, 1972.

DeStefano, Johanna. *Language, Society, and Education: A Profile of Black English.* Charles A. Jones, 1973.

Hook, J. N. *The Story of American English.* Harcourt Brace Jovanovich, 1972.

Littell, Joseph Fletcher, ed. *Dialects and Levels of Language.* McDougal, 1971.

———. *How Words Change Our Lives.* McDougal, 1971.

Thonis, Eleanor W. *Literacy for America's Spanish Speaking Children.* IRA, 1976.

Trudgill, Peter. *Sociolinguistics: An Introduction.* Pelican, 1974.

4

Promoting Intergroup Relations

If Negro freedom is taken away, or that of any minority group, the freedom of all the people is taken away.

Paul Robeson

Few countries are made up of such a diverse culture as is the United States. Our pluralistic society is seen as a strength; yet we do not always take full advantage of this energy. If we truly value pluralism and diversity, then we could well provide a model to demonstrate to the world the strength of our belief.

Beginning with the miniature society within each classroom, you can work toward this end. You and your students can achieve some inspiring and rewarding results. The ideas included in this book have been selected to assist you in moving in that direction. The activities in this chapter are designed specifically to help you and your students to (1) explore the concept of diversity, (2) break down stereotyped thinking, and (3) study groups in our society.

This approach should permeate the entire elementary school curriculum. It is especially appropriate for social studies and language arts classes, and multicultural literature should be present in every reading program. Promoting intergroup relations is a basic consideration, not an extra, something tacked on to the curriculum. In the following pages we will explore strategies that can be used in any classroom.

EXPLORING THE CONCEPT OF DIVERSITY

Students often have the misconception that being different is synonymous with "bad." We need to see that we are all different, and that this is not bad or undesirable.

Explore the concept of diversity with your students. Begin with ideas that are familiar, nonthreatening, and easily accepted: for example, the recognition of personal difference in fingerprints. Extend student perceptions of diversity into other areas such as beliefs and values. Lessons based on such significant ideas will have clear applications for your students. Many of the activities presented in Chapter 2 will also be useful in exploring this concept.

What Is Diversity?

It is interesting to begin with the dictionary in discussing the meaning of a concept that may not be totally clear. We find several forms of this word: diverse, diversification, diversify/diversified, and diversity.

Two definitions are given for diverse: (1) of various kinds or forms; multiform; (2) of a different kind, form, character; unlike. Synonyms for diverse are: varied, manifold, divergent; dissimilar or separate.

Diversity, therefore, is the condition of being different, or having differences. In this book we are talking about diversity in terms of ethnic backgrounds—religion, language, culture—all that goes into producing the rich cultural pluralism we have in the United States. This diversity has been our strength to which each different element has contributed.

Personal Indentity

Discuss how our government keeps track of all the millions of different people in this huge, well-populated country. Why is this important? Why is the system complex and often confusing?

Every ten years we take a national census. We have birth certificates, but sometimes these records were not well kept or they have been destroyed by fire. In order to work we have social security numbers which we retain all our lives. The use of the social security number is being extended more and more so that it appears on many forms, such as the income tax report. This single number may soon become an identification number for all purposes, for example, a driver's license.

A number alone, of course, still does not identify the person precisely. Someone could use another person's social security number or create a new identity with a new social security number. What other ways of identifying people are more reliable? Fingerprints and voice prints are examples. What do they look like and who uses them?

Have students find out more about various aspects of identifying people in the United States. Topics to be investigated include the U.S. Census (how-who-when), birth certification (local procedures), the social security system (getting a social security number), and fingerprinting (how it works).

Students may call or visit local offices to obtain information. They might invite someone to visit their class to tell them about a specific topic.

Our Names

Our names are a very important part of our identities. Students in a class may have a variety of different names—some less common than others. They can be very sensitive about what they are called (by teachers and other students). Students in the class who come from different backgrounds may have names that are difficult for English speakers to pronounce. However, it is an insult to these students and their cultural background to force them to anglicize their names. Translating the name because the form is unfamiliar is also demeaning.

Use the presence of different names to talk about how we can say the same name in different ways. Talk about the many different names that can be made out of Edward (Ted, Ned, Eddie) and Elizabeth (Beth, Eliza, Liza, Betty, Betsy). Students will be interested to learn names in different languages. They can also look up the original meaning of English names in a name dictionary.

Give students a list of Spanish names and their English equivalents. Note the similarities and differences. Even when the names are spelled the same, they are pronounced differently. Some Spanish names have no easy English translation or are less common in English. Some English names have no Spanish translation.

Family Names in Different Cultures

Different cultures have different rules for last names or family names. In English-speaking countries, children take the last name of the father. Some countries, on the other hand, use both the mother's and father's names. Other countries give different forms of the father's first and last names to male and female children.

In Spanish, for example, a person's surname consists of the father's family name followed by the mother's family name, thus:

Teresa	Pérez	Gutiérrez
	(father)	(mother)
Carlos	Chavez	Martínez
	(father)	(mother)

Sometimes the word *y* (and) is inserted between the surnames of the father and mother, like this: Juan López y Benavente. Juan would be called Señor López, however, and his name would be under L in the telephone directory.

A woman who gets married keeps her father's name and adds her husband's name preceded by the word *de* (of or belonging to). If Teresa, above, married Carlos, she would be: Teresa Pérez de Chavez (y Martinez). She then is called Señora Chavez.

Origins of Names

Family names are interesting to children when they discover the meanings that lie behind them. They can easily see that those that have "son" or "sen" at the end carry the meaning "son of," for example, Anderson, Christianson, Peterson, and Williamson. The most common name of all is Johnson, son of John. Endings that mean son of in other languages include *ez* (Spanish), *tse* (Chinese), and *wicz* (Polish).

Many last names are associated with a person's line of work, for instance Carpenter, Farmer, Baker, Miller, and Smith (blacksmith). Characteristics of a person often led to the use of other names such as Young, Black, Long, White, and Little.

For names of foreign origin, use a dictionary for that language. Set out on a discovery trip that all can participate in as they help each other find the origins of their family names.

One Name in Many Languages

Students will be interested, too, in discovering that the same name is used in many languages. One illustration is the name John, which can be found in different languages, thus:

John (English)	Evan (Welsh)
Ian (Scotch)	Giovanni (Italian)
Ivan (Russian)	Hans (German)
Iban (Basque)	Jan (Northern Europe, Holland)
Jannis (Greek)	Johan (Norwegian)
Jean (French)	Johannes (German)
Juan (Spanish)	Sean (Irish)
Shane (Irish)	Yohanna (Arabic)

See if they can discover the equivalent in other languages of such names as Peter, James, David, William, Mary, Rose, and Helen.

Lists of Names

Children will be interested in pursuing this study of names. Prepare a list of English names with corresponding names in other languages. If you have many Spanish-speaking children, develop a poster like this:

NAMES IN SPANISH AND ENGLISH

Pedro—Peter	María—Mary
Juan—John	Juana—Jane
Esteban—Stephen	Esperanza—Hope
Luís—Louis	Margarita—Margaret
Carlos—Charles	Josefina—Josephine
José—Joseph	Teresa—Theresa
Ricardo—Richard	Elena—Helen
Roberto—Robert	Susanna—Susan
Jacinto—James	Beatríz—Beatrice
Arturo—Arthur	Carlota—Charlotte
Eduardo—Edward	Emilia—Emily
Jorge—George	Estrelita—Star
Enrique—Henry	Anna—Ann
Alejandro—Alexander	Rosa—Rose
Guillermo—William	Luísa—Louise

Developing a Continuum

Often we describe things in terms of two opposites, for example, good or bad, black or white, big or little, ugly or beautiful.

Students should become aware that most comparisons involve gradations between extremes. Introduce the word continuum, a continuous portion of a spectrum or range. Demonstrate on the chalkboard, using a familiar pair of antonyms, Hot and Cold, thus:

torrid   HOT   steaming   warm   mild   chilly   cool   COLD   freezing

Add other words suggested by the students. Decide at what point on the continuum each should be placed. Observe that the continuum never ends. Although we use the terms hot and cold as opposites, these terms are only points on the continuum which can get hotter and colder.

Painting a Color Continuum

Students can experiment with gradations of color beginning with white and moving toward blue, red, green, black or brown. This experiment yields artistic and mathematical concepts as well as sociological understandings.

Give each student a sheet of paper which is then folded into eighths. Each person selects a shape to place in the eight squares, as shown here:

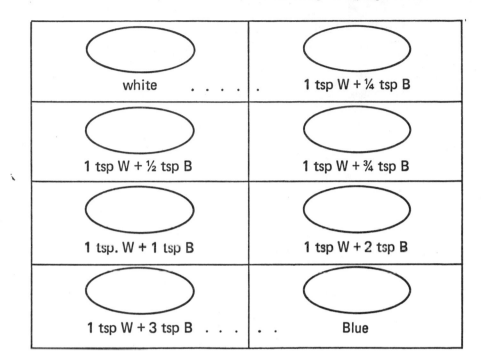

Using measuring spoons, students carefully mix the paint as indicated and paint the shape in each box appropriately.

Between the extremes of white and blue are all gradations of blueness. Obviously, it is not possible to show all the possible gradations of color which are indicated by the omission marks.

This experiment can be carried further by adding a drop of some other color. A drop of red or yellow inserted in the experiment with blue, for example, will make a tremendous difference in the end result.

Help students extend this analogy to skin color. Note that white (in the first box) is the absence of color. Is anyone ever really white? We all have some color in our faces, usually shades of red, yellow, and brown.

Cultural Difference Reflected in Language

Eskimos have many words for snow. Snow is an important part of Eskimo life so there are many words to describe all the different conditions and states of snow. In other cultures rice or millet are important basic foods, so there are many words for variations in these grains.

What can we observe in the English language that reflects a cultural emphasis? One item around which we have developed a rich vocabulary is the automobile. Have students list as many words as possible under the following categories:

Manufacturers' Names	Types	Parts	Related Verbs
Mustang	limousine	fender	drive
Cougar	sedan	carburetor	swerve
Chevrolet	sports car	hood	speed
Cadillac	convertible	trunk	zoom
Honda	taxi cab	tires	race
Volvo	van	steering wheel	crash

After developing these lists, students can discuss such questions as:

1. Why do we have so many words about cars?
2. Are there other similar items that are important to us? (airplane, eating out, clothing, housing)
3. How does our language reveal our values?

The Same Idea in Many Cultures

Proverbs make fascinating study especially if you compare those that say much the same thing in different words. In the United States we often hear the saying: "Actions speak louder than words." Here is much the same idea expressed in proverbs from other countries:

Talk does not cook rice. China

It is one thing to cackle and another to lay an egg.

Ecuador

Fancy words don't butter cabbage.

Germany

Challenge your students to write this saying in still different ways. They might suggest, for instance:

Laudable behavior indicates true brain power.

The big wind only blows down the wheat!

Men and women are not only themselves; they are also the region in which they were born, the city apartment or farm in which they learned to walk, the games they played as children, the old wives' tales they overheard, the food they ate, the schools they attended, the sports they followed, the poems they read, and the God they believed in.

W. Somerset Maugham, *The Razor's Edge*

Borrowing Words

We borrow words from many languages. Sometimes these words were brought to us as people from different countries settled in the land that is now the United States. Sometimes American travelers have brought words back with them.

See how many different foods you can name that come from different countries. Students probably know, for example, sauerkraut, tortillas, and spaghetti.

We have borrowed many words around the world. See if children can discover the origins of the following:

khaki	shanghai
ballet	encore
veldt	parole
opera	corral

More ideas about borrowed words are included in Chapter 3.

Sameness Can Be Dull

Usually we associate spring with pleasure, something to anticipate. Songs express these feelings: "Welcome, sweet springtime: we greet thee with joy!" Poetry, too, presents this idea: "If winter comes, can spring be far behind?" The wonderful thing about spring is obviously the contrast with a cold winter.

Discuss with children what it would be like if we always had spring. Would we continue to appreciate it so much? Do people in warm climates like the contrast of a cool breeze, a little snow?

For fun, and to make a point, teach children this humorous song:

Spring Would Be

Discuss what it would be like if all people were the same.

A Book to Share

An excellent book to read aloud is *Sound of Sunshine, Sound of Rain* by Florence P. Heide (Parents' Magazine Press, 1970). This book is outstanding in terms of both content and the beautiful illustrations by Kenneth Longtemps. This story of a young black boy who is blind offers these possibilities for follow-up:

1. understanding of a handicapped person
2. some grasp of attitudes toward "color"
3. examples of imagery—similes and metaphors
4. development of plot and characterization
5. the family interaction
6. sensory experiences
7. art ideas
8. different points of view
9. discussion of dreams
10. personal feelings

The Ideal American

Discuss what an ideal American might be. Encourage students to share their ideas, recognizing that they will differ. For an individualized approach, use a task card like that shown on page 125, which appears in *Reading across the Curriculum,* by Sharon Belshaw and Candy Carter (Contemporary Press, Box 1524, San Jose, CA 95109, $3.50). These teachers have included many ideas about values in this activity book that is designed for use in learning centers.

A Story to Discuss

THERE'S NOBODY LIKE YOU!

The French poet Jean Cocteau found out early in life why diversity is better than uniformity.

As a young man, M. Cocteau was designing a stage set which required a tree as background. He spent night after night in the theater basement cutting out individual leaves for his creation.

Then a wealthy friend, whose father owned a factory, approached him with another idea.

"Give me the design of the leaf," he said, "and in three days you will have thousands of them here."

After his friend's return, they pasted the multitude of identical leaves onto the branches.

The result, M. Cocteau recalled, was "the most boring package of flat, uninteresting forms one can see."

At last he understood why each leaf of a tree and each man in the world are different from any other.

Christopher News Notes, no. 187, May 1971

The Ideal American

You are to make a Wanted Poster for The Ideal American in a particular period of history. By using history books and other sources, you are to describe the perfect American for one of the periods of history below:

(Check the one you will do)

_____ 1700	_____ 1900
_____ 1750	_____ 1950
_____ 1800	_____ 1970
_____ 1850	_____ 1980
_____ 2000	

> Remember, this does not have to be a real person! The person should, however, represent the ideal person for the period of history which you choose.

A. Place a drawing, photograph or magazine picture of the ideal American on a sheet of colored construction paper. Put the answers for B below the picture.

B. Supply the following information about your Ideal American:
Age
Sex
Religion
Address
Race
Occupation
Economic class
Married?   Single?   Divorced?
Number of children
Years of schooling
Interests or hobbies
Ten qualities or personality characteristics which make this person the Ideal American for this period of history.

What Things Are Unique?

Discuss diversity in nature. The snowflake is a good example, for no two snowflakes are alike. Locate a discussion of snowflakes in a science book. Examine real snowflakes when it snows.

Show students how to cut paper snowflakes, to demonstrate the variety produced.

Step 1:   Fold a paper in fourths

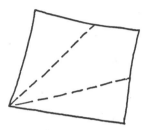

Step 2:   Fold that paper in thirds

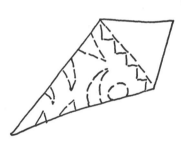

Step 3:   Cut away pieces

Step 4:   Open up the snowflake

Display the snowflakes on the bulletin board with the caption: No Snowflakes Are Alike.

BREAKING DOWN STEREOTYPES

The classroom is a laboratory for human relations, a miniature society in which students experiment daily with the interaction of individuals with different backgrounds, values, ways of looking at life.

In this section we focus on valuing other people as classmates and friends, as human beings. We also stress valuing the contributions of others in the classroom as well as in the larger society. The activities in this section are selected to help break down the stereotyping that results in prejudice. Classroom experiments should help students learn:

1. to view each person as an individual
2. to question generalizations based on race, sex, or age
3. to respect the beliefs of others

What Is Stereotyping?

The development of a generalization that becomes a stereotype is a natural result of the thinking processes that lead us to categorize or to group objects or people. Human perception, as Maureen Mansell points out in "Seeing the Other Point of View" (*Elementary English,* April, 1975), "works to achieve well-ordered categories." Stereotyping results as these categories become "narrow category systems" resulting from limited experience. Categorizing and generalizing cannot be eliminated from our thinking.

We can, on the other hand, help students, and ourselves, to become more aware of the negative effects that can result from overgeneralizing. We can stress the importance of seeing each person as an individual, not just part of a group. We can avoid making generalizations about persons as groups. Just talking about this topic will open the door to further investigation and changing attitudes.

Stereotyped Ideas of Animals

Over the years we have developed stereotyped ideas of what animals are like. You may be surprised at how well these stereotypes have already been passed to children. Ask students to describe the following animals with one or two words: mouse, fox, deer.

Focus on one animal such as the wolf. Have students describe this animal. Record what they say in writing or on a cassette. Then read a story that portrays a sympathetic picture of the wolf such as *The Friendly Wolf* by Dorothy and Paul Goble, *Mowgli and His Brothers* by Rudyard Kipling, or *Julie and the Wolves* by Jean Craighead George.

After completing the story(ies), ask students to comment about what wolves are like. Record this session also. Play the first recording for the class. Has there been a change of opinion? Why?

Color Associations

Talk about the associations we have with one specific color. Ask "What do you think of when you think *red*?" List the ideas on the board, thus: fire, anger, burning, blood.

Then discuss how children feel about red. Is it a *good* color? They may, for example, conclude that red is not a good color, but it is exciting or it signals danger.

Follow this discussion by thinking about our use of the word red in expressions in our language. List those named, for example:

> to get red with anger
> blood red, as red as blood
> to be a Red (Communist)

See page 132 for more ideas related to this topic.

Small Group Exploration of Color

Have the class break into groups of five or six that will explore associations with one specific color. They can collect ideas related to these topics:

Things associated with the color
Kinds of feelings associated with the color
Expressions using this color

The object of this exploration is to demonstrate that we have developed stereotyped ideas about color. What do we mean when we say, for example, "I am blue"?

Blue is sad. (I am blue.)
Yellow means cowardice. (I am yellow.)
Green means young or unskilled. (I am green.)

Ask students to consider how these stereotyped ideas might have developed. If there are students in the class from different backgrounds, they may have very different associations with these colors. Discuss how such stereotypes can vary from culture to culture.

If White Means Good, Then Black Means . . .

Children quickly learn to make the association between white = good, and black = evil, and to transfer this association to black people. The many references in our society that represent black as evil or bad serve to reinforce this association. Help students become more aware of how their attitudes are conditioned by discussing expressions that include black. List examples given by students on the board. How many of them are positive, how many negative?

blackmail	blackhead
black flag	black-hearted
black rage	black magic
blackball	black sheep
Black Death	blacken
black eye	black market
black lie	black mark
black mood	black humor
blackout	in the black
in black and white	black depression

What does black mean in each of these expressions? What does black mean when we are talking about a person's skin color? Does the word black used in *Black Power* and *Black is beautiful* have any connection with the expressions listed? These are important questions for students to discuss in order to eliminate the stereotype that black is bad.

Perception of Others

A group that has been together for a period of time will benefit from sharing their perceptions of each other. Prepare a chart like this on which students record information as indicated:

	Color	Food	Car	Building
Joe				
Terry				
Sara				
Linda				
Juanita				
Felipe				

Each child has a copy of this chart which he or she completes for everyone in the group. Then the group shares their perceptions. One person volunteers to begin, thus: "I see myself as orange because I'm always active. I see myself as a burrito because I'm 'full of beans' and I'm a little plump but not too much. I see myself as a Datsun pickup because I'm pretty practical and not fussy. I see myself as a house in the middle of the woods because I like to be alone outdoors."

Going around the circle, each person then tells the items he or she has written in the columns for this person. Naturally they will differ, but the items selected and the reasons given provide interesting insights that add to each person's understanding of his or her own self.

If you are working with a small group of students, include your own name on the chart. The students will be interested in how you perceive them, and their perceptions of you will be enlightening.

Sex Stereotypes

A stereotype that is easy for students to observe and one that directly affects all of them involves sexism. Ask students, for example, to make individual lists of characteristics of men and women. After each has had time to write a number of items, ask each one to contribute something to add to a class compilation of these characteristics. The lists may include items like this:

Men	*Women*
Support the family	Do the cooking for the family
Take care of the car	Do the grocery shopping
Like sports	Wear dresses

Discuss the items on the lists to determine if these characteristics are true of all men or women. Do some women support a family? Do some men cook? Let children respond freely from personal experience.

Role Reversals

Try one of these experiments to help children become more aware of stereotyped thinking:

1. Tell children that you have invited a doctor to visit your classroom one day soon. Have them draw a picture of the doctor. What will the doctor look like? (Chances are, the drawings will be of men. Have a woman doctor visit, if possible. Discuss the pictures.)
2. Have students pretend to be two sets of parents having dinner together. Have girls play the father roles while boys play the role of mothers. Discuss how they felt about reversing roles. Discuss differences in male and female behavior as well as differences in the usage of language.

Sexism in Books

Frequently you will find examples of stereotyped thinking about sex roles in children's books. It is impractical to remove all such books from the library, but we should help students read critically. An example of such stereotyping is found in *Sylvester and the Magic Pebble* by William Steig (Simon & Schuster, 1969). The mother donkey wears an apron and plays the "helpless female" while father donkey is strong and sits smoking his pipe and reading the evening paper while mother sweeps under his feet. A positive approach to such stereotyped thinking is recognition of such writing as a "period piece" that would not be written today.

Share with students books that portray more realistic pictures of men and women. Old favorites that are outstanding include *Madeline* by Ludwig Bemelmans and *Pippi Longstocking* by Astrid Lindgren. New books that you will enjoy sharing include:

Petronella by Jay Williams (Parents, 1974)

Where the Lilies Bloom by Vera and Bill Cleaver (Lippincott, 1967)

Julie and the Wolves by Jean Craighead George (Harper & Row, 1972)

Mom, the Wolf Man and Me by Norma Klein (Avon, 1974)

Especially good for primary grades are the following:

Mommies at Work by Eve Merriam (Knopf, 1955)

Girls Can Be Anything by Norma Klein (Dutton 1973)

A Woman Is . . . and *A Man Is . . .* by Elizabeth Pellett et al. (Aardvark Media, 1974)

The Terrible Thing That Happened at Our House by Marge Blaine (Parents, 1975)

An idea book that will be helpful along these lines is *Teaching for Liberation* by Iris Tiedt (Contemporary Press, Box 1524, San Jose CA 95109, $1.50).

Families Differ

Discuss the topic: What is a typical family? Students will probably arrive at the stereotyped perception of a family as a mother, father, and two children. They may even feel that the boy is the older of the two children.

Is this what families are really like? How many families represented in the classroom consist of two parents and two children? What other arrangements do the children know about? List them on the board, thus:

    Father   Mother   One Child
    Father   Mother   More than Two Children
    Mother   One Child
    Grandmother   Three Children
    Father   Two Children
    Father   Mother   One Child   Grandfather

The point of this discussion is to show children that families differ. It also opens up an opportunity for students to talk about their own families, something about which they may have felt uncomfortable. It helps to know that other parents have been divorced or that someone else's parent may have died.

Topics that are related that can be discussed without evaluation include:

    Some mothers work and some do not.
    Sometimes relatives live together.
    What constitutes a family?

Books about Different Family Arrangements

Children's books are helpful in exposing children to different family arrangements. It is helpful for all children to have a broadened perspective of this institution which is rapidly changing in our society. Here are a few titles that you might want to order for your library:

Primary Grades

I Love My Mother, Paul Zindel (Harper & Row, 1975). Mother and boy.

Jenny's Revenge, Anne N. Baldwin (Four Winds, 1974). Mother and daughter; babysitter.

Me Day, Joan Lexau (Dial, 1971). Young black boy visits with divorced father.

Upper Elementary

Ludell, Brenda Wilkinson (Harper & Row, 1975). Grandmother and fifth grade girl; unwed mother does not live with them.

The Family Tree, Margaret Storey (Nelson, 1973). Orphaned girl lives with older male cousin.

The Witches of Worm, Zilpha K. Snyder (Atheneum, 1972). Twelve-year-old girl and divorced mother.

I Know You, Al, Constance Greene (Viking, 1975). Girl and divorced mother.

A Month of Sundays, Rose Blue (Watts, 1972). Boy and divorced mother.

Last Night I Saw Andromeda, Charlotte Anker (Walck, 1975). Eleven-year-old girl and mother; father visits.

Reading such stories as part of your regular time for reading aloud to the class will be helpful to students and may open up topics for discussion. Before selecting a book to read aloud, it is important, of course, that you read it first.

What Would It Feel Like?

Help students get into someone else's skin by describing to them the experiment carried out by John Howard Griffin in *Black Like Me* (Houghton Mifflin). Griffin deliberately took drugs that darkened his skin and shaved his head so that people would think he was a Black. Then he went into the South, to experience as intimately as possible what it is like to be a black man in this country.

After the class has talked about how Griffin felt, ask them to imagine themselves in a similar situation. Have them write what they think it would feel like to spend one day as a person with a skin of a different color (Black American, Irish American, Asian American, Mexican American, Native American). Remember, the person inside the skin has not changed but how others react to you, based on skin color, has. Students might make masks to wear to make this experiment more real.

Color Masks for Simulation Games

Have students make masks of red, green, or blue construction paper, distributed arbitrarily. Distribute more green sheets than red or blue. Cut simple features with slits that fit the ears, thus:

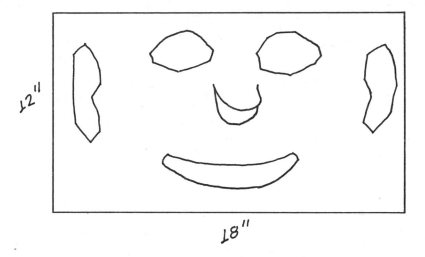

Then create a simulation game in which the students divide into groups according to their mask color. Assign one part of the room to the Reds, Greens, and Blues. Have them move their seats to the designated part of the room.

Explain that the Blues are good. They are the best people in the class, so they each get a piece of candy. They can do anything they want today. The Greens are hard workers, so they are going to do three pages of arithmetic just to keep busy. (Long division or something equally difficult or tedious for the group.) "The Reds are awful. They're so bad I don't even want to talk to them, so they are to sit still and keep quiet."

So the simulation proceeds. Encourage the Blues to walk around and to come up and chat with you. Offer them more candy. Let them play games.

After 15 to 30 minutes, depending on the mutterings of the Greens and Reds, talk about how they feel (with the masks still on). Help them relate the experience to real life. Are there groups that *have* while others *have not,* or groups that are considered *better* while others are *put down?* Which group would they rather belong to? Why? How can groups become more equal?

Wise Words

Display the proverb on p. 134 printed as a poster. Discuss the meaning of this saying.

Students can collect other quotations to display in similar fashion; for example:

"Gently scan your brother man."

Robert Burns, Scottish poet

"What you do not want others to do to you, do not do to others."

Confucius, Chinese philosopher

"Whoever seeks to set one race against another seeks to enslave all races."

Franklin D. Roosevelt, U.S. president

An Experiment in Prejudice

Here is a simple exercise you can use to show students the power of racial prejudice and how strongly it affects how we see people. Clip from the newspaper
an item that describes someone committing a crime such as a mugging or a
burglary. Type two versions of the incident, one describing the criminal as a
white person, the other as a black person. Distribute these versions on dittos to
the students as if they were identical. Give students the assignment of writing
why they think this person committed the crime and whether the person should
be punished and how.

After collecting the papers, tell the class about the difference in the accounts they were given. Read what the students thought about the person who committed this crime. How does the race of the person affect what the students thought? Discuss how people prejudge others by their race, sex, clothing.

Organizing the Classroom Together

Involve students in making important decisions about classroom procedures if you want to avoid instructional problems later. An exciting approach to establishing regulations for a classroom cooperatively has been developed by Faricita Wyatt, of San Francisco, California. Called Improving Motivation Precipitates Affective Classroom Teaching (IMPACT), the program begins with discussing a checklist of items that often cause problems, for example:

1. Entering the classroom (tardies)
2. Talking
3. Gum chewing
4. Grooming
5. Class dismissal
6. Citizenship grade
7. Grade conferences
8. Assignments
9. Folders
10. Test items—errors and comments
11. Make-up tests and assignments
12. Academic grade computation
13. Special help
14. Plagiarism and attendant problems
15. Spelling and vocabulary
16. Text books and classroom materials (care of)
17. Papers returned during student's absence
18. V.I.P.'s
19. Library use
20. Special assignments
21. Schedules
22. Seating (classroom arrangement) flexibility
23. Emergencies
24. Types of evaluations/tests (see #48)
25. Requests to participate in other activities during class period
26. Late work
27. Parent-teacher conferences
28. Interim reports
29. Study periods
30. Student-teacher displays/art work
31. Acknowledgment of student performances in other areas
32. Sharing student papers in oral reading to class—with or without revealing author
33. Sharing current events and experiences applicable to class work
34. Use of films and other media
35. Field trips
36. Assemblies
37. Substitute teachers—cooperation
38. Visitors—dignitaries et al.
39. Group work
40. Counseling
41. Subject-matter scope
42. Classroom illness
43. Administrative classroom interruptions
44. School policies
45. Recommendations
46. Educational games
47. Student teachers
48. Testing procedures
49. Note taking
50. Outside reading and research

Select the items you think may cause you and your students concern during the year. List them as shown and provide copies of the list to students. Discuss each one in turn and have a secretary record the group's decision about how each should be handled. This discussion may be spread over a period of several days. Your class may wish to produce a "Manual for Procedures to be Followed in Room 32." The activity is especially helpful at the begining of the year, but it can be initiated at any time.

The IMPACT program is designed to "evolve a system of classroom organization that is conducive to a feeling of security for each individual, teacher included. It further seeks to organize each class by developing a framework for interaction which will promote the development of the individual student and provide an atmosphere supportive of the learning process."

For more information about this approach send $1.50 for a copy of *IMPACT: A Plan for Classroom Management*, to Contemporary Press, Box 1524, San Jose, CA 95109.

Evaluating Books for Children

How can you evaluate literature for use in the classroom? We need to examine books in terms of (1) realistic portrayals of members of ethnic groups, (2) inclusion of a fair representation of persons that make up our society, and (3) an honest attempt to break down existing stereotypes and prejudices.

You can construct your own checklist especially designed to fit your own purposes. You can also guide students in developing a checklist and in applying this instrument. A simple checklist might be something like this:

Book Title _____

Author _____ Publisher _____ Year _____

Illustrator _____ Pages _____

	Positive images of:			Negative images of:
Story	*Art*		*Story*	*Art*
_____	_____ women		_____	_____ women
_____	_____ men		_____	_____ men
_____	_____ aged persons		_____	_____ aged persons
_____	_____ ethnic groups (list below)		_____	_____ ethnic groups (list below)

This checklist notes only what is present. The lack of checkmarks means, therefore, that there was nothing offensive, but neither was there a positive effort to combat stereotypes.

Comparing Evaluations of Books

Students can compare their evaluation of specific books with evaluations that have been published. The Council on Interracial Books for Children, for example, has published *Human Values in Children's Books,* in which they analyze contemporary books. Older students could easily read this report and discuss the evaluation. Here are sample evaluations for (1) a book ranked outstanding, *Ludell,* and (2) a book that was severely criticized, *Three Fools and a Horse:* [*]

LUDELL[**]

In this sensitive and powerful novel, the positive and the negative sides of growing up in a rural southern Black community are revealed through the eyes of fifth-grader Ludell. The place is Waycross, Georgia, in the 1950s where Ludell Wilson lives with her grandmother ("Mama"). Next door is the Johnson crew: Mrs. Johnson, sixteen-year-old Mattie and her child, Ruthie Mae (Ludell's best friend), Willie, Hawk and Cathy.

Ludell's keen perceptions expose the harsh underside of life in Waycross—the poverty, the selfishness and unconcern of her teachers in the segregated school she attends, the constant reminders that both Mama and Mrs. Johnson work as maids in white people's homes. Whenever racism and oppression are manifest, it is commented upon and clearly defined.

Each experience, whether humorous or tragic, contributes to Ludell's growing awareness of herself and of others. The reader can sense that one day her aspirations will lead her to seek a life outside of Waycross and to exercise more control over her destiny.

Author Wilkinson effectively captures the subtle nuances of Black southern dialect and draws readers inside the Black experience. In addition she provides a truly positive role model for young Black readers. Ludell has a keen sense of who she is, shares with those less fortunate than herself and is shown overcoming adversities in her life.

	ART	WORDS		ART	WORDS		ART	WORDS	N.A.
anti-Racist		✓	non-Racist			Racist omission / commission			
anti-Sexist			non-Sexist		✓	Sexist			
anti-Elitist		✓	non-Elitist			Elitist			
anti-Materialist			non-Materialist		✓	Materialist			
anti-Individualist		✓	non-Individualist			Individualist			
anti-Ageist			non-Ageist		✓	Ageist			
anti-Conformist			non-Conformist		✓	Conformist			
anti-Escapist		✓	non-Escapist			Escapist			
Builds positive image of females/minorities		✓	Builds negative image of females/minorities						
Inspires action vs. oppression			Culturally authentic		✓				

	Excellent	Good	Fair	Poor
Literary quality	✓			
Art quality				

---

[*] SOURCE: *Human Values in Children's Books.* Council on Interracial Books for Children, Inc., 1841 Broadway, N.Y., N.Y.

[**] By Brenda Wilkinson, Harper & Row, $5.95, 170 pages, grades 5-up.

THREE FOOLS AND A HORSE*

The Foolish People were an imaginary group invented by the Apaches as an object of humor. *Three Fools and a Horse* chronicles the misadventures of three of the Foolish People of Two Dog Mountain—Little Fool, Fat Fool and Fool About. The trio decide they must have one of the horses of the "flat land men" (Plains Indians) in order to be "big men, the biggest men of the Foolish People." Little Fool challenges one of the flat land men to a horse race (Little Fool has no horse). Surprisingly, he wins the race and the horse. Unexpected consequences follow from the Fools' attempt to ride horseback.

Native American folk stories should be told by Native Americans, not appropriated from "folklore and anthropology magazines" and then vulgarized by whites. Ms. Baker has no business writing about the Foolish People if their stories are going to be, as they have been in this book, "combined, slightly changed and much elaborated. . . ." The Apache's Foolish People stories are entertaining in their own context, and their misrepresentation here is unethical and racist. Both the Fools (portrayed as ugly and self-seeking) and the Plains Indians (equally ugly and ridiculous) are maligned. The flat land people are differentiated in looks from the Fools only by the addition of leggings, braids, feathers and hook noses.

Though the author claims these stories taught moral lessons to Apache children her book strongly reinforces the "heap dumb Injun" stereotype.

	ART	WORDS		ART	WORDS		ART	WORDS	N.A.
anti-Racist			non-Racist			Racist — omission			
						Racist — commission	√	√	
anti-Sexist			non-Sexist			Sexist			√
anti-Elitist			non-Elitist	√	√	Elitist			
anti-Materialist			non-Materialist	√	√	Materialist			
anti-Individualist			non-Individualist	√	√	Individualist			
anti-Ageist			non-Ageist			Ageist			√
anti-Conformist			non-Conformist	√	√	Conformist			
anti-Escapist			non-Escapist	√	√	Escapist			
Builds positive image of females/ minorities			Builds negative image of females/ minorities	√	√		Excellent	Good	Fair	Poor
Inspires action vs. oppression			Culturally authentic			Literary quality			√	
						Art quality				√

A Chinese-American Author Speaks

Laurence Yep, once a junior college English teacher, wrote *Dragonwings,* which was awarded the 1975 Children's Book Award by the International Reading Association. He explains how he came to write this book about an early Chinese-

---

* By Betty Baker, illustrated by Glen Rounds, Macmillan, $6.95, 62 pages, grades 3-up.

American aviator. You can share this talk which appeared in *Reading Teacher*, January, 1977, with upper elementary and junior high school students:

WRITING *DRAGONWINGS**

Once some anthropologists found a primitive tribe whose artists carved statues of powerful simplicity. When the scientists questioned the artists about their art, the artists would not say that they had sculpted the statues; rather they claimed that the statue already lived within each block of wood and told the artist how to free it.

Something similar happened to me when I tried to write my novel, *Dragonwings*. The story of the early Chinese-American aviator seemed to tell itself to me, but it was possible largely because I kept children in mind as the main reading audience.

But before I can begin to talk about the story of *Dragonwings*, I have to explain my general situation six years before when I first began my general research. Trying to research Chinese-American history—that is, the history of men and women of Chinese ancestry who had been influenced by their experience of America—can be difficult; perhaps I can make some of the problems clearer by presenting an analogy.

Let us suppose a far distant future in which America has become poor and outdated and its men and women forced to migrate to other countries to find work. Further, let's suppose that many of these emigrants leave Mississippi to work in Iran. A very few of them settle there and raise children, and their children raise children. And then one of their descendants decides to write about his ancestors. It is from this scanty material that he must construct a picture of life in Mississippi three generations ago.

These were the types of problems that I first encountered when I tried to understand the background that shaped me. It took some six years of research in the libraries of different cities to find the bits and pieces that could be fitted into Chinese-American history.

I don't have the time to go into any in-depth description of that history, but I should briefly explain some of the general historical background that went into the making of *Dragonwings*. Most of the Chinese who emigrated to America were from Southern China. As a group, the Southern Chinese are culturally and linguistically distinct from the Northern Chinese. Because of immense troubles at home, these Southern Chinese came to America since they could send large amounts of money to their families and clans back home. And for a variety of reasons, including prejudice and fear, it was mostly men who came over. For some eighty years, from the 1850s to the 1930s, it was largely a society of bachelors, for when the original men grew old, they sent for their sons, brothers, cousins, and nephews to take their place.

But a small number of men were able to meet certain special conditions under American law and brought their wives over to join them and start families in America. They created a family society within the shell of the older, larger bachelor society. And this family society, with its determination to sink its roots in America, survived psychologically by selectively forgetting the past history of the bachelor society and the often violent record of confrontations between Chinese and Americans. Ignoring acts of discrimination that happened in their own time, the Chinese-Americans still maintained a discreet distance between themselves and white Americans, choosing to imitate their white counterparts within the confines of Chinatown rather than trying to join the white Americans outside.

---

* Reprinted with permission of Laurence Yep and the International Reading Association.

The third generation, my generation, grew up in households in which little or no Chinese was spoken and Chinese myths and legends were looked upon largely as a source of embarrassment. But now let me try to explain what it's like to grow up within a group that has tried collectively to forget the past and ignore any differences between themselves and others. I found that I was truly like Ralph Ellison's Invisible Man— without form, without shape. It was as if all the features on my face had been erased and I was simply a blank mirror reflecting other people's hopes and fears.

If I wished to see features on my face, I had to put on different masks that I found scattered about in Hollywood prop rooms. I could be pompously wise like Charlie Chan, loveable like Peter, the house boy in *Bachelor Father*. I might be stoic and inscrutable like Cain in *Kung Fu*. Or I might be one of the howling fanatics in *55 Days at Peking* or *Sand Pebbles*. At worst, I might be the sadistically cruel and cunning Fu Man Chu. The best I could really hope for would be if I left Hollywood for literature—then I might become the loveable, dependable sidekick like Lee in Steinbeck's novel, *East of Eden*.

When I tried to replace these stereotypes, I ran into other difficulties. I've already described some of the problems I met trying to find out about my ancestors, but even when I did find material on them, I found that the Chinese-Americans had been a faceless crowd for most writers, providing statistical fodder for historians or abstractions for sociologists. I could give the Chinese population in each of California's counties for a fifty year period; but I could not have told you what any of those Chinese hoped for or feared. I could tell you about the acculturation process as exemplified by the Mississippi Chinese; but I could not have told you what their loneliness must have been like.

One of the few early Chinese-Americans in my notes to have a name was Fung Joe Guey who flew a biplane of his own construction over in Oakland in 1909. The scene of his flight seemed so vivid to me that it was easy to put it on paper, but trying to explain how he got to that field with his biplane was difficult because I could only find two newspaper articles, the September 23, 1909 issues of the San Francisco *Call* and the San Francisco *Examiner*.

Since I wanted to respect his historical integrity, I used his flight as the basis for my novel, *Dragonwings*; and to make my own fictional aviator, Windrider, seem real, I had to recreate the bachelor society itself. However, to do that I discovered that a writer must not be like the anatomist who dictates a record of facts and figures after an autopsy; instead, a writer must be like a necromancer speaking to the shadows of the dead. But in trying to conjure up these spirits from the Chinese-American past, I had no book of spells to guide me. There were no magical formulae, no special chants, no words of power.

If I wanted to write about the Midwest, I would have the work of writers like Hamlin Garland and Sinclair Lewis to show me how to create that space and time. If I wanted to write about New England, I would have Hawthorne and Thoreau to guide me. In their writings, I could find guidelines not only for setting up a fictional world but also its population. I would have a wide range of physical settings and atmospheres to use in making my fictional world. I would know how the people of the world talked, how they dressed, and the kinds of worries they were likely to have. But I have no such guidelines for creating the Chinatown of seventy years ago, which is the time in which *Dragonwings* is set.

So in trying to recreate the world of the past, I was like a child myself who must have the most basic things explained to it. The kitchen god, for instance, was a common god found in many homes and easily recognizable to a Chinese adult of that time, but like a child I had to learn who he was and how I was to treat him. Or if there was a piece of meat on a plate, I had to be told it was duck and that it had been prepared and roasted in a special way.

I had grown up as a child in the 1950s so that my sense of reality was an American one. Now I had to grow up again, but this time in the 1900s, developing a Chinese sense of reality. Milk and cheese had to become exotic to me. An American chessboard would have to seem odd because it would have the river line missing from its middle. The turning point in writing *Dragonwings* came when the checkered tablecloth on a table suddenly seemed strange to me, as if it were too cold and abstract a design because I was used to designs that usually filled up space. So when I chose to describe things from the viewpoint of an eight year old Chinese boy, it was more than simply choosing a narrative device; it was close to the process of discovery I myself was experiencing in writing the story.

But at the same time that I was developing my Chinese sense of reality, I would also have to discover what relationships would be like within that bachelor society—that lonely group of men who spent most of their adult years apart from family and home. So again, it was natural to write about this experience with children as the audience. What were personal relationships like among men who would work for five to ten years or longer before they could visit their families back in China? To all intents and purposes, their families were lost to them. And since I had no guidelines for writing about these social relationships, I would have to project myself back into the past and see how I myself would react to others in that same situation.

And the relationship with which I would most easily empathize would be the most elemental relationship, the relationship between parent and child. And since most Chinese-Americans were men at this time, it would be easiest to describe the relationship between father and son—with the mother present only in the emotions and memories of the man and boy. It was within the strong emotional context of this evolving father-son relationship that the boy's relationships to others would unfold.

Then, too, it would be easier for me to describe the relationship between the boy and his father if I could use the most honest and direct terms. I couldn't be like D. H. Lawrence who described a parent-child relationship in "The Rocking-Horse Winner" by telling the story of a little boy who sat on a rocking horse all day until he rocked himself to death trying to win money for his mother. To be able to write about the relationship in this symbolic way requires a thorough grounding in the basic ways a culture expresses love and affection; but I was unsure of even that much for the early Chinese-Americans.

Speaking more practically, if I kept children in mind as the reading audience, I would keep myself from wandering off into conceptual tangents such as the existential alienation of Chinese-Americans. The important thing, after all, was to give emotional form to the people of that world and not to play intellectual games. The novel would succeed in more fully recreating that world of the past if I could show how Moon Shadow and his father, Windrider, loved and supported one another.

Perhaps I should note here that when I speak of selecting children as the audience for *Dragonwings*, much of that was intuitive, occurring at a preconscious rather than a conscious level. But I had another reason in writing *Dragonwings* for children. Because children are inexperienced and new to the world in general, their vocabulary and their ability to handle complex grammatical structures are both as limited as their ability to handle abstract concepts; yet this same inexperience is also a source of special strength for children's stories. To write for children, one must try to see things as they do; and trying to look at the world with the fresh, inexperienced eyes of a child enables the writer to approach the world with a sense of wonder. (I think I can say this without necessarily sentimentalizing childhood if I add that the sense of wonder produces as many terrors for a child as it does beauties.) Adopting the child's sense of wonder is the reason why—at least for me—the texts of so many picture books approach the lyricism that eludes so many modern poets today with their jaded, world-weary tastes.

I wanted to utilize this sense of wonder when I wrote *Dragonwings* since I wanted to base a large part of the father's motives upon Chinese dragon myths. I could have given the father more ordinary motives. I could have said he was compensating for feelings of inadequacy by proving he could do anything that white Americans could do. Or I could have left the novel simply as a story of "progress on the march": the usual story of a farsighted person among shortsighted people. But the invention with which I was dealing was not a mousetrap or a bottle opener. It was a flying machine, a machine that most people were convinced was impossible to build even several years after the Wright Brothers' original flight. When I wrote of the aeroplane, called Dragonwings, I was actually dealing with the reach of our imagination; for the dream of flight extends far back in time.

The dream of flight has dominated man's imagination from the earliest times. On the cave walls of Lascaux, Stone Age artists attempted to paint a magical man able to transform himself into a bird with the power of flight—a concept which is still widespread in cultures around the world. The Greek legend of Icarus and his wax wings is well known, but of equal antiquity is the story of the legendary ninth emperor of China, Shun, who not only made a successful flight but returned to earth using a parachute-like device (Eliade, 1972; Nicholson, 1960). Later stories claimed that Solomon presented Queen Sheba with the gift of a "vessel whence she could traverse the air." And in twelfth century English tales, King Lear's father, Bladud, supposedly flew with feathered wings, meeting his death. But it was not until 1903, many centuries later, that the dream of powered, controlled flight was made possible by the Wright Brothers. To paraphrase Bronowski (1969), their flight was more than a technological triumph; it was an imaginative triumph as well.

Similarly in *Dragonwings,* Windrider's former life as a dragon symbolizes this same imaginative power in all of us. And so Windrider and his son, Moon Shadow, are engaged not only in the process of discovering America and each other, but also in a pilgrimage, or even a quest for a special moment when they can reaffirm the power of the imagination; that power in each of us to grasp with the mind and heart what we cannot immediately grasp with the hand.

Moreover, children's stories retain a sense of wonder not only toward the world but toward the act of writing itself. Children's writers still enjoy the magic of summoning people and creatures from their imaginations and giving them existence with words or pencil lines or printed colors. They are still in touch with the magical power of words and pictures to capture the world in a way that many who write for adults are not. Adult writers often seem too self-conscious of their own technique. With all the splendid and terrible spirits of myth or of past history to choose from, they would rather conjure up the necromancers of the past in order to talk shop, mistaking an overwhelming self-absorption for a sophisticated complexity.

I am not trying to claim that adult Chinese-American stories are impossible to write; but given my general situation and certain types of story material, it was best to write *Dragonwings* for children. Growing up as I myself did without form or shape, I felt as ghostly as the spirits of the dead and so by giving them form, I was also giving form to myself. And it was only by feeling and seeing and hearing and interpreting things as a child that I could do so.

Laurence Yep

References

Bronowski, Jacob. "The Reach of Imagination." *Modern Essays,* 2nd ed., Russel Nye and Arra Garab, Eds., p. 216. Glenview, Ill.: Scott, Foresman, 1969.

Eliade, Mircea. *Shamanism,* Willard R. Trask, Trans., 1964. Princeton, N.J.: Princeton University, 1972.

LaBarre, Weston. *The Ghost Dance,* p. 177, Garden City, N.Y.: Doubleday & Co., 1970.

Nicolson, Marjorie Hope. *Voyages to the Moon,* p. 10. New York, N.Y.: Macmillan Paperbacks, 1960.

STUDYING GROUPS IN OUR SOCIETY

We all belong to many different groups or categories. Help children realize that we group people in many different ways—by age, sex, religious beliefs, country of birth, the state in which you live, and so on. Beginning with this broad approach provides an opportunity to discuss specific groups as you make an effort to get acquainted with the many interesting groups in our society. The exploratory ideas in this section should help children extend their concept of diversity as well as to break down stereotyped thinking.

Groups in the United States

Talk with students about all the groups in the United States. See how many they can name, for example; Catholics, Mexican Americans, men, women. Accept all suggestions during this brainstorming session, but extend their thinking by asking: "How about all the people that live in our state? What do we call that group?" or "How about all the people over 65? Do we have age groups?"

After the class has named a wide variety of groups, help them make such generalizations as the following:

1. There are many different ways of grouping people.
2. There are many groups in the United States.
3. Everyone belongs to a number of groups.

We All Belong to Many Groups

Ask students to list on a sheet of paper all the groups they belong to. After they have had time to write a number of ideas, ask each person to tell one group they belong to; encourage them to share different ideas as much as possible. As new ideas are suggested, have students add to their individual lists. Then ask children to draw pictures of themselves and to list all the groups they belong to, thus:

Sue Wong is . . .

a girl
a daughter
a member of the Wong family
a Californian
a San Franciscan
a member of this class
a twelve-year-old
a Chinese-American
a U.S. citizen

Display these pictures on the wall. Then they can be bound in a class book: Room 15, the Class of 1980.

Exploring Regions and Cultures

Throughout our country there are located pockets of people who share a unique background and culture. Challenge students to discover such groups as the following: Amish, Pennsylvania Dutch, Mennonites, Creoles, Hudderites, Mormons.

They will discover a variety of interesting ideas, living patterns, and contributions. The Pennsylvania Dutch have developed an attractive and distinctive style of art. They share such folk songs as the following with us:

Johnny Schmoker

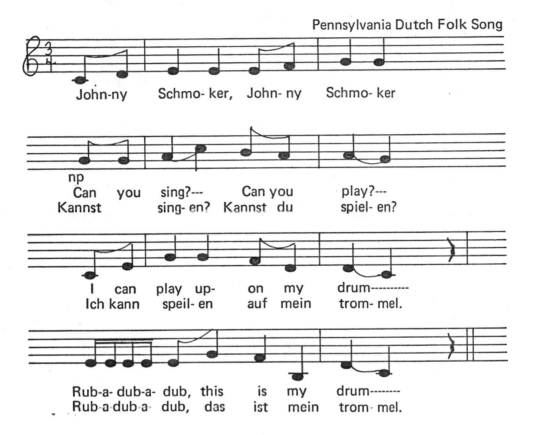

Pennsylvania Dutch Folk Song

John-ny   Schmo- ker,   John- ny   Schmo- ker

np
Can   you   sing?---   Can you   play?---
Kannst   sing- en?   Kannst du   spiel- en?

I   can   play up-   on   my   drum----------
Ich kann   speil- en   auf   mein   trom- mel.

Rub-a- dub-a- dub,   this   is   my   drum--------
Rub-a-dub-a- dub,   das   ist   mein   trom- mel.

Studying Your Community

Students generally accept where they live without really noticing all the characteristics of their community. Help them to think critically about the community
they live in by undertaking an intensive study of the community.

Obtain a city map and have the students mark where they live. What do
they consider the boundaries of their community? This may be a difficult concept
to define. Give them examples of people living in different parts of the area.
Would these people be considered members of the community?

Elicit students' knowledge of the segregated living patterns of the community. Ask them where people of different ethnic backgrounds would be likely
to live, where rich people would probably live, and other similar questions.
What kinds of people live in their community? What groups are represented?
You will probably be surprised at the knowledge reflected in the student
responses.

Observing Your Community Firsthand

Take students on a walking field trip to explore the community they live in. As you walk down commercial streets and residential streets, have them notice who lives there, how they live, and what they do for a living. Pay attention to the age range of the people you see, what occupations are represented, what people do when they are not working.

When you return to the class, discuss what the students saw. Did they see anything during the walk that they had not noticed before? What did they like or dislike about what they saw? Discuss the importance of public transportation. What kinds are available in your community? Do people live near the stores where they shop or far away? What kinds of community services do people depend on—garbage, telephone, television, and so on? What kinds of businesses exist in the community, what kinds of industries?

This discussion may lead to developing a list of problems and issues that are important in your community. Students are usually enough aware of and involved in their community to develop a sophisticated list. Write student suggestions on the board, delaying discussion of individual items until everyone has had a chance to make a suggestion. Class discussion can result in deciding the relative priorities of these items. Discussion should include suggestions for how things might be improved in the community. Concentrate on obtaining specific proposals.

This activity can culminate in a letter-writing campaign. If the class chooses to write letters about the issues identified as most important, students can write to the newspaper to publicize the issue and propose remedies. They can also write to the people or groups considered to have some responsibility for clearing up the problem.

Using the Newspaper

While studying a particular ethnic group, have students begin to collect articles from magazines or newspapers that concern the group, for example, Mexican Americans. Suggest different kinds of articles they might look for: news items about someone with a Spanish surname, stories about local events in the area of town where many Spanish-speaking people live, and articles reflecting the position of Mexican Americans locally and nationally. Allow a month for the collection of these articles while the class is also accumulating historical information. At the end of this time, place the articles on a bulletin board for all the students to read.

Discuss with students the kinds of attitudes toward this group reflected in the articles. What adjectives are used to describe people in the articles? What kind of news is typically reported about Mexican Americans and the Mexican-American community? After they have analyzed the articles, ask whether they think media coverage is prejudiced against this group. This is a good wrap-up activity for any unit on a particular race or ethnic group.

A Poem to Discuss

A leader is best
When people barely know he
  exists.
Not so good when people obey
  and acclaim him,
Worse when they despise him.
"Fail to honor people,
They fail to honor you;"
But of a good leader, who
  talks little,
When his work is done, his
  aim fulfilled,
They will say, "We did this
  ourselves."

Lao-Tse, Chinese Philosopher

Varied Religions

Because Christian holidays have become heavily commercialized, it becomes easy to overemphasize them in the classroom. Help your students to recognize that there are many religions represented in the United States. Bring such books as the following to the classroom as you encourage students to become familiar with varied beliefs that may or not be those of students in the classroom:

Elgin, Kathleen. *The Mormons; The Church of Jesus Christ of Latter-Day Saints.* McKay, 1969.

Elgin, Kathleen. *The Quakers; The Religious Society of Friends.* McKay, 1968.

Fitch, Florence Mary. *Their Search for God; Ways of Worship in the Orient.* Lothrop, 1947.

Fitch, Florence Mary. *Allah, The God of Islam; Moslem Life and Worship.* Lothrop, 1950.

Kettelkamp, Larry. *Religions, East and West.* Morrow, 1972.

Purdy, Susan G. *Jewish Holidays; Facts, Activities, and Crafts.* Lippincott, 1969.

Seeger, Elizabeth. *Eastern Religions.* Crowell, 1973.

Wolcott, Leonard, and Carolyn Wolcott. *Religions around the World.* Abingdon, 1967.

Invite guests to the classroom to talk briefly about a specific religion—a rabbi, a priest, a protestant minister (a woman?).

Life in a Relocation Camp

It is important not to forget what Americans have done to other Americans, of a different race, even in our recent history. Students can learn to appreciate what many Japanese-American children of their own age went through in this country in the 1940s. Several recent books describe life in a relocation camp, where large groups of families were imprisoned for several years, and the effect that this period had on children and the Japanese-American community.

The Moved-Outers, by Florence Means. Houghton Mifflin, 1945.

A Child in a Prison Camp, by Takashima. Morrow, 1971.

Farewell to Manzanar, by Jeanne Houston. Houghton Mifflin, 1973.

Read passages from one of these books to the class. If you have time, read the whole book. Afterward, have the students react to the book. They can draw pictures of what they imagine life in the camp looked like or they can write stories about how they would feel going to a camp, what the people guarding the camp thought about their prisoners, whether this could happen again today, or what the people thought about the United States when they were released from the camp.

Authors Are People

THE GOAL OF A CHILDREN'S AUTHOR

Through the written word I want to give children a love for the arts that will provoke creative thought and activity. All children are creative. They create music, art, poetry, dances, daydreams and nightmares, fads, myths, and—as I'm sure you know—mischief. A strong love for the arts can enhance and direct their creativity as well as provide satisfying moments throughout their lives. . . .

I want to encourage children to develop positive attitudes toward themselves and their abilities, to love themselves . . . I want to write stories that will allow children to fall in love with genuine Black heroes and heroines who have proved themselves to be outstanding in ability and in dedication to the cause of Black freedom . . . I want to be one of those who can choose and order words that children will want to celebrate. I want to make them shout and laugh and blink back tears and care about themselves. They are our future. They are beautiful. They are for loving.

Eloise Greenfield, author of *There She Come Bringing Me That
Little Baby Girl* and *Paul Robeson*

Recognizing Contributions of Others

Focus on broad topics that make it possible to observe the contributions of people from many ethnic groups. Consider such subjects as the following:

Music around the World
Art through the Ages
Folklore and Mythology
Living in the City
Foods of the World

Within such studies students will learn that cultures have their distinctive qualities and contributions. Students will also discover the universals of music and art as well as folklore and mythology. They will discover such human needs as eating and the problems of living together.

Resource Book

Let able students help you prepare a teaching resource book similar to *Bay Area Resources on Japan: A Guide for Teachers* available from Teaching Japan in Schools, Box 2341, Stanford, CA 94305.

Include books, films, activities, field trips, and local resource people. Share with others in your area.

Music—A Universal Language

Music is something that is shared around the world. Demonstrate the universality of music by showing films of dancing performed by different cultures. Here are a few examples:

African Rhythms. 13 minute color. Associated Film, Inc. 1621 Dragon St., Dallas, TX 75207

The Strollers. 6 minute color. The Moiseyev Dance Company in a Russian folk dance.

Negro Spirituals. 17 minute. Helen Tamiris performing to spirituals.

Dancer's World. 30 minute. NET. Martha Graham discusses dancing as her students dance the emotions of hope, fear, joy, and love.

Moving to Music

Encourage students to move to various rhythms by playing recordings of music from different countries around the world. Representative records available include:

Authentic Afro-Rhythms. LP 6060, Kimbo Educational, P.O. Box 246, Deal, NJ 07723. Rhythms from Africa, Cuba, Haiti, Brazil, Trinidad, Puerto Rico.

Authentic Indian Dances and Folklore. Kimbo Educational. Drumming and storytelling by Michigan Chippewa chiefs who narrate history of dances.

Authentic Music of the American Indians. 3 records. Everest. Chesterfield Music Shops, Inc., 12 Warren St., New York, NY 10007.

The Lark in the Morning. Songs and Dances from the Irish Countryside. Everest.

The REAL Flamenco. Everest.

Ethnic Music for Holidays

Make a point of featuring ethnic songs that children can sing together. There are many Negro spirituals that children of all ages enjoy, for example, "Go Down Moses." Here is a spiritual that can be used to recognize Christmas:

Mary Had a Baby

Oh, the peo-ple keep a com-ing   and the   train done gone

More verses . . .

2. What did Mary name him?
3. Mary named him Jesus
4. Where was Jesus born?
5. In a lowly stable
6. Where did Mary lay him?
7. Laid him in a manger

Children can make up more verses if they like.

The following song can be played with melody bells or the xylophone as children sing a song for Hanukkah.

Fair Hanukkah

Hebrew Folk Song

Han- uk- kah   Han- uk- kah   Ho- li- day so   fair.

Glow with light, can- dles bright, hap- pi- ness to   share.

Gai- ly dance,   gai- ly sing   while the drey- dl   whirls,

Round and round, round and round, see how fast it   twirls!

Look through any music books you have available to see which songs they include that you can use. Children can invent movements to accompany the songs as they create a dance.

Oral History

Interviewing the older members of a community is an exciting approach to history. History becomes personal as children interview their grandparents and other old people they know. Questions they might ask include: How long have you lived here? What was this town like when you first came? Where did you live when you were a child about my age? What was school like for you at that time?

Children not only gain information related to social studies through this technique but they also use language abilities. Both oral and written skills are developed as they conduct the interview, report back to the class, and record the results for a class book.

An English teacher in an Appalachian community developed the study of oral history to such an extent that his students have published several collections of their writings. Your students would be interested in reading some of the interviews. Edited by Eliot Wigginton, these attractive paperbound books can be found in most bookstores: *Foxfire 1* and *Foxfire 2* (Doubleday Anchor Books, 1972, 1973). This group also publishes a newsletter, *Foxfire,* Rabun Gap, GA 30568 ($6.00/yr.). A list of such newsletters is published in *Contemporary English in the Elementary School* (Prentice-Hall, 1975) by Iris and Sidney Tiedt, pages 402–403.

An Idea to Share

Observe how this concept is presented in different religions.

THE GOLDEN RULE

Christianity   All things whatsoever ye would that men should do to you, do ye even so to them: for this is the Law and the Prophets.

Matthew, 7, 12

Judaism   What is hateful to you, do not to your fellowmen. That is the entire Law; all the rest is commentary.

Talmud, Shabbat, 31 a

Brahmanism   This is the sum of duty: Do naught unto others which would cause you pain if done to you.

Mahabharata, 5, 1517

Buddhism   Hurt not others in ways that you yourself would find hurtful.

Udana-Varga, 5, 18

Confucianism   Surely it is the maxim of loving-kindness: Do not unto others that you would not have them do unto you.

Analects, 15, 23

Taoism   Regard your neighbor's gain as your own gain, and your neighbor's loss as your own loss.

T'ai Shang Kan Ying P'ien

Zoroastrianism   That nature alone is good which refrains from doing unto another whatsoever is not good for itself.

Dadistan-i-dinik, 94, 5

Islam   No one of you is a believer until he desires for his brother that which he desires for himself.

Sunnah

City Life

Urban living is a broad topic that encompasses many subjects of interest to those who live in the city as well as to children who live in suburban or rural settings. As the subject of city living is explored, an important element to consider is the multiethnic population.

Explore books such as the following about people living in the city:

How the World's First Cities Began by Arthur S. Gregor. Dutton, 1967.

Let's Find Out about the City by Valerie Pitt. Watts, 1968.

New Towns: Building Cities from Scratch by Martha Munzer and John Vogel, Jr. Knopf, 1974.

The Ugly Palaces: Housing in America by Robert A. Liston. Watts, 1974.

An excellent bibliography which might be helpful is *What Is a City? A Multi-media Guide on Urban Living* edited by Rose Moorachian and published by the Boston Public Library in 1969.

Poetry of the City

Share poems about city living as another way of exploring. A useful collection for younger children is *Songs of the City,* compiled by Donald Bissett.

A collection for upper elementary and junior high level is *On City Streets,* selected by Nancy Larrick (Bantam, 1969).

Writing City Poems

Children can write city poems, too. Begin with the words:

A city is . . .

Collectively, or individually, children can add phrases like this to form an unrhymed poem:

A city is . . .
Horns honking—
Red lights,
Green lights—
Traffic on the go!

A city is . . .
People walking—
Down the street,
Up the street—
People everywhere.

Special Centers

Feature specific groups around the room in centers at which students can work independently. Let children suggest groups which might reflect their own group membership, for example:

> Black Americans
> teenagers in America
> Puerto Ricans in New York City
> the problems faced by people in New York

Many of the ideas described in this book will be useful in developing such centers. Check the index for information about specific groups and refer to Chapter 6 for information about making centers and materials for individualized approaches.

Let students develop the centers with your aid as a resource person. You can suggest, for example, that they make a set of large task cards. Providing samples that they can copy will be helpful, for example:

MAKING A TIME LINE

Collect information about significant events that happened in Puerto Rico. Make a time line on a long strip of paper like this:

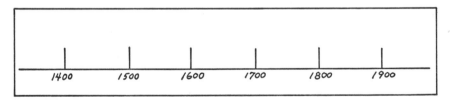

1400	1500	1600	1700	1800	1900

Mark the events that happened above the date. Illustrate your time line in the space above the date.

Where can you find the information you need?

Foreign-Born Americans

Many people that we think of as Americans were actually born in another country. Ask students if they recognize any of the following names: John James Audubon, Alexander Graham Bell, Albert Einstein, Henry Kissinger, or John Muir.

Discuss how people from other countries become known as Americans. The class can maintain a list of names of foreign-born Americans that they discover as they read. Many early citizens of our country were, of course, born in other countries, for example, Thomas Paine. A source of more information is *The People's Almanac Presents the Book of Lists* compiled by David Wallechinsky et al. (Morrow, 1977).

Make a Book of Lists

Have students compile their own Book of Lists related to your multicultural study. Individual students can select one list to compile, for example:

> Black Women Leaders
> Noted Japanese-Americans
> Women in Politics
> Irish-Americans Who Made a Difference
> Leaders in Texas
> Mexican Americans Who Spoke Out

Brief information should be included for each person listed, perhaps their date of birth (death), where they live(d), and their major contribution. Such a book makes fascinating reading. If compiled in a ringed notebook, additions can be made throughout the year.

Living in Other Countries

One of the best ways for students to experience what it is like to live in different countries is to read books about children of their own age who have traveled to a different country or who are growing up in another country. Here are some books you can suggest.

Books about Childhood in Another Country

Egypt   *The 18th Emergency* by Betsy Byars, Viking, 1973.

England   *The Children of Green Knowe* by Lucy Boston, Harcourt Brace Jovanovich, 1955.

Greece   *The Glass Ball* by William Mayne, Dutton, 1962.

Netherlands   *The Wheel on the School* by Meindert DeJong, Harper & Row, 1954.

Spain   *Shadow of a Bull* by Maia Wojciechowska, Atheneum, 1964.

Books about American Children Living in Other Countries

Lebanon   *Crystal Mountain* by Belle D. Rugh, Houghton Mifflin, 1955.

Italy   *Little Leo* by Leo Politi, Scribner's, 1951.

France   *Family Sabbatical* by Carol Ryrie Brink, Viking, 1956.

CONCEPTS TO BE DEVELOPED

Behind the activities described throughout this chapter lie basic assumptions. Whenever possible, make these assumptions explicit. Help students to express them in different ways as they engage in these learning experiences.

1. People are more alike than they are different.
2. People of all races and cultures have contributed to the good of our country.
3. Differing ways of thinking and behaving can be an asset to our society.
4. Prejudice and nonacceptance of others usually is based on lack of knowledge, ignorance.
5. Understanding each other as individuals will help us all to have a better life.

FOCUSING ON ONE GROUP: NATIVE AMERICANS

One approach to the study of groups in the United States is to develop an in-depth study of one group. Elsewhere in this book there are focuses on specific groups such as the Chinese-American (see pages 245–268). Throughout the book there are materials about Black Americans, as the literature related to this group is extensive. One group that has not been as widely studied is the Native American. It may be difficult for teachers to find activities and materials on this subject. Collected here, therefore, are activities and books that will make it easier for you to undertake a study of Indian groups in the United States.

Saturate Your Classroom

An exciting way to develop a study like this is to turn your whole classroom into a learning center focused on Native Americans. Talk with your students as you plan together to saturate your classroom with another culture. There are several ways you might organize this operation, for instance:

Plan A. Imagine that the whole classroom is an Indian campground with a campfire in the middle. Move desks to the outer edges in the "trees." Designate certain areas of the classroom for specific activities such as the horse corral or the chief's teepee. Students will then decide on what tribe they will be, where they will be located geographically, and what the habits of these Indians were.

Plan B. Divide the class into several tribes; the number depends on the amount of space available. Each tribe is located in a specific part of the classroom where they can develop a home typical of the tribe they select. They need to read to discover facts about how the tribe lived and how it got along with other tribes.

Books about Indians

As you develop this study, here are several references you may find helpful:

Brown, Dee. *Bury My Heart at Wounded Knee: An Indian History of the American West*. Holt, Rinehart and Winston, 1970.

Carlson, Ruth Kearney. *Emerging Humanity: Multi-Ethnic Literature for Children and Adolescents*. Brown, 1972.

Henry, Jeannette, and Rupert Costo (ed.). *Textbooks and the American Indian*. Indian Historian Press, 1970.

Townsend, Mary. "Taking Off the War Bonnet: American Indian Literature." *Language Arts,* March 1976, pp. 236–244.

These books for children are some of those which you can obtain at the local library:

Baker, Betty. *A Stranger and Afraid*. Macmillan, 1972.

———. *And One Was a Wooden Indian*. Macmillan, 1970.

———. *Killer-Of-Death*. Harper & Row, 1963.

Carr, Mary Jane. *Children of the Covered Wagon*. Crowell, 1934.

———. *Young Mac of Fort Vancouver*. Crowell, 1940.

Clifford, Eth. *The Year of the Three-Legged Deer*. Houghton Mifflin, 1972.

Embry, Margaret. *Shadi*. Holiday House, 1971.

Fredericksen, Hazel. *He-Who-Runs-Far*. Young Scott Books, 1970.

Gessner, Lynne. *Lightning Slinger*. Funk and Wagnalls, 1968.

Goble, Dorothy, and Paul Goble. *The Friendly Wolf*. Bradbury, 1974.

———. *Horse Raid*. Bradbury, 1973.

James, Harry C. *Ovada: An Indian Boy of the Grand Canyon*. War Ritchie Press, 1969.

Lampman, Evelyn Sibley. *Half Breed*. Doubleday, 1967.

———. *Navajo Sister*. Doubleday, 1956.

———. *The Year of Small Shadow*. Harcourt Brace Jovanovich, 1971.

———. *Witch Doctor's Son*. Doubleday, 1954.

McDermott, Gerald. *Arrow to the Sun*. Viking, 1975.

Moon, Grace. *Chi-Wee: The Adventures of a Little Indian Girl*. Doubleday, 1925.

Nevin, Evelyn. *Captive of the Delawares*. Abingdon-Cokesbury, 1952.

O'Dell, Scott. *Island of the Blue Dolphins*. Houghton Mifflin, 1960.

———. *Sing Down the Moon*. Houghton Mifflin, 1970.

Riggs, Sidney N. *Arrows and Snakeskin*. Lippincott, 1962.

Rubicam, Harry C., Jr. *Pueblo Jones.* Knopf, 1939.

Van Der Veer, Judy. *Higher Than the Arrow.* Golden Gate Junior Books, 1969.

Williams, Barbara. *The Secret Name.* Harcourt Brace Jovanovich, 1972.

Wilson, Carter. *On Firm Ice.* Crowell, 1968.

Stereotyped Ideas about Indians

Before beginning a study of Indians in the United States, use some means of assessing student information and attitudes. This will provide an interesting and instructive comparison at the end of the study. Try some of these ideas:

1. Have each student draw a picture of an Indian engaged in some activity.
2. Ask students to complete this sentence at least three times: An Indian . . .
3. Ask students to list as many Indian tribes as they can.

Put these sheets away until the study is completed. After the study you might have the students repeat the same activities. Then compare the results.

Reacting to the Words of Indians

Read quotations of the words of real Indians who commented on treatment by white men, for example:

I admit that there are good white men, but they bear no proportion to the bad; the bad must be the strongest, for they rule. They do what they please. They enslave those who are not of their color, although created by the same Great Spirit who created us. They would make slaves of us if they could, but as they cannot do it, they kill us! There is no faith to be placed in their words.

Pachgantchilhilas of the Delawares

Children can write their reactions to these words. Share the reactions.

Indian Tribes

Draw a large outline map of the United States on which to locate the various groups of Indian tribes. They can be grouped as follows according to similar modes of living:

Eastern Woodland Area   Algonquin, Delaware, Iroquois, Massachuset, Mohawk, Mohegan, Narraganset, Onandaga, Penobscot, Powhatan, Tuscarora, Passamaquoddy, Pawtuket, Tippecanoe, Wampanoag, Wyandot

Great Lakes Woodland Area   Chippewa/Ojibwa, Huron, Illinois, Kickapoo, Miami, Oneida, Ottawa, Potawatomi, Sauk and Fox, Seneca, Shawnee, Winnebago

Southeastern Area   Catawba, Cherokee, Creek, Lumbi, Natchez, Seminole, Yuchi

North Central Plains Area   Arapaho, Arikara, Assiniboin, Blackfeet, Cheyenne, Cree, Crow, Gros Ventre, Mandan, Pawnee, Shoshone, Sioux/Dakota

South Central Plains Area   Caddo, Chickasaw, Choctaw, Comanche, Iowa, Kaw/Kansa, Kiowa, Omaha, Osage, Ponca, Quapaw

Southwest Area   Apache, Hopi, Maricopa, Navajo, Papago, Pima, Pueblo, Zuñi

California Area   Chumash, Hoopa, Maidu, Mission, Modoc, Mohave, Mono, Pit River, Pomo, Tule River, Wailaki, Yahi, Yokuts, Yuma, Yurok

Northwestern Plateau Area   Bannock, Cayuse, Coeur D'Alene, Colville, Flathead, Kalispel, Klamath, Kootenai, Nez Percé, Paiute, Puyallup, Spokane, Ute, Walla-walla, Wasco, Washoe, Yakima, Nisqually

Northwest Pacific Coast Area   Aleuts, Eskimo, Haida, Lummi, Makah, Muckle-shoot, Nootka, Quinault, Salish, Shoalwater, Snohomish, Suquamish, Tlingit

Speakers of Indian Languages

Figures are listed only for languages for which there are more than 1000 speakers. Eskimo languages are grouped together.

Language	Number of Speakers	Location
Navaho	almost 100,000	Arizona, New Mexico, Utah, Colorado
Ojibwa-Ottawa-Algonquin-Salteaux	40,000–50,000	Montana, North Dakota, Minnesota, Wisconsin, Michigan, Canada (Sask., Man., Ont., Que.)
Cree	30,000–40,000	Montana, Canada
Eskimo	15,882	Alaska
Papago	11,000	Arizona
Teton	10,000–15,000	Colorado
Apache	10,100–14,000 includes:	
	San Carlos (8,000–10,000)	Arizona
	Mescalero (1,000–1,500)	New Mexico
	Jicarilla (1,000–1,500)	New Mexico
	Chiricahua (100–1,000)	Arizona, New Mexico
Cherokee	10,000	(North Carolina)
Muskogee (Creek)	7,000–8,000	(Escambia Co., Alabama)
Keres	7,000	New Mexico Rio Grande pueblos
Choctaw	6,722	Oklahoma (near Philadelphia, Miss.)
Blackfoot-Piegan-Blood	5,000–6,000	Montana, Canada (Alta.)
Shoshone-Gosiute	5,000	California, Nevada, Idaho, Oregon, Wyoming
Hopi	4,800	Northeast Arizona

Language	Number of Speakers	Location
Cheyenne	under 4,000	Oklahoma, Montana
Yuman	3,900	Arizona, California
Zuni	3,500	West New Mexico
Santee	3,000–5,000	Washington
Tiwa	3,000	New Mexico
Yaqui	3,000	Arizona
Crow	3,000	Montana
Chickasaw	2,000–3,000	Oklahoma
Sahaptin	2,750	
Tewa	under 2,500	New Mexico, Arizona
Ute	2,000–4,000	(Colorado, Utah)
Seneca	2,000–3,000	New York, Canada (Ont.) (Erie, Chautauqua, Cattaraugus, Genesee Co., N.Y.)
Northern Paiute-Bannock-Snake	2,000	N. Paiute—East California, Nevada; Bannock—Idaho; Snake—East Oregon
Kiowa	2,000	Oklahoma
Pima	2,000	Arizona
Comanche	1,500	Oklahoma
Towa	1,200	New Mexico
Arapaho-Atsina-Nawathinehena	1,000–3,000	Wyoming, Oklahoma
Winnebago	1,000–2,000	Nebraska, Wisconsin
Oneida	1,000–2,000	New York, Canada (Ont.) (Onondaga Co., N.Y.)
Tlingit	1,000–2,000	Southeast Alaska
Mohawk	1,000–2,000	New York, Canada (Ont., Que.) (Franklin and St. Lawrence Co., N.Y.)
Assiniboin	1,000–2,000	Montana
Yankton	1,000–1,200	Nebraska
Aleut	1,000–1,200	Alaska
Omaha	1,000+	Nebraska
Cayuga	1,000+	(Erie, Chautauqua, Cattaraugus, Onondaga Co., N.Y.)
Fox-Sauk	1,000	Oklahoma
Flathead-Pend d'Oreille-Kalispel-Spokan	600–1,200	Montana, Washington

SOURCE: C. F. and F. M. Voegelin, "Languages of the World: Native American Fascicle One." Locations in parentheses, except for Canadian provinces, from Department of the Interior, Bureau of Indian Affairs. *Indians of the Lower Plateau. Indians of the Gulf States. Indians of the Great Lakes Area. Indians of the Eastern Seaboard.*

English Words from Indian Languages

Many words in English can be traced back to Indian languages. Develop a chart of these words, for example:

chipmunk	hominy
raccoon	succotash
skunk	hickory
woodchuck	moccasin
moose	powwow
muskrat	squash

Indian Place Names

Many state names such as Massachusetts originated in Indian languages. So also do names of many rivers such as the Ohio and Mississippi and the names of cities such as Pontiac, Michigan, and Chicago, Illinois.

Prepare a map on which to locate Indian place names.

Gifts from the Indians

Students will be interested in learning of the many things we gained from the Indians. They knew the best trails and ways of traveling across the country by canoe and by snowshoe. They invented hammocks. The Indians were the first, too, to grow and use tobacco and also rubber. They introduced white men to the following foods that we use today:

corn	chicle (for chewing gum)
sweet potatoes	beans
peppers	chocolate
pineapples	maple sugar
squash	grits
tomatoes	hominy
vanilla	popcorn
avocados	succotash
peanuts	

Have several students prepare an illustrated chart of these foods. You may experiment with preparing hominy or grits, dishes that are easy to make in the classroom.

Making Navaho Fry Bread

Create a learning center at which children can take turns making a semiauthentic version of fry bread. (Teacher supervision is necessary for this activity.)

Directions

Fill the electric skillet half full of oil. Turn on high to heat.
Measure into bowl

> 4 C flour
> 3 tsps. baking powder
> 1 tsp. salt
> 1½ C water

Gradually add the water as you stir.

Knead the dough until it does not stick to your hands. Add a little more flour as needed. Divide the dough into small balls. Then flatten them until thin and make a hole in the center like a doughnut. Slide into hot oil. Fry on each side until light brown. Remove and drain on layer of paper towels. Eat while warm.

Indian Folklore

Folklore from the various Indian tribes is great for storytelling activities. Explore some of the following:

American Indian Mythology by Alice Marriott and Carol Rachlin. Crowell, 1968.
Winter-telling Tales by Alice Marriott and Carol Rachlin. Crowell, 1969.

An excellent bibliography is *Folklore of the North American Indians,* compiled by Judith Ullom for sale by the Superintendent of Documents, U.S. Government Printing Office ($4.05). This annotated bibliography comes out of the Children's Book Section of the Library of Congress.

A Story to Act Out

Here is an original Indian tale by Ann Frimann that students can act out. Read the story aloud. Then have students plan to dramatize the action as several readers present the story itself.

"WAH-HOO-WAH"*

Long, long ago when the world was first formed, it took a long time before everything was completed. In the beginning you could only feel the wind brush against your cheek, or see it move the leaves on the trees or make ripples on the water—but, it made no sound.

In those days California Yahi Indian daughters never tired of hearing this story told by their mothers. It is the story of a young Indian maid who lived in northern California —in the beginning.

It was early springtime. The snows were melting on mighty Waganupu (Mt. Lassen), filling the streams and rivers with cold, fresh waters that held countless fish. Many new berries, grasses and roots reappeared throughout the forests. The trees were pushing out new leaves or pine needles from the tips of their branches. All the animals and birds returned to renew their quest for food for their hungry offspring.

A young Indian girl came bounding down the hillside, leaping from rock to rock, calling out to her mother, "Smiling Moon! Smiling Moon!"

Smiling Moon sat grinding acorns in front of their hut in their village that was nestled in a valley below a plateau of Waganupu. Hearing her daughter's call Smiling Moon looked up, smiling, and thought, "How well we named our 'Babbling Brook.' She comes down the hillside like a lively brook and has not ceased babbling since the moment of birth." Smiling Moon chuckled to herself. This lovely, lively child was the only child of Smiling Moon and her husband, Great Hunter. Smiling Moon's eyes were pleased just to look upon the radiant daughter who brought such joy to her parents and all the tribal family.

Babbling Brook was eleven summers old. Her skin was the color of an autumn sunset. Her hair was so black and shiny that it made crow's feathers look pale in comparison. Her eyes matched the color of her hair and were always wide open, as if afraid they would miss something. Her voice made the ear happy that it could hear.

When Babbling Brook reached her mother she was out of breath and could hardly speak; but Smiling Moon could see that something was disturbing her daughter greatly. "What, dear daughter, has you so sad, yet angry?"

Pouting, Babbling Brook began, "Oh Smiling Moon! It isn't fair! It just isn't fair!"

Reaching up, Smiling Moon took her daughter's hand and Babbling Brook sat down next to her mother. Smiling Moon, pushing her daughter's silky hair from her face, said, "Now slowly, tell me what is not fair."

"Oh, dear mother, everyone knows I can run as swiftly as any of the boys my age. I can shoot an arrow as high and true as any of them. I can catch a fish in any stream as

---

* Reprinted with permission of Anne Frimann.

fast as any boy in our village. And now, the boys are preparing to go on their three-day 'time of testing.' When they return they will get a new name and take their place among the men. I'm as good as any of them and I will still be just a girl! It's just not fair!"

The Indian boy's "time of testing" was an initiation journey into manhood. Every boy, at the age of eleven, had to spend three days and three nights alone in the forest, surviving by his skill and courage. On returning to the village he was given a new, grown-up name and was no longer considered to be a boy, but a man.

Smiling Moon was amused by what had disturbed her lovely daughter and said, patiently, "But, Babbling Brook, it is good to be a girl. One day you will be a woman. It is in a man's nature to hunt and protect. But, it is a woman's nature to bring comfort and peace."

As Babbling Brook looked up at her mother she tried very hard to understand what her mother meant by "a woman's nature." All she could think of was the largeness of her mother's body and the sweet smile on her mother's moon-shaped face. She also thought of how nice and soft it was to snuggle next to her mother, in the evening, around the fire pit. Wherever Babbling Brook put her head on her mother, it was like sinking into a nest of eagle feathers. Was that what Smiling Moon meant by "comfort and peace?"

Still puzzled, Babbling Brook went on, "But mother, it still isn't fair! The boys get a new name and a great feast! Why can't I have a 'time of testing' also and get a new name? I don't even ask for a feast. I just want to show that I can be grown up too!"

Sighing softly, Smiling Moon told Babbling Brook that she would speak to her father, Great Hunter, about it.

Later that day, Smiling Moon told Babbling Brook that her father, Great Hunter, and the men of the village had been surprised by her request to have a "time of testing." They decided that if she truly wanted to, she could go on a journey for one day. They knew of her skills and had great faith that she could care for herself, alone, in the forest.

As Smiling Moon watched her young daughter depart, she said, "Remember, dear one, there is great courage in a woman's nature that makes her able to bring comfort and peace." Returning for a final touch to Smiling Moon's soft, round face, Babbling Brook eagerly ran into the forest with only a small bow and arrow.

As the sun was setting on the far side of the mountains, Babbling Brook had reached Beaver Lake on the plateau above her village. She looked down on her village, proud that she had reached such a great height so quickly. She decided to spend the night there, by Beaver Lake, on the edge of the plateau. There she had all the water she needed to drink, for all other food was forbidden during the "time of testing."

Babbling Brook looked at the deserted beaver dam that spanned the end of the lake and held the water so that only a trickle went over the edge, feeding the valley below. She remembered hearing her father say that the men must come up to repair the dam and make sure it held fast. The beavers had used up all the young birch and aspen trees around the lake and had moved elsewhere, in early spring, to make a new home. Now it was up to the Indian men to keep the dam in good repair.

Gathering pine boughs, Babbling Brook prepared her bed by the edge of the plateau. Then she bathed herself and lay down as night came over the world. Below, in her village, she watched the smoke circle up from the fire pits as the evening meal of acorn mush was being prepared. She realized her hunger as she thought she could even smell the food cooking in her own family's fire pit. Then Babbling Brook nestled deeper into the pine boughs, remembering how much softer and warmer it was next to Smiling Moon. Quickly she said to herself, "I will put such thoughts out of my head! For by tomorrow, I too will have great courage and be grown-up!" Very sleepy, she felt a soft breeze caress her cheek. As she looked up on a night sky sprinkled with blinking stars beyond number and a half moon, she drifted off to sleep.

It was a sharp, grinding sound that woke Babbling Brook. Instantly, she was on her feet, wide awake, standing on the edge of the plateau. All was dark, but by the moonlight she saw that the beaver dam was breaking up, and it took away her breath when she realized that the waters of the melted mountain snow would be pushing Beaver Lake over the plateau, into the valley below, destroying her village and her people!

With her eyes wider than ever, Babbling Brook was aware that she had nothing but her voice to help save her people. But the sound of the dam breaking up was louder than her voice! As a breeze brushed her cheek she thought, "I will use the wind!" So, from the high plateau, she put her voice on the wind and told the wind to carry her voice down to her village.

Smiling Moon wakened, startled, as she heard, "Smiling Moon! Great Hunter! Smiling Moon! Great Hunter! Wake up! Run! Run! My people! Run! Save yourselves!" Hearing the voice of their daughter as the wind came into their hut, Smiling Moon and Great Hunter got up, and once outside, called to their people to run up the hillside. Everyone in the village was fleeing for high ground. They heard a final crash as the whole dam, all the waters of Beaver Lake and the edge of the plateau thundered down, burying the village!

As dawn of the new day came, Smiling Moon and Great Hunter found that all the members of their village had been saved. They gathered on the hillside to await the return of Babbling Brook from her "time of testing." They wanted to celebrate her having saved all the tribal family. They waited all day. But Babbling Brook did not return. As the sun set, they realized that lovely Babbling Brook would never return to them. All was silent, except for the breeze that now drifted across the valley making the loveliest of sounds as it moved through the tops of the trees.

Smiling Moon stood up and spoke to all the people of their village. "My daughter has passed her 'time of testing' and has returned to us with great courage, now grown up. Listen, and you will hear her voice on the wind as she put it on the wind the night she saved her people. Now her voice is soft and sweet. From this day on, Babbling Brook will be called 'Wah-hoo-wah,' which means, 'She who brings comfort and peace.' "

The next time you are camping out, all snuggled in your sleeping bag and ready to go to sleep, listen for a moment. Blowing softly in the tops of the pine trees you will hear the wind. If you listen very carefully, you can hear that it sounds almost like a lullaby, bringing comfort and peace, as is a woman's nature.

Anne Frimann

Writing Indian Folktales

Many of the Indian folktales are "pourquoi" tales, stories that answer "why" something happened, for example:

> Why the rabbit has a short tail
> Why the sun rises in the east and sets in the west
> Why the moon is a full circle at times and only a sliver or crescent at others

These stories represent attempts to explain things that are important to people.

Read aloud a number of pourquoi tales such as the following:

Thunderbird and Other Stories by Henry Chafetz (Pantheon, 1964)

Down from the Lonely Mountain retold by Jane Louise Curry (Harcourt Brace Jovanovich, 1965)

Then have children tell or write their own pourquoi tales. Collect them on a tape or in a book of tales to be shared with others.

Sports from the Indians

Many of the sports we know today originated in games the Indians first played. They played shinny, a game with a puck that was played on ice, similar to ice hockey. Indian children played such games as hide and seek, follow-the-leader, crack-the-whip, prisoner's base, and blindman's bluff. They also had games not unlike hopscotch, marbles, and jack straws.

For more information about Indian sports and how to play them, look for *Sports & Games the Indians Gave Us* by Alex Whitney (McKay, 1977). This author shows children how to make Indian gaming equipment for use in the games described. Stick dice are easy to make, for example. Use a stick about one-half inch wide and four inches long. With a knife round off the ends of the stick. Paint one side red and paint a multicolor design on the other side. With the red side counting as one point and the design as two, see who can get twenty points first.

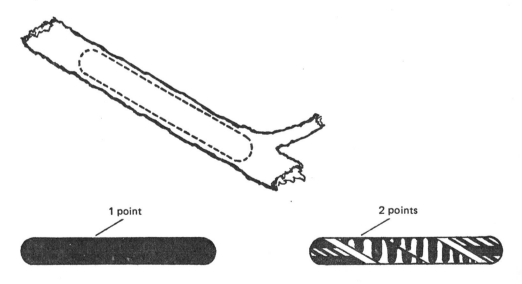

1 point

2 points

Investigating Relations between Indians and Early Settlers

When the class is discussing the role of Indians in American history, use this exercise to increase their awareness of the Indians' point of view. Divide students into five to six small groups. Each group is to represent the Indians of a particular area of the country that had some contact with white people. The groups need to research exactly what contact their tribe or tribes had with what kinds of white people—trappers, missionaries, settlers, prospectors. Each group then roleplays their Indian group and discusses whether they feel threatened by the whites and what they think should be done about the whites. After the groups have decided, a representative from each is sent to an imaginary Indian council meeting where students can argue over what Indian policy toward whites should be.

There is no right answer in this exercise and the solutions reached may not represent historical accuracy. (In historical roleplay, students cannot argue that something is right just because that is how it turned out.) The purpose is to enable students to appreciate the diversity of Indian reactions to whites encroaching on their land and understand why the Indian-white conflict developed as it did.

A Weaving Center

Weaving is an art that has been practiced by many cultures. You may wish to construct one or two large looms on which students can create a decorative piece of cloth cooperatively. Students can create miniature looms on which they can work individually. Directions given are for the large loom, but small looms can be made in similar fashion.

Obtain two lightweight logs about five feet long. Cut off any branches, but leave the rough ends sticking out. Suspend one log from the ceiling to simulate the limb of a tree. The second log is then suspended from the first by rough rope as shown here:

If suspending the log from the ceiling is not possible in your classroom, fasten four logs together with rope to form a loom frame, as shown here:

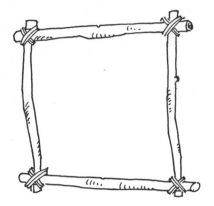

Thread the loom with heavy rug yarn choosing natural colors as much as possible rather than the bright, artificial colors. Using black or beige, loop the yarn around the log to keep it from sliding, thus:

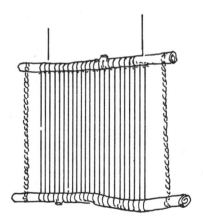

Students can make wooden shuttles of flat pieces of wood. They can alternate colors to form stripes of varied widths.

Simulated Weaving

Graph paper can be used to simulate more complex Indian designs seen in weaving or beadwork. Obtain books that show Indian art to provide students with ideas for appropriate designs. Graph paper that has ten squares to the inch is a good size. Use felt pens or colored pencils to achieve such effects as this:

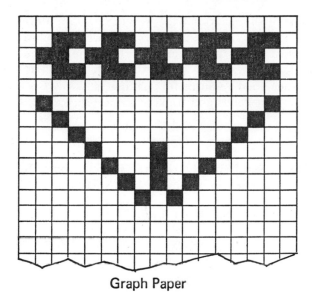

Graph Paper

An interesting supply of drawings and designs is included in *A Coloring Book of American Indians* (Bellrophon, 153 Stewart St., San Francisco, CA 94105).

Indian Masks

Begin a study of Indian masks by showing the excellent film, *The Loon's Necklace,* an Indian legend told by the artful filming of authentic masks from a museum. (Britannica Films, 11 min.)

Then students can create their own masks from heavy cardboard. Folding the cardboard in half makes it fit the child's face more closely. A piece of elastic holds it securely in place, as shown:

The shape of the mask and the way the eyes are developed serve to suggest the person or animal. It is not necessary, however, to be overly realistic. Masks should then be used to tell Indian tales, perhaps the pourquoi tales the children have written.

Another good resource for making masks is *Creative Masks for Stage and School,* by Joan Peters and Anna Sutcliffe (Plays, Inc., 1975).

Indian Poetry

Share these poems with the children in your room. Because they are short, you might print one or two on posters for display in the classroom.

SONG OF FAILURE

A wolf
I considered myself,
But the owls are hooting
and the night
I fear.

> Teton Sioux

SPRING SONG

As my eyes search the prairie,
I feel the summer in the spring.

> Chippewa

GLYPH

Truly buzzards
Around my sky are circling!

For my soul festers,
And an odor of corruption
Betrays me to disaster.

Meanness, betrayal and spite
Come flockwise,
To make me aware

Of sickness and death within me.
My sky is full of the dreadful sound
Of the wings of unsuccesses.

> Washoe-Paiute

MAY I WALK

On the trail marked with pollen may I walk,
With grasshoppers about my feet may I walk,
With dew about my feet may I walk,
With beauty may I walk,
With beauty before me, may I walk,
With beauty behind me, may I walk,

With beauty above me, may I walk,
With beauty under me, may I walk,
With beauty all around me, may I walk,
In old age wandering on a trail of beauty, lively, may I walk,
In old age wandering on a trail of beauty, living again, may I walk,
It is finished in beauty.

Navajo

Child's Night Song
Very much, very much,
I of the owl am afraid,
Sitting alone in the wigwam.

— Chippewa

SOURCE: Reading Songs, May, 1978.

Children Write Poetry

After reading the anonymous Indian poems, encourage children to write similar poetry. Discuss the kinds of topics an Indian child might present in poetry and why. Notice that the out-of-doors is present in each of the poems. Animals are included in several of the poems. Observe, too, that there is no rhyming in this poetry so the stress is on the ideas expressed. Here is a poem that one child wrote which you might find useful as an example:

As I walk in the woods,
I feel the eyes of the forest around me.

Danny Richards

An excellent collection of poetry written by young American Indians is *The Whispering Wind* edited by Terry Allen (Doubleday, 1972). Included in the collection is poetry that would be suitable for all age levels.

A Mural of Indian Life

After students have gained information through reading and discussing topics related to Indian life, have them plan a large mural to which each one can contribute. The space of the mural might be considered similar to the map of the United States. Roughly, then, space could be allocated to activities associated with the Plains Indians, those of the Southwest, the Pacific Northwest, and so on. Sketch this plan on the chalkboard.

Bring in books with pictures that suggest scenes to be included. Crayons can be used for the figures and the background can be painted in with pale brown tempera or light green, as appropriate.

When the mural is completed, display it in the school hall or the multi-purpose room where all can see it.

An All-School Assembly

Plan a school assembly to share the results of your study. Let students discuss various ways they can present an informative and entertaining program. Consider some of the following activities:

1. An introduction: the purpose of your study and some of the things you learned.
2. Presentation of the mural with an explanation of the many Indian tribes in what is now the United States.
3. Reader's theater presentation of Indian folklore which might include music or drum beating.
4. Demonstration of Indian sports, dances, etc.
5. Creative dramatization of an Indian story.
6. Invite students to visit your room to see the things you have made.

Sources of Information

Collect pictures for display in the classroom. Two good sources are:

Society for Visual Education, 1345 Diversey Parkway, Chicago, IL 60614

Arizona Highways, 2039 W. Lewis, Phoenix, AZ 85009

Sources of recordings are:

Folkways/Scholastic Records, 50 W. 44th St., New York, NY 10036

Music Division, Library of Congress, Washington, D.C. 20540

A variety of information can be obtained from these sources:

The American Indian Museum of Natural History, Central Park West and 79th Street, New York, NY 10024

Bureau of Indian Affairs, Department of Interior, Washington, D.C. 20242. Ask for their list of penpals.

Museum of the American Indian, Broadway at 155th St., New York, NY 10032

Also refer to sources listed in Chapter 7.

SOURCES TO INVESTIGATE

California Indian Education Association, Inc., Education Center, Fresno Unified School District; Title IV, Indian Education Act; Tulare and M Streets, Fresno, CA 93721.

Epstein, Charlotte. *Intergroup Relations for the Classroom Teacher.* Houghton Mifflin, 1968.

Grambs, Jean Dresden. *Intergroup Education: Methods and Materials.* Prentice-Hall, 1968.

Group for Environmental Education (GEE!). *Yellow Pages of Learning Resources.* MIT Press, 1972.

Linskie, Rosella, and Howard Rosenburg. *A Handbook for Multicultural Studies in Elementary Schools: Chicano, Black, Asian, and Native American.* (3 books) R & E Research Association, 1976.

Nichols, Margaret S., and Margaret N. O'Neill. *Multicultural Bibliography for Preschool through Second Grade: In the Areas of Black, Spanish-speaking, Asian American, and Native American Cultures.* Multicultural Resources, P.O. Box 2945, Stanford, CA 94305, 1972.

Reid, Virginia M., ed. *Reading Ladders for Human Relations.* American Council on Education, 1972.

Stone, James C. and Donald P. DeNevi, eds. *Teaching Multi-cultural Populations.* D. Van Nostrand, 1971.

5

Teaching with a Multicultural Calendar: Activities and Information

*It is the individual who knows how little he
knows about himself who stands a reasonable
chance of finding out something about himself
before he dies.*

S. I. Hayakawa

A multicultural calendar can be the means of introducing
your students to people from many ethnic groups. Celebrating the birthdays of
specific men and women can bring these people to life as students learn about
their contributions. Focusing on events significant in the history of various ethnic
groups in the United States is an effective way of informing all students about
this country's multiethnic heritage. Information about these groups will provide
the minority-group student special opportunities to identify with his or her history. The multicultural calendar provides you with a useful teaching aid that
you can utilize for reference and display immediately.

Throughout this chapter we have included specific activities that focus on
the achievements of ethnic groups in the United States. Using the suggested
learning experiences in this chapter alone will give you a good start toward developing a multicultural approach in your curriculum whether you are in a
bilingual program or not. This chapter is organized in the following parts: Creating a Multicultural Calendar, Activities and Information for a Multicultural
Calendar, and Exploring Calendars and Cultures.

In developing the multicultural calendar for this chapter, the following
sources were especially helpful in providing information:

The Elementary Teacher's Ideas and Materials Workshop, Parker Publishing Company, West Nyack, NY 10994. (Request a sample copy; includes a very complete calendar for the classroom each month.)

Notable American Women, Harvard University. A complete encyclopedia of women including short biographical entries, edited by Edward T. James.

World Book Encyclopedia, Field Enterprises Educational Corporation, 1975. Entries for each month list events and dates that can be added to a calendar as desired. This encyclopedia is also especially good for outlining multicultural topics you might plan to study.

CREATING A MULTICULTURAL CALENDAR

The multicultural calendar can be created for use in the classroom in varied ways. Groups of two to three students might work on reproducing the calendar for presentation in a large class book entitled "Multicultural Events and People on the Calendar." Each group could work on one month, copying the information given in this chapter. Encourage students to investigate additional items to be included. They could add other quotations and illustrations as well. This class book would then be useful as a reference tool for studies throughout the year.

Displaying the Calendar

One of the best ways to display the multicultural calendar is to reproduce it directly on a large bulletin board. Divide the display space into squares or rectangles using thick colored yarn or strips of colored construction paper as shown here:

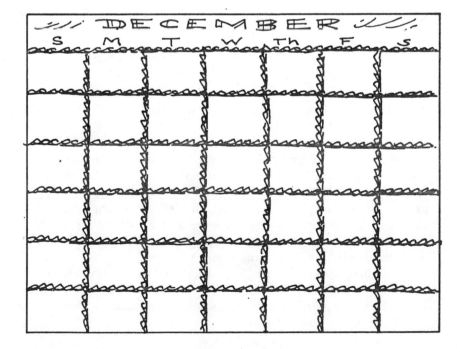

Make the spaces as large as possible. (Challenge several students to solve this measurement problem!) Cut large block letters for the days of the week and the names of the months. Cut a set of numbers from 1 to 31. Both letters and numbers can be made easily if you use graph paper as shown on the following page. To enlarge these letters, simply use graph paper with bigger blocks or double the number of blocks for each pattern. Cut a few samples to check the size against the display space after it is organized. Although the same numbers and many of the letters can be used for each month, you might want to use different colors for variety.

Developing the Calendar

Students can type or print the names and dates on slips of colored construction paper or unlined file cards to mount in the appropriate block for each month. Be sure that they check the current calendar so that the number 1 is placed under the correct day of the week; the rest of the dates will then fall in place accordingly. Add events that occur locally or dates of personal interest to your students such as their birthdays. If the blocks for each day are big enough, you can include pictures and quotations wherever possible.

Quotations are of special interest for the multicultural calendar. Find as many as possible for people whose names appear for that month. Begin with the quotations presented throughout this book. Additional sources of quotations include:

Quotes for Teaching by S. Tiedt (Contemporary Press, Box 1524 San Jose, CA 95109, $1.50)

The Great Quotations by G. Seldes (Lyle Stuart, New York City, $15.00)

Your public library will be able to supply numerous books of quotations. Advanced readers will enjoy poring over these books which they probably have not yet explored.

Pictures add a special dimension to the calendar. Although they are not always easily found, you can gradually build up a collection. Let other teachers know that you are searching for multiethnic pictures for this purpose. Include pictures of people as well as places and events. Keep your eyes open as you look at the daily newspaper or magazines, and it is surprising how many suitable pictures you will find. If you have a large bulletin board on which to display the calendar, you might place a ring of pictures around the calendar. Challenge students to identify the people and events pictured.

Encourage students to add to the calendar. As they discover new dates or information, these can be added. They can conduct research specifically for this purpose as they search the newspapers, their textbooks, library reference books,

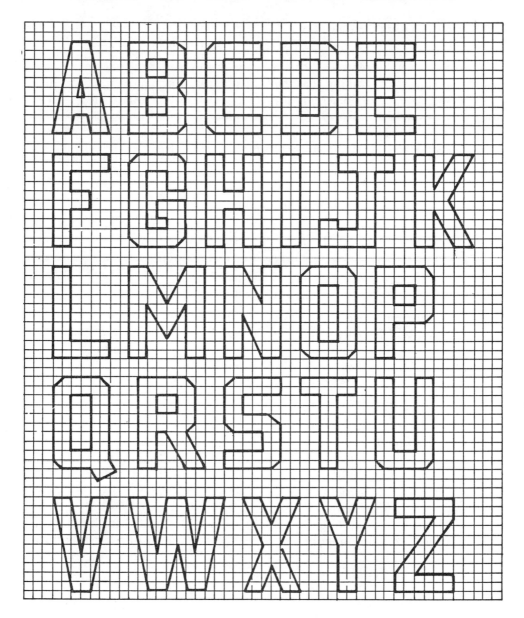

and fiction they read. Let them become *Investigators* with each one exploring a specific group or topic.

Students may also add appropriate motifs around the edge of the calendar. Hearts for February and pumpkins or leaves for the fall months add to the attractiveness of the display. Other motifs include shamrocks, flowers, snowflakes, or kites.

Strategies for Using the Calendar

In the next section of this chapter we present specific ideas about individual people and events as they appear on each calendar. Here we are providing suggestions for teaching that may extend over a period of time not limited to one day or month. Sometimes a more extensive study is triggered by a single event or even a series of dates on one calendar. Such studies as the following cross subject areas as well as periods of time and require students to use various affective and cognitive abilities:

> The Contributions of American Women
> How Native Americans Live Today
> Living in the City
> California, A Fast-growing State
> Spanish Speakers in the United States
> Americans of Italian Descent
> Ethnic Foods across the Country
> Holidays and Celebrations
> Religions of the World

Almost any topic that you study in the elementary and junior high school classroom will lend itself to a multicultural approach. As you plan, therefore, consider the ways you can bring out the kinds of understandings that will promote better human relations in our country. Point to the contributions of various groups—ethnic, religious, young and old, male and female—as a strength of our society. Described here are representative strategies that will add stimulus to your curriculum.

Illustrated Lecture. Upper-grade students can prepare a formal lecture to present to the class. Students select a subject from the calendar to research. They prepare the lecture including appropriate illustrations to make their presentation more effective: for example, pertinent newspaper clippings mounted on a poster, a time-line displayed on the bulletin board, transparencies showing statistics, or a list of words that might be new to their listeners. If these lectures are presented over a period of months, the selection of topics will be larger and the class will not get tired of hearing "lectures." Emphasis should be placed on making the presentation informative and stimulating.

Class Books. Periodically, plan a "big book" to which everyone can contribute. A large tablet of inexpensive drawing paper, which may have a convenient spiral binding, makes a good book. The cover can be made attractive with bright contact paper. Focus on a general topic such as A Person Who Made a Difference or Personalities in Our Community. Students can collect clippings from magazines and newspapers or they can write brief reports of television coverage or draw original pictures for the book.

Notebook on a Theme. Similar to the above idea is the individual notebook. Each student chooses a topic or theme that he or she would like to explore: for example, Families, Pollution, The Development of Parks, Changing to the Metric

System, A Career as a Doctor, Minority Groups in Our Town, The History of This Community, or How People Make a Living Around Here. Students can put anything they like in these notebooks—thoughts they have, questions, notes based on reading or interviews, clippings or sketches. Provide times for discussion and sharing of the ideas being investigated. Encourage students to talk things over together and to contribute to each other's concerns.

Play a Role. Students select someone they would like to know more about. After researching information about the person's life and achievements, they share what they have discovered by playing the role of that person. They might begin by saying, "I am Coretta Scott King." Continuing throughout in the first person, they tell about the life of the person selected. For a variation, students might deliberately avoid revealing the person's name. They end their talk with: "Who am I?"

In the Words of ... Similar to the above role playing, students could pretend to be someone from the past who has suddenly entered your community. How might George Washington, for example, react to many of the problems of today? What would he think of New York City? How would he react to being introduced to Barbara Jordan or Shirley Chisholm? Students write a diary for the person from the past, which includes an account of such personal reactions. Naturally they can select the topics or situations that interest them.

Great Interviews. Students can play the roles of Barbara Walters or David Frost as they interview anyone they choose, past or present. Two or more students will need to develop this activity together as they plan the best questions and appropriate responses. Students can also have several people being interviewed, perhaps from different times. They should, however, try to play these roles as authentically as possible.

Conversations. Imagine a conversation between Presidents Lincoln and Jimmy Carter. Imagine a conversation among Abigail Adams, Eleanor Roosevelt, Harriet Beecher Stowe, Shirley Chisholm, and Yvonne Braithwaite Burke. Students could have fun selecting the groups of people to engage in a conversation as well as participating in the conversations. Tape the conversations for later evaluation.

Letters. Encourage students to write letters to pen pals who live in different countries. They can write letters to the editor of the local newspaper when there is an issue on which they have an opinion. They can also write letters to people from whom they would like information—congressmen or women, authors of articles or books, leaders of groups or movements.

Collage. Have each student choose one person or group represented on the multicultural calendar about which to develop a collage. They might choose César Chávez and his activities, black women in the United States, author Alex Haley, or Japanese Americans. Pictures, words, maps, poetry, small objects—almost anything can be included in this composite picture.

Personality of the Month

At the beginning of class, write the name of a famous person born that month on the board. Tell students something about the person to get them started.

Example: Knute Rockne, born March 4, 1888. This famous American football hero was born in Norway. How old was he when he came to the United States?

Give students a set period of time in which to find information about this person. You may wish to give them specific questions for them to answer. Provide a variety of reference books and sources for them to use so that each student can find something interesting to write down. When the time is up, each student reads to the class what she or he has found. Afterward, the papers are displayed on the bulletin board around the subject's name with pictures or illustrations students have found or drawn.

ACTIVITIES AND INFORMATION FOR A MULTICULTURAL CALENDAR

This section presents a calendar that features people and events important in the history of ethnic groups in the United States. Included are:

birth dates and death dates of Americans from major ethnic groups
people from other countries who have influenced Americans
Independence Days of countries throughout the world
legislation affecting ethnic groups
national and religious holidays
significant events for different groups

Since it is impossible to include all ethnic groups, we have focused on representatives of the largest minority groups: Native Americans, Black Americans, Spanish-speaking Americans, and Asian Americans. It is important for students in multicultural studies to become familiar with the names and contributions of people from groups that are not well represented in school texts.

The information presented for each month has been drawn from many sources and has been accumulated over a period of time; yet, it is far from an exhaustive compilation. It is very difficult to develop a calendar that includes many different groups and cultures because there is so little information on the achievements of Americans from minority backgrounds. Even when the contributions of major groups are recognized, individuals responsible are rarely singled out. For this reason, we may know the names of historically interesting people without knowing their birth date or any specific date associated with them. This is especially true for Native Americans and Blacks born in slavery. In addition, since different groups use different calendars, it is difficult to list holidays and celebrations on the calendar because the dates vary every year.

People are usually listed under their birth date. If the person is living or the year of death unknown, the birth year alone is given, thus: 1899–. As you develop your study of multilingual/multicultural education, you will find many items to add. Following each month is a compilation of classroom activities specific to the events on that calendar.

To facilitate presentation we have not prepared the calendar for one specific year. You will need to make slight adaptations to correct the dates accordingly. For each month, too, there are certain special weeks or holidays that occur on variable dates. July and August are included in the calendar also so that you can present information about these dates during the rest of the school year.

We begin with September and the opening of the school year.

September Activities

9   Write the quote for September by Mao Tse-tung on the board and read it to the students. What was his involvement with revolution? What does he mean by revolution? Discuss various ways the word "revolution" is used today (in advertising, for example). A revolution usually means a revolt against something. Have some students research the Chinese revolution and report to the class. Who and what were the Chinese revolting against? Did they win? What happened afterwards? Compare the Chinese Revolution to the American Revolution. List the similarities and differences.

16   Prepare the class for Mexican Independence Day by featuring Mexico in the classroom. Use all available materials to create an atmosphere of Mexico. Travel

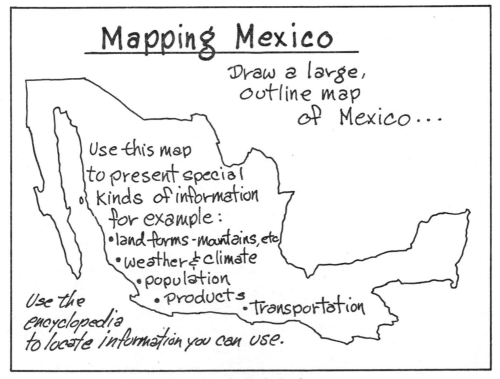

Sample Task Card

SEPTEMBER

1	2	3	4	5	6	7
	Liliuokalani, 1838–1917, last sovereign of Hawaii	Henry Hudson discovered Manhattan, 1609			Independence Day (Swaziland) Marquis de Lafayette, 1757–1834	Brazil's independence from Portugal, 1822
8 Antonin Dvorak, 1841–1904 Second Sunday National Hispanic Week begins	9 Sarah Douglass, 1806–1882, black teacher and abolitionist Mao Tse-tung died, 1976	10 Alice Davis, 1852–1935, Seminole tribal leader	11 Jenny Lind, "Swedish Nightingale," first U.S. concert, 1850	12 Henry Hudson named Hudson River, 1609	13 Maria Baldwin 1856–1922, Black educator and civic leader	14 Ivan Pavlov, 1849–1936
15 Porfirio Díaz, President of Mexico, 1830–	16 Mexican Independence Day, 1810	17 Citizenship Day Constitution Day Steuben Day Constitution Week begins	18 Independence Day (Chile), 1810 Quebec surrendered to English, 1759	19 Lajos Kossuth Hungarian patriot, 1802–1915	20	21
22 First French republic established, 1792	23	24 Francis Watkins Harper, 1825–1911, Black author and reformer	25 Balboa discovered Pacific Ocean, 1513 Columbus began second trip to America, 1493	26 George Gershwin, 1898–1937	27 American Indian Day	28
29 Enrico Fermi, 1901–1954	30					

Revolution is not a dinner party, nor an essay, nor a painting, not a piece of embroidery; it cannot be advanced softly, gradually, carefully, considerately, respectfully, politely, plainly and modestly.

Mao Tse-tung

I am a red man. If the Great Spirit had desired me to be a white man he would have made me so in the first place. He put in your heart certain wishes and plans, in my heart he put other and different desires. Each man is good in his sight. It is not necessary for eagles to be crows.

Sitting Bull

posters, clothes, and objects from Mexico will contribute a festive appearance. Display books about Mexico. Older students can write reports on different aspects of Mexico to put around the room. Use a map of Mexico as a focus for featuring facts about Mexico. Have students research information to construct a time-line of significant events in Mexican history. Why is Mexican Independence Day important? What are other dates that are celebrated in Mexico? Make task cards such as the one shown on p. 181 for individualized approaches.

17   The importance of citizenship is recognized on the anniversary of the signing of the Constitution (1787). Do students know what it means to be a citizen of a country? Ask them what a citizen can do that a noncitizen cannot. Discover how someone becomes a citizen. If possible, arrange for the class to visit the government offices that handle immigration and naturalization. Find out what countries the people are from who want to become citizens. Read portions of the Constitution, for example, "The Bill of Rights" on page 184. Discuss how the Constitution came to be written. Read the second paragraph of the Declaration of Independence:

We hold these truths to be self-evident,
That all men are created equal,
That they are endowed by their Creator with certain inalienable rights,
That among these are life, liberty, and the pursuit of happiness—
That to secure these rights, governments are instituted among men, deriving their just
   powers from the consent of the governed....

The Declaration talks about "men." Ask students who they think the term refers to. Does it include women, poor people, and nonwhite Americans? Who did the writers of the Constitution mean to include? (Property-owning men, free, white, and of a specific age.)

27   American Indian Day is a good time to focus attention on Native Americans. Ask students how many tribes they can name. Have students watch the newspaper for items about current activities of Native American groups. Check your library for books about various Indian tribes. Look for *The Friendly Wolf* (Bradbury, 1974) and *Horse Raid* (Bradbury, 1973) by Dorothy and Paul Goble, beautifully illustrated stories that cross grade levels. A chart showing the present geographic location of different tribes is given in Chapter 4.

In celebrating American Indian Day, take time to combat stereotype images that students may have picked up about Indians from television or other sources. Instead of featuring generalized symbols such as the teepee or war bonnet, concentrate on showing how the tribes differ in clothing, housing, food, and other aspects of their life. Read the well-written biography, *Woman Chief,* the story of a Crow chief, by Rose Sobol (Dial, 1976). Have students discover what tribe(s) once lived in your area. How did they live? What happened to them?

UNITED STATES BILL OF RIGHTS

Amendment 1

Congress shall make no law respecting an establishment of religion, or prohibiting the free exercise thereof; or abridging the freedom of speech, or of the press; or the right of the people peaceably to assemble, and to petition the government for a redress of grievances.

Amendment 2

A well-regulated militia being necessary to the security of a free State, the right of the people to keep and bear arms shall not be infringed.

Amendment 3

No soldier shall, in time of peace, be quartered in any house without the consent of the owner; nor in time of war but in a manner to be prescribed by law.

Amendment 4

The right of the people to be secure in their persons, houses, papers and effects, against unreasonable searches and seizures, shall not be violated, and no warrants shall issue but upon probable cause, supported by oath or affirmation, and particularly described the place to be searched, and the persons or things to be seized.

Amendment 5

No person shall be held to answer for a capital or otherwise infamous crime, unless on a presentment or indictment of a grand jury, except in cases arising in the land or naval forces, or in the militia, when in actual service in time of war or public danger; nor shall any person be subject for the same offense to be twice put in jeopardy of life or limb; nor shall be compelled in any criminal case to be witness against himself, nor be deprived of life, liberty, or property, without due process of law; nor shall private property be taken for public use, without just compensation.

Amendment 6

In all criminal prosecutions the accused shall enjoy the right to a speedy and public trial, by an impartial jury of the State and district wherein the crime shall have been committed, which district shall have been previously ascertained by law, and to be informed of the nature and cause of the accusation; to be confronted with the witnesses against him; to have compulsory process for obtaining witnesses in his favor, and to have the assistance of counsel for his defense.

Amendment 7

In suits at common law, where the value in controversy shall exceed twenty dollars, the right of trial by jury shall be preserved, and no fact tried by a jury shall be otherwise reexamined in any court of the United States than according to the rules of the common law.

Amendment 8

Excessive bail shall not be required, nor excessive fines imposed, nor cruel and unusual punishments inflicted.

Amendment 9

The enumeration in the Constitution of certain rights shall not be construed to deny or disparage others retained by the people.

Amendment 10

The powers not delegated to the United States by the Constitution, nor prohibited by it to the States, are reserved to the States respectively, or to the people.

OCTOBER

1	**2** Mohandas K. Gandhi, 1869–1948 First Pan American Conference—Washington, 1889	**3**	**4** Independence Day (Lesotho) Jean Francois Millet, 1814–1875	**5** Tecumseh (Shawnee) died, 1813	**6** Le Corbusier, 1887–1965 Jenny Lind, 1820–1887	**7** Imanu Amiri Baraka (LeRoi Jones), 1934– Niels Bohr, 1885–1962
8	**9** Leif Erikson Day Mary Shadd Cary, 1823–1893, Black teacher, journalist, lawyer Independence Day (Uganda, Ecuador)	**10** Shawnees defeated in Battle of Point Pleasant (WV), 1774, ends Lord Dunmore's War Chinese Revolution began, 1911	**11** Eleanor Roosevelt, 1884–1962 Pulaski Memorial Day	**12** Columbus lands at San Salvador, 1492	**13** Rudolf Virchow, 1821–1902	**14** Eamon de Valera, Irish president, 1882–
15 3rd Week, Black Poetry Week Friedrich Nietzsche, 1844–1900	**16** Sarah Winnemucca died, 1891, Paiute Indian leader David Ben Gurion, Israeli leader, 1886– Alaska Day Festival	**17** Albert Einstein came to U.S., 1933	**18** First Chinese opera performed in U.S.—San Francisco, 1852 Canada PM, Pierre Trudeau, 1919–	**19**	**20**	**21** U.N. founded in San Francisco, 1945 Alfred Nobel, 1833–1896
22 4th Week, United Nations Week Franz Liszt, 1811–1886	**23** Hungarian Freedom Day, 1956	**24** United Nations Day	**25** Pablo Picasso, 1881–1973 Georges Bizet, 1838–1875	**26** Mahalia Jackson, 1911–1972	**27** Ah Nam, first Chinese in California, baptized, 1815 Dylan Thomas, 1914–1953	**28**
29	**30**	**31** Black Hawk died, 1838, Sauk Indian leader Roberta Lawson, 1878–1940, Delaware civic leader				

If you think the world is all wrong, remember that it contains people like you.
— Gandhi

185

October Activities

2   The Pan American Conference marks the recognition that the countries of the Americas have shared needs and should support each other. Display a map of North, Central, and South America, showing the names of the countries and their capitals. Illustrate it with the flags of the different countries. Discuss what these countries have in common. They were all colonized by Europeans, for example, although descendants of the original inhabitants still live in all the countries. Ask students what languages are spoken in these countries. (English and French in Canada; Spanish in Central America and most South American countries; Portuguese in Brazil) Do these countries share problems? The countries depend on each other for imports and exports. Research information to add to the map. What does the United States import from these countries? What does it export to them?

12   Columbus Day celebrates the landing of Columbus at San Salvador in 1492. Locate San Salvador on the map. Trace Columbus's journey from Spain to the New World. Where did he go after San Salvador? Why did he call the people he met "Indians"? People usually refer to Columbus as the discoverer of America. Is that true? After all, the Indians were there first. Research how the first people to arrive "discovered" America. It is possible that Scandinavian explorers landed in America before Columbus (Leif Erikson Day, October 9). So if Columbus was not the first, why was his discovery particularly important?

14   Explore the history of Ireland and the Irish Americans in this country. To find out more about the country of Eamon de Valera, examine a map of Ireland, showing the political division into Northern Ireland and the Republic of Ireland (Eire). Ireland has a long history of war. What do students know about the basis of the present conflict in Ireland? Research—through books, newspapers, and magazines—the issues involved. Talk about the similarities and differences with other wars over religion.

   Ask students whether any of them are part Irish. When did their ancestors come over from Ireland and why? What kinds of attitudes did the Irish encounter in this country? Have students ask their parents about stereotypes of the Irish immigrants. Compare those attitudes to today's. Is there still prejudice against Irish-Americans? Look at the Kennedy presidential campaign for examples of people's attitudes.

18, 27   Less than forty years elapsed between the first baptism of a Chinese in California (before California was part of the United States) and the performance of a Chinese opera. Have students read accounts of the Chinese immigration to this country in order to see how this rapid change occurred. How did the discovery of gold and the building of the railroad affect Chinese immigration?

   Elicit from students statements about special characteristics of the early Chinese immigrants. Some examples might be:

They were primarily single, young men.

They maintained close ties with their family back in China.

They saved their money and sent it home.

Discuss the consequences of these facts. Include some of the following:

Families in San Francisco's Chinatown now occupy single rooms that were built as dormitories for the original bachelor immigrants.

Many Chinese who live in all-Chinese ghettos (Chinatowns) do not speak English.

21, 24   The organization of countries called the United Nations was founded in San Francisco, at the end of World War II, and succeeded the League of Nations. Have students discover what countries signed the UN Charter. How many countries belong to the United Nations now? Can they find these countries on a world map? (You will need an up-to-date map, especially of Africa.) Where are most of the new countries located? Why? Are there any countries that do not belong to the UN? Write to this address for further information about the UN and its activities: United Nations Information Center, Suite 209, 2101 L Street NW, Washington, D.C. 20037.

November Activities

2   Father Junípero Serra is famous as the builder of the California missions. He is an important part of California history from the period before it became a state. Have students investigate the history of Father Serra and the California missions. Prepare a display with a map of California showing the locations of the missions, pictures of the buildings, and the route of El Camino Real (The King's Highway) that connected them. The missions were part of the Spanish effort to Christianize the local groups of Indians. (Find out what happened to the Indians in California.) Missions were built in other parts of the Southwest as well.

4   Everybody is ignorant, only on different subjects.

Will Rogers

Here is an unusual approach to education. If we are all ignorant about some things then we can all learn something from each other. Discuss with the class what this might mean. Whom do they learn from? Can they learn something from other students? What kinds of things?

Set up a learning exchange center in your class. Post a chart on the board. On one side, students can write down the skills and information that they know, for example:

taking care of a guinea pig
sewing patches on pants
making paper airplanes

NOVEMBER

1	2	3	4	5	6	7
Benvenuto Cellini, 1500–1571	Gaspar de Portola discovered San Francisco Bay, 1769 Father Junípero Serra, a Spanish explorer, 1713–1784		Will Rogers, 1879–1935	Shirley Chisholm, first Black woman was elected to House of Representatives (NY); 1968		William Harrison defeated the Shawnee Prophet at Tippecanoe (IN), 1811 Marie Curie, 1867–1934
8	**9**	**10**	**11**	**12**	**13**	**14**
Edward Brooke, first Black U.S. senator in 85 years, elected (MA), 1966	W. C. Handy, 1873–1958 Benjamin Banneker, 1731–1806	Martin Luther, 1483–1546	Fyodor Dostoyevski, 1821–1881	Dr. Sun Yat-sen, 1866–1925 Auguste Rodin, 1840–1917		Freedom for Philippines, 1935 Jawaharlal Nehru, 1889–1964
15	**16**	**17**	**18**	**19**	**20**	**21**
	Paul Hindemith, 1895–1963	Opening of Suez Canal, 1869	First Thanksgiving, Pilgrims and Massasoit, chief of Wampanoags, 1777 Louis Jacques Daguerre, 1789–1851	Indira Gandhi, 1917–	Atahualpa, Inca of Peru, filled room with gold for Pizarro, 1532	Voltaire, 1694–1778
22	**23**	**24**	**25**	**26**	**27**	**28**
Independence Day (Lebanon) Charles de Gaulle, 1890–1970		Spinoza, 1632–1677 Toulouse-Lautrec, 1864–1901		Sojourner Truth died, 1883		
29	**30**					
	Shirley Chisholm, 1924– Winston Churchill, 1874–1965					

Life is something like this trumpet. If you don't put anything in it you don't get anything out. And that's the truth.

W. C. Handy

embroidering designs on shirts
making tortillas
whistling
singing a new song
knowing a secret way to school
speaking Spanish
growing a plant

Encourage everyone to list one thing so that they can feel proud of what they know.

Then have students sign up for what they would like to learn. Depending on the age level and types of skills listed, they may want to sign up for one or two items on the list. Give the students time to get together and work out arrangements with each other for learning what they would like to know. These "teaching" sessions can take place during class, after school, or at home. Be sure to have students report back on what they have learned.

5   I have been discriminated against far more because I am a female than because I am black.

Shirley Chisholm

Here is a provocative quote for students to discuss. Why would her statement be true? Shirley Chisholm was the first black woman elected to the House of Representatives. Was it harder for her to get elected than for a black man? Read portions from her autobiography, *Unbossed and Unbought* (Houghton Mifflin, 1970), showing her struggles to overcome race and sex prejudice.

Shirley Chisholm was elected in 1968. Now there are more Blacks, men and women, in the House of Representatives. Do students think that race prejudice still affects whether people are elected to Congress? If not, why are there not *more* Blacks in Congress (or women and members of other ethnic minorities)?

12   To understand is hard. Once one understands, action is easy.

Sun Yat-sen

Tell students about Sun Yat-sen, leader of the fight for China's independence. This quote reflects the emphasis on *understanding* common to Asian philosophers, as opposed to the Western obsession with *action*. Ask students to describe what this quote means to them. What would they like to understand—about themselves, other people, the world? Are there times when we act without understanding or thinking?

20   The Incas were one of the major Indian civilizations encountered by the first Spanish explorers of the New World. Have students investigate the Incas and their culture. The Spaniards were amazed at the achievements of the Incas. How were the Incas more advanced than the Spaniards? How did the Spanish treat the Incas and what happened to them? Have students make a model of the mysterious Inca city, Macchu Picchu.

4th Thurs.   Thanksgiving is a time to recognize all that we are grateful for and to give thanks. Ask students to think of what they are thankful for. Have them write individual statements of "I am thankful for..." and illustrate them. Display these "thanksgivings" on the board so that everyone can appreciate them.

Discuss the first Thanksgiving—why was it held? The Pilgrims were grateful for surviving in the new land. How did the Indians feel? Why do you suppose the Indians helped the Pilgrims? How did the Pilgrims feel about the Indians? The first Thanksgiving must have been a strange sight with the groups of Indians and Pilgrims eating together. Have students research this historic event— what the Pilgrims looked like, how the Indians dressed—and draw pictures of how they imagine the first Thanksgiving.

26   In 1851, Sojourner Truth said:

The man over there says women need to be helped into carriages and lifted over ditches, and to have the best place everywhere. Nobody ever helps me into carriages or over puddles or gives me the best place...ain't I a woman? Look at my arm! I have ploughed and planted and gathered into barns and no man could head me—ain't I a woman?

I could work as much and eat as much as a man—when I could get it—and bear the lash as well! And ain't I a woman? I have born 13 children and seen most of 'em sold into slavery, and when I cried out with my mother's grief, none but Jesus heard me . . . and ain't I a woman?

Who was Sojourner Truth? Investigate her life with the class. Here is a strong black woman, whose name we remember from a period when Blacks were mostly anonymous. Ask students why we do not know her birth date, when we know the birth dates of the white women she worked with. Look up information on the life of women and of Blacks at that time. Why did Sojourner Truth fight for the women's movement and women's right to vote? What might she say about today's women's movement?

December Activities

1   Invite students to "discover" Portugal. Use travel folders and books to plan a trip to this country that lies west of Spain, part of the Iberian Peninsula. How far is Lisbon from New York? How far is it from where you live? How much does it cost to fly there?

2   Have several students research the Monroe Doctrine. This document, signed by President James Monroe, stated: "The American continents are henceforth not to be considered as subjects for future colonization by any European powers." Display a map of Central and South America as students identify the names of these countries.

10   Human Rights Day celebrates the Proclamation of the Universal Declaration of Human Rights by the United Nations (1948). This day provides an opportunity for students to discuss what Human Rights are. Ask each one to complete this sentence: Every human being has the right to . . .

15   Related to Human Rights is the Bill of Rights, the first ten amendments to the U.S. Constitution. A group of students can present the Bill of Rights as part of a special program. They can prepare it as a reader's theater presentation. See page 184.

Send for free teaching materials about the Bill of Rights from Standard Oil of California, 225 Bush Street, San Francisco, CA 94120 or *Boys Life Magazine,* New Brunswick, NJ 08903.

18   The Ratification of the thirteenth Amendment meant the official end of slavery. Begin reading a book such as *The Slave Dancer,* by Paula Fox (Bradbury, 1973), which won the Newbery Award in 1974, an excellent historical novel for grades 5–9.

25   Provide new perspectives of Christmas as you consider how this Christian holiday is celebrated in different countries. What is the origin of different practices such as the piñata, the Christmas tree, or the Yule log?

Point out, too, that many words associated with Christmas come from other languages, for example:

DECEMBER

1	2	3	4	5	6	7
Independence Day (Portugal)	Monroe Doctrine, 1823 Georges Seurat, 1859–1891		Vasili Kandinsky, 1866–1944	Phyllis Wheatley died, 1784, Black poet	Feast of St. Nicholas	Bombing of Pearl Harbor by Japanese, 1941
8	**9**	**10**	**11**	**12**	**13**	**14**
2nd Week, Human Rights Week Diego Rivera, 1886–		U.S. acquired Cuba, Guam, Puerto Rico, Philippines, 1898 Human Rights Day Universal Declaration of Human Rights ratified 1948	Aleksander Solzhenitsyn, 1918–	Kenya Independence, 1963		Roald Amundsen reached South Pole, 1911
15	**16**	**17**	**18**	**19**	**20**	**21**
Bill of Rights Day Bill of Rights ratified, 1791	Ludwig von Beethoven, 1770–1827	Maria Stewart died, 1879, Black teacher and lecturer	Ratification of 13th Amendment ended slavery, 1865	Bernice Pauahi Bishop, 1831–1884, Hawaiian leader	Cherokees forced off their land in Georgia because of gold strike, 1835 Sacajawea died, 1812 Shoshoni interpreter	Pilgrims landed at Plymouth (MA), 1620 Henrietta Szold, 1860–1945, Zionist leader
22	**23**	**24**	**25**	**26**	**27**	**28**
Teresa Carreño, 1853–1917, Venezuelan-American concert pianist	First Chinese theater built, San Francisco, 1852 Madame C. J. Walker, 1867–1919, Black businesswoman	Feast of Sacrifice— Moslem Holy Day	Christmas Day	Maurice Utrillo, 1883–1955	Louis Pasteur, 1822–1895	
29	**30**	**31**				
Pablo Casals, 1876–1973	Pocahontas rescued Captain John Smith, 1607	Henri Matisse, 1869–1954				

13th Amendment: Neither slavery nor involuntary servitude, except as a punishment for crime whereof the party shall have been duly convicted, shall exist within the United States, or any place subject to their jurisdiction.

Noel, French, from Latin *natalis.*

Carol, Greek, from *choros* (dance) and *arelos* (flute).

Crèche, French, word for *crib.*

Angel, Greek, *angellos,* means messenger.

Poinsettia, red flower native to Mexico, brought to U.S. by Joel Poinsett, minister to Mexico.

Yule, Norse, *jol,* a feast.

Xmas, Greek letter *chi* (x) stands for Christ.

Merry Christmas around the World

Joyeux Noel—France, Belgium, Switzerland
Kala Hrystoughena—Greece
Glaedelig Jul—Norway
Froeliche Weihnachten—Germany, Austria
Stretan Bozic—Yugoslavia
Buon Natale—Italy
Feliz Navidad—Spain, Mexico
God Jul—Sweden
Merry Christenmass—Scotland
Um Feliz Natal—Portugal
Nodlaig Mhaith Dhuit—Ireland
Boldog Karacsony Unnep—Hungary
Wesolych Swiat—Poland
Kung ho shen tan—Chinese
Vrolyk Kerstmis—Holland
S Rozhdestvom Christovom—Russia

January Activities

The name of this month comes from the Roman god Janus, who had two faces and looked back into the past and forward into the future. Janus guarded doorways and had special charge over the beginnings of undertakings. It is very appropriate, therefore, to take time at the beginning of the year to consider where we have been and where we are going. Talk with the class about the history of

JANUARY

1	2	3	4	5	6	7
Emancipation Proclamation, 1863 / Haiti Independence, 1804 / Commonwealth of Australia established, 1901	Emma, 1836–1885, Queen of Hawaii		Burma Independence Day / Louis Braille, 1809–1852 / Jacob Grimm, 1785–1863	George Washington Carver Day, 1864–1943 / Sissieretta Jones, 1869–1933, Black singer	Celebration of King's Day—Pueblo Dances	
8	**9**	**10**	**11**	**12**	**13**	**14**
Charles de Gaulle became president of France, 1959		First U.N. General Assembly, London, 1946 / League of Nations founded, 1920, Geneva	Eugenio de Hostos, 1839–1903, Puerto Rican patriot / Chad National Day	Adah Thoms, 1863–1943, Black nursing leader	Charlotte Ray, 1850–1911, first Black woman lawyer	Carlos Romulo, Philippine leader, 1901– / Albert Schweitzer, 1875–1965
15	**16**	**17**	**18**	**19**	**20**	**21**
Martin Luther King, Jr., 1929–1968, Black minister and civil rights leader		Anton Chekov, 1860–1904		Paul Cezanne, 1839–1905		Fanny Jackson-Coppin died, 1913, Black educator / Eliza Snow (Smith), 1804–1887, "Mother of Mormonism"
22	**23**	**24**	**25**	**26**	**27**	**28**
	24th Amendment barred poll tax in federal elections, 1964 / Amanda Smith, 1837–1915, Black evangelist	Eva del Vakis Bowles, 1875–1943, Black youth group leader	Florence Mills, 1895–1927, Black singer and dancer	Republic of **India** established, **1950**	Vietnam War ended, 1973 / Wolfgang Mozart, 1759–1796	Auguste Picard, 1884–1962
29	**30**	**31**				
	Mohandas Gandhi (India) killed, 1948 / Franklin Roosevelt, 1882–1945					

It may be true that the law cannot make a man love me, but it can keep him from lynching me, and I think that's pretty important...

Martin Luther King, Jr.

194

this country. Have them list ways in which the country has changed: inventions, attitudes, and people. Then ask them to face forward and think about what might change in the future. What would they like to see happen? Will people be any different? Use the excitement of speculating about the future to show the importance of finding the roots of the future in the past.

1   Australia has a special fascination since it is "down under." Have students discover as much as possible about this island continent in a class search that begins in the library. Teach them a song from Australia such as "Waltzing Matilda." Discuss the words and phrases presented in this song. Would you call this English? Why might people speak English differently in different countries?

WALTZING MATILDA

Once a jolly swagman camped by a billabong
Under the shade of a coolibah tree,
And he sang as he watched and waited till
   his billy boiled,
"You'll come a-waltzing Matilda with me!"

Chorus:
Waltzing Matilda, Waltzing Matilda,
You'll come a-waltzing Matilda with me!

And he sang as he watched and waited till
  his billy boiled,
"You'll come a-waltzing Matilda with me!"

Down came a jumbuck to drink at the billabong,
Up jumped the swagman and grabbed him with
  glee,
And he sang as he stowed that jumbuck in
  his tucker bag,
(Chorus)

Up rode the squatter, mounted on his thorough-bred,
Down came the troopers, one, two, three,
"Where's that jolly jumbuck you've got in
  your tucker bag?"
(Chorus)

Up jumped the swagman, sprang into the billabong,
"You'll never catch me alive," said he,
And his ghost may be heard as you pass by that
  billabong.
(Chorus)

10   Discuss the difference between the League of Nations and the United Nations. How did the United States get involved in each? Find out what the United Nations does. Students can write to the different groups (WHO, UNESCO, UNICEF) for information on their work and material to use in multicultural studies.

World Health Organization, Avenue Appia, 1211 Geneva 27, Switzerland

UNESCO, 7 and 9 Placedefontenoi, 75700 Paris, France

UNICEF, 866 United Nations Plaza, New York City, NY 10017

15   Discuss with students the quote by Martin Luther King, Jr. What do they think was the context of this statement? Martin Luther King was a leader in the civil rights movement. What point of view was he arguing for and what was he arguing against? What does civil rights mean? Students have opinions on the strategies used in the civil rights movement. List some of these and encourage students to comment on the results of these strategies. You might include legislation, nonviolent demonstrations (sit-ins), riots, education, and voter registration.

Martin Luther King is remembered for his "I have a dream" speech. Locate the text of this speech and read it to the class or have students prepare it for group presentation.

Vietnam

27   The Vietnam War is a powerful and painful memory for most adults today. But what do students know about it? Talk with the students about their impressions of Vietnam and the role of the United States in that country. What have they heard other people saying and what are their opinions? Students may find it hard to remember or imagine the emotions aroused by the United States involvement in Vietnam. Use old news magazines such as *Time* and *Newsweek,* and read selected portions about the war to the class. History books are now being written that refer to the war and its conclusion. As an exercise in living history, have students write a short description of the Vietnam War as they think it should appear in their history books. What would they like to know about the war? What part of the U.S. involvement is most difficult to understand? Possible sources for students to use in preparing this report include: (1) interviews with adults of different views, (2) newspapers and magazines for facts and editorials, (3) recent history books that mention Vietnam, and (4) talks with Vietnamese living in the area.

What is Vietnam like? Explore the following books:

Buell, Hal. *Viet Nam; Land of Many Dragons.* Dodd, Mead, 1968.

Graham, Gail. *Cross-Fire: A Vietnam Novel.* Pantheon, 1972.

Lifton, Betty Jean, and Thomas Fox. *Children of Vietnam.* Atheneum, 1972.

Cooke, David D. *Vietnam; The Country, the People.* Norton, 1968.

Nielsen, Jon, with Kay Nielsen. *Artist in South Vietnam.* Messner, 1969.

30 Although Gandhi lived in another country, students should know something about his life and his ideas because he influenced so many people in the United States. Feature several quotations from Gandhi:

Ahimsa ("harmlessness" or nonviolence) means the largest love. It is the supreme law. By it alone can mankind be saved. He who believes in nonviolence believes in a living God.

All humanity is one undivided and indivisible family, and each one of us is responsible for the misdeeds of all the others. I cannot detach myself from the wickedest soul.

All amassing of wealth or hoarding of wealth above and beyond one's legitimate needs is theft. There would be no occasion for theft and no thieves if there were wise regulations of wealth, and social justice.

My nationalism is intense internationalism. I am sick of the strife between nations or religions.

Discuss his ideas. Gandhi is credited with forcing the British to give India its independence. How have his methods of nonviolence (demonstrations) and passive resistance (sit-ins and hunger strikes) been translated to this country? How effective have they been?

Gandhi and his ideas were very powerful; yet he led a simple life. Students can read biographies such as *The True Story of Gandhi, Man of Peace,* by Reginald Reynolds, Children's Press, 1964. Or read them selections from an excellent book written for adults in which people who knew Gandhi describe his life: *Mahatma Gandhi and His Apostles,* by Ved Mehta, Viking, 1977.

FEBRUARY

1	2	3	4	5	6	7
Langston Hughes, 1902–1967, National Freedom Day; Louis S. St. Laurent, French-Canadian P.M. of Canada, 1882–; Treaty of Guadeloupe Hidalgo, 1848	Candlemas Day	Felix Mendelssohn, 1809–1847	Philippine Rebellion against U.S. began 1899	Constitution Day (Mexico); Roger Williams, 1603–1683	Senate ratified treaty ending Spanish-American War, 1899	Mardi Gras
8 Week of Feb. 12, Black History Week	**9**	**10** Leontyne Price, 1927–; End of French and Indian War, 1763	**11**	**12** Chinese Republic, 1912; Fannie Williams, 1855–1944, Black lecturer and civic leader; Thaddeus Kosciusko, Polish patriot, 1746–; Abraham Lincoln, 1809–1865	**13**	**14** Frederick Douglass, 1817–1895; Valentine's Day
15 Galileo Galilei, 1564–1642; Week of Feb. 19, Brotherhood Week	**16**	**17** Marian Anderson, 1902–	**18** Independence Day (Gambia); Alessandro Volta, 1745–1827	**19** Nicolaus Copernicus, 1473–1543	**20** Birthday of the Prophet (Mohammed)	**21** Malcolm X Day, 1925–1965
22 Gertrude Bonnin, 1876–1938, Sioux author and reformer; Frederic Chopin, 1810–1849	**23** W.E.B. DuBois, 1868–1963; George Frederic Handel, 1685–1759	**24** William Grimm, 1786–1859	**25** First Negro in Congress, Hiram Revels (Miss), 1870; Independence Day (Kuwait); José de San Martín (the great liberator), 1778–1850	**26** Victor Hugo, 1802–1885	**27** Independence Day (Dominican Republic)	**28**
29 Emmeline Wells, 1828–1921, Mormon leader and feminist; Mother Ann Lee, 1736–1784, Founder of the Shakers	**30**					

...A world I dream where blacks or whites,
Whatever race you be,
Will share the bounties of the earth
And every man is free . . .
Where wretchedness will hang its head
And joy, like a pearl,
Attend the needs of all mankind
Of such I dream—our world!

Langston Hughes

February Activities

1   Feature the poetry of Langston Hughes. An attractive collection is *Don't You Turn Back* compiled by Lee Bennett Hopkins (Knopf, 1969). Langston Hughes's poetry lends itself to graphic presentation. Have students create posters featuring a selection from a poem. Encourage them to use calligraphy and art on the poster in order to celebrate the poem. Begin reading his biography on this date; for example: *Langston Hughes, Poet of His People* by Elizabeth Myers (Garrard, 1970).

4   Display a world map. Point out the location of the Philippines. (Note the spelling of this name.) Have students make a replica of the Philippine flag and discuss the history of this group of islands. Why did the United States get involved with the Philippines? Is the United States still involved? When and why did groups of Filipinos come to this country? What languages do people speak in the Philippines?

5   Celebrate Mexico's Constitution Day. Create a learning center on Mexico. (Let students contribute ideas.) Explore your library for nonfiction and fiction about Mexico as well as stories about Mexican Americans or Chicanos. For example:

Graciela: A Mexican-American Child Tells Her Story by Joe Molnar (Watts, 1972)

Viva Chicano by Frank Bonham (Dutton, 1970)

Develop task cards that focus on Mexico for reading in the content areas. See page 181.

12   Have students prepare a bulletin board display about Abraham Lincoln, a president who has become a folk hero. He symbolizes the poor boy who rose to leadership, the person who freed the slaves. Feature quotations by Lincoln around his picture, for instance:

The ballot is stronger than the bullet.

Any people anywhere, being inclined and having the power, have the right to rise up and shake off the existing government, and form a new one that suits them better. This is a most valuable, a most sacred right—a right which we hope and believe is to liberate the world.

A house divided against itself cannot stand. I believe this government cannot endure, permanently half *slave* and half *free*.

As I would not be a *slave,* so I would not be a *master*. This expresses my idea of democracy. Whatever differs from this, to the extent of the difference, is no democracy.

Have students prepare "The Gettysburg Address" for choric speaking. Plan a short program using this address, quotations, and poetry about Lincoln. One or two students might tell a story about Abe.

Variable Dates

Black History Week

This special week is sponsored by the Association for the Study of Negro Life and History founded by black historian, Carter G. Woodson. First observed in 1926, it falls during the week in February that includes the birthdays of Abraham Lincoln (12) and Frederick Douglass (14). Request from the association a publication list of materials to be used at this time: 1538 Ninth St., NW, Washington, D.C. 20001.

Use an activity such as "Celebrating Black Americans" on the accompanying page.* Feature books about the achievements of Black Americans such as:

From Lew Alcindor to Kareem Abdul Jabbar by James Haskins, Lothrop, 1972.

Frederick Douglass: Slave-fighter-Freeman by Arna Bontemps, Knopf, 1959.

W.E.B. DuBois; a Biography by Virginia Hamilton, Crowell, 1972.

A special activity for this week would be to learn James Weldon Johnson's song "Lift Every Voice and Sing," also known as the Negro National Anthem. Students will be interested in learning more about the man who wrote this song. Offer them the biography, *James Weldon Johnson,* by Harold Felton (Dodd, 1971), which includes the song.

22   ### Brotherhood Week

Celebrated during the week that includes George Washington's birthday (22), this week was initiated by Father McNenamin of Denver, Colorado, in 1929. It is sponsored by the National Conference of Christians and Jews, 43 W. 57th St., New York, NY 10019. Feature books about promoters of peace and understanding such as Martin Luther King, Jr., or Ralph Bunche.

Explore different interesting ways to present quotations in your classroom. Students might, for example, use quotations related to the topic of brotherhood, such as those shown below, to form a heart. Other topics will suggest appropriate forms such as the silhouette of Washington or Lincoln made of quotations related to freedom or patriotism or a cornucopia formed from quotations related to thankfulness.

QUOTES FOR BROTHERHOOD WEEK

We have committed the Golden Rule to memory;
let us now commit it to life.

Edwin Markham

No man is an Island, entire of itself.

John Donne

Gently scan your brother man.

Robert Burns

Whoever seeks to set one race against another
seeks to enslave all races.

Franklin D. Roosevelt

---

* Answers to the puzzle: Ellington, Bunche, Washington, Anderson, Woodson, Bethune, Smith, Gillespie, Poitier, Chisholm, Horne, Mays, Baldwin, Turner, Hughes, King.

Celebrating Black Americans

Fill in the last names of famous Black Americans to solve this puzzle.
The First name is given as a clue.

```
_ _ _ _N_ _ _ _           Duke _____
_ _ _ _ _E               Ralph _____
_ _ _ _ _ _ _G_ _ _      Booker T. _____
_ _ _ _R_ _ _            Marian _____
_ _O_ _ _ _              Carter G. _____

_ _ _H_ _ _              Mary McLeod _____
_ _I_ _                  Bessie _____
_ _ _ _ _ _S_ _ _        Dizzy _____
_ _ _T_ _ _              Sidney _____
_ _ _ _ _O_ _            Shirley _____
_ _R_ _                  Lena _____
_ _Y_                    Willie _____
_ _ _ _W_ _              James A. _____
_ _ _ _E_                Nat _____
_ _ _ _E_                Langston _____
K _ _ _                  Martin Luther _____ , Jr.
```

1) Find out why each person is famous.
2) List 5 other Black Americans who are known in their fields.

SOURCE: *Reading Ideas,* February 1977.

If our brothers are oppressed, then we are
oppressed. If they hunger, we hunger. If their
freedom is taken away, our freedom is not secure.

Stephen Vincent Benet

The world is my country;
All mankind are my brethren.

Thomas Paine

The world is my mankind are my country. All brethren. Thomas Paine... We dare not just look back to great yesterdays. We must look forward to great tomorrows. Adlai E. Stevenson... Beware, as long as you live, of judging people by appearances. La Fontaine... If you have built castles in the air, your work need not be lost. Now put foundations under them. Osa Johnson... Until you have become really in actual fact, a brother to everyone, brotherhood will not come to pass. Fyodor Dostoyevsky... You must look into people as well as at them. Lord Chesterfield... True friendship is a plant of slow growth. George Washington... Coming together is a beginning; keeping together is progress; working together is success. Henry Ford... He has a right to criticize who has a heart to help. Abraham Lincoln... Democracy is based upon the conviction that there are extraordinary possibilities in ordinary people. Henry Emerson Fosdick!... while democracy must have its organization and controls, its vital breath is individual liberty. Charles Evans Hughes. Whoever seeks to set one race against another seeks to enslave all races. Franklin D. Roosevelt... Nothing happens unless first a dream. Carl Sandburg... No man is an Island, entire of itself. John Donne... Breathes there the man with soul so dead, who never to himself hath said, "This is my own, my native land." Sir Walter Scott... Ask not what your country can do for you; ask what you can do for your country. John F. Kennedy... No man is good enough to govern another man without that others consent. Abraham Lincoln... Gently scan your brother man. Robert Burns...

MARCH

1	2	3	4	5	6	7
Ralph Ellison, 1914– , Black author; Peace Corps est., 1961	Texas declares independence from Mexico, 1836	Doll Festival (Japanese)	Knute Rockne, 1888–1931; Death of Stalin, 1953		Independence Day (Ghana); Fall of the Alamo, 1836; Michelangelo, 1475–1564	Tomás Masaryk (Czech patriot), 1850–1937; Maurice Ravel, 1875–1937
8	**9**	**10**	**11**	**12**	**13**	**14**
International Women's Day	Amerigo Vespucci, 1451–1512, Italian navigator	Harriet Tubman's death, 1913; Hallie Q. Brown, 1850–1949, Black teacher and women's leader		Independence Day (Mauritius)	Birthday of the Prophet (holy day commemorating birth of Mohammed)	Albert Einstein, 1879–1955; Johann Strauss, 1825–1899
15	**16**	**17**	**18**	**19**	**20**	**21**
	G.S. Ohm, 1787–1854; Goddard's first rocket flight, 1926	St. Patrick's Day	Hawaii's Statehood, 1959		Harriet Beecher Stowe's *Uncle Tom's Cabin* published, 1852; Independence Day (Tunisia)	Benito Juárez, Mexican leader, 1806–1872; Johann Sebastian Bach, 1685–1750
22	**23**	**24**	**25**	**26**	**27**	**28**
Emancipation Day (Puerto Rico); Marcel Marceau, 1923–		Robert Koch discovered TB germ, 1882; Andrew Mellon, 1855–1937	Arturo Toscanini, 1867–1957; Seward's Day (Alaska)	Kuhio Day (Hawaii)	Wilhelm Roentgen, 1845–1923	
29	**30**	**31**				
	1st Amendment Right to Vote passed, 1870; U.S. purchased Alaska from Russia, 1867; Vincent Van Gogh, 1853–1890	Elizabeth Greenfield died, 1876, Black singer; First treaty U.S.–Japan, 1854; U.S. took possession of Virgin Islands from Denmark, 1917				

All novels are about certain minorities:
The individual is a minority.

Ralph Ellison

203

March Activities

1   Discuss the quotation (at the bottom of the calendar) by Ralph Ellison, author of *The Invisible Man*. The idea of each person as a minority of one will probably be new to students. Ask students to think of what makes them unique. How are they a minority of one? Have them draw a picture or write a story describing themselves as a minority of one.

8   Celebrate the achievements of American women. Here is an opportunity to point out the achievements of women of all races and creeds. Make a point of including lesser known persons. An excellent resource is: *Notable American Women,* ed. Edward T. James (Belknap Press, 1974), 3 volumes.

9   Our country is named after Amerigo Vespucci. Some people thought it should have been named after Christopher Columbus. Do students know that *Columbia* is sometimes used to refer to this country? ("Columbia, the Gem of the Ocean"). What other countries does *America* refer to? North, Central, and South America are all called the *Americas*. People living in South America rightly resent the use of *America* to refer to the United States alone. Who is an American?

    The name of a country is important. Ask students if they can suggest reasons why this country is called "The United States of America." What other names might have been proposed at different times? (Columbia, New India)

10   **Who was Harriet Tubman?** Pose a question like this on the board occasionally and give a reward (fifteen minutes of free time) to the student who discovers information about the person featured. A good biography of Harriet Tubman was written by Ann Petry (Crowell, 1955).

13   Encourage students to research information about different religions. Have students clip articles about countries where Mohammedanism or the Moslem religion (Islam) is part of the culture—Saudi Arabia, Iran, Egypt. Discuss the importance of these countries today. What are some of the similarities and differences between the Arab culture and ours? Some Arabs are Christian believers, not Moslem. Are there any Muslims in this country? Who are the Black Muslims and what do they believe?

17   Although highly commercialized, St. Patrick's Day offers a good opportunity to recognize Irish Americans and the many Irish customs that we are familiar with. What Irish folk beliefs can students name? The leprechaun is the most familiar although the meaning of this figure has changed. One did not trifle with real leprechauns! Other symbols common around this time include the shamrock. Students can look up the origins and real versions of these symbols and beliefs and report their findings to the class.

    Read aloud Irish folktales from such collections as the following:

Favorite Fairy Tales Told in Ireland retold by Virginia Haviland (Little, Brown, 1961).

The King of Ireland's Son by Padraic Colum (McGraw-Hill, 1966).

Irish Sagas and Folktales retold by Eileen O'Favlain (Walck, 1954).

Have students prepare stories for dramatization, assigning parts and rewriting the dialogue.

22   Have students research the history of Puerto Rico's relationship to the United States and the significance of this Emancipation Day. Read stories aloud. A story for younger children about Puerto Ricans in the United States is *Friday Night Is Papa Night* by Ruth Sonneborn (Viking, 1970). A book for older students is *Magdalena* by Louisa Shotwell (Viking, 1971).

The puzzle on page 206 features the municipalities into which the island of Puerto Rico is divided. Display a map of the island as students discover the following names:

Adjuntas	Hatillo
Aguada	Isabela
Aguadilla	Jayuya
Aguas Buenas	Juana Diaz
Arecibo	Juncos
Barceloneta	Lares
Barranquitas	Loiza
Bayamón	Manati
Caguas	Moca
Camuy	Naranjito
Carolina	Orocovis
Cayey	Patillas
Ceiba	Ponce
Cidra	Rincón
Coamo	Sabana Grande
Corozal	Salinas
Culebra	San Sebastián
Dorado	Santa Isabel
Fajardo	Toa Alta
Florida	Vega Alta
Guánica	Villalba
Guayama	Yabucoa
Gurabo	Yauco

Exploring Puerto Rico

Puerto Rico is an island that is divided into many municipalities. See how many of their names you can find hidden in the puzzle on page 206. Words go vertically or horizontally in either direction or they can be diagonal.

```
S A N S E B A S T I A N J L A J A S B
A A D J U N T A S R A L L I D U A G A
N R B A R C E L O N E T A B F A D G R
T E A A B L W S J C G I J L H N U U R
A C Y C N V E G A A L T A A K A L A A
I I A I M A N P Y Y R A G Z D D O R N
S B M N Z Y G V U E T N U O S I D A Q
A O O A A F B R Y Y C A A R D A A B U
B F N U O A C O A M O M S O N Z R O I
E G J G C J H P L N P R B C M R O S T
L T V G U A Y A M A D Y U Z C I D R A
Y B D F B R C T A R G E E J U N C O S
T M O C A D J I N A P O N C E C A L E
O C U A Y O N L I N R T A S B O M D C
A D I R O L F L L J F H S C G N U L A
A R B E L U C A O I S A B E L A Y O G
L A R E S P T S R T H A T I L L O I U
T V I L L A L B A O R B G B H M S Z A
A Z O D A U T U C P S O S A N I L A S
```

Use an encyclopedia to help you. Forty-seven of the 78 municipalities are included in the puzzle. Which ones are not included? *

Looking at the calendar for this month you will notice a number of dates related to the U.S. acquisition of territory. Some of the areas acquired later became states (Texas, Alaska, Hawaii) and other areas have not (Puerto Rico and Virgin Islands). Discuss with students how and when territories have become states. (How did your area become a state?) Some had been part of other countries first—which ones? Many people who speak different languages and are from different backgrounds became part of this country when territories became states. Students can research who was living in each of these areas before the United States acquired them. What happened to these people? Did they become citizens? The language spoken in these areas reflects their history. For example, because the Virgin Islands were once owned by Denmark, the language has been influenced by Danish. Why have some areas become states and not others? Have students look up information on other U.S. possessions and territories (Samoa, for example).

1	2	3	4	5	6	7
Spring Corn Dances (Pueblos)	Ponce de Leon landed in Florida, 1513; Hans Christian Andersen, 1805–1875		Martin Luther King, Jr., killed, 1968; Liberation Day (Hungary)	Booker T. Washington, 1856–1915; Pocahontas married John Rolfe, 1614	Peary and Henson reach North Pole, 1909; Joseph Smith founded Mormon Church, 1830	
8	**9**	**10**	**11**	**12**	**13**	**14**
First synagogue in America founded in NYC, 1730; Buddha's birthday	Civil War ended, Treaty of Appomattox, 1865	Joseph Pulitzer, 1847–1911		Civil War began Ft. Sumter, 1861	Lucy Laney, 1854–1933, Black educator	Pan American Day; Abraham Lincoln assassinated, 1865
15	**16**	**17**	**18**	**19**	**20**	**21**
Bessie Smith, 1894–1937, Black blues singer	Mary Eliza Mahoney, 1845–1926, first Black nurse; Charles Chaplin, 1889–1977	Independence Day (Syria); Nikita Khrushchev, 1894–1971		Revolutionary War, 1775	Joan Miro, 1893–	Spanish-American War began, 1898
22	**23**	**24**	**25**	**26**	**27**	**28**
Lenin (Vladimir Ilyich Ugyanov), 1870–1924	William Shakespeare, 1564–1616; Sergei Prokofiev, 1891–1953		Ella Fitzgerald, 1918–; UN founded, 1945; Guglielmo Marconi, 1874–1937	Gertrude (Ma) Rainey, 1886–1939, Black blues singer; Syngman Rhee, 1875–1965	Independence Day (Togo)	
29	**30**					
Emperor's birthday (Japanese); Duke Ellington, 1899–1974	Louisiana Territory purchased, 1803					

The wisest among my race understand that the agitation of questions of social equality is the extremest folly, and that progress in the enjoyment of all the privileges that will come to us must be the result of severe and constant struggle rather than of artificial forcing.

Booker T. Washington

April Activities

2   Ponce de Leon was supposedly searching for the Fountain of Youth when he landed in Florida. Have students write on the topic "How life might be changed if there really were a Fountain of Youth." Consider the advantages and problems that would arise.

Let's play hide and seek!

4   Refer to January 15.

5   You can't hold a man down without staying down with him.

Booker T. Washington

What does this mean? Washington was talking about the problem of race relations—what does this quote indicate about this point of view? Taking this statement and the quote given on the calendar, what do students think Booker T. Washington would do about the racial problems today? Have students identify some problems and suggest different approaches to them. How is Washington similar to and different from some of today's black leaders?

9, 12   Someone once said that the Civil War is the longest war in history. It began in 1861 and is still going on today. Discuss this with students. Do they agree? What does it mean to say the war is still going on? What kind of a "war" is it? Are people being killed?

29 April 29 marks the Emperor of Japan's birthday. This is a major holiday in Japan as is Constitution Day on May 3. Japan's national anthem is "Kimigayo" ("The Reign of Our Emperor"). At one time the emperor was considered a god, but the constitution of 1946 begins with these words: "The Emperor shall be the symbol of the State and of the unity of the people, deriving his position from the will of the people with whom resides sovereign power." The Emperor of Japan is a ceremonial position which is inherited, but the position carries no governmental powers.

Ask students to assess how much they know about Japan. They can name products we get from Japan and Japanese foods that they may have eaten. Begin lists on the board to which students can add.

This is a good time to explore writing Japanese haiku poetry. Introduce them to examples from the old masters found in such collections as *Cricket Songs* by Harry Behn (Harcourt Brace Jovanovich, 1964). Students can then experiment with this seventeen-syllable verse form: Line 1: 5 syllables, Line 2: 7 syllables, Line 3: 5 syllables.

> Rain dripping slowly
> Soaks thirsty trees and bushes.
> Spring blossoms open.

Black Blues

Three important blues singers were born this month—Ma Rainey, one of the first blues performers; Bessie Smith, a major influence on all subsequent blues singers; and Ella Fitzgerald, a contemporary singer whose repertoire includes the blues. The blues is an important part of American history, particularly of Black American history.

Ask students what the term "the blues" means to them. Discuss the following quote:

> The whites just *startin'* to get the blues
> John Lee Hooker

He's not just talking about blues music. What does he mean?

Bring records of the blues to school to play for students. Try to get early recordings by singers such as Bessie Smith and Billie Holiday as well as current singers like Ray Charles and Aretha Franklin. What are some recurring themes in these songs? Why are most of the blues singers Black?

After students have talked about what makes the blues different, suggest some books about blues people for them to read.

Big Star Fallin' Mama; Five Women in Black Music by Hettie Jones (Viking, 1974). (Includes Ma Rainey, Bessie Smith, Mahalia Jackson, Billie Holiday, and Aretha Franklin)

Ray Charles by Sharon Bell Mathis (Crowell, 1973).

William C. Handy: Father of the Blues by Elizabeth Rider Montgomery (Garrard, 1968).

MAY

1	2	3	4	5	6	7
Loyalty Day Law Day		Golda Meir, 1898– Constitution Day (Japan)		Children's Festival (Japanese) Kapiolani died, 1841, high chiefess of Hawaii Cinco de Mayo	Chinese Exclusion Act passed, 1882 Rudolph Valentino, 1895–1926	Johannes Brahms, 1833–1897 Peter Tchaikovsky, 1840–1893
8	9	10	11	12	13	14
First resolution adopted to expel Chinese from mines Tudeomne County (CA), 1852 V-E Day, 1945	Liberation Day (Czechoslovakia)	Chinese labor helped complete Transcontinental Railroad, Utah, 1869	Constitution Day (Laos) Salvador Dali, 1904–		Joe Louis, 1914–1972 Congress declared war on Mexico, 1846	State of Israel proclaimed, 1948 Gabriel Fahrenheit, 1686–1736
15	16	17	18	19	20	21
Pierre Curie, 1859–1906	William H. Seward, 1801–1872	Supreme Court declared racial segregation in schools unconstitutional, 1954	Hispanic Society of America founded, 1904	Malcolm X, 1925–1965 I Am an American Day	National Day (Cameroon)	Albrecht Durer, 1471–1528
22	23	24	25	26	27	28
Richard Wagner, 1813–1883		Ynes Mexia, 1870–1938, Mexican-American botanical explorer	African Freedom Day Independence Day (Jordan)	Susette LaFlesche Tibbles died, 1903, Omaha Indian rights advocate	Victoria Matthews, 1861–1907, Black author and social worker Independence Day (Afghanistan) Freedom's Constitution Day (Turkey)	
29	30					
John F. Kennedy, 1917–1963	Hernando de Soto landed in Florida, 1589					

What other countries have taken three hundred years or more to achieve, a once dependent territory must try to accomplish in a generation if it is to survive.

Kwame Nkrumah (Ghana)

May Activities

3   Display a picture of Golda Meir. Have students collect articles from the news-
         paper featuring this prominent world leader. Ask if they know she taught school
         in Milwaukee, Wisconsin, where she lived until going to Palestine. Suggest books
         for those interested in learning more about her life such as *Israel's Golda Meir:
         Pioneer to Prime Minister* by Iris Noble (Messner, 1972).

5   Cinco de Mayo marks the victory of Mexican forces over the French at Puebla,
         Mexico, on May 5, 1862. It is celebrated today in Mexican-American communi-
         ties in the United States as the occasion for a fiesta, with a parade, dancing, and
         other activities. Find out whether any festivities are being held in your area. If
         not, you can hold a fiesta in your room. It won't be a fiesta without music,
         dancing, and food. Bring records of Mexican popular music, folk songs, or
         Mexican-Indian music. The music will make anyone want to move and dance.
         Let the students prepare party food such as tortillas, guacamole, or buñelos.

6, 8, 10 Here are several important dates in the history of the Chinese in the United
         States. This month would be a good time to feature the learning module pre-
         sented in Chapter 6, pages 245–268. An amusing but significant comment is at-
         tributed to the Chinese-American philosopher and writer, Lin Yutang: "I have
         a hankering to go back to the Orient and discard my necktie. Neckties strangle
         clear thinking." Discuss the meaning of this quotation.

14   Related to Golda Meir (above) is the founding of the state of Israel. She served
         as the new state's first minister to Moscow in 1948 and later became its prime
         minister, the first woman in the world to hold such a position. Students will be
         interested in learning about the history of Israel. Discuss the establishment of a
         Jewish state, which has been a controversial international issue since World War
         II, when very few countries would take in the great numbers of Jewish refugees.

25   African Freedom Day offers an opportunity to discuss the origins of Afro-
         Americans. Explore such books as:

         Primary
         Bernheim, Marc and Evelyne. *In Africa.* Atheneum, 1973.
         Feelings, Muriel. *Jambo Means Hello; Swahili Alphabet Book.* Dial, 1974.

         Upper Grades
         Murphy, E. Jefferson. *Understanding Africa.* Crowell, 1969.
         Ojigbo, A. Okion. *Young and Black in Africa.* Random House, 1971.
         Students can investigate early African civilizations. Too many books picture
         Africa as a land of barbaric people who were captured and taken to the civilized
         world.

26   Susette LaFlesche is an important spokesperson for Native American rights. Read
         her biography which is included in *American Indian Women* by Marion Gridley
         (Hawthorne, 1974). Another biography is *Susette LaFlesche: Voice of the Omaha
         Indians* by Margaret Crary (Hawthorne, 1973).

JUNE

1	2	3	4	5	6	7
Brigham Young, 1801–1877 First Week, National Flag Week		DeSoto claimed Florida for Spain, 1539 Roland Hayes, 1887–		English colonists massacre Pequot village in Pequot War, 1637 Kaahumanu died, 1832, Hawaiian ruler	Evacuation of Japanese-Americans into concentration camps completed, 1942 Sarah Remond, 1826–1887?, Black lecturer and physician	Gwendolyn Brooks, 1917–, Black poet Paul Gauguin, 1848–1903

8	9	10	11	12	13	14
		Italy became a republic, 1946	Kamehameha Day (Hawaii) Addie W. Hunton, 1875–1943, Black youth group leader	Philippine Independence Day		Hawaii organized as territory, 1900 Harriet Beecher Stowe, 1811–1896

15	16	17	18	19	20	21
Rembrandt, 1606–1669	Flight of Valentina Tereshkova (first woman in space), 1963	Crazy Horse (Sioux) defeated General Crook, Battle of the Rosebud, 1876 Susan LaFlesche Picotte, 1865–1915, Omaha physician	War of 1812 declared against Great Britain, 1812	Statue of Liberty arrived in New York Harbor, 1885	Start of French Revolution, 1789 Announced purchase of Alaska from Russia, 1867	

22	23	24	25	26	27	28
Slavery abolished in Great Britain, 1772	U.S. entered Korean War, 1950 William Penn signed treaty with Indians, 1683	San Juan Day (Puerto Rico)	Crazy Horse (Sioux) defeated Custer—Battle of the Little Bighorn, 1876	Pearl S. Buck, 1892–1973 UN Charter signed, 1945	Paul Dunbar, 1872–1906, Black writer Joseph Smith, Mormon prophet, killed 1844 Charles Parnell, Irish patriot, 1846	World War I began, 1914 Peace Treaty signed, 1919

29	30
First African church in the U.S. (Philadelphia), 1794 Azalia Hackley, 1867–1922, Black singer Jose Rizal, 1861–1896	Zaire established, 1960

We wear the mask that grins and lies,
It hides our cheeks and shades our eyes,—
This debt we pay to human guile;
With torn and bleeding hearts we smile,
And mouth with myriad subtleties.

Paul Laurence Dunbar

June Activities

7   Gwendolyn Brooks received the Nobel Prize for poetry. She also wrote poetry for young people; for example, *Bronzeville Boys and Girls* (Harper & Row, 1956). Read some of these city poems about black children which will appeal to all students. Encourage students to write their own poems about familiar places and events. These can be collected into a class booklet, titled, and distributed to all students.

11   Discover Hawaii, the fiftieth state, with your students. One of the attractions of the fiftieth state is its multicultural, multilingual heritage. Investigate the history of Hawaii. How and when did it become a state? People from many different countries are represented in Hawaii. What are some of them? Are there native Hawaiians?

Ask students to find examples of unusual words used in Hawaii, for example, words for different foods. Here are a few words used commonly in Hawaii:

ae	(eye)	yes
aloha	(ah *loh* hah)	greetings
hale	(*hah* lay)	house
haole	(*how* lay)	foreigner (white person)
hula	(*hoo* lah)	dance
kamaaiana	(*kah* mah *ai* nah)	oldtimer
kane	(*kah* neh)	man
kaukau	(*kow* kow)	food
keiki	(*kay* kee)	child
lani	(*lah* nee)	sky
lei	(lay)	wreath
luau	(loo ah oo)	feast
mahalo	(mah *hah* loh)	thanks
malihini	(*may* lee *hee* nee)	newcomer
mauna	(*mou* nah)	mountain
moana	(moh *ah* nah)	ocean
nani	(*nah* nee)	beautiful
ohana	(oh *hah* nah)	family
pehea oe	(pay *hay* ah *oy*)	How are you?
wahine	(wha *hee* nay)	woman

20   Investigate Alaska, the forty-ninth state. Only a few hundred thousand people (328,000 in 1975) inhabit this huge territory. Who are they? Read about Alaska in such books as *Julie of the Wolves* by Jean George (Harper & Row, 1972), the story of an Eskimo girl.

Alaska's flag was designed by Benny Benson, a thirteen-year-old schoolboy. The flag is deep blue with seven gold stars, which represent the gold found in Alaska and form the Big Dipper. The eighth star is, of course, the North Star, which symbolizes Alaska's northern location close to the North Pole.

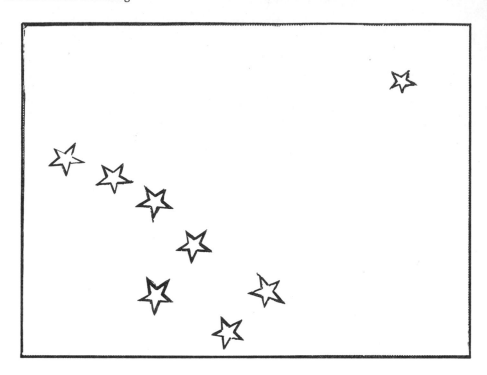

Alaska's song is "Alaska's Flag," which describes the flag and what it stands for. Sing or speak the words by Marie Drake:

> Eight stars of gold on a field of blue—
> Alaska's flag. May it mean to you
> The blue of the sea, the evening sky,
> The mountain lakes, and the flow'rs nearby;
> The gold of the early sourdough's dreams,
> The precious gold of the hills and streams;
> The brilliant stars in the northern sky,
> The "Bear"—the "Dipper"—and, shining high,
> The great North Star with its steady light,
> Over land and sea a beacon bright.
> Alaska's flag—to Alaskans dear,
> The simple flag of a last frontier.

Variable Dates

Listed here are holidays or events that fall on different dates each year. Add them to the appropriate months. Note also that many holidays are being celebrated on a Monday or Friday to provide a holiday weekend.

United States Holidays or Special Days

Mother's Day	2nd Sunday in May
Armed Forces Day	3rd Saturday in May
Memorial Day	last Monday in May
Father's Day	3rd Sunday in June
Labor Day	1st Monday in September
Election Day	1st Tuesday after 1st Monday in November
Veteran's Day	4th Monday in October
Thanksgiving Day	4th Thursday in November

Jewish Feasts and Festivals

Because the Jewish calendar (described in the next section) is different from the school calendar used in this country, the dates of Jewish holidays vary each year. The following chart gives the names and dates for the holidays by year and shows the corresponding Jewish calendar year under Rosh Hashanah, when the new year begins. Note that each holiday actually begins at sunset on the preceding day.

Year	Purim (Feast of Lots)	Passover (Festival of Freedom)	Shevuos (Feast of Weeks)	Rosh Hashanah (New Year)	Yom Kippur (Day of Atonement)	Succos (Feast of Tabernacles)	Hanukkah (Feast of Dedication)
1977	Mar. 4	April 3	May 23	Sept. 13 5738	Sept. 22	Sept. 27	Dec. 5
1978	Mar. 23	April 22	June 11	Oct. 2 5739	Oct. 11	Oct. 16	Dec. 25
1979	Mar. 13	April 12	June 1	Sept. 22 5740	Oct. 1	Oct. 6	Dec. 15
1980	Mar. 2	April 1	May 21	Sept. 11 5741	Sept. 20	Sept. 25	Dec. 3
1981	Mar. 20	April 19	June 8	Sept. 29 5742	Oct. 8	Oct. 13	Dec. 21
1982	Mar. 9	April 8	May 28	Sept. 18 5743	Sept. 27	Oct. 2	Dec. 11
1983	Feb. 27	Mar. 29	May 18	Sept. 8 5744	Sept. 17	Sept. 22	Dec. 1
1984	Mar. 18	April 17	June 6	Sept. 27 5745	Oct. 6	Oct. 11	Dec. 19
1985 ©	Mar. 7	April 6	May 26	Sept. 16 5746	Sept. 25	Sept. 30	Dec. 8

July Activities

1, 3   Recognize Canada on Dominion Day. Display its symbol, the maple leaf, with pictures of Canada from travel folders. (See pages 240–245 for ideas specific to Quebec.) Sing the song "The Maple Leaf Forever." Included here is the chorus of this song:

JULY

1	2	3	4	5	6	7
Dominion Day (Canada) Independence Day (Burundi) Independence Day (Rwanda)	Thurgood Marshall, 1908–	Champlain founded Quebec, 1608	Edmonia Lewis, 1845–?, Black-Cherokee sculptor Lucy Slowe, 1885–1937, Black teacher and administrator Giuseppe Garibaldi, 1807–1882	Independence Day (Venezuela), 1811	Independence Day (Malawi)	
8	**9** Independence Day (Argentina), 1816	**10** Mary McLeod Bethune, 1875–1955	**11**	**12**	**13**	**14** **Bastille Day** (France), 1789
15 Maggie Walker, 1867–1934, Black insurance & Banking executive	**16** Ida Barnett-Wells, 1862–1931, Black journalist and civic leader Mary Baker Eddy, 1821–1910, Founder, Christian Science	**17** Spain transferred Florida to U.S., 1821	**18** Miguel Hidalgo, 1753–1811, Father of Mexican independence	**19** Alice Dunbar Nelson, 1875–1935, Black author, teacher	**20**	**21** Independence Day (Belgium)
22	**23**	**24** Simon Bolívar, 1783–1830 Mormons settled Salt Lake City, 1847	**25** Puerto Rico became Commonwealth, 1952	**26** Netherlands Independence, 1581	**27** Korean War ended, 1953	**28** Independence Day (Peru) through 29, 1821
29	**30**	**31** Sarah Garnet, 1831–1911, Black educator and civic worker				

The drums of Africa still beat in my heart. They will not let me rest while there is a single Negro boy or girl without a chance to prove his worth.

Mary McLeod Bethune

The Maple Leaf Forever

Chorus   Alexander Muir

The   Ma- ple   Leaf   our   em- blem   dear

The   Ma- ple   Leaf   for-   ev-   er,

God   save   our   King   and   Heav-en   bless

The   Ma- ple   Leaf   for-   ev-   er.

4   Independence Day for the United States can be recognized in many ways. Prepare a program that includes songs such as "America," "The Star-spangled Banner," "America the Beautiful," and "Columbia, the Gem of the Ocean." Students can read some of the great poetic prose written by the patriots who drew up the Constitution as well as such eloquent words as those of Lincoln in "The Gettysburg Address":

Four score and seven years ago our fathers brought forth on this continent, a new nation, conceived in liberty, and dedicated to the proposition that all men are created equal.

Now we are engaged in a great civil war, testing whether that nation, or any nation so conceived and so dedicated, can long endure. We are met on a great battlefield of that war. We have come to dedicate a portion of that field, as a final resting place for those who here gave their lives that that nation might live. It is altogether fitting and proper that we should do this.

But, in a larger sense, we can not dedicate—we can not consecrate—we can not hallow—this ground. The brave men, living and dead, who struggled here, have consecrated it, far above our poor power to add or detract. The world will little note, nor long remember, what we say here, but it can never forget what they did here. It is for us the living, rather, to be dedicated here to the unfinished work which they who fought here have thus far so nobly advanced. It is rather for us to be here dedicated to the great task remaining before us—that from these honored dead we take increased devotion to that cause for which they gave the last full measure of devotion—that we here highly resolve that these dead shall not have died in vain—that this nation, under God, shall have a new birth of freedom—and that government of the people, by the people, and for the people, shall not perish from the earth.

10   Who was Mary McLeod Bethune? The featured quote by her suggests her concern with education. Challenge students to find out about her life and achievements. Suggest biographies and other sources of information such as *She Wanted to Read; The Story of Mary McLeod Bethune* by Ella Kaiser Carruth (Abingdon, 1966).

Discuss significant aspects of the struggle for education for Blacks as you discuss Mary Bethune. Do students know that it was illegal to teach slaves to read and write? Do they know that schools were completely segregated for a long time with the Black schools considerably poorer and inferior compared to the white schools?

14   Students can learn "La Marseillaise" for Bastille Day, celebrating the liberation of prisoners from the hated Bastille (prison) during the French Revolution. See the music on the following pages.

LA MARSEILLAISE

A la Marcia.   ROUGET DE LISLE.

16   Disease is an experience of so-called mortal mind. It is fear made manifest on the body.

Mary Baker Eddy

Mary Baker Eddy founded the religion of Christian Science. Are there any Christian Scientists in the class? What do students know about Christian Science? One of the unusual aspects of this religion is its treatment of disease. Discuss the quote with the class. What are some implications of this statement for disease and for medicine?

August Activities

2   The fear I heard in my father's voice . . . when he realized that I really *believed* I could do anything a white boy could do, and had every intention of proving it, was not at all like the fear I heard when one of us was ill or had fallen down the stairs or strayed too far from the house. It was another fear, a fear that the child, in challenging the white world's assumptions, was putting himself in the path of destruction.

James Baldwin

James Baldwin grew up in Harlem (New York) and became a writer but had to leave this country in order to develop his writing abilities. He settled in Paris, as had other Black American exiles. What do the quotes indicate about Baldwin's opinion of the position of Blacks in American society? Why would someone like Baldwin leave the United States? What does "going into exile" mean?

7   I was offered the ambassadorship of Liberia once, when that post was earmarked for a Negro. I told them I wouldn't take a Jim Crow job.

Ralph Bunche

Discuss this comment with students. Ralph Bunche was a famous black diplomat. Ask students whether they know what a "Jim Crow job" is. Can they guess? Why would the ambassador to Liberia be expected to be Black? What would it feel like to go to Africa, after being treated as an inferior in this country, and find people like yourself in positions of power?

12   Who were the Aztecs and why did the Spanish conquer them? Pose such questions to the students and have them search for the answers. The Aztec civilization is particularly interesting because it was so advanced and yet we know very little about it because the Spanish destroyed most of the records. Investigate the Spanish treatment of the Aztecs and compare it to the way the English settlers treated the Indian groups they met.

Have students research the Aztec calendar. The Aztecs were excellent astronomers and developed a calendar that was more accurate than the one the Spaniards used; yet they had not discovered the wheel. Prepare a display featuring the accomplishments of the Aztecs. Obtain pictures of the pyramids and Aztec cities. Show the Aztec circular calendar.

Students who are fascinated by pyramids might work cooperatively to make a sand table model of a pyramid. This can stimulate extensive research on the Aztecs and make this ancient civilization come alike for all students.

AUGUST

1	2	3	4	5	6	7
	James Baldwin, 1924–			Independence Day (Bolivia) thru 7th	U.S. bombed Hiroshima, Japan, 1945	Ralph Bunche, 1904–
8 U.S. bombed Nagasaki, Japan, 1945 Roberto Clemente, 1934–1973	**9** Janie Porter Barrett, 1865–1948, Black social welfare leader	**10**	**11** U.S. annexed Hawaii	**12**	**13** Spanish conquered Aztecs, 1521	**14** Japan surrendered, World War II, 1945
15	**16**	**17** Charlotte Forten (Grimke), 1837–1914, Black teacher and author Independence Day (Gabon, Indonesia)	**18**	**19** Mammy Pleasant, 1814–1904, Black California pioneer	**20** Bernardo O'Higgins, Chilean patriot, 1778	**21**
22	**23**	**24** Lucy Moten died, 1933, Black educator	**25** Independence Day (Uruguay)	**26**	**27** Rose McClendon, 1884–1936, Black actress	**28**
29	**30**	**31** Josephine Ruffin, 1842–1924, Black leader				

The wonder is not that so many Negro boys and girls are ruined but that so many survive.

James Baldwin

EXPLORING CALENDARS AND CULTURES

Calendars themselves are interesting cultural phenomena. Many children may assume that the calendar they use daily has always been the way it now is. They will be interested in learning the historical development of the calendar as well as the fact that there are still ongoing efforts for calendar reform. They can discover, even within their own classroom, information about other calendars that are still being used for different purposes, for example, the Jewish, Muslim, and Chinese calendars.

Marking Time in Different Cultures

As we begin an exploration of calendars, we might first discuss ideas about marking time in general. Students may be surprised to find that not every culture has the same concept of day, for example, that we do. We accept the concepts of day, hour, minute, and second as well as week, month, and year with little question. Let us examine a few ideas that you might discuss as examples of varied ways of considering time within different cultures.

What is a day? Our idea of day is a 24-hour period that includes both light and darkness. Is it not strange that we count a day from the middle of a night to the middle of the next night? In some cultures there is no word that means just that. Many primitive cultures recognized a single event such as dawn, the rising of the sun, and spoke of so many dawns or suns. Other cultures used the night and spoke of "sleeps." Gradually the light period was broken up with terms related to the sun: daybreak, sunrise, noon, afternoon, twilight, and sunset. The crowing of cocks, the yoking of oxen, and siesta are other examples of ways of marking the time of day. For some peoples day began with dawn, but, for example, in Israel it begins in the evening. Dividing the day into hours is a modern concept brought about by industrialization.

Beginning the day at midnight and having two sets of times designated one to twelve are arbitrary decisions that are not always followed. Many students will have heard of 24-hour clocks which are used in many countries and in some cases, such as military organizations, in the United States. They might not know, however, that astronomers begin their day with twelve noon in order to use the same date for observations made at night.

Our determination of months and weeks is also an arbitrary decision. Months roughly correspond to the cycle of the moon, which is 29½ days. Early societies noted the phases of the moon and used them as measures of time from new moon to full moon. The moon is still the basis for some calendars as we will discuss in the next section. Today, we use a calendar that divides the year into months of 30–31 days to fit the solar year so the phases of the moon occur at different times of the various months.

The seven-day week is another interesting phenomenon that began when people who were trading needed some regular arrangement. The week, as the interval between trading or market days, has varied from four to ten days. It is thought that the selection of seven days as the "magical" number does, indeed, have something to do with the significance of the number *seven*. This hypothesis is supported by our use of the names of gods and goddesses to name the days of the week, thus:

Latin Name	French Name	Saxon Name	English Name
Dies Solis	Dimanche	Sun's day	Sunday
Dies Lunae	Lundi	Moon's day	Monday
Dies Martis	Mardi	Tiw's day	Tuesday
Dies Mercurii	Mercredi	Woden's day	Wednesday
Dies Jovis	Jeudi	Thor's day	Thursday
Dies Veneris	Vendredi	Frigg's day	Friday
Dies Saturni	Samedi	Seterne's day	Saturday

The Saxon names which reflect Norse mythology are carried into our English names. In the French and Latin names which are related, you can find Mars, Mercury, Venus, and Jupiter (Jove).

Although we now take for granted the knowledge of astronomy on which we base our year, this concept of year is a relatively new idea. Gradually, primitive peoples found a need for longer designations of time than market days or lunar months. This need was chiefly to count the ages of people and to compare these ages. Some of the following measures were used:

> family generations
> momentous events—plague, famine, war
> reign of monarchs or chiefs
> cycle of seasons
>> monsoons
>> wet and dry periods (rains)
>> summer and winter (summers, snows)
>> agricultural changes
>> animal migration

Folklore provides a wealth of information related to these concepts of time. Encourage students to search out such ideas. They might begin with expressions or beliefs related to time; for example, Friday is a bad day, and Friday the thirteenth is the worst of all days! Students might pursue the study of cultural beliefs and superstitions in such books as *Cross Your Fingers, Spit in Your Hat* by Alvin Schwartz (Lippincott, 1974).

How Calendars Developed

Encourage students to investigate the history of calendars. They can learn, for example, the origins of the word which goes back to the Latin "calendarium" which means account book. Calendars are associated, therefore, with the payment of debts, marking times when payments were due. A calendar, as generally used, is a system for recording the passage of time. Congress, for instance, has a calendar or schedule of events.

Before we had formal ways of measuring time, humans marked time by observing the rising and setting of the sun, the different phases of the moon, and the passage of the seasons. The first calendars, created by the Babylonians, were based on moons (months), the periods of time when the moon completed its full cycle of phases. Twelve moons make a 354-day year. When it was observed that every four years the year needed an adjustment to make the calendar fit the seasons, the Babylonians added another moon or month. This calendar was adapted by the Egyptians, Semites, and Greeks.

The Egyptians modified this calendar by basing their calculations on the regular rising of the Nile River which occurred each year just after Sirius, the Dog Star, appeared. They developed a calendar that more nearly matched the solar year, using 365 days, which was still a little off from the 365¼ days we now consider accurate. Considering that they created this system more than 4000 years B.C., however, they were amazingly exact. They worked with 12 months of 30 days each and simply added 5 days at the end of the year.

The Roman calendar, introduced by Romulus around 700 B.C., was derived from that used in Greece. The Romans had ten months: Martius, Aprilis, Maius, Junius, Quintilis, Sextilis, September, October, November, and December. The names of the last six months correspond to the Latin number names—five, six, seven, eight, nine, and ten. One king, who wanted to collect more taxes, added two more months, Januarius and Februarius. Needless to say, the calendar soon became very confused and did not correspond with the solar year.

Then came the Julian Calendar which Julius Caesar created in 46 B.C. to correct the inaccuracy of the Roman Calendar. He divided the year into 12 months of 30 and 31 days except for February which he gave 29 days plus one every fourth year, so his year was a few minutes longer than the solar year. He changed the beginning of the year to January 1st instead of March 1st and changed the month of Sextilis to August, named after Emperor Augustus. The month Quintilis was changed to Julius in honor of Caesar. Thus, we have the origins of our names for the twelve months. The Julian Calendar was used for more than 1500 years. The Gregorian Calendar was created to correct the error in the Julian Calendar which had become ten days off in 1580. The Gregorian Calendar was gradually adopted until it has become standard throughout much of the world.

Students might like to investigate further efforts to reform the calendar. The Thirteen-Month Calendar would contain thirteen months of equal length. The Perpetual Calendar is another fascinating topic to explore.

The Christian Calendar

The calendar that Christians use is the Gregorian Calendar which was developed by Pope Gregory around 1580. Students may know the old verse that helps them remember the number of days in each month according to this calendar:

Thirty days has September,
April, June, and November.
All the rest have thirty-one
Except February alone
Which has twenty-eight
Until Leap Year gives it one day more.

This Christian Calendar is based on the year Jesus Christ was born. Dates before his birth are marked as B.C. (before Christ). Dates after his birth are marked as A.D. (*anno Domini*—in the year of our Lord). Non-Christians sometimes use the markings B.C.E. (before the Christian era) and C.E. (Christian era). On this Christian calendar there are certain fixed dates such as Christmas. Movable feast days include Easter and Thanksgiving.

Christian Holidays

	Ash Wednesday	Easter Sunday
1977	February 23	April 10
1978	February 8	March 26
1979	February 28	April 15
1980	February 20	April 6
1981	March 4	April 19
1982	February 24	April 11
1983	February 16	April 3
1984	March 7	April 22
1985	February 20	April 7

Easter falls on the first Sunday following the arbitrary Paschal Full Moon, which does not necessarily coincide with a real or astronomical full moon. The Paschal Full Moon is calculated by adding 1 to the remainder obtained by dividing the year by 19 and applying the following:

1—April 14	6—April 18	11—March 25	16—March 30
2—April 3	7—April 8	12—April 13	17—April 17
3—March 23	8—March 28	13—April 2	18—April 7
4—April 11	9—April 16	14—March 22	19—March 27
5—March 31	10—April 5	15—April 10	

Thus, for the year 2000 the key is 6 or April 18. Since April 18th in the year 2000 is a Tuesday, Easter Sunday is April 23rd. *Caution*—If the Paschal Full Moon falls on a Sunday, Easter is the following Sunday. The earliest Easter can fall is March 23rd and the latest is April 25th.

Lent begins on Ash Wednesday which comes 40 days before Easter, excluding Sundays.

The Hebrew Calendar

Another calendar that is still widely used today is the Hebrew, or Jewish, Calendar, based on the Creation, which preceded the birth of Christ by 3760 years and 3 months. The Hebrew year begins in September rather than January. From the fall of 1980 to the fall of 1981, therefore, the Hebrew year will be 5741.

Based on the moon, the Hebrew year usually contains 12 months. Periodically, an extra month is inserted to adjust this calendar, as shown here:

Months in the Hebrew Calendar	Important Dates
Tishri	1–2 Rosh Hashanah (New Year)
Heshvan	10 Yom Kippur (Day of Atonement)
Kislev	25 Hanukkah (Feast of Dedication)
Tebet	2 or 3 Hanukkah ends
Shebat	
Adar	14–15 Purim (Feast of Lots)
(Veadar)	
Nisan	15–22 Pesach (Passover)
Iyar	5 Israel Independence Day
Sivan	6–7 Shabuoth (Pentecost)
Tammuz	
Ab	
Elul	

The Islamic Calendar

Also based on the moon, the Islamic or Muslim Calendar dates from Mohammed's flight from Mecca, called the Hegira, which took place in A.D. 622. The year has only 354 days so that its New Year moves with respect to the seasons. It makes a full cycle every 32½ years. The names of the Islamic months are:

Muharram	Rajab
Safar	Shaban
Rabi I	Ramadan
Rabi II	Shawwal
Jumada I	Zulkadah
Jumada II	Zulhijjah

Clarify terminology for students who may be confused as they read news reports from the Near East. The word *Moslem* comes from an Arabic word *muslim* which means "one who submits" (to Allah or God). The words are used interchangeably. Arabic is the language spoken by the majority of Muslims or Moslems, and Islam is the chief religion. (In the United States many Muslims follow the Christian religion.) The mosque with its minarets is the typical house of worship.

Other Calendars of the World

Students who are interested in calendars can research other systems that have been developed. The Chinese Calendar, consisting of a twelve-year cycle based on Jupiter's positions in relationship to the constellations, is discussed on page 252. Other calendars that students can investigate include Hindu, Assyrian, Greek, and Maya.

Sources of Information on Important Asians

Chinn, Thomas, ed. *A History of the Chinese in California. A Syllabus.* Chinese Historical Society of America, 1969.

Hosokawa, Bill. *Nisei: The Quiet Americans.* Morrow, 1969.

Kitano, Harry. *Japanese Americans.* Prentice-Hall, 1969.

Ritter, E., Ritter, H., and Spector, S. *Our Oriental Americans.* McGraw-Hill, 1965.

Sources of Information on Important Native Americans

Gridley, Marion, ed. *Indians of Today.* Towerton Press, 1960.

Hoffman, Virginia, and Johnson, Broderick. *Navajo Biographies.* Rough Rock, Arizona, Dine, and the Board of Education, the Navajo Curriculum Center, 1970.

Josephy, Alvin M., Jr., ed. *The American Heritage Book of Indians.* American Heritage, 1961.

Klein, Bernard, and Icolari, Daniel, eds. *Encyclopedia of the American Indians.* B. Klein, 1967.

United States Department of the Interior. Bureau of Indian Affairs. *Famous Indians: A Collection of Short Biographies.* Government Printing Office, 1966.

United States Department of the Interior. Bureau of Indian Affairs. *Indians of the Northwest.* Government Printing Office, 1968. *You Asked About Prominent American Indians.* 1969. *American Indian Calendar.* 1977.

Sources of Information on Important Blacks

Adams, Russell. *Great Negroes Past and Present.* Afro-Am Publishing Co., 1964.

Bennett, Lerone. *Before the Mayflower: A History of Black America.* Johnson Publishing Co., 1966.

Bergman, Peter. *The Chronological History of the Negro in America.* New American Library, 1969.

Calendar of Great Blacks. Progressive Black Associates, 1969.

Davis, John, ed. *American Negro Reference Book.* Prentice-Hall, 1966.

Haskins, James. *A Piece of the Power; Four Black Mayors.* Dial, 1972.

Hayden, Robert C. *Eight Black American Inventors.* Addison-Wesley, 1972.

Meier, August, and Rudnick, Elliott, eds. *The Origins of Black Americans.* Atheneum, 1969.

Metcalf, George. *Black Profiles.* McGraw-Hill, 1968.

Ploski, Harry and Roscoe Brown, eds. *Negro Almanac.* Bellwether, 1967.

Rollins, Charlemae. *They Showed the Way: Forty American Negroes.* Thomas Crowell, 1965.

Schraff, A. E. *Black Courage.* Macrae Smith, 1969.

Wesley, Charles H., ed. *International Library of Negro Life and History.* The Association for the Study of Negro Life and History. Publishers Co., 1969.

Young, Margaret B. *Black American Leaders.* Watts, 1969.

Sources of Information on Important Mexican Americans

Acuna, Rudolph. *The Story of the Mexican Americans: The Men and the Land.* American Book Co., 1969.

Forbes, Jack. *Mexican-Americans, a Handbook for Educators.* Far West Lab for Educational Research, Berkeley, 1966.

McWilliams, Carey. *North from Mexico: The Spanish-Speaking People of the United States.* Greenwood Press, Westport, 1968.

Nava, Julian. *Mexican Americans: Past, Present and Future.* American Book Co., 1969.

Palacios, Arturo, ed. *The Mexican-American Directory.* Executive Systems Corp., Washington, 1969.

Rivera, Feliciano. *A Mexican American Source Book with Study Guide Outline.* Educational Consulting Associates, Menlo Park, 1970.

6

Creating Teaching Materials for Multicultural Approaches

*It is the supreme art of the teacher to awaken joy
in creative expression and knowledge.*

Albert Einstein

The resourceful teacher can prepare many effective teaching materials to promote multicultural understandings. The advantage of teacher-created materials is that they are specific to your own classroom needs in terms of content presented and ability levels of the students with whom you are working. If you are creating your own materials, too, you will often find that you can involve the children in your classroom in the actual production of learning centers, an additional valuable learning experience.

Materials you create can be used in different types of classroom organization. Activities can be planned for a whole class. Other activities may be designed for interaction in small groups. Many activities will be suitable for a learning center approach where children can work individually or in small groups.

In this chapter you will learn how to:

1. organize a learning center around a specific key issue or group of people
2. develop sets of task cards designed to teach specific understandings or skills
3. create a learning module focused on a single topic

ORGANIZING A LEARNING CENTER

A learning center is a portion of the classroom, large or small, devoted to the study of a specific topic or set of skills. You might have, for example, a language center, a United Nations center, a center for the study of Native Americans, or a center for the study of prejudice. Here are collected books, pictures, and other items related to the center of focus. Here, too, are placed teaching materials and equipment to aid students working in the center as they engage in varied learning experiences.

How to Develop a Center

Plan with your students. First, decide what kind of center is needed. This depends, of course, on the focus of study in your classroom. Give the center a name which can be printed on a large sign to place above the space allocated for this learning center. You may have several centers operating at any one time.

Use your ingenuity in creating a suitable place to focus activities. A reading table can be used to collect materials together. You may have students construct a kind of cubicle, as shown here.

The bottom and sides of a large carton form the back of this center which is placed on a table; varied shapes and sizes of tables are appropriate. This center focuses on Americans from Scandinavia. Feature any kinds of information pertinent to the study.

A corner of the room is easily transformed into a center focusing on Alaska. In this case you might include a map of Alaska, the number of people living in Alaska, and other information. See the ideas beginning on page 213 for more ways to develop a center focusing on this idea.

A Cozy Corner

Invite students to participate in collecting all kinds of pertinent information and materials that might be useful—clothing, postal cards, magazine articles. Brainstorm possible activities, people to contact, places to visit as you develop the study together. Provide paper, pencils and other materials that may be needed as students engage in work at the center. Depending on the type of study being developed, you might consider the following materials and equipment for the center:

tape or cassette recorders
typewriter
stapler
scissors
rulers
various papers
   lined and unlined
   drawing paper
   colored construction paper
   cardboards
   posterboard
   corrugated cardboard for construction

In addition to pictures and information displayed to make the center attractive and inviting, there will be a variety of activities. Planned activities should range from easy to more difficult as well as involve using varied skills—listening, speaking, reading, and writing. Included, too, can be activities that draw from different subject areas and those that stimulate student creativity in music and art. In the following sections of this chapter we will explain how to produce two useful kinds of teaching materials for the learning center—the task card and the learning module.

How to Use the Learning Center

After you and your students have created one or more learning centers, you need to talk about using them. Discuss how many students can work at each center at any one time. The number of seats provided is a good way to indicate how many can work at a center. As a seat is vacated, someone else may come to the center. Students may need to sign up for a particular center.

A good way to begin work at learning centers is to post a schedule so each student has a specific assignment for the day. You can prepare the schedule for a week, two weeks, or a month, depending on how long the study will take and how many centers are available. Working in the library could be one center activity that would accommodate a number of students. Your schedule might look like this for ten days.

Name	M	T	W	TH	F	M	T	W	TH	F
Felipe	1	1	2	2	L	3	3	4	4	L
James	1	1	2	2	L	3	3	4	4	L
Julia	1	1	2	2	L	3	3	4	4	L
Sandra	2	2	L	3	3	4	4	L	1	1
Hope	2	2	L	3	3	4	4	L	1	1
Harold	2	2	L	3	3	4	4	L	1	1
Marisa	3	3	4	4	L	1	1	2	2	L

Enlarging specific centers to provide more activities and seating space will permit additional students to participate. Sometimes, activities can be completed at the student's desk. Adding other learning centers also expands the capacity.

Keeping track of materials at each center is another important part of planning. Here are several tips that may help you.

1. Package all the parts of a game in one large envelope. Label the envelope in big print, thus:

2. Color code everything that belongs at one center. If the center on France is blue, then mark games, task cards, modules, etc., with a blue felt pen. Students soon learn to replace task cards or games at the appropriate center.
3. Hang activities in envelopes or plastic bags on the wall where they are visible. Pegboard is ideal for this purpose, but you can improvise with cork bulletin boards, or strips of wood in which hooks can be placed. If you have

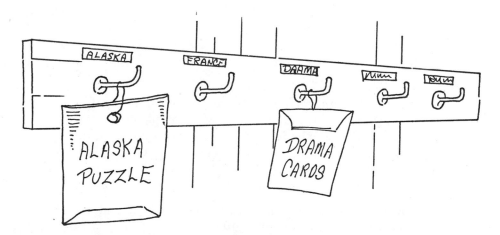

a specially marked hook for each item, you can quickly tell when something is missing at the end of the day.

Whenever there are problems regarding classroom operations, have a class meeting to thresh out the problems and possible solutions. If students decide on the solution, their decision is more likely to carry **weight**, and they will enforce it, not you!

The teacher role in working with learning centers is to help students organize toward a goal and specific objectives. The teacher facilitates and guides the learning experiences and serves as a resource, a person to be consulted when help is needed. The teacher guides the students in assessing their own growth and what they have learned as well as checking their own work. Avoid playing the undesirable role of corrector or grader. Use your talents and expertise rather to respond to student needs, to plan strategies for stimulating further learning, and to explore new resources and materials that come your way.

DEVELOPING TASK CARDS

The task card is one of the most useful and versatile forms of presenting learning activities. Especially appropriate for the learning center and individualized instruction described in the preceding section, task cards can also be used in conjunction with whole class presentations.

Developing sets of cards is well worth the time invested, for the cards can be used repeatedly and in various ways as we will point out. In this section we will suggest ways of working with task cards under the following topics:

How to Make Task Cards
Cards for Multicultural Experiences
Cards for a Specific Learning Center:
    Americans with French Origins

How to Make Task Cards

Task cards are sometimes called job cards or activity cards. They come in various sizes from small ones about 3″ × 5″ to large cards that are 8½″ × 11″ in size. The size you choose depends on the age of the students who will use the cards (young children can handle large cards more easily). It also depends on your instructional purpose.

Making Small Cards. Small cards are excellent for *idea files* to which students refer individually. On the next page, for example, is a set of cards designed for a file called Choice. The ideas on these cards stimulate creativity as well as developing understandings about different people of the world. In addition, you might use small cards for sets focusing on:

Acting Out

On each card a problem situation is described that calls for role playing. Activities could be for small groups.

Books to Read

Each card lists the title and author of a book as well as a short synopsis of the story. Students use this file as they are searching for a book to read about Mexico, living in New York City, or any other topic you want to include.

Have students themselves develop these sets of cards. If you prepare just a few to show them the kinds of ideas they can include, they will soon generate a useful set. Each person can prepare a card, for example, about the book he or she has read. This activity serves a dual purpose—the students have a purpose for reading and they create a set of cards about books other students will find interesting. Preparing *acting out situations* gives students a purpose for writing a short paragraph. Then the students use the set of cards for further educational experience.

Sets of cards can be made easily with purchased, unlined file cards. Either 3″ × 5″ cards or 4″ × 6″ cards are good for this purpose.

CHOICE!

PAINT A PICTURE

of your idea of
The Ideal American

-    Man? Woman?
         Black? Yellow? White? Brown?
         Old? Young?
             Who will it be?

MAKE A COLLAGE

about a group of people in the United States

Native Americans	Women
City Dwellers	Black Americans
Aged Men and Women	Children
Workers	Drivers

Clip words and pictures to picture this group. Glue everything on a large piece of cardboard at least 18″ × 24″ in size.

WRITE A POEM

about something important to you—love, music, sister, time, food, flying

Follow this pattern:

Line 1: 1 word—the subject
Line 2: 2 words—describe the subject
Line 3: 3 words—express a feeling
Line 4: 4 words—describe an action
Line 5: 1 word—refer to the subject

Making Large Cards. Large cards are usually constructed of sturdy poster board so they are stiff and durable. These cards are used to present an activity that one or more students will undertake at different times. Directions must be clear if students are to work independently in an individualized approach.

Accompanying this is a task card for upper-grade students that focuses on the money used in various countries. The names of the coins or bills are given as well as their worth compared to the U.S. dollar based on January 1977 figures. On the other side of the card (page 237), students are directed to work with this informative chart. They are directed, for example, to check the newspaper to see whether the comparative values have changed (figures are posted daily in the business section). This kind of activity encourages reading, involves students in mathematics activities, and provides information about life in other countries. It is a worthwhile activity that provides valuable learning experience.

MONEY FROM OTHER COUNTRIES

Country	Currency	Worth in dollars*
Argentina	peso	.0040
Australia	dollar	1.0925
Austria	schilling	.0605
Belgium	franc	.0276
Britain	pound	1.7100
Canada	dollar	0.9972
Chile	peso	.0750
Colombia	peso	.0300
Denmark	krone	.1720
Ecuador	sucre	.0400
France	franc	.2015
Holland	guilder	.4048
Hong Kong	dollar	.2150
Israel	pound	.1185
Italy	lira	.0011
Japan	yen	.0034
Mexico	peso	.0525
Norway	krone	.1928
Peru	sol	.0155
Portugal	escudo	.0320
South Africa	rand	1.1530
Spain	peseta	.0147
Sweden	krone	.2415
Switzerland	franc	.4060
Uruguay	peso	.2650
Venezuela	bolivar	.2335
W. Germany	deutschmark	.4230

* January 1977.

When material is prepared for your use like this, you can simply copy the material presented. The information about currencies can be typed. Use a primary typewriter if it is available to facilitate reading. Directions can also be typed. If they are short, however, printing with a felt pen is effective. Throughout this book you will find informative material and activities that can be presented in a similar fashion on task cards.

Make these cards more durable by covering them with clear contact paper. They can also be laminated if you have access to a laminating machine. This kind of coating makes it possible to have students write on a card with a grease pencil which can later be wiped off.

MONEY AROUND THE WORLD

Have you ever heard of a guilder?

> In which country would you find this coin? (Look at the chart on the other side of this card.)
> How much is a guilder worth compared to our dollar?

Do other countries use dollars besides the United States?

> Which countries use dollars?
> Are these "dollars" worth the same amount?
> Which "dollar" is worth the most?

Every day this list of currencies appears in the newspaper. See if you can find it in the financial or business section. Compare the values for each coin to see how it has changed since this list was published in January, 1977.

> Why might values of coins or bills go up or down?
> See if you can find information about what determines the value of a piece of currency.

Pretend you are traveling to several different countries. As you enter each country, you exchange $10.00 for the currency of that country.

> How many pesos would you get in Mexico?
> How many francs would you get in France?
> How many pounds would you get in Great Britain?
> How many rands would you get in South Africa?

Find pictures of some of these coins. Perhaps someone you know has money from different countries.

Task Cards for Primary Children

Suggestions throughout this book can be adapted for various levels. Here are sample ideas adapted specifically for primary grades.

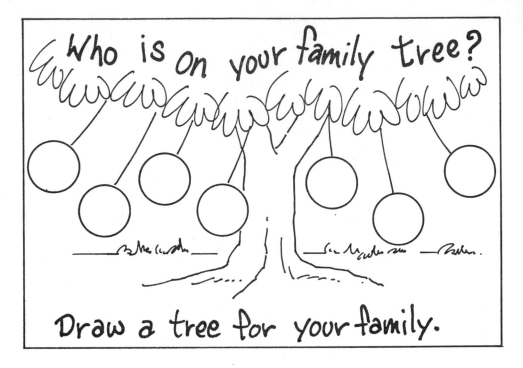

Who is on your family tree?

Draw a tree for your family.

Who lives here?

a city apartment

a farmhouse

a suburban home

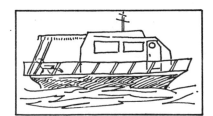

a houseboat

PEOPLE IN THE CITY

Old people, young people;
Red and white,
Black and yellow;
People everywhere.

All kinds of people live in the city. Draw three people you might see on a city sidewalk.

Cards for a Specific Learning Center: Focusing on French Origins

French Canadians and Americans with French backgrounds will be interested in a learning center that focuses attention on the French language and France as the country of origin. Such a study should also be of interest to students who know nothing about France, the French language, or French Canada (Québec).

Create a Center

Several varieties of learning centers are shown in this chapter and elsewhere in this book. The one shown here, therefore, is only one possibility. It can be quickly set up and put into use. Use a reading table, the bigger the better. Create a display like the one shown that focuses on whatever aspect of this study you wish to emphasize: for example, Traveling in Québec, Flying to France!, Parlez-Vous Français? For an attractive display, consider using some of the following: a map of the area, pictures, postcards, items from the newspaper. Students can add to the display as the study progresses. Students can come to the table to work on tasks designed for this study.

Making Cards for the Center

Develop a variety of learning experiences that will lead students to discover facts about France. Develop cards that direct students to discover facts about France or to draw their own map of France as shown on these examples:

FACTS ABOUT FRANCE

1. List as many things as you can that you already know about France.
2. List any words you know that we have borrowed from the French language.
3. Use the encyclopedia to find the answers to these questions:
   How big is France?
   Which other countries touch its borders?
   What products is France known for producing?
   (Add more questions to guide student research.)

Display a map of France on the bulletin board to aid students in drawing their own maps as directed on this card. Divide the map in fourths to assist them.

TRAVELING THROUGH FRANCE

As you prepare to take a trip to France, draw your own map. Use a large sheet of paper.

Step 1: Draw light pencil lines to divide your paper in fourths. This will help you make the map the right size. Then draw the outline of France; notice the harbors and seaports.

Step 2: Locate the larger cities and rivers. Try to place them accurately. The pencil lines will help you.

Step 3: Print in the names of the countries and bodies of water that touch France on all sides. Locate the mountains.

Now choose one of the cities on your map to investigate. Find out as much as possible about it. You may be able to find a book that takes place there. Be ready to tell something about your city. We will record each person's talk on a cassette.

Create a set of small cards that will help students learn French-English vocabulary. Begin with basic vocabulary such as numbers, objects around the room, expressions students can use, for example:

Numbers			*Colors*		
1	un	*uhn*	red	rouge	*roozh*
2	deux	*duh*	yellow	jaune	*zhone*
3	trois	*twah*	blue	bleu	*bloo*
4	quatre	*kat truh*	green	vert	*vair*
5	cinq	*sank*	white	blanc	*blahnk*
6	six	*sees*	black	noir	*nwahr*
7	sept	*set*			
8	huit	*weet*	*Family*		
9	neuf	*nuhf*	mother	mère	*mehr*
10	dix	*dees*	father	père	*pehr*
			sister	soeur	*suhr*
			brother	frère	*frair*

Expressions		
hello	bonjour	*bohn zhoor*
good-by	au revoir	*oh ruh vwahr*
thank you	merci	*mair see*
please	s'il vous plait	*seel voo pleh*

Any standard high school French book will provide an ample vocabulary to introduce to your students. Note that the suggested pronunciations above are only approximate as many French sounds cannot be directly translated into English. We suggest that you find a French teacher or perhaps a parent who can pronounce the words on a tape for you and your students if you do not know French yourself.

Students can use these cards in numerous ways. They will enjoy just using them as flash cards to test each other. For this purpose prepare the cards with the French word or words on one side and the translation in English on the other, as shown here:

maison
(may zohn)

house

To encourage students to use these vocabulary cards, construct a gameboard like this:

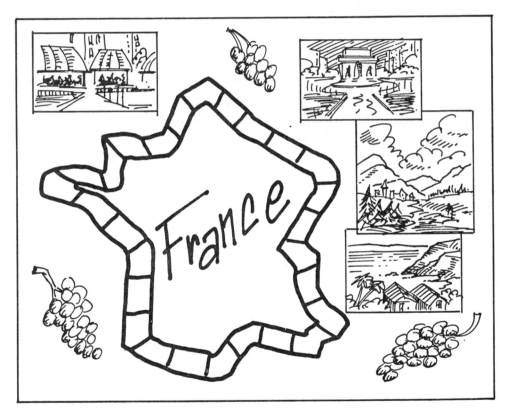

To give the gameboard a French motif, glue pictures from travel brochures around the board. Spaces are colored with alternate colors such as blue and white. Cover the board with clear contact paper or have it laminated. Use a die to determine the number of moves a student is to make. If the student lands on blue, he or she draws a card from the French pile (French words are on top, and the student must supply the English). If the player lands on a white space, he or she draws from the English pile (English words are up, and the player must supply the French word.) Students who are unable to answer correctly move back three spaces. Before they move, however, they read the correct answer, and the card is placed at the bottom of the pile.

Focus a learning center on the Canadian province of Québec which touches our New England states of Maine, New Hampshire, and Vermont as well as New York. See page 240. The largest of the provinces, its capital is Québec City. Québec is especially interesting because of its French origins; 80 percent of its population is French-Canadian. You might develop task cards that involve students in the following activities:

1. Draw a map of Québec. Identify its cities and waterways.
2. Reproduce Québec's flag on paper or cloth.
3. Write letters to obtain information about places of interest such as: Montréal, the Gaspé Peninsula, The Citadel in Québec City, the St. Lawrence River. (Address: Canadian Government Travel Bureau, Ottawa, Ontario, Canada KIA OH6.)
4. Make a poster featuring facts about Québec—the provincial tree, the flower, coat of arms, flag, and so on.
5. Develop a class time-line showing the history of Québec beginning with its discovery by Jacques Cartier in 1534.
6. Read a book set in some part of Québec.

Have a number of books available for student use during this study. In addition to the appropriate volumes of encyclopedias, include both nonfiction and fiction. Following is a list of recommended titles arranged from the easier to the more difficult:

Fiction
Barbeau, C. Marius. *The Golden Phoenix and Other French-Canadian Fairy Tales* Retold by Michael Hornyansky. Walck, 1958.

Carlson, Natalie S. *The Talking Cat and Other Stories of French Canada.* Harper & Row, 1952.

Carlson, Natalie S. *Jean-Claude's Island.* Harper & Row, 1963.

Nonfiction
Boswell, Hazel. *French Canada: Pictures and Stories of Old Quebec.* Atheneum, 1967.

Rockwell, Anne F., ed. *Savez-Vous Planter les Choux? and Other French Songs.* World, 1969.

Schull, Joseph. *Battle for the Rock: The Story of Wolfe and Montcalm.* Macmillan, 1960; St. Martin's, 1960.

Swayze, J. Fred. *Frontenac and the Iroquois: The Fighting Governor of New France.* Macmillan, 1959.

Syme, Ronald. *Champlain of the St. Lawrence.* Morrow, 1952.

Toye, William. *Cartier Discovers the St. Lawrence.* Oxford, 1970; Walck, 1970.

Bishop, Morris G. *Champlain: The Life of Fortitude.* McClelland, 1963.

Costain, Thomas B. *The White and the Gold: The French Regime in Canada.* Doubleday, 1954.

This study of French-speaking Americans or those who have French backgrounds could also include a New Orleans or Louisiana learning center. Another center might focus on French in our language—the many English words borrowed from French (ballet, adroit), place names that are French, or French expressions that we use (R.S.V.P.). This approach to teaching is truly interdisciplinary as students study concepts from the various social studies, mathematics, and literature and develop such skills as reading, writing, painting, and singing.

Notice, too, that you can develop similar learning centers that focus on any group, its locations within the United States, and the country or countries of origin: Swedish Americans—Minnesota, Sweden; Irish Americans—New York City, Ireland; Italian Americans—San Francisco, Italy; Spanish-speaking Americans—California, Southwest USA, Florida, Spain, Mexico, Puerto Rico, Cuba.

Simply follow the steps described in developing a center focusing on Americans who have French backgrounds. Use some of the same activities. Interspersed throughout the chapters of this book you will find additional suggestions for different groups. Check the index as well as the special listing of activities and information related to specific groups. In the following section we present a fully developed study focusing on Chinese-Americans.

THE LEARNING MODULE

The learning module is a booklet focused on a specific topic. The learning module can be used with a learning center approach. It can also be used effectively with small groups that break out from the whole class to study one topic. Sets of modules (five to ten) are useful when small groups are studying topics drawn from a larger unit of study. If the class is studying, for example, Africa, then small groups might be using modules focusing on Egypt, the Union of South Africa, West Africa, and so forth.

What is a module? The term "module" comes to us from electronics, meaning a component of a larger unit. In education, therefore, we can speak of a learning module as being one component in a larger unit of study.

A learning module, as defined here, is a booklet, usually 8½ × 11, that focuses on a single topic. Rather short, about five to twenty pages, the module is designed to teach two to three objectives that are part of an overall goal. Both goal and objectives are stated clearly. The module begins with a simple pretest and concludes with a posttest or culminating activity that aids student self-evaluation. The learning module is self-contained and speaks directly to the student. A teacher's guide is usually included with suggestions for use and such teaching aids as test answers, additional enrichment activities, and recommended resources. Read through the sample module that follows now so that you have a clearer picture of how a module can be used. First we present the student module and then the teacher's guide. The study is appropriate for grades four to nine.

THE YEAR OF THE DRAGON

A Study of Chinese-Americans (Student Module)*

THE YEAR OF THE DRAGON: A STUDY OF CHINESE-AMERICANS

---

* Adapted from *The Year of the Dragon*, a Multicultural Module, Contemporary Press, Box 1524, San Jose, CA 95109 ($1.50).

(cover)

The Year of the Dragon!

The dragon is the spirit of change, and it is expected that nothing but good can come of it, for the dragon is also known as a divine do-gooder.

Gung hay fat choy loong nien!
(Happy year of the dragon!)

With such a fascinating idea before you, we begin a study of China, that mysterious country about which we know so little, and Chinese-Americans, about whom we should know more. China is the third largest country in the world, second only to Russia and Canada, and more than 600 million people speak Chinese.

China's civilization developed long before that of the United States. Our country is an infant compared to such countries that trace their history to the years before Christ (B.C.).

Since China existed so many years before we did, naturally many things we take for granted today came originally from China. Can you name three things that we use today that were gifts from China?

1. _____

2. _____

3. _____

Look at the chart on the next two pages. Here you will discover that we have received many gifts from China.

CHINA'S GIFTS TO THE WEST

CHINA*		THE WEST*
Silk, about 1300		
	—300 B.C.—	
Folding umbrella (?)		
Lodestone, 240		
	—200 B.C.—	
Shadow figures (?)	—100 B.C.—	
	Birth of Christ	
Lacquer		
Paper, 105	—A.D. 100—	Peach and apricot
	—200—	
Tea, 264–273		
Word for porcelain first used	—300—	
Sedan chair		
	—400—	
	—500—	
Kite, 549		Silk, 552–554
	—600—	

---

* Dates in the "China" column indicate approximate date of origin; in "The West" column they indicate approximate date of receiving item described.

Page 2

	CHINA	THE WEST

CHINA		THE WEST
Playing cards	—700—	
Dominoes		
Gunpowder (?)	—800—	
Porcelain described, 851		
First printed book, 868	—900—	
	—1000—	
Movable type, 1041–1049		Orange
Compass		
Zinc in coins, 1094–1098	—1100—	
		Paper, 1150
Explosives, 1161		Compass, 1190
	—1200—	
	—1300—	1330
		Gunpowder and cannon,
		Playing cards, 1377
	—1400	
		Block printing, 1423
		Gutenberg's Bible, 1456
	—1500	
Chaulmoogra oil and ephe-drine described, 1552–78		Zinc described
		Kite, 1589
	—1600—	Sedan chair, tea, folding
		umbrella 1688
	—1700—	Wallpaper manufactured,
		Porcelain, 1709
		Lacquer produced, 1730
		Zinc in industrial
The use of the following		production, 1740
also originated in China		"German silver"
in early times, but cannot		production
be accurately dated: peach,		Chrysanthemum, tea rose,
orange, apricot, lemon,	—1800—	camellia, azalea, China
pomelo, Chrysanthemum,		aster, grapefruit
tea rose, camellia, azalea,		Shadow figures
China aster, gingko, "German		Gingko, tung oil, soy bean,
silver," wallpaper, goldfish.	—1900—	ephedrine, chaulmoogra oil

SOURCE: Derk Bodde. *China's Gifts to the West,* American Council on Education,
Washington, D.C.

Your Own Book about China

Begin a book about China. You can put everything you do in this study in your book. Choose a title for the book.

Select a piece of colored construction paper to use as the cover. Use a brush and black tempera paint to create a Chinese ideograph (a symbol used for a word or idea) to decorate the cover. Look on page 5 for several ideas or you may find some in your encyclopedia or other books about China. Follow the directions given on page 5.

Make a page for the table of contents. You can add titles to this page gradually as you make new pages for your book.

Make a page now about Gifts We Received from China. You can make a chart like the one on pages 2 and 3 or you can simply list the things we received from China.

You can add pages of your own to this book, too. Perhaps you would like to include a picture from a magazine or a newspaper clipping. If you like to draw, you may include some of your own illustrations.

CHINESE BRUSH PAINTING

Combine art with reading and the study of the Chinese culture. Try your hand at the beautiful figures used in classic Chinese writing.

Use white art paper (9″ × 12″), a brush, and black tempera to create the words shown here:

man   beautiful   country

To explore further, find *You Can Write Chinese* by Kurt Wiese in your library.

Exploring China

Find an article about China in an encyclopedia. Read this article to see what you can find out about:

> the people of China
> the land—its boundaries, size
>   comparison with the United States
>   mountains and rivers
> China's government
> the languages of China

Study the map of China. Make an outline of this country. First divide your paper in fourths with light pencil lines. This helps you draw the map in proper proportion. The lines can be erased later.

Locate provinces, major cities, and rivers. Print the names of countries that border China. Identify the bodies of water that touch China.

Page 6

The Puzzling Pagoda: A Chinese Crossword Puzzle

After reading about China and drawing a map of this country, you should be able to complete the crossword puzzle on page 8. If you can not think of an answer, refer again to the encyclopedia.

Definitions

Across

1. The capital of China
4. People's _____ of China
8. Chinese philosopher and scholar
9. Jewel
10. Luxurious cloth
11. Basic Chinese coin
13. Largest city in China
14. Useful cloth produced
16. Leader: _____ En-lai
18. Unique building

Down

2. Tallest mountain
3. Common cereal
5. Kind of government
6. Fishing boat
7. Country larger than China
12. Large woody plant
14. Common fish eaten
15. Prized lumber
17. Precious stone

PUZZLING PAGODA

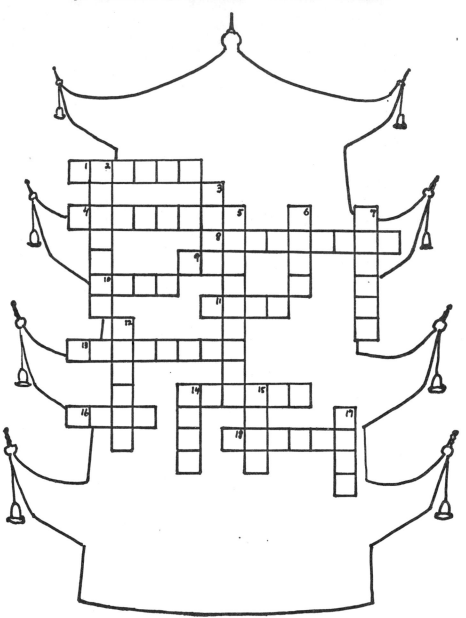

Chinese Folktales

Every country has its share of stories, tales that have been passed down through the years. Here is an interesting fable that comes to us from China.

THE MUSSEL AND THE BIRD

Once upon a time there was a Mussel who lived in the cliffs along the edge of the ocean. After a long winter, sunshine at last reached the rocks, and the Mussel drowsily opened its shell to the warmth. A Bird dropped suddenly from the sky swooping down on the Mussel to snatch a meal from the shell. The Mussel quickly snapped shut, closing tightly on the Bird's beak. The Mussel squeezed the Bird's beak, but no matter how hard the Mussel squeezed the Bird wouldn't leave.

Finally the Bird spoke to the Mussel: "Mussel, if you don't open your shell soon, not in one day, not in two days, but in three days surely you will die." The Mussel made no reply.

Eventually the Mussel spoke to the Bird: "Bird, if you don't take your beak out of my shell, not in one day, not in two days, but in three days surely you will die." The Bird would not heed the Mussel.

Then along came a child on her way to play in the ocean. The Bird saw the child, but still it would not remove its beak. The Mussel also saw the child, but still it would not open its shell. The child spotted the Bird and the Mussel locked together, picked them up, and carried them away for the family stew pot.

Retold by Pamela Tiedt

Can you think of a moral for this story?

Moral: _____

_____

_____

Find another folktale from China. Read it together with a friend. Plan how you can act the story out for others in the class. Invite other people to join you if you need their help.

The Chinese Calendar

The Chinese Calendar is much different from the one which we usually refer to. It is based on ancient traditions. An animal symbol is identified for each year, and persons born in that year are supposedly ruled by this symbolic animal and have characteristics associated with the animal. Twelve symbols are repeated con-

---

IN WHICH YEAR WERE YOU BORN?

Ox (1913, 1925, 1937, 1949, 1961, 1973) You have a calm patient nature. Friends turn to you because you are that rarest of creatures—a good listener. Love bewilders you so many people wrongly consider you cold.

Tiger (1902, 1914, 1926, 1938, 1950, 1962, 1974) You are a person of great extremes. A sympathetic and considerate friend. A powerful and dangerous enemy. In your career you are both a deep thinker and a careful planner.

Hare (1903, 1915, 1927, 1939, 1951, 1963, 1975) You are blessed with extraordinary good fortune and will inevitably provide financial success. This luck of yours not only extends to your business interests, but also to games of chance.

Dragon (1904, 1916, 1928, 1940, 1952, 1964, 1976) Your reputation as a fire-eater is based on your outward show of stubbornness, bluster and short temper. But underneath you are really gentle, sensitive and soft hearted.

Serpent (1905, 1917, 1929, 1941, 1953, 1965, 1977) You Snake people have more than your share of the world's gifts, including basic wisdom. You are likely to be handsome, well formed men and graceful beautiful women.

Horse (1906, 1918, 1930, 1942, 1954, 1966, 1978) Your cheerful disposition and flattering ways make you a popular favorite. Great mental agility will keep you in the upper income.

Ram (1907, 1919, 1931, 1943, 1955, 1967, 1979) You are a sensitive, refined, aesthetic type with considerable talent in all the arts. Indeed success or failure will depend upon whether you can shepherd your ability and energy into a single field.

Monkey (1908, 1920, 1932, 1944, 1956, 1968, 1980) In today's parlance you are a swinger. And because of your flair for decision making and sure-footed feel for finance, you are certain to climb to the top.

Rooster (1909, 1921, 1933, 1945, 1957, 1969, 1981) You either score heavily or lay a large egg. Although outspoken and not shy in groups, you are basically a loner who doesn't trust most people. Yet you are capable of attracting close and loyal friends.

Dog (1910, 1922, 1934, 1946, 1958, 1970, 1982) You are loyal and honest with a deep sense of duty and justice. Can always be trusted to guard the secrets of others.

Boar (1911, 1923, 1935, 1947, 1959, 1971, 1983) The quiet inner strength of your character is outwardly reflected by courtesy and breeding. Your driving ambition will lead you to success.

Rat (1912, 1924, 1936, 1948, 1960, 1972, 1984) You have been blessed with great personal charm, a taste for the better things in life, and considerable self control which restrains your quick temper.

Page 10

tinuously so that 1976 was the year of the Dragon, and the year of the Dragon will come again in 1988.

Examine this chart showing the symbols for the twentieth century. What is your symbol? Do you think the characteristics listed fit you?

Chinese Celebrations

Through the years many Chinese have immigrated to the United States, especially to the West coast. Such cities as San Francisco and Los Angeles have large sections called Chinatown where you can eat Chinese food and visit Chinese shops.

Many Chinese Americans still celebrate the traditional holidays and festivals of China. There is nothing so festive and exciting as a Chinese New Year's parade with the flamboyant dragon leading the way down the streets of Chinatown. Chinese New Year falls on a variable date depending on the moon. It is celebrated as each person's birthday with fireworks, gongs and cymbals, and of course, wonderful delicacies.

Other traditional Chinese holidays include:

Spring Festival Honors the planting season.

The Dragon Boat Festival Sometimes called the Double Fifth, this holiday falls on the fifth day of the fifth month of the Chinese calendar. On this day dragon-shaped boats race, and inhabitants of Chinatown eat *jung,* three-cornered rice dumplings, in the local teahouses.

Ch'ung Yang Festival This summer holiday, celebrated with kite flying, originated with a legend. The story goes that a fortune teller foretold disaster for a certain farmer on the ninth day of the ninth month, so he took his family to a high windy hill. Upon returning home, they found that, indeed, their animals had all perished.

Festival of the Moon This harvest festival is celebrated privately at night. This romantic celebration is the women's festival. They prepare large moon cakes made of flour and brown sugar to resemble the moon and its palaces.

Double Ten Festival On the tenth day of the tenth month, the dragon appears again to celebrate the Chinese Revolution and the fall of the Manchu Empire in the early twentieth century.

Ching Ming Festival Also called the Festival of the Tombs, it falls on the 106th day after the winter solstice. At this time the Chinese go to private cemeteries to honor the dead.

Winter Festival A family celebration, this holiday usually occurs in December shortly before Christmas.

See if you can find out more about these Chinese celebrations. Try one of these means of gathering information:

Page 11

1. Interview someone whose family originated in China. Find out if they celebrate these holidays, and if so, how the celebration is carried out.
2. Read about Chinese holidays in a book in your library.
3. Go to Chinatown to observe a celebration.
4. Write to a Tourist Agency or the Embassy of China to request information.

Write a short report of your findings.

Chinese Come to America

People of Chinese origins have made major contributions to the development of the United States. Many are doctors, college professors, and business executives. As immigrants, however, their life was difficult.

Read this list of events that are significant in the history of Chinese Americans from the first immigration to the present.

1785

First record of Chinese in the United States. Three Chinese seamen from the ship *Pallas* were left stranded in Baltimore.

1815

First record of a Chinese in California. Ah Nam, a cook for Governor de Sola, was baptized as a Christian on October 27, 1815. (California was not yet a part of the United States.)

1849

In the year of the Gold Rush, Chinese in San Francisco recorded as 54; in 1850 there were 787 men and two women. First anti-Chinese riot at Chinese camp, Tuolumne County, California.

1850

First laundry business begun in San Francisco by a Chinese person.

1852

First Chinese opera performed in San Francisco.
First Chinese theater built in San Francisco.
Columbia Resolution expelled Chinese from gold mines in Tuolumne County; followed by similar action in other counties.

1854

First Chinese newspaper in America, *Gold Hill News*.

1869

Completion of Transcontinental Railway. Chinese labor used by Central Pacific. Chinatown established in Deadwood, South Dakota, with discovery of gold. Chinese followed development of the mining industry as well as agriculture, and fishing; resentment by whites.

1871

Chinese massacre in Los Angeles.

1877

Special Report by Joint Committee of Congress investigated the "Chinese Question."
Labor agitation; anti-Chinese movement.

1879

Californian Constitution contained anti-Chinese legislation prohibiting employment of Chinese by corporations and government agencies.

Page 13

1882
Chinese Exclusion Act passed by U.S. Congress; ten-year ban on immigration.
Anti-Chinese riots.
1892
Geary Act extended exclusion for another ten years; required aliens to register.
1893
Anti-Chinese riots grew numerous:
Fresno, California
Napa, California
Redlands, Tulare, Visalia, Ukiah, California
1894
Vacaville, California, riot;
Chinese driven to cities where they formed Chinese ghettos, called Chinatowns.
1902
Exclusion laws extended indefinitely.
1907
Vancouver, British Columbia, riot.
1943
Repeat of Chinese Exclusion Act:
Chinese aliens in U.S. may become citizens.
Chinese immigration quota set at 105 per year.
1965
Quota system repealed. Permits up to 20,000 Chinese to enter United States each year.

Work with others in your class to prepare a time-line on a long strip of paper that looks something like this:

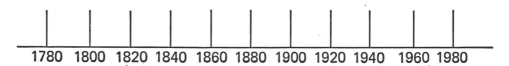

1780   1800   1820 1840   1860   1880   1900   1920 1940   1960 1980

Add illustrations and other information related to the history of Chinese Immigration into the United States.

Challenging the Dragon

Directions to the Student

Here is a fiery dragon whose breath can destroy you or bring you fortune. Which will it be?

This dragon guards a Treasure Chest that you can reach only by performing the many tasks required by the fearsome beast.

At each step roll the dragon's Curious Cube to see how many tasks you must perform. To learn what the tasks will be, draw forth a Cardinal Card for each task. If you can perform the required tasks, the dragon will permit you to move to the next perilous step. If you fail even one of the tasks, you must slide back to the previous step.

You have only a limited time to perform each task. As you complete each task, place the Cardinal Card under the great pile of Arduous Tasks. That task may be assigned to another unlucky challenger who dares to challenge the dragon.

Making the Curious Cube

Copy the pattern shown here to make the cube that will tell how many of the Arduous Tasks you must perform. After cutting the cube pattern from heavy red paper, print the numbers indicated with a felt pen. Then fold the pattern on each line, folding in the same direction each time. Form the six-sided figure and tuck the flaps in after applying glue on each.

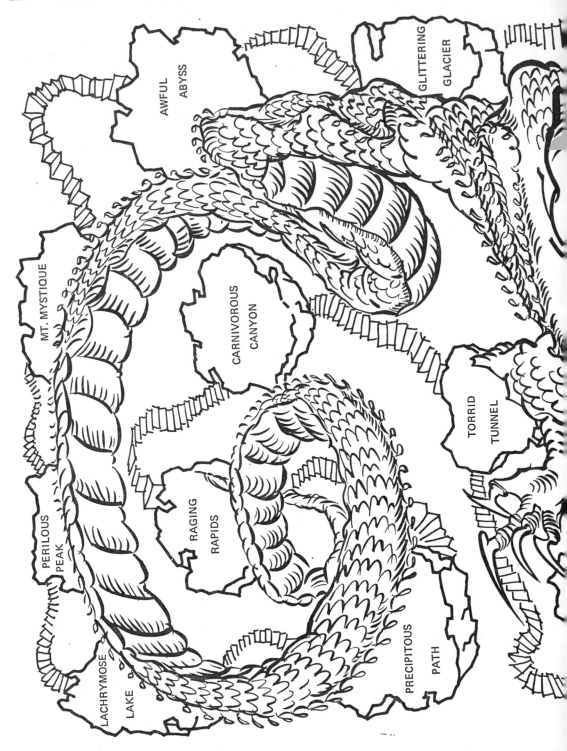

GLITTERING GLACIER

AWFUL ABYSS

MT. MYSTIQUE

CARNIVOROUS CANYON

TORRID TUNNEL

PERILOUS PEAK

RAGING RAPIDS

PRECIPITOUS PATH

LACHRYMOSE LAKE

Page 16

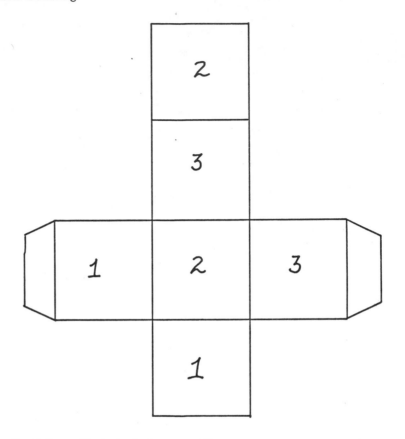

Preparing the Arduous Task Cards (on page 20)

Cut the cards apart. Mount each one on red (cardinal) construction paper that is 3″ × 4″ so the color frames the card.

Playing the Game Alone

This is a good game to play individually as you challenge the dragon alone. You may need a person to serve as Timer and Checker to see if your answers are acceptable. Use any means to discover the correct answer within the time limit, for instance, a dictionary.

Playing the Game with a Friend

You may wish to play this game with a friend or two. In this case do not wait for each person to finish the tasks assigned. If one player finishes a task in a short time, he or she can move to the next step, throw the Curious Cube, draw the Cardinal Cards, and work on the tasks assigned. In this way, each person moves ahead individually depending on the number of tasks received each time and how quickly they are completed. You will want to hurry, of course, if you are to reach the Treasure before someone else gets it away from the Dragon!

1. About how many people live in China?	6. Name the tallest mountain in China.
2. Name the 3 largest countries in the world.	7. Identify the following: a. pagoda b. junk c. carp
3. What kind of cloth was a gift from China?	8. Where did Chinese immigrants first settle?
4. What city is the capital of China?	9. Which of these names is likely to be Chinese? Martin　Chang　Yomura
5. Which city is the largest in China?	10. Name two countries that border China.

Exploring Your Community

What do you know about Chinese Americans in your own community? Begin a survey by turning to your local telephone book. Check the following:

1. The number of persons listed under several common Chinese names such as Wong, Chang, or Yee. What other names might you try?
2. Look under the word "Chinese" to see how many listings begin with that word, for example, Chinese Alliance Church.
3. In the Yellow Pages, look under Restaurants. How many Chinese restaurants are listed?
4. Look under the entry, Physicians and Surgeons, M.D., in the Yellow Pages. How many doctors have Chinese names?

Write a summary of your findings. Then write a paragraph explaining your conclusions about the Chinese in your community.

Do your findings surprise you? How can you find out more about Chinese Americans in your community?

What Do You Know Now?

Write three things that you know about China or Chinese Americans now that you did not know before you began this study:

1. _____
2. _____
3. _____

Examine the answers you gave to the questions on page 1. Would you change any of them now?

Choose one of the following activities to complete your work on this study:

1. Write a poem or story about a person from China.
2. Act out a story set in China that you have read. (You may work with several students on this task.)
3. Plan a Reader's Theater presentation of a folktale from China. (Work with several students.)
4. Make a diorama of a scene from China.
5. Make a table size relief map of China. (Work with another student.)

Your class may want to share your information about China and Chinese Americans with other classes or the whole school. How can you do this?

The Year of the Dragon: A Module about China and Chinese Americans (Teacher's Guide)

1976, our Bicentennial, was the year of the dragon. 1978 is the year of the horse, and 1980 is the year of the monkey. The title of this module could be modified according to the symbol for the year in which you plan to present this unit of study to provide a more contemporary flavor. The dragon, however, is still a useful motif for the gameboard.

Copy the module directly on duplicating masters so that you can produce a number of booklets at one time. Enlarge drawings by projecting them with an opaque projector. Prepare a simple construction paper cover that bears the title and perhaps the head of the dragon. Or, the cover might be decorated with a Chinese ideograph as shown.

Introducing the Study

Saturate your classroom with books, pictures, and other items of interest related to China. Use these materials as a basis for discussion designed to get students involved in the topic to be explored. Ask them, for example, what they know about China or if they know anyone who has lived in China. They might also list all the words they associate with China. Save this list for examination later after they learn more about the land and people. Comparison should show growth and perhaps changed viewpoints. This activity serves as the pretest.

You might begin your study by reading a folktale from China: for example, *Tikki Tikki Tembo,* the story of a little boy who had such a long name that he almost drowned because his little brother had so much trouble repeating the name. This book is also recommended because it is illustrated beautifully by Blair Lent. A film and filmstrip of the story are available from Weston Woods (Weston, Connecticut).

This story is a good example of a pourquoi tale, a story that explains why something has happened: Why the Chinese have such short names. After hearing this story, students of all ages can write original pourquoi (the French word for *why*) tales to explain, for example:

> Why our clock has 12 numbers.
> Why the cherry has a pit.
> Why corn has a tassel on top.
> Why we have stoplights on city streets.

After students have written their pourquoi tales, have them collected in a book entitled: *Pourquoi, ¿Pourque? Why?* Place the book on the reading table where everyone can read them.

Creating a Center of Focus

Create a learning center something like the one shown here which will serve as the center of focus for the study of China and Chinese Americans. Have students help develop the Center for the Study of China.

You can feature any pertinent information to add interest to the center. Here we have presented facts designed to pique student curiosity, such as the fact that 600 million people speak Chinese or that China is the third largest country in the world. The gameboard, Challenging the Dragon, can be presented as part of the module or as a separate activity with the directions displayed where students can read them easily. Place the modules, varied supplies, and numerous resources such as books at this work center.

Collecting Resources

Explore your school library as well as the local public library to see what kinds of resources are available. To accommodate a wide range of reading abilities, include both easy and more difficult fiction. Also bring in the C volumes of several encyclopedias because they also vary in reading difficulty. You can find other nonfiction written for young people. Here is a selection of titles to look for. Ask the assistance of your librarian in discovering other resources.

Fiction

Easy Books

The Story about Ping by Marjorie Flack (Viking).
Mei Li by Thomas Handforth (Doubleday).
Peachblossom by Eleanor Lattimore (Harcourt Brace Jovanovich).
Happy New Year by Yen Liang (Lippincott).
Fish in the Air by Kurt Wiese (Viking).

Short Stories

Shen of the Sea by Arthur Chrisman (Dutton).
The Treasure of Li-Po by Alice Ritchie (Harcourt Brace Jovanovich).

Books for Older Students

The House of Sixty Fathers by Meindert De Jong (Harper & Row).
Ride the Far Wind by Adrienne Jones (Little, Brown).
The Superlative Horse by Jean Merrill (Scott, Foresman).
Li Lun, Lad of Courage by Carolyn Treffinger (Abingdon).

Nonfiction

Let's Visit China Today by John Caldwell (Day).
The Land and People of China by Cornelia Spencer (Lippincott).
The Chinese in America by Betty Lee Sung (Macmillan).
The Yangtze, China's River Highway by Cornelia Spencer (Garrard).
The World of Red China by Hal Buell (Dodd).

An up-to-date resource for teachers is *Studying China in Elementary and Secondary Schools* by Leonard S. Kenworthy (Teachers College Press, 1975).

Preparing the Gameboard

If you choose to prepare the gameboard yourself as a stimulating extra activity for this study, begin by enlarging the drawing with an opaque projector. Have students help you as much as possible because involvement pays off. Examine this part of the module again before reading the following directions so you will understand the instructions.

Duplicate or copy the directions to the student on page 261. Mount these directions on a heavy piece of colored cardboard. Cover the directions with a sheet of clear contact paper to protect the sheet as it is used repeatedly. Pressing this direction board (covered by a sheet of clean paper) with a warm iron will make the protective sheet adhere well.

Have a student construct the curious cube as instructed (page 261). Have several other students finish the cardinal cards (see pages 264 to 266). You will need to prepare additional cards similar to the examples given if a number of students wish to play at once.

Answers:

1. 600 million
2. Russia
   Canada
   China
3. silk
4. Peking
5. Shanghai
6. Mt. Everest

7. a. special kind of building
   b. Chinese boat
   c. kind of fish
8. California
9. Chang

10.	Russia	India	Afghanistan
	North Korea	Bhutan	Mongolia
	North Vietnam	Sikkim	
	Laos	Nepal	
	Burma	Pakistan	

Answers for the Pagoda Puzzle (pages 253–254)

Across	*Down*
1. Peking	2. Everest
4. Republic	3. Rice
8. Confucius	5. Communist
9. Gem	6. Junk
10. Silk	7. Russia
11. Yuan	12. Bamboo
13. Shanghai	14. Carp
14. Cotton	15. Teak
16. Chou	17. Jade
18. Pagoda	

Sources for the Pagoda Puzzle were *China,* edited by Thomas W. Chinn, and *California, A Syllabus.* The Chinese Historical Society of America, 17 Adler Place, San Francisco, CA 94133.

Additional Activities

As students are working on the study of China, you might wish to interject additional interesting activities that can involve the whole group or may be designed for small group interaction. Here are a few suggestions:

1. Invite a parent who was born in China to visit your class to tell about China as they remember it, childhood experiences, coming to the United States, what their life here is like. Students then write these stories together.
2. Prepare a simple Chinese meal of rice and a combination of vegetables— celery, onions, green peppers, canned water chestnuts, soy sauce. See: *Eating and Cooking Around the World; Fingers before Forks* by Erich Berry (Day).
3. Read a version of "Cinderella" that comes from China. See: *Favorite Children's Stories from China and Tibet* by Lotta C. Hume (Tuttle).
4. Write a Chinese play or produce one that is available in the library. See: *7 Plays and How to Produce Them* by Moyne R. Smith (Walck).
5. Learn how Chinese New Year is celebrated. See: *Holidays Around the World* by Joseph Gaer (Little, Brown).
6. Explore Chinese poetry. See: *Chinese Mother Goose Rhymes* edited by Robert Wyndham (World); *The Moment of Wonder* edited by Richard Lewis (Dial).
7. Read stories aloud that are set in China, for the well-told story adds much to our understanding of another culture. You might choose, for example, *Seven*

Magic Orders: An Original Chinese Folktale, beautifully illustrated by Y. T. Mui (Lipincott).

8. Feature interesting quotations in your classroom to provoke discussion. The quotation accompanying this is presented in attractive calligraphy by Dana Cole of Seattle. It can be framed by mounting it on a sheet of 9″ × 12″ red construction paper. You may prefer to frame this quotation in a simple black inexpensive frame that comes in a 9″ × 12″ size with white matting included.

Encourage students to select quotations that they especially like to write or print artfully. This quotation is by an ancient Chinese philosopher and scholar, Lao-tsze (spelling varies). Other quotations from the Chinese that you might present include:

What you do not want others to do to you, do not do to others.

Confucius

It is the great tree that tempts the wind.

Chinese Proverb

Learning is like rowing upstream; not to advance is to drop back.

Chinese Proverb

A man who has committed a mistake and doesn't correct it is committing another mistake.

Confucius

A source of more good quotes for this use is *Quotes for Teaching* ($1.50, Contemporary Press, Box 1524, San Jose, CA 95109). Check the index of this book to discover other ideas related to China and Chinese-Americans that appear in this text.

Chinese Children in Your Classroom

Presenting a study related to the country of origin for students in your class gives them a good feeling of belonging. They can often contribute special information and personal experiences. Their parents may be willing to share in the study, too. The students will learn, too, as they participate in the study. Students who may have arrived recently from China or Hong Kong will be very much interested in finding out about Chinese Americans in the community and in the United States.

As you work with Chinese-speaking children, it is helpful to be somewhat aware of the problems they may experience as they learn English. On the opposite page is a summary of aspects of the Chinese language that may cause problems for children learning English.

Producing a Module

Modules can be produced for any subject area. You must first decide, of course, on what you want to teach. Modules can focus on groups of people, geographic areas, or broad concepts related to multilingual/multicultural studies. Examples of good topics for presentation in modular form are the following:

> Prejudice in America
> Native Americans Today
> Americans from Puerto Rico
> Breaking Down Stereotypes
> The People in New York City

After deciding on the topic that is appropriate for your class, begin with a good encyclopedia such as *World Book* or a reference book on the specific topic you chose. Here you will find a useful outline of the subject to be covered, names of people, important dates, questions to consider. Your task then is to select what information you want to convey to students and learning activities that will be stimulating and effective. The sample module on China included in this chapter demonstrates the kinds of things you might include in other modules.

ASPECTS OF THE CHINESE LANGUAGE THAT MAY CAUSE PROBLEMS FOR CHINESE STUDENTS LEARNING ENGLISH

1. The verb has only one form. Unlike the English verb, the Chinese verb is not conjugated to indicate tense. Tenses are indicated by the use of auxiliaries placed before or after the stable verb form.

2. Nouns are not inflected to indicate plural forms. Plurality is indicated by the use of auxiliaries in the form of specific or general number indicators placed before a noun (e.g., three book, many boy).

3. The Chinese article a is very specific and complex. It refers to the noun that it modifies and varies according to that noun. It is used as a unit of measure rather than as a general article (e.g., a book, a building, a string, a coat, a horse, a pencil).

4. Word order may not be manipulated to change meaning as is done in English. In Chinese the word *is*, for example, may not be repositioned to convert a statement into a question (e.g., "She is a nurse" may not be repositioned to "Is she a nurse?").

5. Spoken Cantonese and spoken Mandarin have an identical spoken sound to represent the pronoun he and she; but the written forms for these and three other singular pronouns in the third person are very distinct when genders are indicated basically by word-radical forms: She (feminine); he (masculine); it (inanimate object); it (animate object); and He (deity).

6. In a Chinese dictionary, words are not arranged in alphabetical order. Instead, they are listed by the number of strokes each character has.

7. There is a tendency for Chinese speakers to drop, glottalize, or add a vowel sound to English endings in the consonants *t, d, s, l, p, b, k, f, g, r,* and *v*.

8. A tone system is used in Chinese as a device for distinguishing word meanings. Words having the same pronunciation may have four different meanings. These meanings are, in turn, represented by four written forms.

9. There is a distinction between *n* and *l* in spoken Chinese; but some speakers, especially the Cantonese, use the letters interchangeably. The difference in pronunciation is particularly distinct in Mandarin.

SOURCE: *Framework in Reading for the Elementary and Secondary Schools of California.* California State Department of Education, 1973.

Prepare the student module first. The module can direct students to engage in varied activities such as viewing a film or filmstrip or recording something on a cassette. Try to include activities that use all of the language skills—listening, speaking, writing, and reading. Art and music add another dimension to learning experiences introduced in the module. Students can be directed to work in small groups at times as well as to work individually.

If you are the only person who will use this module, you may not want to prepare a full teacher's guide such as that included in the sample module. However, you should consider each part presented because you, too, will need a list of books and resources, the answers to activities presented in the student module, some ideas about introducing the study, and additional activities to add stimulus to the study.

SOURCES TO INVESTIGATE

Belshaw, Sharon, and Candy Carter. *Reading across the Curriculum; A Student Activity Book for Reading, Language Arts and Social Studies.* Contemporary Press, Box 1524, San Jose, CA 95109 ($3.50). Incorporates many of the ideas presented in this chapter. Designed as a 64-page module for student use. Ready to go with point system set up. Study varies from two weeks to nine weeks. An exciting approach to U.S. history including such topics as: What Is America?, American Values, The American Language, Contributions from Many Lands, Your Ancestry, The Ideal American.

Carlson, Ruth Kearney. *Emerging Humanity: Multi-Ethnic Literature for Children and Adolescents.* Brown, 1972. ($3.95). Contains good discussions of use of literature to promote multicultural understandings.

Reid, Virginia, ed. *Reading Ladders for Human Relations.* Fifth edition. National Council of Teachers of English, 1972. ($3.95). Lists many annotated resources. Includes many suggestions for using literature in the classroom. See especially, Ladder 3, "Appreciating Different Cultures."

Tiedt, Iris M. *Exploring Books with Children.* Houghton Mifflin, 1979. Includes excellent sections on literature related to various ethnic groups. Throughout there are good descriptions of teaching strategies such as reader's theater, storytelling, teaching a novel, planning lessons.

7

Resources for Multilingual/Multicultural Approaches to Teaching

Knowledge is of two kinds. We know a subject ourselves, or we know where we can find information upon it.

Samuel Johnson

Included in this chapter are resources for the teacher who needs more background information. Here we have gathered an up-to-date listing of books and nonprint media that can be used with students of varied ages. Here, too, are the addresses of organizations and publishers of materials related to this broad area of study.

GENERAL INFORMATION FOR THE TEACHER

The collection of materials listed in this section will provide general information for teachers interested in exploring topics in greater depth. Books are grouped according to (1) those that are language related and (2) those that are related to intergroup relations. Note that books about specific groups such as Black Americans or Mexican Americans are listed separately in the section entitled Materials Related to Ethnic Groups.

Books Related to Student Language

Andersson, Theodore, and Mildred Boyer. *Bilingual Schooling in the United States.* Volumes 1 and 2. U.S. Office of Education, U.S. Government Printing Office, 1970. ($6/set).

Ching, Doris C. *Reading and the Bilingual Child.* IRA.

Spolsky, Bernard. *The Language Education of Minority Children: Selected Readings.* Newbury House.

Stevick, Earl W. *Helping People Learn English: A Manual for Teachers of English as a Second Language.* Abingdon Press.

Thonis, Eleanor W. *Literacy for America's Spanish Speaking Children.* International Reading Association, 1976.

Tiedt, Iris M., and Sidney W. Tiedt. *Contemporary English in the Elementary School.* Prentice-Hall, 1975.

Tiedt, Iris M., and Sidney W. Tiedt. *Language Arts Activities for the Classroom.* Allyn & Bacon, 1978.

Valencia, Atilano A. *Bilingual/Bicultural Education for the Spanish-English Bilingual.* BABEL Media Center.

Books Related to Intergroup Relations

Banks, James A. *Teaching Strategies for Ethnic Studies.* Allyn & Bacon.

Banks, James, ed. *Teaching Ethnic Studies.* National Council for the Social Studies, 1973. Excellent resource for teachers.

CIBC Racism and Sexism Resource Center for Educators. *Human and Anti-Human Values in Children's Books: Guidelines for the Future.* The Council, 1976. Analyzes over 200 books and explores "hidden messages" transmitted to young readers.

Carlson, Robert A. *The Quest for Conformity: Americanization Through Education.* Wiley, 1975. Explains hostility toward nonconformity; gives historical perspective.

Carlson, Ruth Kearney. *Emerging Humanity; Multi-Ethnic Literature for Children and Adolescents.* Brown, 1972. Describes values and criteria for multiethnic literature; suggestions for use.

Cohen, David. *Multi-Ethnic Media: Selected Bibliographies in Print.* ALA.

Coleman, James S., et al. *Equality of Education Opportunity.* Office of Education, U.S. Government Printing Office, 1966. 737 pp. Studies segregation in schools, its cause and effects.

Coles, Robert. *Teachers and the Children of Poverty.* Potomac Institute, 1970. A report showing how teachers and students in thirteen cities see the school's role in integrated education.

Dunfee, Maxine, and Claudia Crump. *Teaching for Social Values in Social Studies.* Association for Childhood Education International, 1974.

Forbes, Jack D. *The Education of the Culturally Different: A Multi-Cultural Approach.* Far West Laboratory for Educational Research and Development, 1969. Explains educational disadvantages of monocultural orientation.

Goodykoontz, William, ed. *Prejudice; The Invisible Wall.* Scholastic, 1968.

Harmin, Merrill, Howard Kirschenbaum, and Sidney B. Simon. *Clarifying Values through Subject Matter: Applications for the Classroom.* Winston, 1973.

Hawley, Robert C., and Isabel L. Hawley. *Human Values in the Classroom.* Hart, 1975.

Hotchkiss, Jeanette, comp. *African-Asian Reading Guide for Children and Young Adults.* Scarecrow, 1976. Listed under separate countries and categories of literary composition.

Keating, Charlotte Matthews, comp. *Building Bridges of Understanding.* Palo Verde, 1967. An annotated bibliography of minority groups.

————. *Building Bridges of Understanding Between Cultures.* Palo Verde, 1971. Annotations are listed by age level in each minority group; companion volume to above listing.

Kelly, Ernece B. *Searching for America.* NCTE, 1972. Contains critiques of twelve English textbooks; provides insights into distortions and exclusions in literature at all levels.

Knowles, Louis, and Kenneth Prewitt. *Institutional Racism in America.* Prentice, 1969. Explains ideological roots of racism; illustrates perpetuation of institutional racism.

Nichols, Margaret S., and Peggy O'Neill. *Multicultural Materials.* Multicultural Resources, Stanford.

————. *Multicultural Bibliography for Preschool through Second Grade.* Multicultural Resources, Stanford.

Portrait: The Literature of Minorities (1970) *and Supplement* (1972). Office of the Los Angeles County Superintendent of Schools. An annotated bibliography of literature by and about four ethnic groups in the United States for grades 7–12. Includes fiction, poetry, nonfiction, anthologies, and background materials for teachers.

Reid, Virginia, ed. *Reading Ladders for Human Relations.* NCTE, 1972.

Rosenthal, Robert, and Lenore Jacobson. *Pygmalion in the Classroom: Teacher Expectation and Pupil's Intellectual Development.* Holt, Rinehart and Winston, 1968. A classic book outlining evidence on importance of teacher expectations of student performance in the classroom. Includes account of devastating study showing effect of self-fulfilling prophecies.

Ryan, William. *Blaming the Victim.* Pantheon, 1971. Exposes myths of racism and social science; well written.

Steinfield, Melvin. *Cracks in the Melting Pot: Racism and Discrimination in American History.* Glencoe, 1970. A collection of readings providing insight into racist practices at many levels.

Stent, Madelon D., William R. Hazard, and Harry N. Rivlin. *Cultural Pluralism in Education: A Mandate for Change.* Appleton, 1973. Excellent collection of papers given at a Chicago Conference by prominent educators and leaders from various cultural groups.

Terry, Robert W. *For Whites Only.* Eerdmans, 1970. Good analysis of the processes of racism; strategies for bringing about changes in the society.

Welton, David A., and John T. Mallan. *Children and Their World: Teaching Elementary Social Studies.* Rand McNally, 1976.

JOURNALS AND NEWSLETTERS

A number of periodicals report current research and promising practices related to bilingual/multicultural education. Request a sample copy and information about subscribing for your school.

The Bulletin, Council on Interracial Books, CIBC Resource Center, Room 300, 1841 Broadway, New York, NY 10023.

The Elementary Teachers Ideas and Materials Workshop. Parker Publishing Company, West Nyack, NY 10994. $20.00 per yearly subscription; 10 months.

The Linguistic Reporter, Center for Applied Linguistics, 1611 N. Kent St., Arlington, VA 22209.

NABE: Journal of the National Association of Bilingual Educators. Alma Flor Ada, ed. Subscription free with membership or $10/yr; quarterly publication. Los Angeles Publishing Co., 40–22 23rd Street, Long Island City, New York, NY 11101.

Reading Ideas. Contemporary Press, Box 1524, San Jose, CA 95109. $15.50/yr.; $18.50 outside USA; published monthly.

TESOL Newsletter; TESOL Quarterly. ($14/yr for both publications), Teachers of English to Speakers of Other Languages, 455 Nevits, Georgetown University, Washington, D.C. 20057.

INSTRUCTIONAL MATERIALS FOR STUDENT USE

This annotated list of instructional materials for student use is far from complete. New books, films, cassettes and other materials appear almost daily so that the supply is slowly growing. The materials listed will support bilingual, English as a second language, and multicultural programs, for these areas clearly overlap in their emphases. Publishers' addresses appear in a separate directory of addresses at the end of this chapter.

Publisher and Title

ACI Productions, Inc. *Look, Listen, and Read Series.* Filmstrips and cassettes for grades K–1; language arts; learning center approach.

ACI Productions, Inc. *Read On Series.* Filmstrips and cassettes for grades 1–4; language arts; teaching/learning tool.

Behavioral Research. *AMANECER.* (Level I–Level II) Laboratories, Inc. Consumable workbooks and teacher's guide criterion reference test for grades K–3; language arts; designed for Spanish-speaking children.

Benefic Press. *American Indian Contributors to American Life.* Textbook (hardbound) for grades 5–8; history-biographical approach to understanding of American Indian; Indian culture.

Benefic Press. *Mi Segundo Libro de Estudios Sociales.* Textbook (hardbound) for grades 2–4; inquiry-questions; Spanish textbook.

Benziger, Bruce & Glencoe, Inc. *Benziger Readers.* Texts for grades K–3; language arts.

BFA Educational Media. *Bilingual Reading Child.* Sound filmstrips for grades K–6; social studies.

Borg-Warner Educational System. *Beginning Language Concepts.* Records for grades K–3; language arts.

Bowmar Publishing Corp. *Beginning Fluency in English As a New Language.* Cassettes, filmstrips, and records for grades K–5; language arts; Inservice in creative dramatics; adopted for ESL.

Bowmar Publishing Corp. *Music of the Black Man in America—Parts 1 & 2.* Filmstrips and cassettes for grades 4–8; music.

Bowmar Publishing Corp. *Para Chiquitines.* Text and records for grades K–4; language arts.

Bowmar Publishing Corp. *Songs of Spanish America.* Records, multigraded; music.

Bowmar Publishing Corp. *Spanish Edition of the Reading Incentive Program.* Multimedia kits for grades 4–8; language arts.

Bowmar Publishing Corp. *Spanish Monster Books.* Readers for grades K–5; language arts.

Continental Press, Inc. (The). *Duplicating Masters for Developing Reading and Reading Readiness Skills.* Duplicating masters for grades K–2; language arts; Spanish language.

Coronet Instructional Media. *Latin American Folktales.* Records and filmstrips for grades 4–6; language arts and social studies.

Coronet Instructional Media. *Seeing Mexico.* Kits for grades 4–6; social studies.

Coronet Instructional Media. *Stories About Color.* Sound and filmstrips for grades K–3; language arts; appropriate audiovisual equipment.

Creative Teaching Association. *NUMBER—NÚMERO.* Card game, multigraded; math, language arts; could be made easily by students.

Creative Teaching Press, Inc. *Escribe Un Cuento, Story Starters Intermediate Level.* Cards for grades 4–6; language arts.

Denoyer-Geppert Co. *Explorations in Gross Motor Skills and Sensory Perception.* Kits for grades K–1; psychomotor.

Denoyer-Geppert Co. *Explorations in Number Concepts.* Kit for grades K–1; math, visual discrimination.

Denoyer-Geppert Co. *Explorations in Shape, Color and Size.* Kit for grades K–1; math, visual discrimination; bilingual suggestions.

Denoyer-Geppert Co. *Maps, Charts & Globes.* Maps, charts and globe for grades 4–6; students' fundamental map-reading skills; Spanish text provided.

Denoyer-Geppert Co. *Un Estudio Del Cuerpo Humano.* Charts for grades 6–8; science.

Dumas and Moore Distributing Co. *Golden Legacy.* Paperback books for grade 4; reading, cultural awareness.

El Dorado Distributors. *A Collection of Mini-Books.* Softbound books, multigraded; to stimulate beginning Spanish learners; Mexican artifacts helpful to reinforce culture.

El Dorado Distributors. *I Will Catch the Sun* and *I Color My Garden.* Softbound books, multigraded; literature, cultural; to be integrated with reading.

Encyclopaedia Britannica. *Fairy Tale Magic.* Sound and filmstrips for grades 1–4; communication, language development; appropriate audiovisual equipment.

Encyclopaedia Britannica. *Now You Know About Plants.* (Spanish and English) books and cassettes for grades K-3; science.

Ginn and Company. *Core English: English for Speakers of Other Languages.* Teachers manual, workbook, wall charts, picture cards, E.S.L. material for grades K–3; four-level oral language arts program approach; very flexible program may be used in varied school situations, adopted for ESL.

Guidance Associates. *Profiles of Black Achievement*. Filmstrip and record for grades 6–8; multicultural.

Guidance Associates. *Series of American Legends and Other Cultural Folktales*. Filmstrips and cassettes, multigraded; audiovisual presentations; proper audiovisual equipment.

Harcourt Brace Jovanovich Inc. *Bilingual Syntax Measure*. Oral proficiency test in English and/or Spanish for grades K–2; diagnostic, prescriptive; determine language dominance.

Houghton Mifflin Co. *Mis Primeras Lecturas*. Text for grades K–1; sequential; all materials are entirely in Spanish.

Motivational Learning Programs, Inc. *Crane Reading System in Spanish*. Reading books for grades K–2; reading, elective; teacher inservice, required.

National Textbook Co. *Bilingual Fables*. Paperbound books for grades K–3; didactic; bilingual English/Spanish.

Nystrom. *Mexico, Central America Wall Map*. Map, multigraded; social science; adopted for ESL.

QED Prod., Inc. *Economia Para Los Grados de Primaria*. Sound and filmstrip for grade 2; economics.

QED Prod., Inc. *Matimaticas Para Primaria: Geometria*. Teacher manual, 6 filmstrips with cassettes, student activity book for grades K–3; geometry; teacher's manual in English or Spanish.

Santillana Publishing Co. *Diccionario Del Lenguaje Usual*. Dictionary for grades 3–8.

Santillana Publishing Co. *Primera Biblioteca Altea*. Nine texts for grades 3–4; nature and ecology; English translation of corresponding series in Spanish.

Santillana Publishing Co. *Who Am I Series*. Nine science books for grades 3–4; nature and ecology, adopted for ESL; English translation of *Primera Biblioteca Altea*.

Santillana Publishing Co. *Santillana Bilingual Series: Programa de Lengua Espanola*. Text workbooks for grades K–6; sequential; inservice needed.

Santillana Publishing Co. *Santillana Bilingual Series: Sistema de Manejo del Programa*. Evaluation and assessment system for grades K–6; reading assessment; inservice needed.

Santillana Publishing Co. *Senda—Spanish Language Arts Development System*. Textbooks for grades 1–8; reading sequential; inservice needed.

Scholastic Magazine, Inc. *Cinco Ninos, Cinco Familias; Puedo Unit I, Puedo Unit II*; Sound filmstrip with mini books for grades K–3; development of basic concepts, language and vocabulary development; appropriate audio-visual equipment.

Scholastic Magazine, Inc. *Cinco Ninos, Cinco Familias; Puedo Unit I, Puedo Unit II; Quien Soy Yo? Como Aprendo?* Filmstrips, cassettes, poster for grades K–3; social studies and language instruction; very effective for use in learning centers.

Scott, Foresman and Co. *Vocabulario Ilustrado: A Bilingual Word Book*. Dictionary, paperback, for grades 2–3; vocabulary development.

Society for Visual Education. *Las Aventuras del Dragon Peletero; Cuentos Clasicos Infantiles; La Caperucita Roja; Nino de la Ciudad*. Sound filmstrips for grades K–6; appropriate audiovisual equipment.

Society for Visual Education. *La Bibliotica de la Escuela Elemental.* Filmstrip and cassettes for grades 3–6; appropriate audiovisual equipment.

Society for Visual Education. *Stories from the Old West.* Filmstrip and cassette for grade 6; history of the Old West.

Society for Visual Education. *The American Indian before Columbus.* Filmstrip and cassette for grade 6; American Indian history before Columbus.

Spanish Language Multimedia, Inc. *Ciencias de la Naturaleza.* Textbook for grades 1–6; science sequential and topical.

Spanish Language Multimedia, Inc. *Cien—Descrubamos el mundo Prescolar.* Textbooks for grades 1–4; sequential.

Spanish Language Multimedia, Inc. *Gramatica Espanola.* Textbook (exercises in text are consumable) for grades 7–8; sequential.

Spanish Language Multimedia, Inc. *Mecanografia 100,* and *Mecanografia 100, Practicas Secretariales.* Textbook and workbook for grade 8; drill.

Spanish Language Multimedia, Inc. *Mi Primer Diccionario Bilingual Edition.* Textbook for grades 1–6; vocabulary builder.

Telefact Foundation. *The Original Constitution of the State of California 1849* and *El Trato de Guadalupe Hidalgo 1848.* Softbound texts for grades 5–8; social science.

FREE AND INEXPENSIVE MATERIALS FOR TEACHING

Listed here is a potpourri of free and inexpensive aids and materials that may add spice to multicultural teaching. Travel folders can add interest to the study of Mexico; recipes for cooking ethnic foods add a new dimension to classroom experiences; directions written in another language provide concrete evidence that many people in the United States speak languages other than English.

Free and Inexpensive Aids

Cooperative Extension Service, Box U-35, The University of Connecticut, Storrs, CT 06268. *Mexican Foods and Traditions* (25¢).

Delmonte Teaching Aids, Box 4007, Clinton, IA 52732. The Big Four Daily Countdown (basic foods). Consuma Diariamente Los Cuatro Alimentos Basicos.

Frito-Lay Tower, Dallas, TX 75235. *Tasty Recipes from Frito-Lay, Inc.*

Multicultural Modules, Contemporary Press, Box 1524, San Jose, CA 95109. *Chinese Americans* ($1.50), *Spanish-speaking Americans* ($1.50), *Black Americans* ($1.50).

National Dairy Council, Chicago, IL 60606. *Una Guia Para Comer Bien*—Chart.

Texas Education Agency, 201 East 11th St., Austin, TX 78701. *El Corrido de Gregorio Cortez.* (Send blank tape, cassette size).

Free and Inexpensive Materials

American Library Association, 50 East Huron St., Chicago, IL 60611. *American Indians: A Bibliography of Sources,* a list of many recent materials, (50¢).

————. *Children's Books of International Interest Printed in U.S.A.,* a selective list, (free).

Asia Society, 112 East 64th St., New York, NY 10021. *Asia: A Guide to Basic Books,* a list of basic books on Asia (50¢).

Baker, Augusta. Office of Children's Services, New York Public Library, 8 East 40th St., New York, NY 10016. *The Black Experience in Children's Books,* a revision that includes 400 titles, (50¢).

California Library Association, 1741 Solano Ave., Berkeley, CA 94707. *American Negro in Contemporary Society,* an annotated list of 121 titles, (free).

Centro Mexicano de Escritores, Apartado Postal 1298, Mexico 1, D.F., Mexico. *Children's Books Mexico,* a list of books for children in Spanish, (free).

Cohen, David, chm. American Association of School Librarians, 50 East Huron St., Chicago, IL 60611. *Multi-ethnic Media: Selected Bibliographies,* (free).

Contemporary Press, Box 1524, San Jose, CA 95109. *Selected Free Materials,* a list of materials and addresses, ($1.50).

Dimitroff, Lillian. National Education Association, Division of Educational Technology, 1201 Sixteenth St., NW., Washington, DC 20036. *An Annotated Bibliography of Audiovisual Materials Related to Understanding and Teaching Culturally Disadvantaged,* (75¢).

Free Library of Philadelphia, 19th and Vine Sts., Philadelphia, PA 19103. *To Be Black in America,* a bibliographic essay arranged in broad categories; materials included suitable for use by junor and senior high school students, (free).

Glancy, Barbara Jean. American Federation of Teachers, AFL-CIO, 1012-14th St., NW., Washington, DC 20036. *Children's Interracial Fiction,* an annotated unselected bibliography identifying 328 books with black characters, ($1).

Information Center on Children's Cultures, United States Committee for UNICEF, 331 East 38th St., New York, NY 10016. *Africa: An Annotated List of Printed Materials Suitable for Children,* evaluation of all in-print English-language materials for children on subject of Africa, ($1).

————. *Latin America: An Annotated List of Materials for Children,* evaluation of all in-print English language materials for children on subject of Latin America, ($1).

Koblitz, Minnie. Center for Urban Education, 105 Madison Ave., New York, NY 10016. *The Negro in Schoolroom Literature: Resource Materials for the Teacher of Kindergarten Through the 6th Grade,* an annotated list of more than 250 books, background materials for teachers, source materials, author and publisher index, (25¢).

Michigan Department of Education, 735 East Michigan, Lansing, MI 48913. *The Heritage of the Negro in America—a Bibliography: Books, Records, Tapes, Filmstrips,* sources of information on contributions of the American Negro in various fields, (free).

National Education Association, 1201 Sixteenth St., NW., Washington, DC 20036. *Index to Multiethnic Teaching Materials and Teacher Resources,* an annotated bibliography in four sections, (35¢).

New York Public Library, Fifth Avenue and 42nd St., New York, NY 10018. *A Touch of Soul,* a selected, annotated listing of the most recent books for children, (free).

————. *Black Films: A Selected List,* a film listing selected from the current film collection in the New York Library for a Black Films Wo. kshop, (free).

————. *Books, Films, Recordings By and About the American Negro,* a selection of 233 titles, films tested with teenagers, recordings of various types of music styles plus spoken recordings, (free).

Oakland Public Library, 1457 Fruitvale Ave., Oakland, CA 94601. *His House Below; Books from the Beach Struggle,* an annotated list of media explaining the black struggle, (free).

Pan American Union, 17th and Constitution Ave., NW., Washington, DC 20006. *Proyecto Leer Bulletin,* quarterly; lists elementary books and other reading and audiovisual materials in Spanish for children and adults, (free).

Pennsylvania Department of Education, Bureau of General and Academic Education, Box 911, Harrisburg, PA 17126. *American Diversity: A Bibliography of Resources on Racial and Ethnic Minorities for Pennsylvania Schools,* an annotated, graded list identifying resources to implement curriculum studies relating to minority groups, (free).

Revelle, Keith. Latin American Library of the Oakland Public Library, 1457 Fruitvale Ave., Oakland, CA 94601. *Chicana: A Selected Bibliography of Materials By and About Mexico and Mexican Americans,* (free).

Rosenfeld, Harriet. Yeshiva University, Amsterdam Ave. and 186th St., New York, NY 10033. *Books to Enhance the Self-Image of Negro Children,* an annotated list of 122 books organized in two parts on American life, Africa and the West Indies, (free).

U.S. Committee for UNICEF, 331 East 38th St., New York, NY 10016. *Photo Set: UNICEF's Children in School,* twelve black and white photographs (12″ × 14″) with captions and illustrating UNICEF aid to education, ($1).

U.S. Department of the Interior, Bureau of Indian Affairs, Washington, DC 20240. *Indian Bibliography,* an annotated listing of part of the collection; contains books written by and about American Indians, (free).

U.S. Office of Education, U.S. Government Printing Office, Washington, DC 20402. *Books Related to Compensatory Education,* a bibliography in three parts, concerning materials about Africa, minority groups, U.S. children with handicaps, (50¢).

Vogel, Virgil J. Integrated Education Associates, 343 South Dearborn St., Chicago, IL 60604. *The Indian in American History,* contributions of the American Indian to American civilization, (50¢).

Weinberg, Meyer. Integrated Education Associates, 343 South Dearborn St., Chicago, IL 60604. *Afro-American History: Separate or Interracial?* a commentary on Negro history, (50¢).

White, Doris. ERIC Clearinghouse on Early Childhood Education, 805 West Pennsylvania Ave., Urbana, IL 61801. *Multi-Ethnic Books for Head Start Children: Black and Integrated Literature,* an annotated list arranged by subject areas, (90¢).

INFORMATION ABOUT COUNTRIES

Write for free materials from addresses given. Use official stationery.

Africa

Ghana: Press Attaché, Embassy of Ghana, 2460 16th St., NW., Washington, DC 20009.

Tunisia: Embassy of Tunisia, 2408 Massachusetts Ave., NW., Washington, DC 20008.

Union of South Africa: Information Service of South Africa, 655 Madison Ave., New York, NY 10021.

Asia

Australia: Australian News and Information Bureau, 636 Fifth Ave., New York, NY 10020.

Burma: Embassy of the Union of Burma, 2300 S St., NW., Washington, DC 20008.

China: Embassy of the Republic of China, 552 National Press Building, Washington, DC 20004.

India: Information Service of India, 2107 Massachusetts Ave., NW., Washington, DC 20008.

Indonesia: Embassy of the Republic of Indonesia, 2020 Massachusetts Ave., NW., Washington, DC 20006.

Iraq: Embassy of the Republic of Iraq, 1801 P St., NW., Washington, DC 20036.

Israel: Consul General of Israel, 105 Montgomery St., San Francisco, CA 94104.

Japan: Information Section, Embassy of Japan, 2514 Massachusetts Ave., NW., Washington, DC 20008.

Jordan: Embassy of the Hashemite Kingdom of Jordan, 2319 Wyoming Ave., NW., Washington, DC 20008.

Korea: Embassy of Korea, 1145 19th St., NW., Suite 312, Washington, DC 20036.

Malaysia: Embassy of Malaysia, 2401 Massachusetts Ave., NW., Washington, DC 20008.

New Zealand: New Zealand Embassy, 19 Observatory Circle, NW., Washington, DC 20008.

Pakistan: Embassy of Pakistan, 2315 Massachusetts Ave., NW., Washington, DC 20008.

Sri Lanka: Embassy of Sri Lanka, 2148 Wyoming Ave., NW., Washington, DC 20008.

Turkey: Turkey Tourism & Information Office, 500 5th Ave., New York, NY 10036.

U.S.S.R.: Embassy of the Union of Soviet Socialist Republics, 1706 18th St., NW., Washington, DC 20009.

Canada

Write the Canadian Government Travel Bureau, Ottawa, Ontario, Canada K1A OH6.

Alberta: Alberta Government Travel Bureau, 1629 Centennial Building, Edmonton, Alberta, Canada. Greater Vancouver Visitors and Convention Bureau, 650 Burrard St., Vancouver, B.C., Canada V6C 2L2.

British Columbia: Dept. of Travel Industry, Govt. of British Columbia, 1019 Wharf St., Victoria, B.C., Canada V8W 2Z2.

Manitoba: Manitoba Tourist Branch, Dept. of Tourism and Recreation, Winnipeg 1, Manitoba, Canada.

Yukon: Yukon Tourism, Travel and Information Branch, Govt. of the Yukon, Box 2703, Whitehorse, Yukon, Canada.

Europe

Denmark: Danish Information Office, 280 Park Ave., New York, NY 10017.

Finland: Embassy of Finland, 1900 24th St., NW., Washington, DC 20008.

France: French Government Tourist Office, 972 Fifth Ave., New York, NY 10021.

Germany: German Information Center, 410 Park Ave., New York, NY 10022.

Ireland: Irish International Airlines, 564 Fifth Ave., New York, NY 10036.

Italy: Italian Government Travel Office-ENIT, 630 5th Ave., New York, NY 10020.

Netherlands: Royal Netherlands Embassy, 4200 Linnean Ave., NW., Washington, DC 20008.

Norway: Norwegian Embassy Information Service, 825 Third Ave., New York, NY 10022.

Portugal: Casa de Portugal, Portuguese National Tourist Office, 570 Fifth Ave., New York, NY 10036.

Spain: Spanish Embassy, Cultural Relations Office, 1629 Columbia Rd., NW., Washington, DC 20009.

Switzerland: Swiss National Tourist Office, 661 Market St., San Francisco, CA 94105.

Yugoslavia: Yugoslav State Tourist Office, 509 Madison Ave., New York, NY 10022.

South America

Colombia: Information Services Staff, Foreign Agricultural Information Division, U.S. Dept. of Agriculture.

Ecuador: Embassy of Ecuador, 2535 15th St., NW., Washington, DC 20009.

Venezuela: Embassy of Venezuela, Institute of Information and Culture, 2437 California St., NW., Washington, DC 20008.

CHILDREN'S BOOKS PUBLISHED ABROAD

Of special interest to children as you conduct studies of other groups will be books published in different languages. These books can be obtained in the original language, such as German, or they may be found in translation. There is a value in having both, but translations are more easily obtained.

Notice that these translations have been published by American publishing companies. All are 1976 publications. The languages listed are the original languages.

Afrikaans

The Lion of the Kalahari, by Sam Hobson & George Hobson (Greenwillow)

Danish

The Golden Future by Thorsteinn Stefansson (Nelson)

The Little Locomotive by Ib Spang Olsen (Coward)

Otto Is a Rhino by Ole Lund Kirkegaard (Addison-Wesley)

Dutch

Cats and Dolls by Margriet Heymans (Addison-Wesley)

Crusade in Jeans by Thea Beckman (Scribner's)

Flemish

The Circus Baron by Willy Vandersteen (Hiddigeigei Books)

The Great Balloon Race by Commaar Timmermans (Addison-Wesley)

The Little White Hen and the Emperor of France by Gommaar Timmermans (Addison-Wesley)

An Island Called Hoboken by Willy Vandersteen (Hiddigeigei Books)

The Merry Musketeers by Willy Vandersteen (Hiddigeigei Books)

The Tender-hearted Matador by Willy Vandersteen (Hiddigeigei Books)

French

The Adventures of Tintin by Hergé (4th series) (Atlantic—Little, Brown)

The Runaway Flying Horse by Paul Jacques Bonzon (Parents')

German

Animal Babies of East Africa by Hans & Monique Dossenbach (Putnam)

A Foal Is Born by Hans Isenbart and Hanns-Jorg Anders (Putnam)

The Giant's Feast by Max Bollinger (Addison-Wesley)

A Hamster's Journey by Luis Murschetz (Prentice-Hall)

The Hare's Race by Hans Baumann (Morrow)

Mister Mole by Luis Murschetz (Prentice-Hall)

Outrageous Kasimir by Achim Broger (Morrow)

When Half-Gods Go by Hannelore Valencak (Morrow)

Japanese

The Foxes of Chironupp Island by Hiroyuki Takahashi (Windmill/Dutton)

My Teddy Bear by Chiyoko Nakatani (Crowell)

Polish

Sister of the Birds and Other Gypsy Tales by Jerzy Ficowski (Abingdon)

Russian

The Air of Mars and Other Stories of Time and Place ed. by Mirra Ginsburg (Macmillan)

Pamalche of the Silver Teeth ed. by Mirra Ginsburg (Crown)

The Silver Crest: My Russian Boyhood by Kornei Chukovsky (Holt, Rinehart and Winston)

Spanish

Black Rainbow (Inca Legends and Peruvian Myths) ed. by John Bierhorst (Farrar, Straus & Giroux)

Swedish

Dan Henry in the Wild West by Stig Ericson (Delacorte/Seymour Lawrence)

Dolphins in the City by Bo Carpelan (Delacorte/Seymour Lawrence)

Elvis and His Friends by Maria Gripe (Delacorte/Seymour Lawrence)

Elvis and His Secret by Maria Gripe (Delacorte/Seymour Lawrence)

In the Time of the Bells by Maria Gripe (Delacorte/Seymour Lawrence)

Pippi on the Run by Astrid Lindgren (Viking)

LISTS OF BOOKS PUBLISHED ABROAD

Orders for these lists should be prepaid with request.

Country	Name, Language and Frequency of List	Order from
Australia	*Reading Time*, Publication No. 1, "Book of the Year and Picture Book Awards 1946–1976," a 16-page pamphlet listing the winners, highly commended and commended titles for these awards since the inception of the awards program.	*Reading Time*, Children's Book Council of Australia, c/o Library Services, 35 Mitchell St., North Sydney 2060, Australia ($1.00 by surface mail; $2.00 by air mail)
Brazil	"Separata" within the quarterly *Boletim Informativo*, with annotated reviews of recommended new books arranged by age level. (Portuguese)	Fundação Nacional do Livro Infantil e Juvenil, rua Voluntários da Pátria 107, ZC-02 Rio de Janeiro, Brazil ($10.00 annually)
France	Annual selection of best children's books appears as part of the last issue each year of *Bulletin d'analyses de livres pour enfants*, published six times a year. Annual subscription is 45 francs; single issue is 8 francs. (French)	la Joie par les Livres, Centre de documentation, 4, rue de Louvois, 75002 Paris, France
Great Britain	"Poetry Books for Children: A *Signal* Booklist," a 32-page annotated selection of over 100 poetry books from the earliest books to the midteens. Alan Tucker. Illustrations.	The Thimble Press, Lockwood Station Rd., South Woodchester, STROUD, Glos. 5EQ, England ($2.00)

Country	Name, Language and Frequency of List	Order from
Israel	"Books from Israel: Suggestions for Publication Abroad," a 1976 catalog prepared for the Frankfurt Book Fair (Children's books pp. 15–23). (English)	International Promotion and Literary Rights Dept., Book Publishers Assn. of Israel, 29 Carlebach St., Tel-Aviv 67-132, Israel (Free)
Sweden	"Vi läser på fritid: Basta bocker for barn och ungdom." Eight-page pamphlet containing annotated listings of approximately 80 best children's books of the year. Illustrations. Published annually in November. (Swedish)	Children's Booklists Ed. Bibliotekstjänst AB, Fack 221 01 Lund, Sweden (25¢)
	"Boknyheter: Barnbocker," an annual selection annotated, of books for libraries, schools and youth organizations. (Swedish)	Address as above. ($4.00)
Switzerland	"Zürcher Klassenleseserien der Schweizerischen Volksbibliothek 1976/77," an annotated listing of under 200 recommended children's books. (German)	Mr. A. Lüthi (Schweizerischer Bund für Jugendliteratur) Newdorfstr. 29 CH 8820 Wädenswil, Switzerland (Free; limited supply)

Booklist, the library buying guide published by American Library Association, has featured such lists in the following issues:

German, March 1, by Sybille Jagusch, Baltimore County Public Library

India (in English), April 15, compiled by Lucretia Harrison from an Indian bibliography

Spanish-Language, May 15, from Proyecto Leer

Greek, June 1, adapted by L. M. Harrison from German-language list of International Youth Library

Polish, September 15, by Anna Bogucka

Arabic, November 1, by Mary Ploshnick, Detroit Public Library

MATERIALS RELATED TO ETHNIC GROUPS

In this section we feature four major ethnic groups of special importance in the United States: Asian Americans, Black Americans, Native Americans, and Spanish-speaking Americans. There are problems inherent in any system of categorization. Many books, for example, group tales of Japan and China together. While the framework used in this presentation is not perfect, it appears to be functional in terms of classroom needs. Books about other national groups are listed under Other Multicultural Books for Children.

**Selected Materials about Asian Americans
(Limited to Chinese and Japanese Americans)**

Background Information for Teachers

General

Chin, Frank, Jeffery Paul Chan, Lawson Fusao Inada, and Shawn Hsu Wong. *Aiiieeeee! An Anthology of Asian-American Writers*. Howard University, 1974. Includes novelists, short-story writers, poets, and playwrights.

Nee, Victor G., and Brett De Bary. *Longtime Californian: A Documentary Study of an American Chinatown*. Pantheon, 1972. Interviews of hundreds of San Francisco's Chinatown people, preceded by narrative introductions.

Ng, Pearl. *Writings on the Chinese in California*. R and E Research Assoc., 4843 Mission St., San Francisco, CA 94112. ($7) Fine study with a 70-page bibliography.

Tachiki, Amy, Eddie Wong, Franklin Odo, and Buck Wong. *Roots: An Asian American Reader*. Asian American Studies Center, University of California at Los Angeles, 1971. Divided into three parts: history, community, and identity; written from a multitude of perspectives.

Thomas, Dorothy, and Richard Mishimoto. *The Spoilage*. Berkeley: University of California Press, 1946. Japanese-American civil and human rights during the World War II period; based on the records of relocation camp inmates and social scientists.

Journals

Amerasia Journal (irregular). Asian American Studies Center, 3232 Campbell Hall, UCLA, Los Angeles, CA 90024.

Asian American Review (irregular). Asian American Studies, 3407 Dwinelle Hall, Berkeley, CA 94720.

Chinese Affirmative Action Newsletter (monthly). 699 Clay St., San Francisco, CA 94111. In English and Chinese.

Intercom (3–5 times a year). The Center for War/Peace Studies, 218 E. 18th St., New York, NY 10003. Articles on issues, resources, and guides for teachers on subjects related to Asia.

Japan Chronicle. The Pacific and Asian Affairs Council, Pacific House, 2004 University Ave., Honolulu, Hawaii 96822.

Nichi Bei Times (daily, except Monday). The Nichi Bei Times Co., 2211 Bush St., San Francisco, CA 94119. A newspaper circulated mainly in the Bay Area and Northern California; printed in Japanese and English.

Nonprint Media

Films on Japan and Its National Life. Japan Information Service, Consulate General of Japan, 1601 Post St., San Francisco, CA 94115. A superior collection of 80 films on Japan; English narration. Free lending library.

Standard Oil Company of California Film Library. Free Loan Films, 25358 Cypress Ave., Hayward, CA 94544. A free film library. Titles include "Avery Brundage Collection of Asian Art" and "Japan the Beautiful."

Children of Asia. U.S. Committee to UNICEF, 331 East 38th St., New York, NY 10016. Slide sets and filmstrips illustrate the lives of children in Asia and include ways in which UNICEF touches their lives; for all ages. Slide set (30 slides), $4; filmstrip (30 frames), $3; both in color.

Organizations

Visual Communications, Asian American Studies Central, Inc., 1601 Griffith Park Blvd., Los Angeles, CA 90026.

UCLA Asian American Studies Center, 3232 Campbell Hall, Los Angeles, CA 90026.

Japanese American Curriculum Project, P.O. Box 367, San Mateo, CA 94401.

Chinese Media Committee of the Chinese for Affirmative Action, 699 Clay St., San Francisco, CA 94111.

Books for Children

Bibliographies

Books for the Chinese-American Child; A Selected List, comp. by Cecelia Mei-Chi Chen. Cooperative Children's Book Center, 1969. A list of books included for their literary quality and honesty.

The Chinese in Children's Books. Prepared by Anna Au Long et al. New York Public Library, 1973.

Posner, Arlene, and Arne J. deKeijzer, eds. *China: A Resource and Curriculum Guide.* University of Chicago Press, 1972. An annotated guide to books about China. Includes films, slides, tapes, records, periodicals and organizations.

Fiction

China and Chinese Americans

Chrisman, A. B. *Shen of the Sea., Chinese Stories for Children.* Dutton, 1968. Short stories.

DeJong, M. *The House of Sixty Fathers.* Harper & Row, 1956.

*Flack, M., and K. Wiese. *The Story about Ping, A Duck Who Lived on a House-boat on the Yangtze River.* Viking, 1933.

*Handforth, T. *Mei Li.* Doubleday, 1938.

*Lattimore, E. *Little Pear, The Story of a Little Chinese Boy.* Harcourt Brace Jovanovich, 1931.

Lewis, E. *Young Fu of the Upper Yangtze.* Holt, Rinehart and Winston, 1973. Rev. ed.

Merrill, J. *The Superlative Horse.* Young Scott Books, 1961.

Ritchie, A. *The Treasure of Li-Po.* Harcourt Brace Jovanovich, 1949. Short stories.

Treffinger, C. *Li Lun, Lad of Courage.* Abingdon, 1947.

Japan and Japanese Americans

Buck, P. *The Big Wave.* Day, 1948; new edition, 1973.

Coatsworth, E. *The Cat Who Went to Heaven.* Macmillan, 1958.

---

* Suitable for primary grades.

*Lifton, B. J. *The Cock and the Ghost Cat*. Atheneum, 1965.

*Lifton, B. J. *The Dwarf Pine Tree*. Atheneum, 1963.

*Matsuno, M. *A Pair of Red Clogs*. Collins, 1963.

*Uchida, Y. *The Forever Christmas Tree*. Scribner's, 1963.

*Uchida, Y. *Sumi & the Goat & the Tokyo Express*. Scribner's, 1969.

*Uchida, Y. *Sumi's Prize*. Scribner's, 1964.

*Yashima, T. *Crow Boy*. Viking, 1955.

Yashima, T. *The Golden Footprints*. World, 1960.

*Yashima, T. *Seashore Story*. Viking, 1967.

Japanese Americans

*Hawkinson, L. *Dance, Dance, Amy-Chan!* Whitman, 1964.

*Politi, L. *Mieko*. Golden Gate Jr. Books, 1969.

Uchida, Y. *The Promised Year*. Harcourt, 1959.

Uchida, Y. *Samurai of Gold Hill*. Scribner's, 1972.

Uchida, Y. *Journey to Topaz*. Scribner's, 1971.

Nonfiction

China and Chinese Americans

Dowdell, Dorothy. *The Chinese Helped Build America*. Messner, 1972.

Gray, Noel. *Looking at China*. Lippincott, 1975.

Hsiao, Ellen. *A Chinese Year*. Evans, 1970.

Jones, Claire. *The Chinese in America*. Lerner, 1972.

Rau, Margaret. *Our World: The People's Republic of China*. Messner, 1974.

Reit, Seymour. *Rice Cakes and Paper Dragons*. Dodd, 1973.

Sasek, M. *This Is Hong Kong*. Macmillan, 1965.

Sidel, Ruth. *Revolutionary China: People, Politics, and Ping-Pong*. Delacorte, 1974.

Spencer, Cornelia. *The Yangtze, China's River Highway*. Garrard, 1963.

Sung, Betty Lee. *The Chinese in America*. Macmillan, 1972.

Japan and Japanese Americans

Ashby, Gwynneth. *Looking at Japan*. Lippincott, 1969.

Boardman, Gwenn R. *Living in Tokyo*. Nelson, 1970.

Dowdell, Dorothy. *The Japanese Helped Build America*. Messner, 1970.

Vaughan, Josephine B. *The Land and People of Japan*. Lippincott, 1972.

*Yashima, Taro. *The Village Tree*. Viking, 1953.

---

* Suitable for primary grades.

Chinese and Japanese Poetry

Baron, Virginia Olsen, ed. *The Seasons of Time; Tanka Poetry of Ancient Japan.* Dial, 1968.

Behn, Harry, comp. *Cricket Songs; Japanese Haiku.* Harcourt Brace Jovanovich, 1964.

———— *More Cricket Songs; Japanese Haiku.* Harcourt Brace Jovanovich, 1971.

Cassedy, Sylvia, comp. *Birds, Frogs, and Moonlight; Haiku.* Doubleday, 1967.

Lewis, Richard, ed. *In A Spring Garden.* Dial, 1965.

Lewis, Richard. *The Moment of Wonder; A Collection of Chinese and Japanese Poetry.* Dial, 1964.

Selected Materials about Black Americans

Background Information for the Teacher

General

Abajian, James de T., comp. *Blacks and Their Contributions to the American West: A Bibliography and Union List of Library Holdings through 1970.* G. K. Hall and Co. ($29.50). Consists of 4,300 entries arranged in classified order; includes books, periodicals, manuscript collections, museum artifacts, etc. Covers all aspects of black life in the western states.

Butcher, Margaret Just. *The Negro in American Culture.* Mentor, 1967. The black man's contributions to American literature, music, art, dance, drama and other areas.

Franklin, John Hope, and Isidore Starr. *The Negro in Twentieth Century America: A Reader on the Struggle for Civil Rights.* Vintage, 1967. Interesting collection of documents on the black man's struggle in the Twentieth Century.

Goldston, Robert. *The Negro Revolution.* Macmillan, 1968. For young readers, the story of the Negro's pilgrimage in America.

International Library of Negro Life and History, Publishers Co., 1967, 1968. Ten volumes treating in detail the cultural and historical background of the Black American.

Jackson, Miles M. *A Bibliography of Negro History and Culture for Young People.* University of Pittsburgh Press, 1969. An annotated list of references.

Koblitz, Minnie W. *The Negro in Schoolroom Literature: Resource Materials for the Teacher of Kindergarten Through Sixth Grade.* The Center for Urban Education, 1967. Excellent list of fiction, reading series, and biography.

Miller, Elizabeth W. *The Negro in America: A Bibliography.* Harvard University Press, 1968. Comprehensive, annotated list of over 3,500 books, documents, articles, and pamphlets.

The Negro Freedom Movement: Past and Present. Wayne County Intermediate School District Desegregation Advisory Project, Detroit, 1967. Comprehensive, annotated bibliography of adult and children's books and audiovisual aids.

The Negro Heritage Library, Educational Heritage, 1966.

Ploski, Harry A., and Roscoe C. Brown. *The Negro Almanac: The Negro—His Part in America.* Bellweather Publishing Co., 1967. Useful reference book containing information on Negro history, biographies, statistical data.

Report of the National Advisory Commission on Civil Disorders, Bantam, 1968. Controversial report contains introduction by Tom Wicker and black history.

Rollins, Charlemae. *We Build Together.* NCTE, 1967. A highly selected list of fiction, history, poetry, music, sports, readable books, etc., dealing with Black Americans. Includes criteria for judging books.

Sloan, Irving. *The Negro in Modern American History Textbooks.* American Federation of Teachers, 1966. An analysis of the treatment of the Negro in sample junior and senior high school history texts; helpful to teachers.

Stanford, Barbara Dodds. *I, Too, Sing America: Black Voices in American Literature.* Hayden, 1971. Prose and poetry selections selected and introduced primarily for high school students or older. Also an excellent source of information on poets and authors for the elementary level.

Yuill, Phyllis, J. *Little Black Sambo: A Closer Look.* The Council on Interracial Books for Children. Insightful analysis of Helen Bannerman's well-known book; invaluable resource for teachers, librarians, students of children's literature.

History

Adams, Russel L. *Great Negroes Past and Present,* 3rd Ed. Afro-Am, 1970. Excellent resource for teachers and pupils; contains drawings and biographies of black heroes.

Aptheker, Herbert. *A Documentary History of the Negro People in the United States.* Citadel, 1968, 2 vols. First volume covers colonial times through Civil War; second volume chronicles the black man's role in American history from Civil War to establishment of the NAACP, 1910.

Banks, James A. *March Toward Freedom: A History of Black Americans.* Fearon, 1970. Valuable reference for teachers; a complete chronological history from African background to the revolt of the 1960's. Includes subject of black militancy, illustrations, index.

Bennett, Lerone, Jr. *Before the Mayflower: A History of the Negro in America, 1619–1964.* Penguin, 1967. Presents a unique point of view; originally published as a series of articles in *Ebony* magazine.

Blaustein, Albert P., and Robert L. Zangrando. *Civil Rights and the American Negro: A Documentary History.* Washington Square Press, 1968. Includes documents usually not found in other histories; contains strong section on constitutional and legal history.

Davidson, Basil. *A History of West Africa.* Doubleday, 1966. West African history from early times to nineteenth century.

Drotning, Philip T. *A Guide to Negro History.* Doubleday, 1968. Detailed discussion of historical sites relevant to the Negro's role in America.

Fishel, Leslie, II., Jr., and Benjamin Quarles. *The Negro American: A Documentary History.* Scott, Foresman, 1967. Includes extensive overview of each historical period written by the editors; contains section on early Africa.

Franklin, John Hope. *From Slavery to Freedom: A History of Negro Americans.* Knopf, 1967. Classic history of Black Americans.

Grant, Joanne. *Black Protest: History, Documents, and Analyses.* Fawcett, 1968. Contains strong section on Black power, documents from 1619 to present.

Harris, Middleton. *The Black Book*. Random, 1974. A scrapbook of black history; written history and folk history. An invaluable source for teachers of all levels; especially recommended.

The History of the Negro in America. Berkeley Unified School District, 1414 Walnut Street, Berkeley, California, 1967. Highly recommended resource unit containing annotated bibliographies for teachers and students.

Hughes, Langston, and Milton Meltzer. *A Pictorial History of the Negro in America*. Crown, 1968. 1,000 prints, engravings and photographs; twelfth printing.

Katz, William L. *Teacher's Guide to American Negro History*. Quadrangle, 1968. Contains brief overview of Negro history, extensive annotated bibliographies of books and other sources.

Osofsky, Gilbert. *The Burden of Race: A Documentary History of Negro-White Relations in America*. Harper & Row, 1967. Includes representative documents from each historical period ranging from a slave voyage to a Stokeley Carmichael statement.

Quarles, Benjamin. *The Negro in the Making of America*. Collier, 1964. Interesting and highly readable.

Salk, Erwin A. *A Layman's Guide to Negro History*. McGraw, 1967. A list of books and teaching aids; valuable resource for the teacher.

Welsch, Edwin K. *The Negro in the United States: A Research Guide*. Indiana University Press, 1966. In-depth guide into Negro history for the scholar.

Curriculum Materials

Archibald, Helen A. *Negro History and Culture: Selections for Use with Children*. Community Renewal Society, 116 South Michigan, Chicago, IL 60630. Undated. Poems, biographies, songs and other selections; for elementary school teachers.

Banfield, Beryle. *Africa in the Curriculum*. Edward W. Plyden Press, 1968. A valuable resource prepared to help teachers plan lessons on Africa.

Gibson, John S. *The Intergroup Relations Curriculum: A Program for Elementary School Education*. The Lincoln Filene Center for Citizenship and Public Affairs, Tufts University, Medford, MA 02155. 1968. For grades K–8, a comprehensive intergroup education program.

Integrated School Books. NAACP Special Contribution Fund, 1790 Broadway, New York, NY 10019. 1967. Primary and elementary school texts and story books recommended by the NAACP Education Department.

Journals

Africana Library Journal: A Quarterly Bibliography and Resource Guide. 101 Fifth Ave., New York, NY 10003. Evaluations of books on Africa published throughout the world; current bibliographies, information on African writers and scholars; children's books and AV materials, adult books.

The Black Scholar. P.O. Box 908, Sausalito, CA 94965. Highly influential black-oriented publication; contains valuable book review section.

Crisis. Organ of the National Association for the Advancement of Colored People. The Crisis Publishing Co., 1790 Broadway, New York, NY 10019. ($1.50/year)

Ebony. Johnson Publishing Co., 1820 S. Michigan Ave., Chicago, IL 60616.

Freedomways. Quarterly Review of the Negro Freedom Movement. Freedomway Associates, 799 Broadway, New York, NY 10013. ($3.50/year)

Jet. Johnson Publishing Co., 1820 S. Michigan Ave., Chicago, IL 60616. ($7/year)

The Journal of Negro History. Published quarterly by the Association for the Study of Negro Life and History, 1538 Ninth Street, NW., Washington, D.C. Contains scholarly articles on Negro culture and history, book reviews, important documents.

Negro-American Literature Forum for School and University Teachers. Indiana State University, Terre Haute, IN 47809. ($2/year)

Negro Heritage. P.O. Box 1057, Washington, D.C. 20013. ($3.75/year)

Negro History Bulletin. The Association for the Study of Negro Life and History, Inc., 1538 Ninth Street, NW., Washington, D.C. 20001. ($3/year)

Sepia. Sepia Publishing Co., 1220 Harding St., Fort Worth, TX 76102. ($2/year)

Nonprint Media

Afro-American Audio-Visual History and Culture Series. Produced and distributed by Buckingham Enterprises Inc., 160-08 Jamaica Ave., Jamaica NY 11432. A series of kits, each one containing drawings of outstanding Black Americans, teacher's manual, filmstrips and recordings, texts, workbooks.

Afro-American History and Culture. Produced and distributed by Folkways/Scholastic Records, 906 Sylvan Ave., Englewood Cliffs, NJ 07632. A set of 27 albums in five units including material written and narrated by Langston Hughes, an anthology of U.S. Negro poets, West African folk tales; booklets accompany material.

Afro-American History Posters. Pittman Publishing Corp, 20 East 46th St., New York. The black man's role in the building of America depicted in a set of fifteen posters.

Afro-American History Program. Educational Division, Encyclopedia Britannica, 425 North Michigan Ave., Chicago. Black American history in four sets of color filmstrips; textbooks available.

Afro-American History Series. AEVAC, Inc., Educational Publishers, 500 Fifth Ave., New York 10036. Black American history presented in set of 18 full-color transparencies with 49 overlays.

Aime Records. Aime Associates, Inc., 123 Manhattan Ave., New York 10025. Various phases of Afro-American history and culture.

Black History. Multi-Media Productions, 580 College Ave., Palo Alto, Calif. Excellent series of 15 filmstrips including review exercises and answers.

Children of Africa. U.S. Committee for UNICEF, 331 East 38th St., New York, NY 10016. Slide set and filmstrip that illustrates needs of children and UNICEF's work in Africa. In color and for all ages. Includes teacher's guide and commentary. Slide set (20 slides), $3; filmstrip (20 frames), $2.

Ellis Photographs and Drawings. Ellis Book Store, 6447 South Cottage Grove, Chicago, IL 60637. Collection of wall-sized photographs and drawings of eminent Black Americans.

Jefferson, Louise E., and James H. Robinson. *Twentieth Century Americans of Negro Lineage.* Friendship Press, 475 Riverside Dr., New York 10027; Vaughn's Book Store, 12123 Dexter, Detroit, MI 48206. Excellent set consists of a portfolio of 24 photographs and a pictomap that tells of the Negro's history in America.

Negro History: Multi-Media Kit. Society for Visual Education, Inc., 1345 Diversey Parkway, Chicago 60614. Collection of teaching aids including seven sound filmstrips, four records, one book, three sets of picture portfolios, and six overhead transparencies.

Photopak. Johnson Publishing Co., 1820 S. Michigan Ave., Chicago 60616. Black and white wall-sized photographs of famous Black Americans plus scenes from everyday life.

A Picture History of the American Negro. Rand McNally Co., Box 7600, Chicago; Pepsi Cola Bottling Companies. A visual kit containing a wall-sized mural and including portraits of 68 famous Americans, a student's booklet, and a teacher's manual; also contains two sound filmstrips in the Pepsi Cola package.

Which Way to Equality: The Afro-American Experience. Scholastic Magazines, 906 Sylvan Ave., Englewood Cliffs, NJ 07632. Includes a teacher's guide, booklets, a record, a filmstrip and a report.

Winslow, Eugene, David P. Ross, and Russel L. Adams. *Afro-Am Portfolios 1, 2,* and *3.* Afro-Am Publishing Co., Inc., 1727 S. Indiana Ave., Chicago 60616, and Society for Visual Education, 1345 Diversey Parkway, Chicago 60614. A set of three portfolios with each set containing 24 wall-sized portraits drawn by Eugene Winslow; brief biographies; highly recommended.

Books for Children

Bibliographies

Baker, Augusta. *Books about Negro Life for Children.* New York Public Library, 1968. An annotated list of children's books with black characters.

Broderick, Dorothy M. *The Image of the Black in Children's Fiction.* Bowker, 1973. Racism in books recommended by established library periodicals and reference sources; an analysis.

Dodds, Barbara, comp. *Negro Literature for High School Students.* NCTE, 1968. Valuable reference guide; suggestions for classroom uses of black literature; extensive bibliography.

Irwin, Leonard, comp. *Black Studies: A Bibliography.* McKinley, 1973. Biographical material, African background, essays and anthologies, and other materials, annotated; for young people and adults.

Latimer, Bettye I., et al., eds. *Starting Out Right: Choosing Books About Black People for Young Children, Pre-School Through Third Grade,* 1972. Distributed by Division for Administrative Services, Wisconsin Hall, 126 Langdon St., Madison, WI 53702. Contains outstanding chapter on criteria for selecting children's literature on black themes; reviews of 300 books.

Lerner, Gerda, ed. *Black Women in White America.* Random House, 1972. A fine documentary history including speeches, letters, essays on various subjects.

McCann, Donnarae, and Gloria Woodward, eds. *The Black American in Books for Children: Readings in Racism.* Scarecrow, 1972. Compilation of 25 articles pinpointing racist attitudes in books; urges involvement of Black Americans in procedures of book production.

Millender, Dharathula H. *Real Negroes/Honest Settings: Children's and Young People's Books about Negro Life and History.* American Federation of Teachers, 1967. Compilation and discussion of a list of fiction, biography and factual books about Negroes; illustrated.

Mills, Joyce White, comp. *The Black World in Literature for Children; A Bibliography of Print and Non-Print Materials.* Atlanta University, 1975. For children 3–13.

Rollins, Charlemae, ed. *We Build Together; A Reader's Guide to Negro Life and Literature for Elementary and High School Use.* 3rd ed. NCTE, 1967. Annotated bibliography of fiction, picture books, history, biography, folklore, poetry, science, music and sports.

Rollock, Barbara, comp. *The Black Experience in Children's Books,* rev. ed. New York Public Library, 1974. Annotated bibliography about black life in America, Africa, the islands, and England; classified by age and subject matter.

Fiction

Agle, Nana Hayde. *Maple Street.* Seabury, 1970.

Armstrong, William H. *Sounder.* Harper & Row, 1969.

Childress, Alice. *A Hero ain't nothin' but a Sandwich.* Coward McCann & Geoghegan, 1973.

*Clifton, Lucille. *Somé of the Days of Everett Anderson.* Holt, Rinehart and Winston, 1970.

Cone, Molly. *The Other Side of the Fence.* Houghton Mifflin, 1967.

Devereaux, Alexis. *Na-ni.* Harper & Row, 1973.

Dorson, Richard M., collector. *American Negro Folktales.* Fawcett, 1967.

Fox, Paula. *The Slave Dancer.* Bradbury, 1973.

*Greenfield, Eloise. *She Come Bringing Me That Little Baby Girl.* Lippincott, 1974.

Graham, Lorenz. *North Town* and other titles. T. Y. Crowell, 1965.

Hamilton, Virginia. *The House of Dies Drear.* Macmillan, 1968.

———. *Zeely.* Macmillan, 1967.

———. *M. C. Higgins the Great.* Macmillan, 1974.

Justus, May. *A New Home for Billy.* Hastings House, 1966.

*Keats, Ezra Jack. *The Snowy Day.* Viking, 1962.

Konigsburg, E. L. *Jennifer, Hecate, Macbeth, William McKinley, and Me, Elizabeth.* Atheneum, 1967.

Krementz, Jill. *Sweet Pea: A Black Girl Growing Up in the Rural South.* Harcourt Brace Jovanovich, 1969.

Petry, Ann. *Tituba of Salem Village.* Crowell, 1964.

Wilkinson, Brenda. *Ludell.* Harper & Row, 1975.

Shearer, John. *I Wish I Had an Afro.* Cowles, 1970.

Steptoe, John. *Marcia.* Viking, 1976.

*———. *Stevie.* Harper & Row, 1969.

---

* Suitable for primary grades.

———. *Train Ride*. Harper & Row, 1971.

———. *Uptown*. Harper & Row, 1970.

Nonfiction

Books listed are for grades 4–8. Titles reveal the subject of biographies.

Abdul, Raoul, ed. *The Magic of Black Poetry*. Dodd, 1972.

Adoff, Arnold. *Malcolm X*. Crowell, 1970.

Adoff, Arnold, comp. *Black on Black*. Macmillan, 1968.

Berg, Jean Horton. *I Cry When the Sun Goes Down: The Story of Herman Wrice*. Westminster, 1975.

Bernard, Jacqueline. *Journey Toward Freedom: The Story of Sojourner Truth*. Norton, 1967.

Brownmiller, Susan. *Shirley Chisholm*. Doubleday, 1970.

Chambers, Bradford. *Chronicles of Negro Protest*. Parents', 1968.

Chittenden, Elizabeth F. *Profiles in Black and White: Stories of Men and Women Who Fought Against Slavery*. Scribner's, 1973.

Clayton, Ed. *Martin Luther King: The Peaceful Warrior*. Prentice-Hall, 1968.

Dahlstedt, Marden. *The Terrible Wave*. Coward McCann & Geoghegan, 1972.

Douty, Esther Morris. *Charlotte Forten: Free Black Teacher*. Garrard, 1971.

Feelings, Tom. *Black Pilgrimage*. Lothrop, 1972.

Folsom, Franklin. *The Life and Legends of George McJunkin, Black Cowboy*. Nelson, 1973.

Graham, Lorenz. *David He No Fear*. Crowell, 1971.

———. *Every Man Heart Lay Down*. Crowell, 1970.

———. *How God Fix Jonah*. Crowell, 1970.

———. *A Road Down in the Sea*. Crowell, 1970.

Greenfield, Eloise. *Paul Robeson*. Crowell, 1975.

———. *Rosa Parks*. Crowell, 1973.

Hamilton, Virginia. *The Time-Ago Tales of Jahdu*. Macmillan, 1969.

Hardwick, Richard. *Charles Richard Drew: Pioneer in Blood Research*. Scribner's, 1967.

Harris, Janet. *The Long Freedom Road*. McGraw, 1968.

Haskins, James. *From Lew Alcindor to Kareem Abdul Jabbar*. Lothrop, 1972.

Hayden, Robert, ed. *Kaleidoscope; Poems by American Negro Poets*. Harcourt Brace Jovanovich, 1967.

Jones, Hettie. *Big Star Fallin' Mama; Five Women in Black Music*. Viking, 1974.

Jordan, June. *Who Look at Me?* Crowell, 1969.

Kaufman, Mervyn. *Jesse Owens*. Crowell, 1973.

Lawrence, Jacob. *Harriet and the Promised Land*. Windmill, 1968.

Mathis, Sharon Bell. *Ray Charles*. Crowell, 1973.

McGovern, Ann. *Runaway Slave: The Story of Harriet Tubman*. Four Winds, 1965.

Meltzer, Milton. *Langston Hughes: A Biography.* Crowell, 1968.

Meyer, Howard. *Colonel of the Black Regiment: The Life of Thomas Wentworth Higginson.* Norton, 1967.

Montgomery, Elizabeth. *William C. Handy: Father of the Blues.* Garrard, 1968.

Moore, Carman. *Somebody's Angel Child; The Story of Bessie Smith.* Crowell, 1970.

Newman, Shirlee P. *Marian Anderson: Lady from Philadelphia.* Westminster, 1966.

Petry, Ann. *Harriet Tubman: Conductor on the Underground Railroad.* Crowell, 1955.

Rollins, Charlemae Hill. *They Showed the Way: Forty American Negro Leaders.* Crowell, 1964.

Rowe, Jeanne. *An Album of Martin Luther King, Jr.* Watts, 1970.

Rubin, Robert. *Satchel Paige: All-time Baseball Great.* Putnam, 1974.

Sterne, Emma Gelders. *Mary McLeod Bethune.* Knopf, 1957.

Tobias, Tobi. *Arthur Mitchell.* Crowell, 1975.

Turk, Midge. *Gordon Parks.* Crowell, 1971.

Williams, John A. *The Most Native of Sons.* Doubleday, 1970.

Wolkstein, Diane. *The Cool Ride in the Sky.* Knopf, 1973.

Yates, Elizabeth. *Amos Fortune: Free Man.* Dutton, 1950.

Young, Bernice E. *Harlem: The Story of a Changing Community.* Messner, 1972.

Young, Margaret E. *The Picture Life of Ralph J. Bunche.* Watts, 1968.

Selected Materials about Mexican American/Chicano Backgrounds

Background Information for the Teacher

Bibliografía about the Chicano. San Jose Unified School District; Mexican American Graduate Studies Department, San Jose State College, San Jose, California.

Ceja, Manuel V. *Methods of Orientation of Spanish-Speaking Children to an American School.* R and E Research Assoc., reprint 1973. ($8)

Chang, Dorothy K. *A Guide to Understanding and Teaching of Mexican-American Adolescents.* R and E Research Assoc., reprint 1973. ($8)

Chicanos in Children's Books. The *Bulletin,* Council on Interracial Books, CIBC Resource Center, Room 300, 1841 Broadway, New York, NY 10023. ($2.50)

Conwell, Mary K., and Pura Belpré. *Libros en Español: An Annotated List of Children's Books in Spanish.* New York Public Library, 1971.

Cooper, Elizabeth K. *Attitude of Children and Teachers Toward Mexican, Negro and Jewish Minorities.* R and E Research Assoc., reprint 1972. ($7)

Drake, Rollen H. *A Comparative Study of the Mentality and Achievement of Mexican and White Children.* R and E Research Assoc., reprint 1972. ($7)

Gould, Betty. *Methods of Teaching Mexicans.* R and E Research Associates, 4843 Mission Street, San Francisco, CA 94112. Reprint 1973. ($8)

Marcoux, Fred W. *Handicaps of Bi-lingual Mexican Children.* R and E Research Assoc., reprint 1973. ($8)

Meguire, K. H. *Educating the Mexican Child in the Elementary School.* R and E Research Assoc., reprint 1973. ($8)

Revelle, Keith. *Chicano.* Oakland Public Library, 1969.

Teachers and Students: Differences in Teacher Interaction with Mexican American and Anglo Students. Report V: Mexican American Education Study. A report of the U.S. Commission on Civil Rights. Superintendent of Documents, U.S. Government Printing Office, Washington, D.C. 20402, 1973.

Journals and Newsletters

Bronze. 1560 34th Avenue, Oakland, CA 94601. ($4/year)

Carta Editorial. P.O. Box 54624, Terminal Annex, Los Angeles, CA 90054 ($3/year)

Chicano Student Movement. P.O. Box 31322, Los Angeles, CA 90031. ($2.50/year)

Compass. 1209 Egypt Street, Houston, TX 77009. (Free)

El Gallo 1265 Cherokee Street, Denver, CO 80204. ($2.50/year)

El Grito del Norte. Rt. 2, Box 5, Espanola, NM 87532. (15¢/copy)

El Hispanoamericano. 630 Ninth Street, Sacramento, CA 95825. ($3/year)

Inside Eastside. P.O. Box 63273, Los Angeles, CA 90063. ($2.50/year)

Lado. 1306 N. Western Avenue, Chicago, IL 60622. ($5/year)

El Macriado. P.O. Box 130, Delano, CA 93215. ($3.50/year)

La Opinion. 1426 S. Main Street, Los Angeles, CA 90015. ($2/month)

La Prensa Libre. 2973 Sacramento Street, Berkeley, CA 94702. ($2/year)

La Raza. 2445 Gates Street, Los Angeles, CA 90031. ($2.50/year)

Times of the Americas. P.O. Box 1173, Coral Gables, FL 33134. ($6/year)

La Verdad. P.O. Box 13156, San Diego, CA 92113. ($3/year)

Proyecto Leer Bulletin. 1736 Columbia Road, NW., St. 107, Washington, D.C. 20009.

Children's Books

Fiction

Babbitt, Lorraine. *Pink Like the Geranium.* Children's Press, 1974.

Balet, Jan. *The Fence.* Delacorte, 1969. (Easy)

*Behn, Harry. *The Two Uncles of Pablo.* Harcourt Brace Jovanovich, 1959.

Bonham, Frank. *Viva Chicano.* Dutton, 1970.

Bulla, Clyde Robert. *The Poppy Seeds.* Crowell, 1955.

Colman, Hila. *Chicano Girl.* Morrow, 1973.

*Ets, Marie Hall. *Bad Boy, Good Boy.* Crowell, 1967.

*———. *Nine Days to Christmas.* Viking, 1959. (Easy)

Flack, Marjorie, and Karl Larrson. *Pedro.* Macmillan, 1940.

---

* Suitable for primary grades.

Forsee, Aylesa. *Too Much Dog*. Lippincott, 1957.

Garrett, Helen. *Ángelo, the Naughty One*. Viking, 1944.

Garthwaite, Marian. *Tomás and the Red-Haired Angel*. Messner, 1966.

Good, Loren. *Panchito*. Coward, 1955.

Hitte, Kathryn, and William B. Hayes. *Mexicali Soup*. Parents', 1970.

Kidwell, Carl. *Arrow in the Sun*. Viking, 1961.

Krumgold, Joseph. *And Now Miguel*. Crowell, 1970.

Lampman, Evelyn S. *Go Up the Road*. Atheneum, 1972.

Lay, Marion. *Wooden Saddles: The Adventures of a Mexican Boy in His Own Land*. Morrow, 1939.

Lewis, Thomas P. *Hill of Fire*. Harper & Row, 1971. (Easy)

Molnar, Joe, ed. Graciela: *A Mexican-American Child Tells Her Story*. Watts, 1972.

Moon, Grace. *Tita of Mexico*. Stokes, 1934.

Morrow, Elizabeth. *The Painted Pig*. Knopf, 1930.

Norman, James. *Charro: Mexican Horseman*. Putnam, 1970.

O'Dell, Scott. *The Black Pearl*. Houghton Mifflin, 1967.

————. *The King's Fifth*. Houghton Mifflin, 1966.

Parish, Helen Rand. *Estebánico*. Viking, 1974.

*Politi, Leo. *Juanita*. Scribner's, 1948.

*————. *The Mission Bell*. Scribner's, 1953.

*————. *Pedro, the Angel of Olvera Street*. Scribner's, 1946.

*————. *Rosa*. Scribner's, 1963.

Ritchie, Barbara. *Ramón Makes a Trade; Los Cambios de Ramón*. Parnassus, 1959.

Sawyer, Ruth. *The Least One*. Viking, 1941.

Schweitzer, Byrd Baylor. *Amigo*. Macmillan, 1963. (Easy)

*Todd, Barbara. *Juan Patricio*. Putnam, 1972.

Treviño, Elizabeth Borton de. *Nacar, the White Deer*. Farrar, Straus, & Giroux, 1963.

Witton, Dorothy. *Crossroads for Chela*. Messner, 1956.

Folklore

Brenner, Anita. *The Boy Who Could Do Anything & Other Mexican Folk Tales*. Young Scott, 1942.

Campbell, Camilla. *Star Mountain, and Other Legends of Mexico*. McGraw-Hill, 1968.

Nonfiction

Books cited are for grades 4–8. Titles reveal the subject of the book.

Bailey, Bernadine. *Famous Latin American Liberators*. Dodd, Mead, 1960.

————. *Picture Book of New Mexico*. Whitman, 1960.

Blecker, Sonia. *The Aztec: Indians of Mexico*. Morrow, 1963.

————. *The Maya: Indians of Central America*. Morrow, 1961.

Discoverers of the New World, by the editors of American Heritage. American Heritage, 1960.

Epstein, Sam. *The First Book of Mexico.* Watts, 1967.

Glubok, Shirley. *The Art of Ancient Mexico.* Harper & Row, 1968.

Goetz, Delia. *Neighbors to the South.* Harcourt Brace Jovanovich.

Grant, Clara Louise. *Mexico, Land of the Plumed Serpent.* Garrard, 1968.

Hogner, Dorothy Childs. *Children of Mexico.* Heath, 1942.

Jacobs, W. J. *Hernando Cortés.* Watts, 1974.

McNeer, May. *The Mexican Story.* Ariel, 1953.

Neurath, Marie. *They Lived Like This in Ancient Mexico.* Watts, 1971.

Rose, Patricia. *Let's Read about Mexico.* Fideler, 1955.

Syme, Ronald. *Cortés of Mexico.* Morrow, 1951.

———. *Juárez: The Founder of Modern Mexico.* Morrow, 1972.

Wilson, Barbara Kerr. *Fairy Tales of Mexico.* Cassell, (London)-Dutton, 1960.

Mexicans in the United States

De Garza, Patricia. *Chicanos; The Story of Mexican Americans.* Messner, 1973.

Franchere, Ruth. *César Chavez.* Crowell, 1970.

Katz, William Loren. *Modern America, 1957 to the Present.* Watts, 1975.

———. *Years of Strife, 1929–1956.* Watts, 1975.

Marcus, Rebecca B., and Judith Marcus. *Fiesta Time in Mexico.* Garrard, 1974.

Newlon, Clarke. *Famous Mexican-Americans.* Dodd, 1972.

Sechrist, Elizabeth Hough. *Christmas Everywhere.* Macrae Smith, 1962.

———. *It's Time for Brotherhood.* Macrae Smith, 1973.

Weiner, Sandra. *Small Hands, Big Hands.* Pantheon, 1970.

Nonprint Media

Children of Latin America. U.S. Committee for UNICEF, 331 East 38th St., New York, NY 10016. Slide set and filmstrip showing the lives of children in Latin America and the work of the Children's Fund on their behalf. For all ages and in color; includes teacher's guide and commentary. Slide set (30 slides), $4; filmstrip (30 frames), $3.

Ramirez, A. R. *Teaching Reading to Spanish Speakers.* Rental or purchase fees. The JAB PRESS, INC., P.O. Box 213, Fair Lawn, NJ 07410. Available in English or Spanish narrative versions. A visual report of an experiment undertaken which introduced reading in their native language to Spanish speakers in kindergarten.

Ramirez, A. R. *Teaching English in Kindergarten—ESL.* Rental or purchase fees. The JAB PRESS, INC. Available in English or Spanish narrative versions. A view of kindergarten students in a class where the major language spoken in the home is Spanish.

Selected Materials about Native Americans

Background Information for the Teacher

Bahr, Howard M., Bruce A. Chadwick, and Robert C. Day. *Native Americans Today: Sociological Perspectives.* Harper & Row, 1972.

Beauchamp, William M. *A History of the New York Iroquois.* Friedman, 1968.

Brown, Dee. *Bury My Heart at Wounded Knee.* Holt, Rinehart and Winston, 1970.

Burnette, Robert and John Koster. *The Road to Wounded Knee.* Bantam, 1974. Analysis of events leading up to Wounded Knee, 1973.

Byler, Mary Gloyne. *American Indian Authors for Young Readers.* Association on American Indian Affairs, 432 Park Ave., South, New York, NY 10016 An annotated bibliography.

The Council on Interracial Books for Children. *Chronicles of American Indian Protest.* A collection of documents recounting the American Indian's struggle for survival. Offers supplemental reading assignments for classes.

Deloria, Vine, Jr. *Custer Died for Your Sins.* Avon, 1970.

Fenton, William N., ed. *Parker on the Iroquois.* Syracuse University Press, 1968.

Foreman, Grant. *Indian Removal.* University of Oklahoma Press, 1932.

Graymont, Barbara. *The Iroquois in the American Revolution.* Syracuse U. Press, 1972.

Hagan, William T. *American Indians.* University of Chicago Press, 1961.

LaPointe, Frank. *The Sioux Today.* Macmillan, 1972. Stories of young Indians.

Lenarcic, R. J. *Pre-Columbian Indians: New Perspectives.* Community College Social Science Assoc., 1974.

Oswalt, Wendell H. *This Land Was Theirs.* Wiley, 1966. Pre-Columbian cultural aspects.

Prucha, Francis Paul. *American Indian Policy in the Formative Years.* University of Nebraska Press, 1962. Trade and Intercourse Acts, 1790–1834.

Strensland, Anna Lee. *Literature By and About the American Indian: An Annotated Bibliography for Jr. and Sr. High School Students.* NCTE.

Van Every, Dale. *Disinherited.* Morrow, 1966. Removal of the Cherokee.

Wilson, Edmund. *Apologies to the Iroquois.* Vintage, 1959. Historical and contemporary problems.

Journals

AAIA, 432 Park Ave., New York, NY 10016. General and legislative information; newsletter.

Akwesasne Notes. Mohawk Nation via Rooseveltown, NY 13683. ($8/year) Indian paper; current events and activities. Donation, publishes calendar.

American Indian Media Directory. American Indian Press Association, Room 206, 1346 Connecticut Ave., NW., Washington, D.C. 20036. ($10) Listing press, radio, TV/video, film, theater.

Wassaja. American Indian Historical Society, 1451 Masonic Ave., San Francisco, CA 94117. Monthly newspaper; significant events.

Sources of Materials

Alaska Rural School Project, Univ. of Alaska, College, AK 99701

Navajo Curriculum Center, Rough Rock Demonstration School, Rough Rock, AZ

Navajo Social Studies Project, College of Education, The Univ. of New Mexico, Albuquerque, NM 87106

Senate Committee on Labor and Public Welfare, Washington, D.C.

South Central Regional Ed. Lab. Corp., 408 National Old Line Bldg., Little Rock, AR 72201

Nonprint Media

Bibliography of Nonprint Instructional Materials on the American Indian prepared by the Instructional Development Program for the Institute of Indian Services and Research, Brigham Young University. Brigham Young University Printing Service, Provo, Utah 84601, 1972. A 220-page publication including films of all types, slides, recordings, varied visual teaching aids, and multimedia kits. Entries are annotated and indexed with a reference to the grade level.

Books for Children

Fiction

Bales, Carol Ann. *Kevin Cloud; Chippewa Boy in the City.* Reilly & Lee, 1972.

Baker, Betty. *And One Was a Wooden Indian.* Macmillan, 1970.

Baylor, Byrd. *When Clay Sings.* Scribner's, 1972.

Beatty, Patricia. *The Bad Bell of San Salvador.* Morrow, 1973.

*Benchley, Nathaniel. *Small Wolf.* Harper & Row, 1972.

Clark, Ann Nolan. *Blue Canyon Horse.* Viking, 1954.

Clifford, Eth. *The Year of the Three-Legged Deer.* Houghton Mifflin, 1972.

Clymer, Eleanor. *The Spider, the Cave and the Pottery Bowl.* Atheneum, 1971.

*Dalgliesh, Alice. *The Courage of Sarah Noble.* Scribner's, 1954.

Fife, Dale. *Ride the Crooked Wind.* Coward, 1973.

Forman, James. *The Life and Death of Yellow Bird.* Farrar, Straus & Giroux, 1973.

Goble, Paul, and Dorothy Goble. *Lone Bull's Horse Raid.* Bradbury, 1973.

———. *Red Hawk's Account of Custer's Last Battle.* Pantheon, 1970.

Griese, Arnold A. *At the Mouth of the Luckiest River.* Crowell, 1973.

Harris, Christie. *Raven's Cry.* Atheneum, 1966.

Houston, James. *Eagle Mask.* Harcourt Brace Jovanovich, 1966.

———. *Ghost Paddle.* Harcourt Brace Jovanovich, 1972.

Jones, Weyman. *Edge of Two Worlds.* Dial, 1968.

Lampman, Evelyn Sibley. *The Year of Small Shadow.* Harcourt Brace Jovanovich, 1971.

*McDermott, Gerald. *Arrow to the Sun: A Pueblo Indian Tale.* Viking, 1974.

*Monjo, F. N. *Indian Summer.* Harper & Row, 1968.

O'Dell, Scott. *Island of the Blue Dolphins.* Houghton Mifflin, 1960.

———. *Sing Down the Moon.* Houghton Mifflin, 1970.

Peake, Katy. *The Indian Heart of Carrie Hodges.* Viking, 1972.

---

* Suitable for primary grades.

Sleator, William. *The Angry Moon*. Little, Brown, 1970.

Sneve, Virginia Driving Hawk. *Betrayed*. Holiday House, 1974. Fictional account of historical episode.

Williams, Barbara. *The Secret Name*. Harcourt Brace Jovanovich, 1972.

Wolf, Bernard. *Tinker and the Medicine Man: The Story of a Navajo Boy of Monument Valley*. Random House, 1973.

Nonfiction

Allen, Terry, ed. *The Whispering Wind*. Doubleday, 1972. Poetry written by young Eskimo, Aleut, and American Indian students.

Armstrong, Virginia Irving, ed. *I Have Spoken*. Sage Books, 1971.

Bailey, Paul D. *Ghost Dance Messiah*. Westernlore, 1970.

Baker, Betty. *At the Center of the World*. Macmillan, 1973. Based on Papago and Pima myths; includes six myths about the Arizona Indians.

Baldwin, Gordon C. *How Indians Really Lived*. Putnam, 1967.

Baylor, Byrd. *Before You Came This Way*. Dutton, 1969.

———. *They Put on Masks*. Scribner's, 1974.

———. *When Clay Sings*. Scribner's, 1972.

Bealer, Alex W. *Only the Names Remain: The Cherokee and the Trail of Tears*. Little, Brown, 1972.

Beauchamp, William M. *A History of the New York Iroquois*. Friedman, 1968.

Beck, Barbara L. *The First Book of the Aztecs*. Watts, 1966.

Bierhorst, John, ed. *In the Trail of the Wind; American Indian Poems and Ritual Orations*. Farrar, Straus & Giroux, 1971.

Bleeker, Sonia. *The Cherokee: Indians of the Mountains*. Morrow, 1952.

———. *The Crow Indians: Hunters of the Northern Plains*. Morrow, 1951.

———. *The Delaware Indians: Eastern Fishermen and Farmers*. Morrow, 1953.

———. *Indians of the Longhouse: The Story of the Iroquois*. Morrow, 1950.

———. *The Maya*. Morrow, 1961.

———. *The Mission Indians of California*. Morrow, 1956.

———. *The Navajo: Herders, Weavers and Silversmiths*. Morrow, 1958.

———. *The Sioux Indians: Hunters and Warriors of the Plains*. Morrow, 1962.

Bringle, Mary. *Eskimos*. Watts, 1973.

Brown, Dee. *Bury My Heart at Wounded Knee*. Holt Rinehart and Winston, 1970.

Bulla, Clyde. *Pocahontas and the Strangers*. Crowell, 1971.

Burt, Jesse Clifton. *Indians of the Southeast: Then and Now*. Abingdon, 1973.

Clark, Ann Nolan. *Circle of Seasons*. Farrar, Straus & Giroux, 1970. Describes ceremonies of the Pueblo Indians.

Collier, John. *The Indians of the Americas*. Norton, 1947.

Collier, Peter. *When Shall They Rest? The Cherokees' Long Struggle with America*. Holt, Rinehart and Winston, 1970.

Coy, Harold. *Man Comes to America*. Little, Brown, 1973.

Crary, Margaret. *Susette La Flesche: Voice of the Omaha Indians*. Hawthorne, 1973.

D'Amato, Janet. *American Indian Craft Inspirations*. Evans, 1972.

Daniels, Walter M., ed. *American Indians*. Wilson, 1957.

David, Russell, and Brent Ashabranner. *Chief Joseph, War Chief of the Nez Percé*. McGraw-Hill, 1962.

Dorian, Edith. *Hokahey! American Indians Then and Now*. McGraw-Hill, 1957.

Eastman, Charles A. *Indian Boyhood*. Dover, 1971.

Ehrlich, Amy. *Wounded Knee: An Indian History of the American West*. Holt, Rinehart and Winston, 1974.

Elting, Mary. *The Hopi Way*. Evans, 1969.

Erdoes, Richard. *The Pueblo Indians*. Young Readers' Indian Library, 1967.

———. *The Sun Dance People*. Knopf, 1972.

Fenton, William N., ed. *Parker on the Iroquois*. Syracuse University Press, 1968.

Folsom, Franklin. *Red Power on the Rio Grande: The Nature of the American Revolution of 1680*. Follett, 1973.

Foreman, Grant. *Indian Removal*. University of Oklahoma Press, 1932.

Glubok, Shirley. *The Art of Ancient Mexico*. Harper & Row, 1968.

———. *The Art of the North American Indian*. Harper & Row, 1964.

———. *The Art of the Northwest Coast Indians*. Macmillan, 1975.

———. *The Art of the Southwest Indians*. Macmillan, 1971.

Grant, Bruce. *American Indians Yesterday and Today*. Dutton, 1958.

Graymont, Barbara. *The Iroquois in the American Revolution*. Syracuse U. Press, 1972.

Gridley, Marion E. *American Indian Women*. Hawthorne, 1974. Describes the lives of 19 women ranging over a period of 300 years.

———. *Indian Tribes of America*. Hubbard, 1973.

Gurko, Miriam. *Indian America: The Black Hawk War*. Crowell, 1970.

Hagan, William T. *American Indians*. University of Chicago Press, 1961.

Hamilton, Charles. *Cry of the Thunderbird*. Macmillan, 1950.

Haverstock, Mary Sayre. *Indian Gallery*. Four Winds, 1973. A biography of artist George Catlin who traveled among the Indian tribes painting Indian subjects and collecting materials for an Indian museum.

Hays, Wilma P. *Foods the Indians Gave Us*. Washburn, 1973.

Hirsch, S. Carl. *Famous American Indians of the Plains*. Rand McNally, 1973.

Hofmann, Charles. *American Indians Sing*. Day, 1967.

Hofsinde, Robert. *Indian Arts*. Morrow, 1971.

———. *Indian Music Makers*. Morrow, 1967.

———. *Indian Warriors and Their Weapons*. Morrow, 1965.

Houston, James. *Songs of the Dream People*. Atheneum, 1972. A collection of songs and chants.

Hunt, W. Ben. *The Complete Book of Indian Crafts and Lore*. Golden, 1976.

Indian Culture Series. Montana Reading Publications, Level 4, Stapleton Building, Billings, MT 59101. Series written and illustrated by Indian children for Indians.

Jacobson, Daniel. *Great Indian Tribes*. Hammond, 1970.

Johnston, Johanna. *The Indians and the Strangers*. Dodd, Mead, 1972.

Jones, Hettie, comp. *The Trees Stand Shining; Poetry of the North American Indians*. Dial, 1971.

Josephy, Alvin. *The Nez Percé Indians and the Opening of the Northwest*. Yale University Press, 1965.

Jones, Jayne Clark. *The American Indian in America*. Lerner, 1973.

——. *Red Power: The American Indians' Fight for Freedom*. American Heritage Press, 1971.

——. *The Patriot Chiefs*. Viking, 1958.

Katz, William Loren. *Early America, 1492–1812*. Watts, 1974.

——. *Reconstruction and National Growth, 1865–1900*. Watts, 1974.

Kirk, Ruth. *David, Young Chief of the Quileutes: An American Indian Today*. Harcourt Brace Jovanovich, 1967.

Kroeber, Theodora. *Ishi: Last of His Tribes*. Parnassus, 1964.

La Farge, Oliver. *The American Indian*. Golden, 1960.

——. *Pictorial History of the American Indian*. Crown, 1956.

Lenarcic, R. J. *Pre-Columbian Indians: New Perspectives*. Community College Social Science Assoc., 1974.

McNeer, May. *The American Indian Story*. Ariel, 1963.

McSpadden, J. Walker. *Indian Heroes*. Crowell, 1950.

Marcus, Rebecca. *The First Book of the Cliff Dwellers*. Watts, 1968.

Marriott, Alice. *The First Comers*. Longman's, 1960.

——. *Indians on Horseback*. Crowell, (1968 c1948).

Martin, Patricia Miles. *Indians, the First Americans*. Parents', 1970.

Matson, Emerson N. *Legends of the Great Chiefs*. Nelson, 1972. Focuses on the Pacific Coastal tribes.

May, Julian. *Before the Indians*. Holiday, 1969.

Momaday, N. Scott. *The Way to Rainy Mountain*. Ballantine, 1970. A poetic mixture of retellings of Kiowa tales, stories for the history of the Kiowa, and the author's memories of his grandmother.

Nurge, Ethel, ed. *The Modern Sioux*. University of Nebraska Press, 1970.

Parish, Peggy. *Let's Be Indians*. Harper & Row, 1962.

Parker, Arthur C. *Skunny Wundy: Seneca Indian Tales*. Whitman, 1970. Useful for practicing creative storytelling for students of all ages.

Payne, Elizabeth. *Meet the North American Indians*. Random House, 1965.

Pine, Tillie S. *The Indians Knew*. McGraw-Hill, 1957.

Porter, C. Fayne. *Our Indian Heritage: Profiles of 12 Great Leaders*. Chilton, 1964.

Powers, William K. *Here Is Your Hobby: Indian Dancing and Costumes*. Putnam, 1966.

Reit, Seymour. *Child of the Navajos*. Dodd, Mead, 1971.

Robertson, Thomas L. *The Yellow Cane*. Steck, 1956.

Robinson, Maudie. *Children of the Sun: the Pueblos, Navajos, and Apaches of New Mexico*. Messner, 1973.

Rounds, Glen. *Buffalo Harvest*. Holiday House, 1952.

Scheele, William E. *The Mound Builders*. World, 1960.

Siegel, Beatrice. *Indians of the Woodland Before and After the Pilgrims*. Walker, 1972.

Shapp, Charles and Martha. *Let's Find Out About Indians*. Watts, 1962.

Showers, Paul. *Indian Festivals*. Crowell, 1969.

Steiner, Stan. *The Tiguas: The Lost Tribe of Indians*. Collier, 1972.

Tobias, Tobi. *Maria Tallchief*. Crowell, 1970.

Van Every, Dale. *Disinherited*. Morrow, 1966.

Vlahos, Olivia. *New World Beginnings; Indian Cultures in the Americas*. Viking, 1970.

Warren, Betsy. *Indians Who Lived in Texas*. Steck, 1970.

Wilson, Charles Morrow. *Gerónimo*. Dillon, 1973.

Wilson, Edmund. *Apologies to the Iroquois*. Vintage, 1959.

Witt, Shirley Hill. *The Tuscaroras*. Crowell-Collier, 1972.

Wood, Nancy. *Hollering Sun*. Simon and Schuster, 1972.

The World of the American Indian. National Geographic Society, Washington, D.C., 1974.

Wyatt, Edgar. *Cochise, Apache Warrior and Statesman*. McGraw-Hill, 1973.

Yellow Robe, Rosebud. *An Album of the American Indian*. Watts, 1969.

Folklore

Belting, Natalia. *Whirlwind Is a Ghost Dancing*. Dutton, 1974.

Chafetz, Henry. *Thunderbird and other Stories*. Pantheon, 1964.

Curry, Jane Louise. *Down from the Lonely Mountain*. Harcourt Brace Jovanovich, 1964. California Indian Tales.

Fisher, Anne B. *Stories California Indians Told*. Parnassus, 1957.

Harris, Christie. *Once More upon a Totem*. Atheneum, 1973.

Jones, Hettie. *Coyote Tales*. Holt, Rinehart and Winston, 1974.

Marriott, Alice, and Carol K. Rachlin. *American Indian Mythology*. Crowell, 1968.

Whitney, Alex. *Stiff Ears: Animal Folktales of the North American Indian*. Walck, 1974.

Poetry

Allen, Terry. *The Whispering Wind*. Doubleday, 1972. Poetry by young American Indians.

Belting, Natalia. *Our Fathers Had Powerful Songs*. Dutton, 1974.

Bierhorst, John. *In the Trail of the Wind.* Farrar, Straus & Giroux, 1971. American Indian poems and ritual orations.

Houston, James. *Songs of the Dream People.* Atheneum, 1972. Chants and images from the Indians and Eskimos of North America.

Jones, Hettie. *The Trees Stand Shining.* Dial, 1971. Poetry of the North American Indians.

Longfellow, Henry Wadsworth. *The Song of Hiawatha.* Dutton, 1960.

OTHER MULTICULTURAL BOOKS FOR CHILDREN

In addition to the more detailed lists of books for children for important minority groups presented in the preceding pages, here are collections of recommended books about specific countries or areas of the world.

India

Arand, Mulk Raj. *Indian Fairy Tales.* Bombay: Bhatkal, 1966. 104 pp. Colorful tales; good illustrations.

*Babbitt, Ellen C. *The Jatakas, Tales of India.* Appleton, 1940. 92 pp. Animal stories from India.

Panday, Daulat. *The Tales of India.* India: Ashram, 1963. 126 pp. Descriptive text; good illustrations.

Picard, Barbara Leonie. *The Story of Rama and Sita.* London: Harrap, 1960. 90 pp. Exciting legend; good color illustrations.

Middle East

Davis, Russell, and Brent Ashabranner. *Ten Thousand Desert Swords.* Little, Brown, 1960. 158 pp. Good adventure story.

*Economakis, Olga. *Oasis of the Stars.* Coward, McCann & Geoghegan, 1965. 29 pp. Text vague and derogatory, nonfactual; good illustrations.

*Tashjian, Virginia A. *Three Apples Fell from Heaven.* Little, Brown, 1971. 78 pp. Entertaining stories; excellent illustrations.

*Walker, Barbara K. *The Courage of Kazan.* Crowell, 1970. 42 pp. Well-written story; beautiful illustrations.

Leipold, L. E. *Folktales of Arabia.* Denison, 1973. Six of the best-known Arabian tales are retold in a simplified form.

Philippines

*Bartosiak, Janet. *A Dog for Ramón.* Dial, 1966. 44 pp. Good story; complementary illustrations.

---

* Suitable for primary grades.

Gartler, Marion, et al. *Understanding the Philippines.* Laidlaw, 1963. 64 pp. Good source book; good color photos and maps.

Spencer, Cornelia. *Seven Thousand Islands, The Story of the Philippines.* Aladdin, 1951. 105 pp. Interesting and readable.

Puerto Rico

*Belpré, Pura. *Juan Bobo and the Queen's Necklace.* Warne, 1962. 40 pp. Pleasant story and illustrations.

Puerto Ricans in New York City

Fiction

*Belpré, Pura. *Santiago.* Warne, 1969.

*Keats, Ezra, Jack, and Pat Cherr. *My Dog Is Lost!* Crowell, 1960.

Mann, Peggy. *The Street of the Flower Boxes.* Coward, McCann & Geoghegan, 1966.

Shotwell, Louisa R. *Magdalena.* Viking, 1971.

Puerto Ricans in the United States

Fiction

*Barth, Edna. *The Day Luis Was Lost.* Little, Brown, 1971.

*Blue, Rose. *I Am Here: Yo Estoy Aquí.* Watts, 1971.

*Sonneborn, Ruth A. *Friday Night Is Papa Night.* Viking, 1970.

Nonfiction

Buckley, Peter. *I Am from Puerto Rico.* Simon, 1971.

Colorado, Antonio, J. *The First Book of Puerto Rico.* Watts, 1972.

Kurtis, Arlene Harris. *Puerto Ricans.* Messner, 1969.

Secrist, Elizabeth Hough. *It's Time for Brotherhood.* Macrae Smith, 1973.

Sterling, Philip, and Maria Brau. *The Quiet Rebels.* Doubleday, 1968. Factual material accompanied by fictional dialogue.

Folklore

Alegría, Ricardo E. *The Three Wishes.* Harcourt Brace Jovanovich, 1969.

Belpré, Pura. *Dance of the Animals.* Warne, 1972.

————. *Once in Puerto Rico.* Warne, 1973.

————. *Oté.* Pantheon, 1969.

————. *Perez and Martina.* Warne, 1961.

————. *The Tiger and the Rabbit.* Lippincott, 1965.

ADDITIONAL MULTICULTURAL MATERIALS

U.S. Committee for UNICEF, 331 East 38th St., New York, NY 10016.

Child of UNICEF. Eight children, each from a different country, tell of their experiences with UNICEF in separate booklets. $2.

Folk Crafts for World Friendship, by Florence Temko. Instructions for making items from around the world; for fun, gifts, celebrations. Photographs and colorful drawings; for ages 9 and up, $4.

Folk Toys Around the World: And How to Make Them. Includes history and complete instructions for making toys from 22 countries. Colorful pictures, hard cover; for ages 9 and up. $3.50.

Lingo. Names of nutritious foods in English, Spanish, and French are used in a game similar to Bingo. $2.50.

Many Hands Cooking. Full-color drawings, spiral binding; delicious, nutritious, easy recipes from 40 countries. 64 pages, $4.

Sing, Children, Sing. Music with original words and translations. Includes 35 songs, dances, and singing games from 34 countries. Introduction by Leonard Bernstein. For all ages; $3.50.

UNICEF Wall Calendar (1979 issue). Colorful 32-page calendar with a child's painting on each page. More than 400 holidays are listed on the calendar with 24 described in detail.

SOURCES OF MULTILINGUAL/MULTICULTURAL INFORMATION

Listed here are varied sources of published materials for multilingual/multicultural programs. When writing to any source, *request their publication list* which may suggest other items of interest to you. Also, be sure to *specify the language(s)* that you are interested in. You will find the greatest quantity of materials available are for working with Spanish and English.

Dissemination Centers

Two national centers funded by Title VII prepare and disseminate instructional materials at cost to schools.

The National Assessment and Dissemination Center for Bilingual/Bicultural Education (385 High St., Fall River, MA 02720) has Spanish, Portuguese, Oriental, Native American, Greek, Italian and French materials.

The Dissemination Center for Bilingual/Bicultural Education (6504 Tracor Lane, Austin, TX 78721) has Spanish, Navajo, Portuguese and French materials.

Another center funded by the National Institute of Education (NIE) and the Educational Products Exchange Institute (EPIE) has published the following informative volumes:

Volume 1: Selector's Guide for Bilingual Education Materials: Spanish Language Arts

Volume 2: Selector's Guide for Bilingual Education Materials: Spanish "Branch" Programs

Volume 3: Selector's Guide for Bilingual Education Materials: Programs in Chinese, Japanese, Korean, and Vietnamese.

Available from: EPIE Institute, 463 West St., New York, NY 10014 ($10 each).

Directory of Organizations and Publishers

Abelard, Schuman, Ltd., 666 Fifth Ave., New York, NY 10019

Abingdon Press, 201 Eighth Ave., South, Nashville, TN 37202

Aci Films, 35 West 45 Street, New York, NY 10036

Addison-Wesley Publishing Co., Reading, MA 01867

Aid/Rocap Textbook Program, c/o American Embassy, San Salvador, El Salvador

Aims, 20 East 30th Street, New York, NY 10016

Aims Instrumental Media Services, P.O. Box 1010, Hollywood, CA 90028

Aleut League, Star Route A, Box 289, Spenard, AK

Allyn and Bacon, Inc., 470 Atlantic Avenue, Boston, MA 02210

American Association for Jewish Education, 101 Fifth Ave., New York, NY 10003

American Council for Judaism, 309 Fifth Ave., New York, NY 10016

American Council for Nationalities Service, 20 W. 40th St., New York, NY

American Council on Education, 1785 Massachusetts Ave., NW., Washington, D.C. 20036

American Federation of Teachers, AFL-CIO, 1012–14th St., NW., Washington, D.C. 20025

American Folklore Society, Univ. of Texas Press, Box 7819, Austin, TX 78712

American Friends Service Committee, Children's Program, 160 N. 15th St., Philadelphia, PA 19102

American Heritage Press, 1221 Avenue of the Americas, New York, NY 10020

American Library Association, Publishing Services, 50 E. Huron St., Chicago, IL 60611

American Lithuanian Community, 6804 South Maplewood Ave., Chicago, IL 60629

American Personnel and Guidance Association, 1712 I St., NW., Washington, D.C., 20009

American-Scandinavian Foundation, 126 East 73rd St., New York, NY 10021

American School Foundation, A.C., Calle Sur 136, No. 135, Mexico 18, D.F.

Anti-Defamation League of B'nai B'rith, 315 Lexington Ave., New York, NY 10016

Applied Language Research Center, 1116 E. Yandell Dr., El Paso, TX 79902

Asia Society, 112 E. 64th St., New York, NY 10021

Aspira, Inc., 296 Fifth Ave., New York, NY 10001

Association for Childhood Education International, 3615 Washington Ave., NW., Washington, D.C. 20016

Association for the Study of Negro Life and History, 1538 9th St., NW., Washington, D.C. 20001

Association of Mexican-American Educators, Inc. (AMAE), California State College at San Bernardino, 5500 State College Pkwy., San Bernardino, CA 92407

Association on American Indian Affairs, Inc., 432 Park Ave., S. New York, NY 10016

Atheneum Publishers, 122 E. 42d St., New York, NY 10017

Avon Books, 959 Eighth Ave., New York, NY 10019

Babel Media Center, 1033 Heinz St., Berkeley, CA 94710

Barr Films, P.O. Box 7-C, Pasadena, CA 91104

Basque Studies Program, Univ. of Nevada, Reno, NV 89507

Behavioral Publications, 2852 Broadway, New York, NY 10025

Bell & Howell, 2201 West Howard, Evanston, IL 60202

Bilingual Demonstration and Dissemination Center, 2nd Floor—Navarro Elem. Sch., 623 South Pecos, San Antonio, TX 78207

Bilingual Educational Services, P.O. Box 669, 1603 Hope St., South Pasadena, CA 91030

Bobbs-Merrill Co., 4300 W. 62d St., Indianapolis, IN 46268

Books for the People Fund, Inc., Pan American Union, Washington, D.C. 20006

Boston Public Library, Copley Square, Boston, MA 02116

Stephen Bosustow Productions, 1649 11th St., Santa Monica, CA 90404

The R. R. Bowker Co., Xerox Education Group, 1180 Avenue of the Americas, New York, NY 10036

Bowmar Publishing Corp., 622 Rodier Dr., Glendale, CA 91201

Bradbury Press, 2 Overhill Rd., Scarsdale, NY 10583

British Council, English-Teaching Information Centre, State House, 63 High Holborn, London W.C. 1, England

Bro-Dart Foundation, 1609 Memorial Ave., Williamsport, PA 17101

Broadcasting Foundation of America, 52 Vanderbilt Ave., New York, NY

Bureau of Jewish Education, 72 Franklin St., Boston, MA 02110

California Test Bureau (Div. of McGraw-Hill), Del Monte Research Park, Monterey, CA 93940

California Library Association, 1741 Solano Ave., Berkeley, CA 94707

Canada Council, Humanities and Social Sciences Div., 140 Wellington St., Ottawa, Ontario, Canada

Catholic Library Association, 461 W. Lancaster Ave., Haverford, PA 19041

Center for Applied Linguistics, (ERIC Clearinghouse for Linguistics), 1717 Massachusetts Ave., NW., Washington, D.C. 20036

Center for Curriculum Development in Audio-Visual Language Teaching, The Irvin Building, Philadelphia, PA

Center for Inter-American Relations, 680 Park Ave., New York, NY 10021

Center for Urban Education, 105 Madison Ave., New York, NY 10016

Central American Regional Textbook Prog., (Centro Regional de Libros de Textos), Departamento de Asuntos Culturales y Educativos, Organización de Estados Centro-americanos (ODECA), San Salvador, El Salvador

Centro Mexicano de Escritores, Apartado Postal 1298, Mexico D.F., Mexico

Centron Educational Films, 1621 W. Ninth, Lawrence, KS 66044

Changing Times Education Service, 1729 H Street, NW., Washington, D.C. 20006

Child Development Evaluation and Research Center, The Univ. of Texas at Austin, Austin, TX 78712

Child Study Assn. of America, Publications Dept., 9 E. 89th St., New York, NY 10028

Children's Book Council, Inc., 175 Fifth Ave., New York, NY 10010

Children's Music Center, Inc., 5373 West Pico Blvd., Los Angeles, CA 90019

Children's Press, 1224 W. Van Buren St., Chicago, IL 60607

Christopher News Notes, 12 E. 48 St., New York, NY 10017

Churchill Films, 662 N. Robertson Blvd., Los Angeles, CA 90069

Citation Press, 50 W. 44th St., New York, NY 10036

Clearvue, 6666 N. Oliphant Ave., Chicago, IL 60631

William Collins & World Publishing Co., 2080 W. 117th St., Cleveland, OH 44111

Columbia University Press, 562 W. 113th St., New York, NY 10025

The Combined Book Exhibit, Inc., Scarborough Park, Albany Post Rd., Briarcliff Manor, NY 10510

Commission on the Humanities in the Schools, P.O. Box 15212, Steiner St. Station, San Francisco, CA 94115

Committee for the Yiddish Schools, 426 West 58th St., New York, NY 10019

Contemporary Press, Box 1524, San Jose, CA 95109

Continental Book Co., 11-03 46th Ave., Long Island City, NY 11101. Resources for Sp.-Eng. bilingual curriculum (Mexico & Puerto Rico)

Coronet Instructional Media, 65 E. South Water St., Chicago, IL 60601

Council on International Educational Exchange, 777 United Nations Plaza, New York, NY 10017

Council on Interracial Books for Children, Inc., 1841 Broadway, New York, NY 10023

Coward, McCann & Geoghegan, 200 Madison Ave., New York, NY 10016

Thomas Y. Crowell Co., 666 Fifth Ave., New York, NY 10019

Crowell-Collier Press, 640 5th Ave., New York, NY 10019

The John Day Co., 666 Fifth Ave., New York, NY 10019

Delacorte Press, 1 Dag Hammarskjold Plaza, 245 E. 47th St., New York, NY 10017

Department of Foreign Languages, 1201 Sixteenth St., NW., Washington, D.C. 20036

The Dial Press, 1 Dag Hammarskjold Plaza, 245 E. 47th St., New York, NY 10017

Dillon Press, 106 Washington Ave. N., Minneapolis, MN 55401

Disney, Walt, Educational Materials, 800 Sonora Ave., Glendale, CA 91201

Dodd, Mead & Co., 79 Madison Ave., New York, NY 10016

Doubleday & Co., 245 Park Ave., New York, NY 10017

Doubleday Multimedia, 1371 Reynolds Ave., Santa Ana, CA 92705

E. P. Dutton & Co., 201 Park Ave. S., New York, NY 10003

Early Childhood Bilingual Education Project, Yeshiva U., 55 Fifth Ave., New York, NY 10003

East-West Center, Institute of Advanced Projects, Univ. of Hawaii, Honolulu, HI 96822

Editorial La Muralla, S.A., Carretas, 14, 5. 1–2, Madrid 12, Spain

Educational Development Corp., 202 Lake Miriam Dr., Lakeland, FL 33803

Educational Testing Service, Rosedale Rd., Princeton, NJ 08540

EMC Corp., 180 E. Sixth St., St. Paul, MN 55101

Encyclopaedia Britannica Educational Corp., 425 N. Michigan Ave., Chicago, IL 60611

English for Speakers of Other Languages Program (ESOL), Center for Applied Linguistics, 1717 Massachusetts Ave., NW., Washington, D.C. 10036

Enoch Pratt Free Library, Baltimore, MD 21201

ERIC (Educational Resources Information Center) (Central ERIC Headquarters) U.S. Office of Education, Dept. of Health, Ed., and Welfare, 400 Maryland Ave., SW., Washington, D.C.

ERIC Clearinghouse on Adult Education, Syracuse Univ., Syracuse, NY 13210

ERIC Clearinghouse on Counseling and Personnel Services, Univ. of Michigan, Ann Arbor, MI 48104

ERIC Clearinghouse on the Disadvantaged, Teachers College, Columbia Univ., New York, NY 10027

ERIC Clearinghouse on Early Childhood Education, 805 W. Pennsylvania Ave., Urbana, IL 61801

ERIC Clearinghouse on Educational Administration, Univ. of Oregon, Eugene, OR 97403

ERIC Clearinghouse on Educational Facilities, Univ. of Wisconsin, Madison, WI 53703

ERIC Clearinghouse on Educational Media and Technology, Stanford Univ., Stanford, CA 94305

ERIC Clearinghouse on Exceptional Children, The Council for Exceptional Children, Washington, D.C. 20036

ERIC Clearinghouse on Higher Education, George Washington Univ., Washington, D.C. 20006

ERIC Clearinghouse on Junior Colleges, Univ. of Calif. at Los Angeles, Los Angeles, CA 90024

ERIC Clearinghouse on Library and Information Sciences, Univ. of Minnesota, Minneapolis, MN 55404

ERIC Clearinghouse on Linguistics, Center for Applied Linguistics, 1717 Massachusetts Ave., NW., Washington, D.C. 10036

ERIC Clearinghouse on Reading, Indiana Univ., Bloomington, IN 47401

ERIC Clearinghouse on Rural Education and Small Schools, New Mexico State Univ., Box 3AP, Univ. Pk. Branch, Las Cruces, NM 88001

ERIC Clearinghouse on Science Education, Ohio State Univ., Columbus, OH 43221

ERIC Clearinghouse on Teacher Education, American Association of Colleges for Teacher Education, Washington, D.C. 10005

ERIC Clearinghouse on the Teaching of English, National Council of Teachers of English, Champaign, IL 61820

ERIC Clearinghouse on the Teaching of Foreign Languages, Modern Language Association of America, 62 Fifth Ave., New York, NY 10011

ERIC Clearinghouse on Vocational and Technical Education, Ohio State Univ., Columbus, OH 43210

ESL Demonstration Project Center, 2950 National Ave., San Diego, CA 92113

M. Evans & Co., 216 E. 49th St., New York, NY 10017

Farrar, Straus & Giroux, 19 Union Square West, New York, NY 10003

F. W. Faxon Co., 15 Southwest Park, Westwood, MA 02090

The Feminist Press, Box 334, Old Westbury, NY 11568

Follett Publishing Co., 1010 W. Washington Blvd., Chicago, IL 60607

Foreign Language Education Center, Sutton Hall 417, The Univ. of Texas at Austin, Austin, TX 78712

Foreign Language Innovative Curricula Study (FLICS), 550 City Center Building, 220 E. Huron, Ann Arbor, MI 48108

Four Winds Press, 50 W. 44th St., New York, NY 10036

Free Library of Philadelphia, 19th and Vine St., Philadelphia, PA 19103

Freedomway Associates, Inc., 799 Broadway, New York, NY 10003

Garfield Elementary School, Del Rio ISD, Del Rio, TX

Garrard Publishing Co., 1607 N. Market St., Champaign, IL 61820

General Educational Media, 350 Northern Blvd., Great Neck, NY 10021

Gessler Publishing Co., Inc., 131 East 23rd St., New York, NY 10010

Golden Gate Junior Books, 1247½ N. Vista St., Hollywood, CA 90046

Golden Press (Western Publishing Co.), 850 Third Ave., New York, NY 10022

Goldsholl Associates, 420 Frontage Rd., Northfield, IL 60093

Grant, Allan, Productions, 808 Lockearn St., Los Angeles, CA 90049

Grosset & Dunlap, 51 Madison Ave., New York, NY 10010

Guidance Associates, 41 Washington Ave., Pleasantville, NY 10570

Hachette Teacher's Showroom and French Book Guild, 595 Madison Ave., New York, NY 10022

G. K. Hall & Co., 70 Lincoln St., Boston, MA 02111

Hammond, Dr., 211 S. Main, McAllen, TX 78501

Harcourt Brace Jovanovich, 757 Third Ave., New York, NY 10017

Harper & Row, Publishers, 10 E. 53rd St., New York, NY 10022

Harvey House, 20 Waterside Plaza, New York, NY 10010

Haskell Institute, Lawrence, KS 66044

Hastings House Publishers, 10 E. 40th St., New York, NY 10016

Hawthorn Books, 260 Madison Ave., New York, NY 10016

Heffernan Supply Co., Inc., 926 Fredericksburg Rd., Box 5309, San Antonio, TX 78201

Hispanic-American Publications, Inc., 252 East 51st St., New York, NY 10022

Holiday House, 18 E. 56th St., New York, NY 10022

Holt, Rinehart & Winston, 383 Madison Ave., New York, NY 10017

Houghton Mifflin Co., 2 Park St., Boston, MA 02107

HRD/ROCAP, U.S. Embassy, Guatemala, Guatemala

Indian Rights Association, 1505 Race St., Philadelphia, PA 19102

Information Center on Children's Cultures, U.S. Committee for UNICEF, 331 E. 38th St., New York, NY 10016

Institute for Personality and Ability Testing, 1602 Coronado Dr., Champaign, IL 61820

Institute for Research in Language Teaching, Central Corporus 108, 15 Agebacho, Shinjuku-ku, Tokyo, Japan

Institute of Language Teaching, Waseda Univ., No. 647, 1-Chome, Totsuka-Machi, Shinjuku-ku, Tokyo, Japan

Instituto Lingüístico de Verano (Summer Inst. of Linguistics), Box 1960, Santa Ana, CA 92702

Integrated Education Associates, 343 S. Dearborn St., Chicago, IL 60604

Inter-Agency Committee on Mexican American Affairs, 1800 G St., NW., Washington, D.C. 20506

Inter-American Ed. Center, Inter-American Institute, 2525 Tower Life Bldg., San Antonio, TX 78205

Inter-American Institute, The Univ. of Texas at El Paso, El Paso, TX 79999

Inter-American Prog. for Linguistics and Lang. Teaching/Programa Internacional de Lingüística y de Enseñanza de Idiomas (PILEI), El Colegio de Mexico, Guanajuato 125, México 7, D.F.

International Center for Research on Bilingualism, Cité Universitaire, 4530 Bibliothèque Générale, Ste-Foy 10, Québec, Canada

International Film Bureau, Inc., 332 S. Michigan Ave., Chicago, IL 60604

International Reading Association, Box 695, Newark, DE 19711

Jewish Education Committee, 426 West 58th St., New York, NY 10019

Alfred A. Knopf, 201 E. 50th St., New York, NY 10022

Kosciuszko Foundation, 15 East 65th St., New York, NY 10021

Language Arts, Inc., 1205-C.W. 34th St., Austin, TX

Language Research Associates, 300 North State St., Chicago, IL 60610

Language Study Center, Philippine Normal College, Manila, Philippines

Learning Corp. of America, 711 Fifth Ave., New York, NY 10022

Learning Resources Co., P.O. Box 3709, 202 Lake Mirian Dr., Lakeland, FL 33803

Learning Tree Filmstrips, 934 Pearl St., P.O. Box 1590 Dept. 105, Boulder, CO 80302

Lerner Publications Co., 241 First Ave. N., Minneapolis, MN 55401

Libraries Unlimited, Box 263, Littleton, CO 80120

J. B. Lippincott Co., 521 Fifth Ave., New York, NY 10017

Little, Brown & Co., 34 Beacon St., Boston, MA 02106

Lorraine Music Co., P.O. Box 4131, Long Island City, NY 11104

Lothrop, Lee & Shepard Co., 105 Madison Ave., New York, NY 10016

L'Union Saint-Jean Baptiste D'Amérique, 1 Social Street, Woonsocket, RI

Macrae Smith Co., Lewis Tower Bldg., 225 S. 15th St., Philadelphia, PA 19102

Macmillan Publishing Co., 866 Third Ave., New York, NY 10022

McGraw-Hill Book Co., 1221 Avenue of the Americas, New York, NY 10020

David McKay Co., Publishers, 750 3d Ave., New York, NY 10017

Maestros Para Mañana (Teachers for Tomorrow), 1705 Murchison Dr., Burlingame, CA 94010

Media and Methods Institute, 134 N. 13th St., Philadelphia, PA 19107

Merrill, Charles E., Publishing Co., 1300 Alum Creek Dr., Columbia, OH 43216

Julian Messner (A Division of Simon & Schuster), 1 W. 39th St., New York, NY 10018

Mexican-American Educators Coordinating Council, State Dept. of Ed., 721 Capitol Mall, Sacramento, CA 95814

Miller-Brody Productions, 711 Fifth Ave., New York, NY 10022

Modern Language Association, 62 Fifth Ave., New York, NY 10011

Modern Language Center, The Ontario Institute for Studies in Education, 102 Bloor St. West, Toronto 5, Ontario, Canada

William Morrow & Co., 105 Madison Ave., New York, NY 10016

Multicultural Resources, Box 2945, Stanford, CA 94305

Multi-Media Approach to Library Services for the Spanish Surnamed, Colorado State College, Greeley, CO

National Association for the Advancement of Colored People, 1790 Broadway, New York, NY 10019

National Association of Language Laboratory Directors, Brown Univ., Box E, Providence, RI 02912

National Carl Schurz Association (NCSA), 339 Walnut St., Philadelphia, PA

National Conference of Christians and Jews, 43 W. 57th St., New York, NY 10019

National Congress of American Indians, 1346 Connecticut Ave. NW., Washington, D.C. 20036

National Council for the Social Studies, 1201 Sixteenth St. NW., Washington, D.C. 20036

National Council of Teachers of English, 1111 Kenyon Rd., Urbana, IL 61801

National Council of Teachers of Mathematics, 1906 Assoc. Dr., Reston, VA 22091

National Education Association, 1201 Sixteenth St., NW., Washington, D.C. 20036

National Instructional Television, Box A, Bloomington, IN 47401

Negro Bibliographic and Research Center, Inc., 117 R St., NE., Washington, D.C. 20002

Negro Book Club, 160 W. 85th St., New York, NY 10024

Thomas Nelson, 407 7th Ave., Nashville, TN 37203

Newbury House Publishers, 68 Middle Rd., Rowley, MA 01969

Newsweek, 444 Madison Ave., New York, NY 10022

New York Library Association, Children and Young Adult Services Section, 230 W. 41st St., Suite 1800, New York, NY 10036

New York Office of State History, State Education Dept., 99 Washington Ave., Albany, NY 12210

Nordmanns Förbundet, Minneapolis Chapter, 529 E. Minnehaha Parkway, Minneapolis, MN 55419

Northern Arizona Supplementary Education Center (NASEC), Northern Arizona Univ., Box 5618, Flagstaff, AZ 86001

Norwegian-American Historical Association, Northfield, MN

Nuffield Foundation, Nuffield Foreign Languages, Teaching Materials Project, 5 Lyddon Terrace, The University, Leeds 2, England

Oakland Public Library, 1457 Fruitvale Ave., Oakland, CA 94601

J. Philip O'Hara, 20 E. Huron St., Chicago, IL 60611

Oxford Films, 1136 North Las Palmas Ave., Los Angeles, CA 90036

Pan American Union, 17th and Constitution Ave., NW., Washington, D.C. 20006

Pantheon Books, 201 E. 50th St., New York, NY 10022

Parents' Magazine Press, 52 Vanderbilt Ave., New York, NY 10017

Parnassus Press, 4080 Halleck St., Emeryville, CA 94608

Pathescope Educational Films, 71 Weyman Ave., New Rochelle, NY 10802

Peace Corps, 806 Connecticut Ave., NW., Washington, D.C. 20515

S. G. Phillips, 305 W. 86th St., New York, NY 10024

Pied Piper Productions, P.O. Box 320, Verdugo City, CA 91046

Plays, 8 Arlington St., Boston, MA 02116

Platt & Munk, Publishers, 1055 Bronx River Ave., Bronx, NY 10472

Polish-American Congress, 1520 West Division, Chicago, IL 60622

Polish-American Journal, 409–415 Cedar Ave., Scranton, PA 18505

Polish Institute of Arts and Sciences, 59 East 66th St., New York, NY 10021

Polish Teachers Assn. in America, 2653 W. Logan Blvd., Chicago, IL 60647

Portal Press, Inc., Publishers, 605 Third Ave., New York, NY 10016

Practical Drawing Co., 2205 Cockrell, Dallas, TX 75222

Prentice-Hall, Englewood Cliffs, NJ 07632

Project Head Start, The Office of Economic Opportunity, 1111 18th St., NW., Washington, D.C. 10036

Project Libro, The Galton Institute, 319 S. Robertson Blvd., Beverly Hills, CA 90211

Proyecto Leer, La Casita, Pan American Union, Washington, D.C. 20006

Psychological Corporation, 304 E. 45th St., New York, NY 10017

Psychological Test Specialists, Box 1441, Missoula, MT

Puerto Rican Forum, Inc., 156 Fifth Ave., New York, NY 10010

Pyramid Films Corporation, P.O. Box 1048, Santa Monica, CA 90406

Q-ED Productions, P.O. Box 1608, Burbank, CA 91507

Rand McNally & Co., P.O. Box 7600, Chicago, IL 60680

Random House Educational Media, Order Entry Department-Y, 400 Hahn Road, Westminster, MD 21157

The Reilly & Lee Co., 114 W. Illinois St., Chicago, IL 60610

Rosenzweig, Dr. Saul, 8029 Washington St., St. Louis, MO 63114

St. Martin's Press, 175 Fifth Ave., New York, NY 10010

Salinger Educational Media, 1635 12th St., Santa Monica, CA 90404

Santillana, S.A. de Ediciones, Elfo, 32, Madrid 17, Spain

Scarecrow Press, 52 Liberty St., Box 656, Metuchen, NJ 08840

Schloat Productions, 150 White Plains Rd., Tarrytown, NY 10591

Schmitt, Hall & McCreary Co., 110 N. Fifth St., Minneapolis, MN 55403

Scholastic Magazines, Audio Visual and Media Dept., 50 West 44th St., New York, NY 10036

Schools for the Future, P.O. Box 349, Cooper Station, New York, NY 10003

Science Research Associates, Inc., 259 East Erie St., Chicago, IL 60611

Scott, Foresman & Co., Educational Publishers, 1900 E. Lake Ave., Glenview, IL 60025

Screen Education Enterprises, 3220 16th Avenue West, Seattle, WA 98119

Charles Scribner's Sons, 597 Fifth Street, New York, NY 10017

Scroll Press, Publishers, 129 East 94th St., New York, NY 10028

The Seabury Press, 815 Second Ave., New York, NY 10017

See Hear Now! Ltd., 49 Wellington St., East, Toronto M5E 1C9 Canada

Simon & Schuster, Publishers, 630 5th Ave., New York, NY 10020

Society for French Amer. Cultural Services & Educational Aids (FACSEA), 972 Fifth Ave., New York, NY

Society for the Advancement of Scandinavian Studies, Northeastern Univ., Evanston, IL

Sons of Norway Intl. Hdqtrs., 1455 West Lake St., Minneapolis, MN 55408

Southeastern Educational Corp., Box 10867, Airport Branch, Atlanta, GA 30304

Southern Regional Council, Inc., 5 Forsyth St., NW., Atlanta, GA 30303

Southwest Council for Biling. Ed., Box 497, The Univ. of Texas at El Paso, El Paso, TX 79999

Southwest Ed. Dev. Lab., Suite 550, Commodore Perry Hotel, Austin, TX 78701

Steck-Vaughn Co., Division of Intext Publishers Group, Box 2028, Austin, TX 78767

Studyscopes Productions, Box 25943, Los Angeles, CA 90025

Summer Institute of Linguistics, Wycliffe Bible Translators, Inc., Box 1960, Santa Ana, CA

Superintendent of Documents, U.S. Government Printing Office, Washington, D.C. 20402

Teachers of English to Speakers of Other Languages (TESOL), School of Languages and Linguistics, Georgetown Univ., Washington, D.C. 20007

Teaching Research Division, Oregon State System of Higher Education, Monmouth, OR

Teaching Resources Films, Station Plaza, Bedford Hills, NY 10507

Technicolor, 299 Kalmus Dr., Costa Mesa, CA 92626

3M Company, Visual Products Division, Box 334, 3M Center, St. Paul, MN 55101

Trans-World Films, Inc., 332 South Michigan Ave., Chicago, IL 60604

Troll Associates, 320 Route 17, Mahwah, NJ 07430

United Japanese Society of Hawaii, Honolulu, HI

United States Aid Mission to Bolivia, Casilla 673, La Paz, Bolivia

U.S. Committee for UNICEF, P.O. Box 1618, Church St. Station, New York, NY

U.S. Dept. of Health, Education, and Welfare, U.S. Office of Education, 400 Maryland Ave., SW., Washington, D.C. 20202

U.S. Dept. of Interior, Bureau of Indian Affairs, 1951 Constitution Ave., NW., Washington, D.C. 20242

U.S. Dept. of State, U.S. Mexico Commission for Border Development and Friendship, 1800 G St., NW., Washington, D.C. 20525

U.S. Inter-Agency Committee on Mexican American Affairs, 1800 G St., NW., Washington, D.C. 20506

University of Chicago Press, 5801 Ellis Ave., Chicago, IL 60637

University of Pittsburgh Press, 127 N. Bellefield Ave., Pittsburgh, PA 15213

The Vanguard Press, 424 Madison Ave., New York, N.Y. 10017

Van Nostrand-Reinhold Co., 450 W. 33d St., New York, NY 10001

The Viking Press, 625 Madison Ave., New York, NY 10022

Villa Jones, Centro Cultural Internacional, A.C., Chilpancingo 23, México 11, D.F.

Visual Instruction Bureau, Division of Extension, 18th and Sabine Sts., The Univ. of Texas at Austin, Austin, TX 78712

Henry Z. Walck, Publishers, 19 Union Square W., New York, NY 10003

Walker & Co., 720 5th Ave., New York, NY 10019

The Ward Fitchie Press (Anderson, Ritchie & Simon), 3044 Riverside Dr., Los Angeles, CA 90039

Frederick Warne & Co., 101 5th Ave., New York, NY 10003

Ives Washburn, 750 3d Ave., New York, NY 10017

Franklin Watts, 730 5th Ave., New York, NY 10019

Western Psychological Services (A Division of Manson Western Corp.), 12031 Wilshire Blvd., Los Angeles, CA 90025

Westminster Press, Witherspoon Building, Philadelphia, PA 19107

Weston Woods, Weston, CT 06880

Albert Whitman & Co., 560 West Lake St., Chicago, IL 60606

The H. W. Wilson Co., 950 University Ave., New York, NY 10452

Windmill Books, 201 Park Avenue South, New York, NY 10003

Xerox Films, 245 Long Hill Road, Middletown, CT 06457

Young Scott Books, Reading, MA 01867

APPENDIX A

A Linguistic Evaluation of Bilingual Education Programs

by Pamela Tiedt
Stanford University, 1977

Language is an important but often neglected part of bilingual education programs. Despite the fact that demands for these programs demonstrate recognition of the importance of language, bilingual education programs take many language related issues for granted. Statements of good intentions are not sufficient. Bilingual programs and program proposals must be evaluated **not** only by what they claim to provide but in how they carry out their **intentions,** particularly in the areas directly related to language.

How can we assess the bilingual nature of bilingual education programs? By discussing language-related features, we can develop a method of evaluating and comparing various programs. The areas to be examined are the following: (1) the language of the students; (2) the language of the teachers; (3) the language used in curriculum materials; and (4) the program goals with respect to language. All of these are important factors to take into account in order to develop an effective program. Although examples used are specific to the Spanish-English bilingual programs because they are most widespread and fully developed, the approaches presented are applicable to all bilingual programs.

It should be noted that there are equally important aspects of program planning and development that are not language-related. Political considerations rising out of the need to balance community demands against administrative inertia have always been foremost in program planning. Other factors such as teachers' years of experience and whether the programs are designed to begin early enough and last long enough are undeniably relevant to any full discussion of the success of bilingual education. But bilingual education has been seen first as a political issue and not a linguistic one. I would like to show in this discussion that not only is attention to language-related issues an essential foundation for any program, but that language itself is a highly political issue that cannot be disregarded.

In describing and proposing bilingual education programs, we need to be careful to match the stated goals of the program against their implementation. Listing the effects one intends to accomplish is not the same as showing what these goals imply for every aspect of the program. By not expanding how they expect to accomplish these goals, program directors reveal that they are assuming that everyone agrees on the best method of accomplishment. Gaarder (1970) points out the extent to which program goals and practice often conflict, in his description of the first bilingual programs funded: "Many profess to aim for equal emphasis on the two languages and seek to develop in their pupils equal competence in the two. Here it is evident in most cases that, whether consciously or unconsciously, the emphasis is very far from equal" (p. 164).

One of the basic steps in clearing up the ambiguities surrounding these programs is to define the terms we use. Cohen (1975) notes: "Although the terms 'bilingualism' and 'bilingual' are frequently used, the users rarely define what they mean when they use the terms. Individuals are referred to as 'bilinguals' as if there were some fixed notion of what that meant" (p. 7). Nor do people define what they mean when they refer to the Spanish language. We will discuss later the possible variation in what variety is meant. We must recognize how the assumption that we know what we are talking about without having to define our terms obscures the fact that this assumption may not be shared by others or may be incorrect.

Clear statements of goals help to begin specifying what information about language is needed in order to propose and develop these programs. We will discuss language from the perspective of students, teachers, curriculum materials, and program results in order to suggest what should be done to fill the demonstrated lacks. Description of what programs should consider will be proposed as ways to increase the effectiveness of present and future bilingual education programs.

LANGUAGE OF THE STUDENTS

Program planners need to know how many students in the school district speak Spanish in order to justify a bilingual program. A count of the Spanish-surnamed children is frequently the only information available. This is dangerously inadequate because we cannot assume that all Spanish-surnamed children speak Spanish. Campbell (1970) points out that "we assume a uniformity of proficiency in

Spanish on the part of these children that may be illusory. There is some evidence that their competence in Spanish ranges over a broad continuum from complete competence to only passive knowledge of a small amount of Spanish." What we really want to know is the language of the home. Riley (quoted in Cohen, 1975) found a difference in the Spanish and English proficiency among bilinguals from two different Spanish-speaking communities. The children in one community were reportedly encouraged to use Spanish in the home while children in the other community were not. "Data analysis indicated how much these environments influenced the measured bilingualism of the children, dispelling the myth that all Spanish-surnamed children are bilingual in Spanish and English in the same way" (Cohen, 1975).

Programs cannot assume that Spanish-speaking children enter school with the same degree of exposure to English. Schools include students with limited English-speaking abilities as well as non-English-speaking students. Even children who watch television may have developed a limited comprehension of English. It is necessary to create a means to assess the linguistic knowledge of the students in both English and Spanish for all the language arts skills. The variety of English the students have been exposed to is also an important part of their language knowledge. Children may hear other people speaking a nonstandard dialect of English and pick up nonstandard features themselves. However, the presence of a "Chicano English" has been questionable. Hernandez, Cohen, and Beltramo (1975) suggest that rather than an institutionalized nonstandard dialect that all children would be exposed to, the nonstandard features are the result of imperfect **learning** and would not be maintained across generations. The implication **is that** some children would be exposed to nonstandard features and others to Standard English.

An important point that is rarely recognized is the need to determine the variety of Spanish spoken by the students. There are dialect differences in the Spanish spoken in this country just as there are differences throughout the Spanish-speaking world. The features distinguishing the dialects include differences in the pronunciation of various sounds, vocabulary differences, and grammatical differences, for example, in the verb forms. These differences cannot be interpreted as indications of the gradual corruption of Spanish in this country by contamination with English, but represent archaisms or trends of language change found in other Spanish-speaking areas (Hernandez, Cohen, and Beltramo, 1975). Cárdenas (1975) claims that the majority of the Spanish speakers in the Southwest came from two dialect areas of Mexico. He divides presentday Southwest Spanish into four areas: (1) Texas, (2) New Mexico and Southern Colorado, (3) Arizona, and (4) California, with the homogeneity of the area along the United States-Mexico border representing constant influence from Mexico. Despite the speech differences that separate these areas, the speakers share norms of what constitutes standard Spanish—usually based on standard Mexican Spanish (and distinct from Puerto Rican or Cuban Spanish). In asking what variety the students speak, we are interested in what regional dialect is used by their families and also what the local norms for standard speech are.

The question of the variety used by students is important because schools must decide what variety of Spanish to use in order to reach the Spanish-speaking students. The basic argument appears to be between those who think that standard Spanish (presumably, although not stated, Mexican standard) should be used and those who argue in favor of the local variety. The first group bases their case on the assumption that nonstandard dialects are inferior to standard dialects. Children must learn the standard so as not to be handicapped. However, this approach weakens the professed aim of presenting material to students in their own language. Students would have to learn standard Spanish as well as English. Those who want the local variety used in the schools feel that the standard variety is only useful as a part of the children's knowledge of several varieties and speech styles. Garcia (1975) notes that "if the Chicano is to learn the standard dialect, it should not be at the expense of the legitimacy of his home dialect. . . . Schooling must add to the children's repertoire of learned speech behaviors, but any attempt to subtract from the Chicanos' speech repertoire makes the ultimate ends of schooling more difficult and in many cases impossible to attain." Negative attitudes toward the speech used by children need to be counteracted. Cohen (1975) points out that "one variety of a Chicano's speech viewed by an outsider as mixing of English and Spanish, is viewed by the speaker as a language in its own right." Lance (1975), looking at dialect and nonstandard features in Texas Spanish, comments that "on the whole, no justification was found for the common belief held particularly by monolingual Anglos, but also by many Mexican Americans that Texas Spanish is impoverished in its vocabulary and grammar and is generally 'corrupt.' " Use of the standard variety in schools, to the exclusion of the local variety, would negate any intention of helping the children feel accepted. Not only would they feel discriminated against for not speaking English, but they would be told that even their own language was bad and incorrect.

Knowledge of community attitudes toward the relative roles of Spanish and English and the varieties of each language is also important to the success of bilingual programs. What variety of Spanish do the Spanish-speaking parents want taught in the schools? Ornstein (1971) considers information on community attitudes toward the local varieties of Spanish and English and the maintenance of these languages essential for sociolinguistic research in Spanish-speaking areas. Knowledge of parental attitudes and language use can prevent schools from teaching a variety that the students do not know or a variety that is considered so prestigious the students are not comfortable with it. Many families come from rural areas of Mexico and may have had no exposure to standard Mexican Spanish. Parents may express concern that schools should not teach "inferior" varieties of Spanish like Pachuco, or the "mixed" varieties such as Pocho. But Hernandez, Cohen, and Beltramo (1975) note that Pachuco is no longer identified as the speech of "delinquents." Pachuco has influenced all levels of Spanish as spoken in the Southwest. Garcia's plea for acceptance of the Chicano's home dialect is a plea for recognizing Pocho as an important language variety for use in education. Without information on community attitudes toward local varieties, it would be difficult to determine precisely what varieties exist. "What counts as a language boundary cannot be defined by any purely linguistic measure. Attitudes and social meanings enter in as well" (Hymes, 1970).

The Mexican-American community comprises four language groups. One group speaks no English, one speaks more Spanish than English, another speaks more English than Spanish, and the last speaks no Spanish. Studies show considerable regional diversity in the use of Spanish and English and their varieties. We need to know more about where and when the different varieties of Spanish and English are used in a single community. Barker (1975) looked at how membership in a group within a Mexican-American community and the social context of speech interacted to determine the language/variety choice in a particular situation. He identified four varieties of Spanish in the community of Tucson: (1) standard Mexican Spanish, (2) local dialect (Arizona Spanish), (3) Yaqui dialect of Spanish (from Mexico), and (4) Pachuco, spoken by a specific subgroup. We need a sociolinguistics study for the Chicano that can identify the varieties available for use and the conditions under which they are used.

Use of Spanish in the schools must be seen in the context of use of Spanish in the community. Whether Spanish is being maintained in the community affects the success of Spanish in the schools. Recent immigrants from Mexico will continue to bring Spanish into the community, but the language is only maintained if those who have lived in the country for longer periods of time have learned English and continue to speak Spanish. There is little practical point in setting up *bilingual* education programs if the students will eventually switch to English completely. Gaarder (1970) points out the need to consider whether Spanish is being maintained or English is replacing Spanish and lists a number of factors that affect language maintenance/language shift. Cohen (1975) attempted to supply some of this information for the Redwood City bilingual education project through questionnaires on the language use and proficiency of families and the "language loyalty" of the parents.

Spanish language maintenance requires that Spanish and English have established, but different, functions in the community. Fishman (1970) comments: "Socially patterned bilingualism can exist as a stabilized phenomenon *only* if there is functional *differentiation* between two languages rather than merely global dominance or balance" (p. 560). Barker's (1975) Tucson study found that English was used· more in certain domains or fields ·of personal relations and Spanish was used more in others. Greenfield (1972) claimed that the amount of Spanish and English reported by Puerto Rican bilinguals for conversational use with other bilinguals differed according to the domain of interaction, which was related to differences in person, place, and topic.

In order to obtain the information that has been argued to be necessary for any bilingual education program, we would need an ethnographic/sociolinguistic survey of the community in question. The survey would have to determine where the Spanish speakers are from and how long they have lived in this country, in order to provide a measure of the homogeneity or heterogeneity of the community. A homogeneous Spanish-speaking community makes the task of choosing one variety as a medium of instruction easier. The linguistic characteristics of the varieties used need to be described so that the differences between varieties are clear. Research on where Spanish and English are used will show the functional distribution of the languages. The basic sociolinguistic question is who uses what language or variety to whom and when. Fishman and Lovas (1970) have emphasized the importance of investigating language use and proficiency by domain and identifying community attitudes to the different varieties and the changing language situation. No such complete surveys have been done for bilingual communities, yet this information is an essential foundation for bilingual programs in the schools.

LANGUAGE OF THE TEACHERS

Who should teach in a bilingual program? The usual answer is, of course, bilingual people, but the question becomes whom we consider to be bilingual. Gaarder's (1970) summary of the program proposals for the first bilingual projects shows the lack of agreement.

Forty-nine call for mere "bilingualism," or "conversational ability" in the other tongue. Six want "fluent" bilinguals; at least one specifies the ability to read, write, and speak the two languages; some say the teachers will be "hopefully" or "preferably" bilinguals. On the other hand, eleven either identified or demanded well qualified people; and in fifteen there is at least one person educated abroad and some were seeking one or more such teachers. (p. 165)

Even when Gaarder criticizes these programs, he fails to define what he considers "well-qualified" or even what he means by bilingual. The problem most programs face is having to make do with the people available. This frequently means that they hire bilingual aides to assist monolingual teachers. However, this does not avoid the necessity for defining what is meant and what is desired by bilingualism.

Many of the bilingual teachers hired for these programs will be non-native speakers of Spanish. It is important to know how and when they learned Spanish. Some bilingual programs place great emphasis on the acquisition of college credits in Spanish. Unfortunately such training may equip one to teach Spanish literature or the Spanish language but will hardly ever help one learn how to teach *in* Spanish. Learning Spanish through courses also encourages the development of artificial standards of correctness, particularly correct grammar, rather than conversational ability. The worst deficiency is that they do not provide experience in speaking Spanish in a variety of contexts and about various topics. Ideas learned in such an environment about "correct" Spanish could interfere with the goal of providing for the Spanish-speaking students a teacher who understands them and their background and is able to make school comprehensible for them. Any intention of using and promoting the local variety is nullified and the Spanish-speaking students may feel as alienated as they do with an English monolingual teacher.

The Spanish native speakers available are frequently classroom aides from the community. Although these people are presumably familiar with the local variety, they may not be fluent in English. Since many teachers are unfamiliar with the use of aides in the classroom, an aide may be treated as a fellow teacher or a menial laborer. Imagine how the Spanish-speaking students feel about the demonstrated status of Spanish-English bilinguals. Clearly, to speak only English is to have higher status. Aides are generally expected to develop materials for use with the Spanish-speaking students, usually by adapting English materials into Spanish. However, this can be a particularly difficult task for many of them because, although fluent in Spanish conversation, they were educated in English and may not be comfortable with the necessary academic vocabulary in Spanish.

The variety of Spanish and English spoken by the teachers (and aides) is a particularly crucial point. Although teachers and students may theoretically speak the same language, attitude differences can affect even mutual comprehension. Making an effort to find trained staff who are familiar with the local variety of speech would be rewarding in that these people would be less likely to try to impose alienating standards of correct speech. The fact that many people, both teachers and students, in the classroom do speak different varieties is not a difficulty; rather the problem is the tendency to categorize speech into "bad" and "good." Those who automatically claim that teachers should speak (and teach in) the standard variety are falling into the trap of assuming a value judgment on speech. It is not clear how the programs described in Gaarder (1970) expect to handle the difference between local and standard varieties, "One plan states that its bilingual teacher aides will be trained in 'Standard South American Spanish.' The exception noted calls for someone to prepare 'material in barrio Spanish,' but not to the exclusion of standard writings" (p. 168).

We expect bilingual teachers to function equally well in both languages. An ideal or balanced bilingual is one who learned both languages as a child, has practiced both of them in all contexts since, and is comfortable speaking, reading, and writing both equally well. Such a paragon probably does not exist, although "there is a common belief that the person who speaks two languages can say anything in one that he can say in the other" (Gaarder, 1970). Native Spanish speakers may rarely read or write Spanish and speak Spanish only in certain contexts, such as talking with their family. Those who have learned Spanish as a second language may also use it in limited contexts. If they took courses in the language, they may not speak it well. If they did not study it in schools, they may not have learned to read or write the language fluently and expressively. Hence, the need to establish the teachers' and students' proficiency in both Spanish and English across a number of contexts. This is frequently referred to as language dominance because one's native language is not necessarily one's strongest language or the language used in many contexts.

An ability to use both languages across contexts means that the person possesses a full repertoire of speech styles. One of the requirements for communicative competence in a language is to have access to a number of different styles. A bilingual teacher must be able to switch from a formal to an informal speech style in the weaker language as naturally and unconsciously as this is usually performed in the dominant language. As has been remarked before, if speakers' experience with their native language is relatively limited, their capacity to handle different styles in the first language may be less than in the second language because they use the second more often. In fact, as an "ideal" bilingual is rare, it is also rare to have access to a variety of speech styles equally well in both languages. What this means for the classroom teacher is that some bilinguals will be comfortable either teaching a lesson or discussing topics with the class in one language but prefer to switch into the other language for the opposite situation.

Successful bilingual education programs depend on the development of bilingual teacher-training programs. We need to develop programs that will provide teachers who can model bilingual behavior for students. The first step is to recognize that since we expect bilingual teachers to teach in both languages, they must be given practice in teaching in both languages. "Teacher talk" is a distinct speech style that needs to be learned, particularly in the second language. Teacher talk includes specialized vocabulary and grammatical constructions that we can take for granted in our first language but are not normally part of learning a foreign language.

Practice teaching in both languages will prepare teachers by giving them the requisite vocabulary so that they are prepared to teach the total curriculum equally easily in each language. In general, teacher training should aim to provide experience in all aspects of language skills in the largest possible variety of contexts. The goal is to produce teachers who feel at home in both languages. This is important if educators want students to become bilingual, for teachers should be able to demonstrate the strengths and advantages of bilingualism and serve as models and motivators for students to learn Spanish and English.

A recognized part of normal Spanish-English bilingual behavior is code-switching. Code-switching refers to the fact that speakers may switch from one language to another in the course of an utterance or during the same conversation. Since this occurs between bilinguals, it is sometimes thought of as reflecting an inability to keep the languages separate. But as Hernandez, Cohen, Beltramo (1975) point out: "Switching is not a breakdown in the ability to maintain the languages apart but rather a complex ability commanded by some bilinguals which reflects the intricate socio-cultural situation of language contact" (p. xiii).

Code-switching serves a communicative function for bilinguals. Because teachers need to understand how and when bilingual students code-switch, they will be at a disadvantage if they themselves are not comfortable with code-switching. Teacher-training programs can counteract the negative stereotypes of "Tex-Mex" or "Spanglish" by providing examples of expected bilingual behavior —spontaneous code-switching in natural environments. Again, we need to expect the same bilingual abilities from teachers that we want to foster in students.

LANGUAGE OF MATERIALS

The choice of curriculum materials is an important issue for any program. Although programs frequently operate on the principle of accepting whatever material they can obtain, it is necessary both to begin to set standards of acceptability and to begin developing appropriate materials. Fortunately, more bilingual materials are being produced as bilingual programs increase. The materials used in schools come from three sources. They are produced (1) in the United States, (2) in other countries, and (3) by local school districts. Each of these sources poses particular problems. Materials from this country are written in a particular variety of Spanish. This variety may or may not be the variety the students are comfortable with. Teachers should be familiar with and able to discuss differences that may arise. Materials produced in other countries also face the problem of differences in speech varieties. The lexical, grammatical, and cultural differences may interfere considerably with student comprehension. The material, however, does have the advantage of being designed for use in teaching content areas *through* the language. Locally produced material is commonly used as a stop-gap measure for meeting an immediate need. The person expected to produce this material is all too often the teacher or aide who has regular classroom responsibilities. Such material is usually translated directly from English into Spanish, thereby raising the problem of English influence on the Spanish style and structure. Translated material is less likely to reflect natural Spanish writing style and more likely to represent English sentences put into Spanish word for word.

How shall evaluation of bilingual materials proceed and what kinds of materials would we like to see developed? First, the language used in the curriculum materials should match as closely as possible the language used in the classroom. This, of course, requires that the language to be used in the classroom be clearly specified. The teacher cannot use several varieties indiscriminately, completely confusing the students so that they cannot tell what variety to use and when. Teachers must be conscious of the fact that the variety of Spanish used in the classroom may differ from that of the book and be prepared to explain the differences to students. Second, the language used in the materials should contain as little English influence as possible. Naturally, the Spanish spoken in the United States has borrowed considerably from English. It is necessary to read the prepared materials critically and have them evaluated by different people in order to determine whether the language used represents how Spanish speakers would write naturally. Depending on their sensitivity to fine distinctions of appropriate speech, it should be possible to produce materials that can represent Chicano Spanish and not be English with Spanish words substituted. Third, the language should be consistent with the goals of the program. Material designed for teaching Spanish, which includes much of the material produced in this country, is not suitable for teaching other subjects through Spanish. In a bilingual program, the content areas are of major concern. Teaching with the language serves as another, highly effective method of language teaching.

INSTRUCTIONAL GOALS

All bilingual programs need to begin with a clear, well-designed statement of their intentions. Many programs are either avowedly bilingual or English as a second language. It is important to maintain a distinction between these, both in terms of instructional goals and in the means of achieving them. The problem frequently becomes the definition of bilingual and/or bilingual education. Cohen (1975) states clearly what he means by bilingual education:

"Bilingual education" is the use of two languages as media of instruction for a child or group of children in part or all of the school curriculum ... Bilingual education usually implies that more than just language is being taught in the second language. (p. 18)

However, programs ranging from completely bilingual to purely ESL are frequently labeled "bilingual," probably because ESL is increasingly recognized as inadequate for the needs of Spanish-speaking students. Guidelines for interpreting the Title VII (ESEA) Bilingual Education Program specify how the government defines bilingual education:

The use of two languages, one of which is English, as mediums of instruction for the same pupil population in a well-organized program which encompasses part or all of the curriculum and includes the study of the history and culture associated with the mother tongue. (p. 1)

It is important to look closely at many different features of a "bilingual" program in order to see whether it meets the definition of bilingual (Kjolseth, 1972). Programs intended to produce people who can function in two languages are language-maintenance programs and are opposed to programs designed to assimilate Spanish-speaking students into the English-speaking majority language and culture.

Examples of the way that intention and practice can conflict and contradict each other are shown in the discussions of languages of instruction. In considering what bilingualism meant for teachers, we made the point that they needed to be able to handle both languages in all situations. Naturally, we would expect bilingual students to be able to do this as well. However, this would not happen if some subjects were taught in Spanish and others in English. While a functional specialization of language of instruction (teaching from one to one-half of the subjects in one language, the rest in the other) may be easier on the schools, it does not fit the definition or the stated goals of bilingual education.

If we want to have all subjects taught in both languages, there are several program models possible. These include: (1) simultaneous translation, where the material is presented in one language and then immediately translated; (2) repeated teaching, where material is introduced in one language and summarized later in the other (and then these are reversed); and (3) alternate days, where all of the material is presented in one language on one day and the other language the next day. The alternate days model is one of the oldest and most popular program models. It is effective because of the temporal separation. Students and teachers know that one day is for Spanish, another for English, and the distinction is clear. In the simultaneous translation model, teachers become confused by interference between the languages and have trouble switching quickly back and forth. The repeated teaching model makes it easy for students to avoid learning the other language. When all of the content material is given in both languages, they have only to wait in order to hear it presented in a language they understand.

CONCLUSION

I have described and discussed several of the most basic linguistic aspects of bilingual education in order to provide a means of measuring and evaluating bilingual programs. It is important to take into consideration the language background of the students in planning a bilingual program. The language of teachers is presented as an example of the necessity for establishing clear definitions of bilingualism. Despite the fact that instructional materials are hard to find, the language used in these materials might have considerable influence on bilingual programs and what we would hope for in creating these materials. The need to make definite statements about program goals and consistent implementation of them is illustrated by examples of how program models must be tied to particular instructional goals. All of the factors and the linguistic concepts raised in connection with them must be considered by those proposing and carrying out a bilingual education program.

BIBLIOGRAPHY

Alatis, James, ed. 1970. *Georgetown University Round Table on Languages and Linguistics 1970.* Washington: Georgetown University Press.

Andersson, Theodore, and Mildred Boyer. 1970. *Bilingual Schooling in the United States.* 2 Vol. Washington: U.S. Government Printing Office.

Barker, George. 1975. "Social Functions of Language in a Mexican-American Community," in Hernandez, Cohen, Beltramo, eds.

Campbell, Russell. 1970. "English Curricula for Non-English Speakers," in Alatis, ed.

Cardenas, Daniel. 1975. "Compound and Coordinate Bilingualism/Biculturalism in the Southwest," in Hernandez, Cohen, Beltramo, eds.

Cohen, Andrew. 1975. *A Sociolinguistic Approach to Bilingual Education.* Rowley, Mass: Newbury House.

Fishman, Joshua. 1971. "Sociolinguistic Perspective on the Study of Bilingualism," in Fishman, Cooper, Ma.

Fishman, Joshua, Robert Cooper, and Roxana Ma. 1971. *Bilingualism in the Barrio.* The Hague: Mouton.

Fishman, Joshua, and John Lovas. 1970. "Bilingual Education in Sociolinguistic Perspective." TESOL Quarterly 4:3.

Gaarder, A. Bruce. 1970. "The First Seventy-Six Bilingual Education Projects," in Alatis, ed.

Garcia, Ernest. 1975. "Chicano Spanish Dialects and Education," in Hernandez, Cohen, Beltramo, eds.

Greenfield, Lawrence. 1972. "Situational Measures of Normative Language Views in Relation to Person, Place, and Topic among Puerto Rican Bilinguals," in Fishman, Joshua, ed. *Advances in the Sociology of Language*. The Hague: Mouton.

Gumperz, John. 1970. "Verbal Strategies in Multilingual Communication," in Alatis, ed.

Hernandez, Eduardo, Andrew Cohen, and Anthony Beltramo. 1975. *El Lenguaje de los Chicanos*. Washington: Center for Applied Linguistics.

Hymes, Dell. 1970. "Bilingual Education: Linguistic vs. Sociolinguistic Bases," in Alatis, ed.

Kjolseth, Rolf. 1972. "Bilingual Education Programs in the United States: For Assimilation or Pluralism?," in Spolsky, ed.

Lance, Donald. 1975. "Dialectal and Nonstandard Forms in Texas Spanish," in Hernandez, Cohen, Beltramo, eds.

Ornstein, Jacob. 1971. *Sociolinguistics and the Study of Spanish and English Language Varieties and their Use in the U.S. Southwest, with a Proposed Plan of Research*. Albuquerque: SWCEL.

Spolsky, Bernard, ed. 1972. *The Language Education of Minority Children: Selected Readings*. Rowley, Mass: Newbury House.

U.S. Commission on Civil Rights. 1975. *A Better Chance to Learn: Bilingual-Bicultural Education*. Clearinghouse Publication #51. Washington: U.S. Government Printing Office.

U.S. Office of Education. 1971. *Programs under Bilingual Education Act (Title VII, ESEA): Manual for Project Applicants and Grantees*. Washington: IIEW.

Handling Dialects in the Classroom

A Position Paper from the National Council of Teachers of English, Support for Learning and Teaching of English Committee (SLATE), September, 1976.

Copyright © 1976 by the National Council of Teachers of English. Reprinted with permission

THE ISSUES

People complain that the schools aren't teaching students to "talk correctly," and people are confused about what "correct talk" is.

Does "talking correctly" mean making geographical variations conform to local practice? Does it mean getting rid of such symbolic colloquialisms as "he don't" or "ain't got no" in every speech situation? Does it mean distinguishing between "lie" and "lay," or "lend" and "loan," and learning not to say "It was between John and myself"? Or, does "correctness" vary with the audience and the situation?

What people mean by "correctness" will depend on where they grew up, how much education they have had, what ambitions they hold for their children, and/or what social barriers they want to enforce.

PROFESSIONAL VIEWPOINTS: NCTE/RESEARCH

In November 1974, the National Council of Teachers of English passed a resolution emphasizing that students have a right to speak and learn in their own language, in the dialect that makes them comfortable and gives them a sense of their own identity and worth. That resolution was passed because NCTE members know something about the nature of language and how people learn it; they have some information not shared by the general public.

As language scholars, we know that language changes, slowly but inevitably, and that what was a solecism a century ago—splitting an infinitive, for instance—is now common practice among our best writers and speakers.

We know that everybody speaks a dialect—there's nothing pejorative about the term. Dialects can be regional or socioeconomic, and include pronunciation, vocabulary, and syntax. All children master the basic elements of their own dialect before they start school.

We know that people learn the language they hear spoken. Young children have an enormous capacity to absorb language, an ability that begins to diminish with adolescence and has diminished so much by adulthood that changing ingrained patterns is a slow and often painful process.

We know that speakers of any dialect can add new words whenever they need them, usually without shifting the major features of their dialects.

We know that children who read a lot, both in and out of school, probably gain more syntactic flexibility and broader vocabularies than children who roam the playgrounds or sit glued to television.

We know that there's no such thing as an absolute standard of correctness. What's right for one situation may be quite "wrong," or unsuitable, in a different situation. Language choices cannot be measured as "right" or "wrong" in the way that yardsticks can be checked to see whether their inches are the proper length.

We know that all speakers adjust their language choices to the situation they find themselves in. Students don't talk on the playground the way they talk in the classroom, or speak to their friends as they speak to their teachers. This ability to shift styles shows a genuine skill in using language—the same skill that adults use in adapting to the requirements of the job, the cocktail bar, or a funeral service.

We know that people, young and old, do make changes in their language habits, but they make those changes only when they get an immediate benefit. High grades or success in school is often not enough to provide the motivation they need.

We know that people *think* in language, and that people can think logically or illogically in any dialect. We know that the ability to think clearly is more important than minor dialect variations, and most of us suspect that time spent on clarity of thought is better spent than time devoted to shifting dialect patterns.

But we also know that people judge others by the language choices they make. Such judgments are harmless enough when they are limited to "Are you from Australia?" or "You sound like a Chicagoan," but they can be damaging when they result in judgments such as "poor white trash," "uneducated (and probably stupid)," or "socially unacceptable." We tell students they will be judged by their language habits, just as they are judged by their dress and their table manners.

STRATEGIES FOR ACTION

We can help the public understand what we're trying to do if we:

1. emphasize that practice in using language by sharing experiences, role-playing, and other devices, is a better route to flexibility and effectiveness than having a teacher

correct mistakes. In other words, discussions of appropriateness, clarity, and intelligibility are more useful than "chasing errors."

2. explain that drills in usage are more likely to teach nervousness and self-consciousness than change in language. Such drills can teach people to fill in the blanks or name the parts, but seldom teach them to speak or write better.

3. remind parents that schools can supply only a small part of the language learning that goes on. Children spend only seven hours a day in school for five days a week; the rest of their waking hours they are bombarded with language that seems more real to them than the language they hear in the classroom.

4. ask for specific examples from people who are troubled about how language is taught. Deal with each objection separately rather than attempting a general defense of what we do.

5. remind people that the National Assessment results showed that mechanics (usage choices, spelling, syntax, etc.) have not declined but have slightly improved; what declined were sentence flexibility, creativity, and coherence—just the qualities that we're trying to teach.

6. make clear what standardized tests actually measure and what the scores actually mean. Explain what a "norm" is, what a "percentile score" is.

7. show parents some actual assignments and explain what those assignments aim for. Invite them to visit classes and see that most activities are actually more demanding than older methods.

8. urge school boards and legislators to provide classes small enough that every student can have the language practice necessary for real progress.

9. demonstrate that what's "basic" about English is the ability to communicate. Successful communication can take place in many different ways, in many different situations, and depends on the good will of the listener as well as on the skill of the speaker.

RESOURCES

Arnoled, Lois V. "Writer's Cramp and Eyestrain—Are They Paying Off?" *English Journal* (January, 1964), pp. 10–15.

Braddock, Richard, et al. *Research in Written Composition.* Urbana, Ill.: National Council of Teachers of English, 1963.

Britton, James. *Language and Learning.* Miami, Fla.: University of Miami Press, 1970.

Clark, Virginia P., et al. *Introductory Readings in Language.* New York: St. Martin's Press, 1972, especially Part Four, "Americans Speaking."

Dixon, John. *Growth Through English.* Reading, England: National Association for the Teaching of English, 1967.

Laird, Charlton. *Language in America.* Englewood Cliffs: Prentice-Hall, 1970.

Lloyd, Donald J. "Our National Mania for Correctness," in W. Bruce Finnie and Thomas Erskine, *Words on Words.* New York: Random House, 1971.

Miller, George A. *Language and Communication.* New York: McGraw Hill, 1951, especially Chapters 7 and 8, "Verbal Behavior of Children" and "The Role of Learning."

Moffett, James. *Teaching the Universe of Discourse.* New York: Houghton Mifflin, 1968.

National Council of Teachers of English, Conference on College Composition and Communication. *Students' Right to Their Own Language.* Annotated bibliography. Urbana, Ill.: NCTE, 1974.

Piaget, Jean. *Language and Thought of the Child.* New York: New American Library, 1955.

Schauch, Margaret. "Social Aspects: Class, Taboos, Politics." In *Perspectives on Language,* edited by J. A. Rycenga and J. Schwartz. New York: Ronald Press, 1963.

Index